Peugeot 504 1968-74 Autobook

By Kenneth Ball
Associate Member, Guild of Motoring Writers
and the Autopress Team of Technical Writers.

Peugeot 504, 1796 cc, 1968-70
Peugeot 504, 1796 cc, Fuel Injection 1968-70
Peugeot 504, 1971 cc, 1970-74
Peugeot 504 SL, 1971 cc, 1970-74
Peugeot 504, 1971 cc, Fuel Injection 1970-74

AUTOBOOKS

Autopress Ltd. Golden Lane Brighton BN1 2QJ England

The AUTOBOOK series of Workshop Manuals is the largest in the world and covers the majority of British and Continental motor cars, as well as all major Japanese and Australian models. For a full list see the back of this manual.

CONTENTS

ISBN 0 85147 522 1

First Edition 1972
Second Edition, fully revised 1972
Third Edition, fully revised 1973
Fourth Edition, fully revised 1974

783

Printed and bound in Brighton England for Autopress Ltd by G Beard & Son Ltd B

ACKNOWLEDGEMENT

My thanks are due to Peugeot Ltd. for their unstinted co-operation and also for supplying data and illustrations.

I am also grateful to a considerable number of owners who have discussed their cars at length and many of whose suggestions have been included in this manual.

Kenneth Ball
Associate Member, Guild of Motoring Writers
Ditchling Sussex England.

INTRODUCTION

This do-it-yourself Workshop Manual has been specially written for the owner who wishes to maintain his car in first class condition and to carry out his own servicing and repairs. Considerable savings on garage charges can be made, and one can drive in safety and confidence knowing the work has been done properly.

Comprehensive step-by-step instructions and illustrations are given on all dismantling, overhauling and assembling operations. Certain assemblies require the use of expensive special tools, the purchase of which would be unjustified. In these cases information is included but the reader is recommended to hand the unit to the agent for attention.

Throughout the Manual hints and tips are included which will be found invaluable, and there is an easy to follow fault diagnosis at the end of each chapter.

Whilst every care has been taken to ensure correctness of information it is obviously not possible to guarantee complete freedom from errors or to accept liability arising from such errors or omissions.

Instructions may refer to the righthand or lefthand sides of the vehicle or the components. These are the same as the righthand or lefthand of an observer standing behind the car and looking forward.

CHAPTER 1

THE ENGINE

1:1 Type, capacity and features

The engine is mounted at the front of the vehicle and is inclined to the right at an angle of 45 deg. This has the effect of reducing engine height and centre of gravity and enables the engine mountings to be designed to give smoother running conditions. It also provides easier access to auxiliary equipment.

As shown in the sectional views in **FIG 1:1**, the engine is basically of the four cylinder in-line overhead valve type with a forged steel five-bearing crankshaft transmitting the drive to the rear wheels. The valves are inclined at different angles to the centre line of the engine, the inlet valves having the greater bias. Operation is from a single side camshaft through crossed pushrods and two rocker shafts.

In 1970 the size of the engine was increased from 1796 cc to 1971 cc. This increase was obtained by enlarging the bore to 88 mm from 84 mm, the stroke remaining at 81 mm.

Removable wet cylinder liners are incorporated in a cast iron cylinder block with a cross-flow aluminium alloy head. Fuel delivery may be either by means of a Solex carburetter or by the Kugelfischer indirect fuel injection system and the cylinder blocks vary in detail according to the system used. In the carburetter version the feed is to a common induction chamber, but the injection unit has four separate ports. Other modifications with fuel injection are concerned with differences in camshaft, timing gear, fuel pump, oil and air filters, ignition coil, plugs and type of alternator, as well as a higher final drive ratio. In all models a particular feature is the Peugeot magnetically-clutched fan coupling employed in the cooling system, by which the fan is automatically disconnected or reconnected at certain temperatures.

Lubrication is by a gear-type oil pump. Oil is drawn from the sump through a strainer screen and after circulating through a fullflow-type external oil filter is discharged to the main oil gallery located lengthwise through the crankcase. Lubrication is thus provided to the crankshaft, connecting rod and camshaft bearings, from the rear of which the oil continues to be circulated to the rockers and rocker shafts.

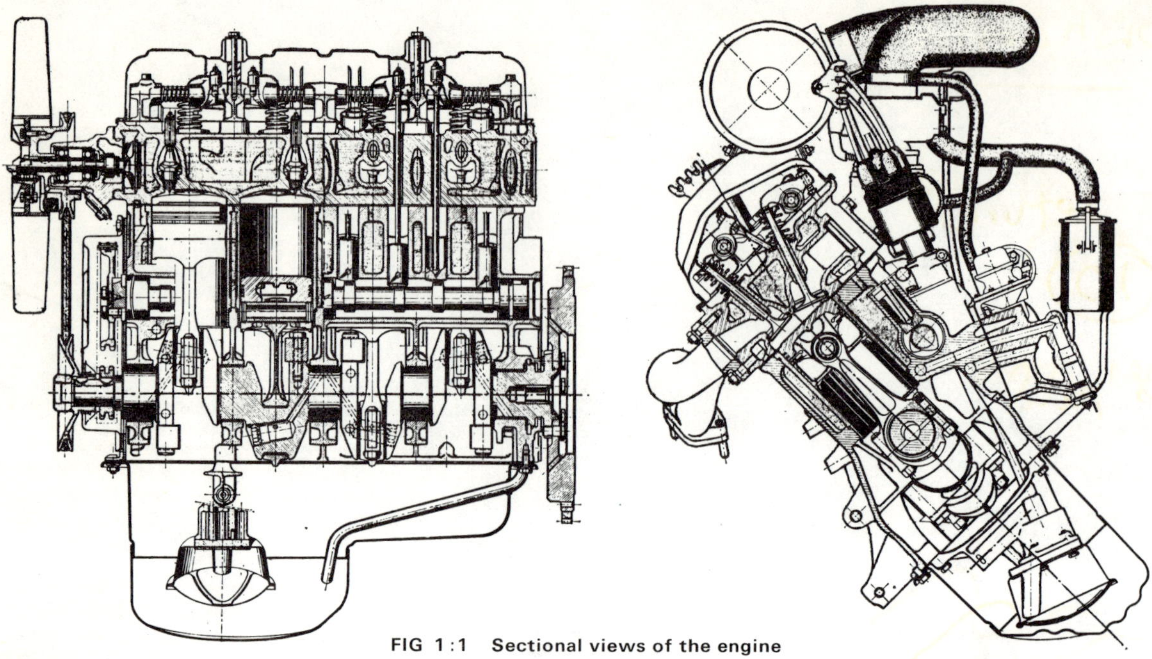

FIG 1:1 Sectional views of the engine

1:2 Working on engine in car

Apart from normal running adjustments to the fuel and ignition systems and the fan belt tension, other work which can be undertaken without the removal of the engine includes such matters as changing the lubricating oil, removing the cylinder head, decarbonizing and attention to valves, removing the water pump and thermostat and magnetic fan clutch, also the distributor and carburetter as necessary. Instructions on these matters are given in this and later chapters.

The engine lubricating oil should be changed every 5000 km. Drain the oil by removing the drain plug, then refit the plug with a new joint. Remove the cap and hose complete from the filler tube and refill with a recommended lubricant to the maximum level on the dipstick. The capacity of the sump is 4 litre and the minimum level is 2.5 litre. The oil filter, situated horizontally between the oil pump and circulation system, has a capacity of approximately .5 litre. It contains a renewable cartridge which should be changed every 10,000 km, or at more frequent intervals of 1000 and 5000 km when running-in a new engine.

For working underneath the car it is often necessary to jack it up at front or rear. In all these operations special care needs to be observed to see that the car is **firmly supported** by suitable blocks to make sure that it will not be shaken off the jacking arrangements by such jolting as is inseparable from the work being undertaken.

1:3 Removing the engine

Preliminary operations for the removal of the engine assembly are to chock the wheels of the car, protect the wings with suitable covers and disconnect the battery. Drain the cooling system by removing the radiator cap and opening the drain taps below the radiator and on the side of the cylinder block. Retain the liquid if it contains antifreeze. Further operations are as follows:

1 Remove the bonnet after disconnecting the upper pivot of the bonnet articulated stay. Remove the battery and its supporting bracket.

2 Disconnect the radiator hoses, the heater hoses from the engine, the carburetter heater pipe from the three-way union near the scuttle, the fuel feed pipe and the servo vacuum pipe from the inlet manifold.

3 Disconnect also the wiring for the alternator, the oil pressure switch, the ignition coil, the thermostatic connector, the starter switch, the self-disengaging fan switch and the choke and accelerator controls.

4 Remove the radiator, the ignition coil, the starter motor and the sheet metal flywheel protector plates.

5 Remove the two Allen screws securing the steering rack housing to the front crossmember, using an 8 mm Allen key. Turn the steering wheel to the left to lower the housing.

6 Detach the three nuts securing the exhaust pipe to the manifold, also the nut securing the damper to the propeller shaft tube and disengage the lug.

7 Remove the three Allen screws securing the clutch housing, using the special key 8.0202 shown in **FIG 1:2**.

8 Attach suitable lifting tackle on the engine. The arrangements used in service are shown in **FIG 1:3**.

9 Remove the four bolts securing the engine supports to the crossmember. Ensure that the front righthand brake fluid feed hose is held against the crossmember to avoid damage.

10 Raise the engine with the lifting tackle until the gearbox abuts on the propeller shaft tunnel. Position a jack or the special apparatus 8.0125 (see **FIG 1:4**) under the gearbox to hold it against the tunnel.

11 Separate the engine from the gearbox by jerking lightly, **without altering the position of the lifting tackle.** Then raise the tackle and withdraw the engine from the engine compartment.

Automatic transmission:

Engine removal from cars fitted with automatic transmission will be the same as above, but it will also be necessary to remove the air filter and the metal bracket retaining the filler tube.

After removing the four bolts securing the converter to the flywheel, be careful to disengage the converter as it **must not** be removed with the engine.

1:4 Lifting the head

The cylinder head must be removed when the engine is cold to avoid the possibility of deformation. If the engine remains in the car, preliminary operations as described in **Section 1:3** are first undertaken, followed by removing the distributor cap and the sparking plug leads, the sparking plugs, the fan belt, the fitting for the heater hose on the wing valance, the rocker cover and the air filter, the carburetter and the inlet manifold, the rocker lubrication pipe and the oil vapour recirculating unions. Disconnect the exhaust pipe bracket from under the car.

Remove the upper front and rear cylinder head bolts and engage in the holes the cylinder head guides 8.0115 Z. Screw them in completely. These two piece guides have an upper part with a lefthand thread which unscrews when the lower part of the guide (see Z in **FIG 1:6**) is screwed in completely. Remove the remaining cylinder head bolts in the reverse order of their tightening shown in **FIG 1:7.**

Withdraw the cups and seals from the sparking plug tubes, then unscrew the rocker shaft bolts evenly and lift off the rocker assembly shown in **FIG 1:5.** Take out the pushrods and keep them aside in their correct order, then carefully lift off the cylinder head and gasket. If the head does not come away freely, tap it lightly along each side with a mallet, or if the sparking plugs are refitted and the engine turned over the head should free itself. Lock the cylinder liners in place with the two retaining screws 8.0104D as shown in **FIG 1:19.**

Later engines (XN1, XN2, XM7):

On later engines with compressed liners the head removal procedure has a few points of difference from the above and if fuel injection equipment is fitted the injector lines and air distribution chamber will have to be removed.

After removing the pushrods, remove the head guide from bolt hole No. 8 (see **FIG 1:7**) and **pivot the head** to separate it from the block and cylinder liners, then remove the head and gasket and take out the second head guide.

1:5 Servicing the head, attention to valves

With the cylinder head removed, decarbonizing may be undertaken. Most of the scraping should be done with the valves in place so that the seats are not damaged. The cylinder head bolts should be temporarily refitted to avoid carbon particles entering the holes, also the two oil return holes situated at each end of the cylinder block should be suitably protected. To prevent dirt getting between the pistons and liners a used piston ring may be inserted on top of the pistons. The manufacturers advise that the piston crowns should not be decarbonized. Ensure that the 1 mm diameter petrol drainage hole on the cylinder block is not obstructed. Remove all traces of old gasket material from the cylinder head faces and finally clean with paraffin and petrol.

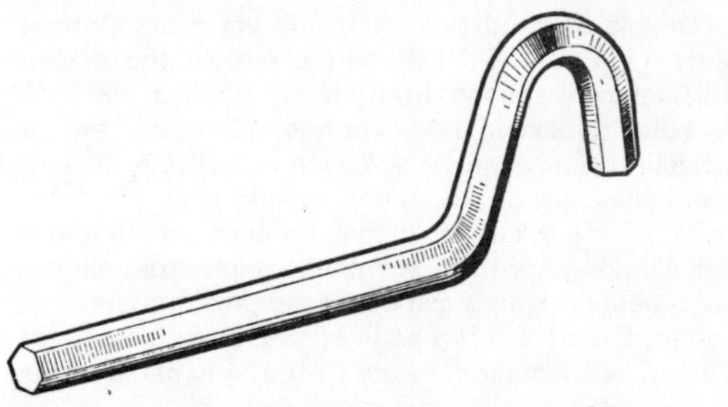

FIG 1:2 Allen key No. 8.0202 for clutch housing screws

FIG 1:3 Lifting tackle 8.0102X in position

FIG 1:4 Support base 8.0125 used in removing engine

Details of the rocker shaft and valve components are shown in **FIG 1 : 5.** To dismantle, remove the lock springs and tension springs from the shaft and slide off the rockers, brackets and springs. Remove the rocker adjusting screws and place each rocker and its parts in a numbered rack or take other steps to ensure that they go back in the same locations. Proceed to compress the valve springs with a suitable compressor, remove the split collars, spring caps and springs and remove the valves. Each valve has an internal and an external spring, which are identical for both inlet and exhaust valves.

Check the rocker shaft and the rocker bores for scores and wear. Inspect the cups and bottom contact faces of the pushrods for excessive wear. Withdraw the valve tappets and keep them in correct order for refitting, if serviceable, in their original bores.

Try each valve in its guide for undue side movement, indicating wear of either bore or valve stem or both. The valve guides are renewable and if the valve stem clearance in the bore exceeds the specified maximum valves with oversize stems are available. Valve seats may be refaced to the specified angles if necessary by a valve refacing machine. Each valve should be ground in to its appropriate seat, using a light application of medium or fine grinding paste. Clean away all abrasive on completion. Thoroughly flush out the cylinder head water passages and refit the valve assemblies by reversing the sequence of removal operations. Lubricate the valve stems and fit new valve springs if required, also new oil seal washers, before fitting the split collars. Reassemble the tappets if removed.

To refit the cylinder head, clean the contacting faces of head and block with a cloth dipped in petrol to eliminate any trace of grease. Use a new gasket making sure that the correct gasket is being used, and handle it with clean hands. Referring to **FIG 1 : 6,** remove the liner retaining screws and locate the gasket on the cylinder block with the tab 1 on the left. Centre the gasket with the lower ends of the guides Z in their respective bolt holes. Locate the cylinder head on the block and engage the exhaust manifold fitted with a new gasket. Refit the pushrods in their original locations. Reassemble the rocker gear, lubricating the shaft and rockers and assembling the components in the order of their removal. Do not fully tighten the bracket bolts. Refit the cylinder head bolts and flat washers in the order shown in **FIG 1 : 7** and tighten moderately. Remove the guides Z with their upper ends and fit the corresponding cylinder head bolts. Tighten the cylinder head bolts in the order shown in **FIG 1 : 7,** first to a torque of 6 kg m (43.8 lb ft) and finally to a torque of 8.25 kg m (60.2 lb ft). Tighten the rocker shaft nuts to a torque of 1.5 kg m (10.9 lb ft).

The method of adjusting the valve clearances is to turn the crankshaft until the valves indicated in the first column of the following table (see also **FIG 1 : 8**) are open, when the rocker arms shown in the second column may be checked and adjusted as required.

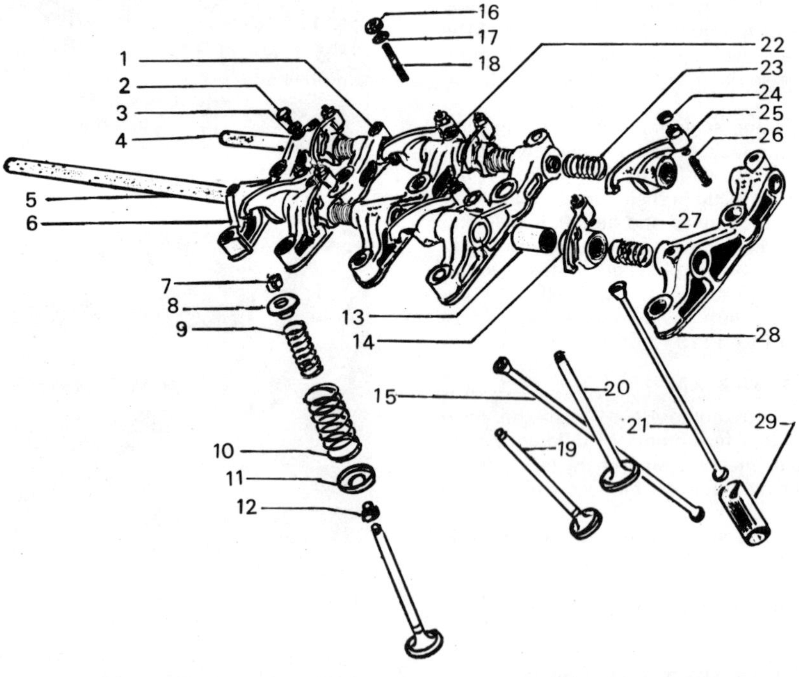

FIG 1 : 5 An exploded view of the rocker shaft and valve components

Key to Fig 1 : 5 1 Rocker shaft bracket, intermediate 2 Rocker shaft lock screw 3 Shakeproof washer 4 Inlet valve rocker shaft 5 Exhaust valve rocker shaft 6 Rocker shaft bracket, rear 7 Split collet 8 Spring seat 9 Inner spring 10 Outer spring 11 Spring seat 12 Oil seal 13 Bush 14 Exhaust valve rocker 15 Exhaust valve pushrod 16 Nut 17 Shakeproof washer 18 Stud 19 Exhaust valve 20 Inlet valve 21 Inlet valve pushrod 22 Rocker shaft bracket, centre 23 Spring 24 Locknut 25 Inlet valve rocker 26 Tappet adjusting screw, inlet 27 Tappet adjusting screw, exhaust 28 Rocker shaft bracket, front 29 Tappet

Valve wide open	*To adjust the rockers*
E1	In.3 E4
E3	In.4 E2
E4	In.2 E1
E2	In.1 E3

The rocker arm gaps for the first 1000 km (600 miles) should be set at inlet .15 mm (.006 inch) and exhaust .30 mm (.012 inch). Subsequently retighten the cylinder head bolts to the torque of 8.25 kg m (60.2 lb ft) and adjust the rockers to their normal gaps of inlet .10 mm (.004 inch), exhaust .25 mm (.010 inch).

Refit the rocker cover, the carburetter and other equipment originally removed for access, according to the extent of other overhaul work which may be intended.

With compressed liners, first pretighten the head bolts to 5 kg m (36 lb ft) and then tighten the rocker shaft support nuts to 1.5 kg m (11 lb ft).

Place the double socket tool 8.0129 on the two central bolts as shown in **FIG 1:27**, slacken off bolt No. 1 completely and retighten it to 2 kg m (15 lb ft). Hold the torque wrench under tension and place the pointer (inset 11) opposite the notch 0 on the quadrant of the double socket by pushing on the lower prong of the spring.

Continue tightening until the pointer 11 is in line with notch 90 on the quadrant and then repeat the operation on bolt No. 2.

Place the double socket on the other bolts in order 3–4, 5–6 etc., and tighten them in the same manner as above.

If there is any doubt about the tightening of any one bolt slacken off completely and repeat ALL the above operations.

When the head has been refitted the valve clearances may be adjusted as described earlier to: inlet .15 mm (.006 inch), exhaust .30 mm (.012 inch).

The cylinder head should be retightened when cold after 600 miles (1000 km) using the above procedure. Note that it may be necessary to move the brake servo unit forward, to gain access to bolt No. 9, without disconnecting the brake pipes from the master cylinder.

FIG 1:6 Refitting the cylinder head

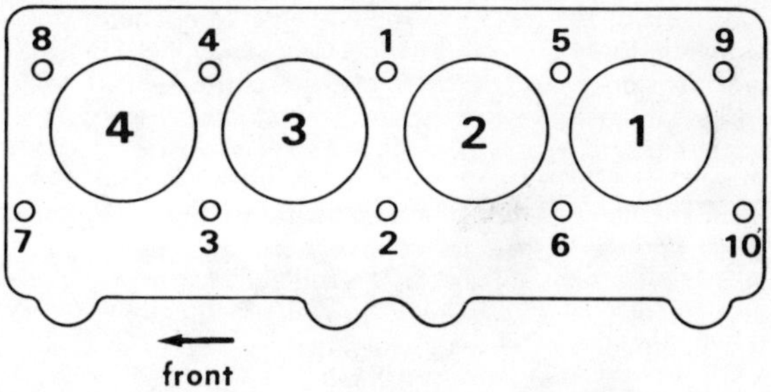

FIG 1:7 Cylinder head bolt tightening sequence

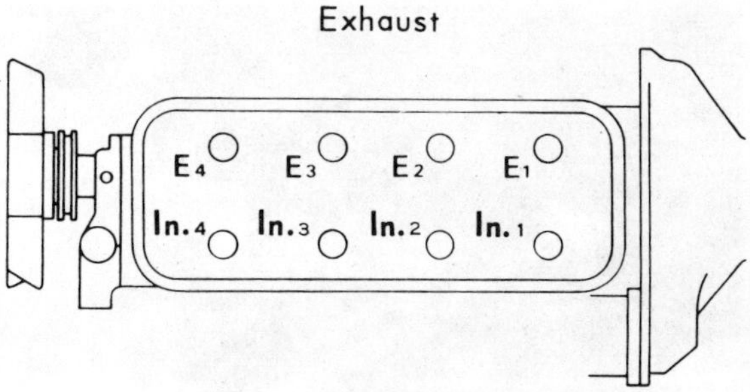

FIG 1:8 Valve locations

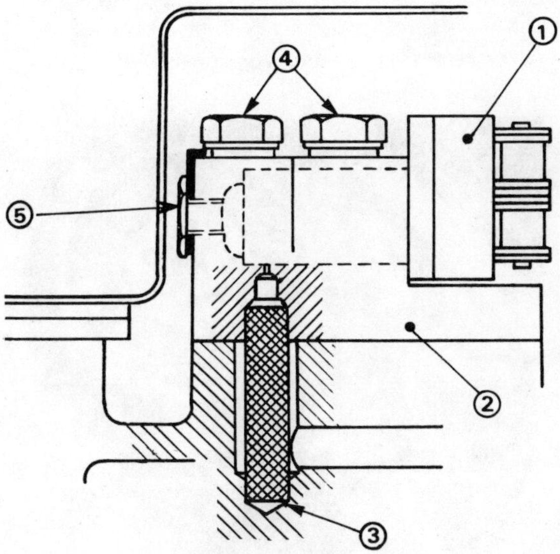

FIG 1:9 A sectional diagram of the chain tensioner

Key to Fig 1:9 1 Pad 2 Body 3 Filter 4 Securing bolts 5 Stopper bolt

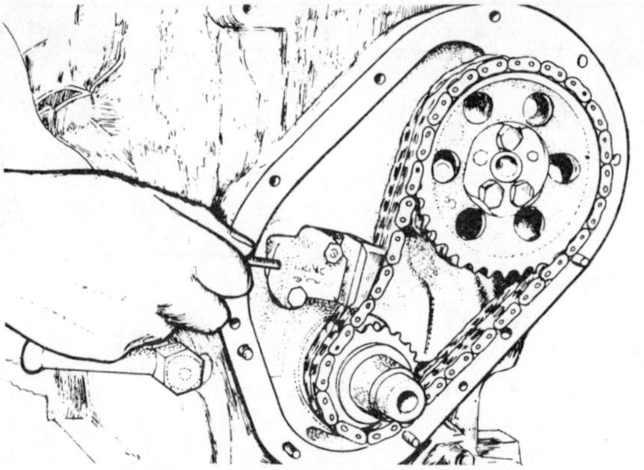

FIG 1:10 Removing the chain tensioner

FIG 1:11 Withdrawing the camshaft

FIG 1:12 Valve timing marks

Retighten the rocker shaft support nuts and then adjust the valve clearances to: inlet .10 mm (.004 inch), exhaust .25 mm (.010 inch).

Retighten the exhaust and inlet manifolds and also the carburetter.

1:6 Removing timing gear and camshaft

With the engine removed from the car as in **Section 1:3**, remove the fan belt, the fan and pulley as described in **Chapter 4.** Proceed as follows:

1 Remove the crankshaft pulley and its key, also the timing gear housing.

2 Unscrew the stopper bolt 5 (see **FIG 1:9**) from the chain tensioner and through the orifice insert a 3 mm Allen key into the plunger. Turn the key to the right to release the pad from the spring, as shown in **FIG 1:10.** Remove the tensioner and its filter 3 in **FIG 1:9.**

3 Proceed to remove the camshaft pinion, the timing chain, the washer and the crankshaft pinion. Incline the engine and remove the tappets, keeping them in correct order for reassembly.

4 Remove the sheet steel timing gear support plate, the gasket and the front stop. Carefully withdraw the camshaft as shown in **FIG 1:11.**

1:7 Refitting timing gear and camshaft

Before reassembly all parts should be examined for wear. If the skew gear is badly worn or damaged the drive gear may also have to be renewed. Compare the shape of the teeth on the timing wheels with those on a new wheel, as worn teeth will cause rapid wear on a new chain. Operations for reassembly are as follows:

1 Lubricate and refit the tappets in the same order as removed and ensuring that each tappet is fully home.

2 Smear the cams with graphited oil and carefully insert the camshaft.

3 Fit the crankshaft pinion with its key and thrust washer. As shown in **FIG 1:12,** marks are inscribed on the crankshaft and camshaft pinions which must be brought into line in the positions indicated.

FIG 1:13 Refitting timing gear housing. **A** indicates the centring bush No. 0.0128

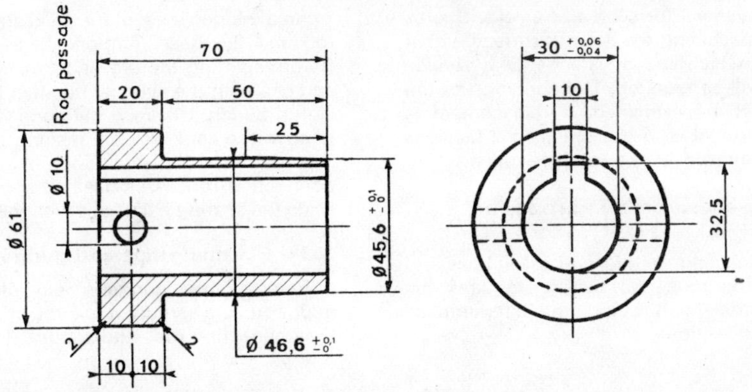

FIG 1:14 Centring bush for timing gear housing. Dimensions are in mm

4 Locate the chain on the camshaft pinion with the two cadmium-plated links enclosing the marked tooth on the pinion.

Retain this assembly and fit the chain on the crankshaft pinion with the marked tooth coinciding with the cadmium-plated link. Rotate the engine as necessary to bring the marks into the positions indicated and secure the camshaft pinion. Use a new lockwasher and tighten the bolts to a torque of 2.25 kg m (16 lb ft).

Fit the chain tensioner. Locate the plunger and spring against the pad 1 (see **FIG 1:9**) and secure the plunger by inserting the 3 mm key and turning it to the right. Position the pad in the body 2 to ensure its free movement and check that the filter 3 is unobstructed. Fit the retaining bolts 4 and reload the tensioner, using the Allen key and turning it to the right until it engages. Fit and lock the stopper bolt 5.

Refit the oil thrower bowl and the timing gear housing, using a new gasket. Centre the housing using the bush A.0.0128 (see **FIGS 1:13** and **1:14**) and tighten the bolts to a torque of 1 kg m (7.2 lb ft). Fit the crankshaft pulley, a new sheet steel locking washer and the securing nut tightened to 17 kg m (123 lb ft). The sheet steel locking washer was discontinued in October 1968 and for later cars the fitting of a locking washer PN.0518.05 is advised.

1:8 Removing and refitting the oil pump

With the engine removed from the car, the oil drained from the sump and the cylinder head removed, incline the engine and remove the tappets (see **Section 1:6**). Turn the engine upside down as shown in **FIG 1:15** and remove the sump. Withdraw the oil pump after taking out the three retaining screws.

To refit the pump, locate the centring pins 1 (see **FIG 1:15**) in the cylinder block and the O-ring 2 in the oil pump. Then locate the pump in position, ensuring that the drive blade is correctly in place and turning the crankshaft if necessary. Tighten the retaining bolts to a torque of 1 kg m (7.2 lb ft). Ensure that the mating faces of the sump and crankcase are thoroughly clean, then refit the sump with a new gasket. Tighten the bolts to a torque of 1 kg m (7.2 lb ft) and the drain plug to a torque of 4.25 kg m (31 lb ft).

Details of the construction of the oil pump and the external oil filter are shown in **FIG 1:16**. The pump is of the gear-type incorporating driving and driven impellers and is driven from the camshaft by skew gears, one of which is secured to the pump impeller driving spindle. The bottom cover provides attachment for a gauze screen. A spring-loaded oil pressure relief valve is fitted. A similar relief valve is incorporated in the external oil filter, ensuring the continued circulation of oil if the filter cartridge becomes obstructed.

1:9 Removing clutch and flywheel

To remove the clutch it is necessary to remove the engine as described in **Section 1:3**. Then proceed as follows:

1 Mark the clutch cover and flywheel relationship.

2 Unscrew the six retaining screws and remove the clutch assembly and disc (see **FIG 1:17**). Use an Allen key of 6 mm across the flats and slacken the screws gradually by diagonal selection until the spring pressure is released.

Unscrew the retaining bolts securing the flywheel. Support the latter and tap it off the crankshaft flange evenly, using a copper or lead hammer. Examine the

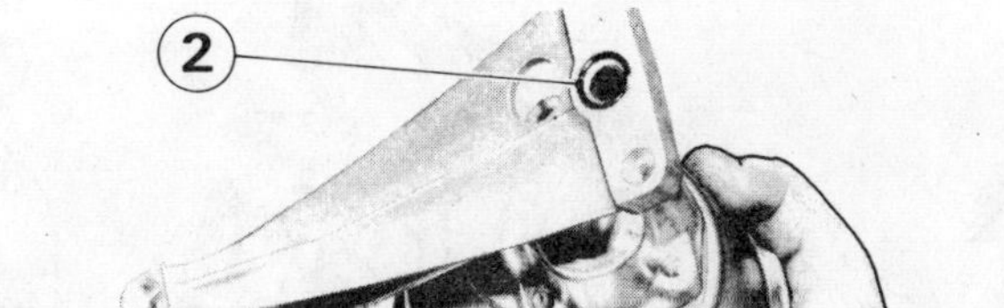

FIG 1:15 Refitting the oil pump. 1 indicates the centring pins and 2 the O-ring

friction face of the flywheel for scores or cracks. Scores can be removed by machining the bearing surface within specified limits, for which the assistance of a service agent with a lathe will be required. The condition of the ring gear should also be examined. If replacement is necessary it is also advisable to use the special facilities and experience at the disposal of a service workshop.

1:10 Splitting big-ends, removing rods and pistons

Access to the connecting rod big-end assemblies and removal of connecting rods and pistons requires the removal of the cylinder head, sump and oil pump as described in previous Sections.

An exploded view of the crankshaft, piston, connecting rod and flywheel components is shown in **FIG 1:18.** Before splitting the big-ends, mark each connecting rod and cap with the cylinder number, but do not use a file or centre punch. Unscrew the connecting rod cap nuts and remove the caps and the bearing half shells. Keep these aside in order of dismantling. Then withdraw the piston-connecting rod assemblies as shown in **FIG 1:19.** Set aside the bearing half shells with their corresponding caps.

1:11 Pistons, rings and gudgeon pins

Remove the gudgeon pin circlips, withdraw the gudgeon pins and uncouple the connecting rods. Lay out the connecting rods and pistons with their gudgeon pins

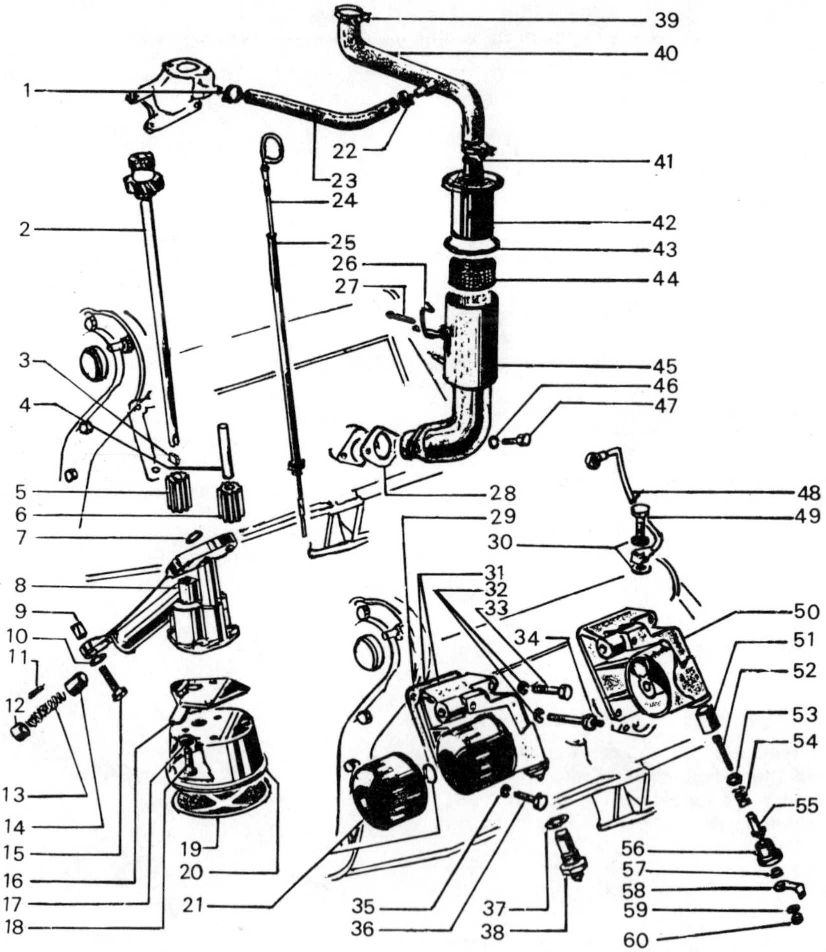

FIG 1:16 Exploded views of the oil pump and external oil filter

Key to Fig 1:16 1 Clip 2 Oil pump drive shaft 3 Key 4 Idler shaft 5 Oil pump drive pinion 6 Oil pump idler pinion 7 O-ring 8 Pump housing 9 Split bush 10 Washer 11 Splitpin 12 Relief valve spring retainer 13 Relief valve spring 14 Relief valve 15 Screw 16 Pump cover and stand pipe 17 Lockwasher 18 Screw 19 Strainer 20 Bottom cover 21 Filter cover 22 Clip 23 Pipe 24 Dipstick 25 Dipstick tube 26 Spring clip 27 Splitpin 28 Washer 29 Washer 30 Washers sealing 31 External filter casing assembly 32 Spring washers 33 Bolt 34 Stud 35 Spring washer 36 Bolt 37 Washer 38 Filter bypass valve assembly 39 Clip 40 Pipe 41 Clip 42 Oil filter cap 43 Washer 44 Strainer and flame trap 45 Oil filter casing 46 Spring washer 47 Screw 48 Oil pipe 49 Bolt 50 Oil filter casing 51 Filter bypass valve 52 Bolt 53 Guide 54 Spring 55 Pressure release valve 56 Plug 57 Washer 58 Clip 59 Washer 60 Nut in the order in which they were removed. The gudgeon pin/piston pairing must never be altered as it is established during production with precision apparatus.

If required, remove the retaining screws 8.0104D and the early type of liner. With compressed liners the owner is advised to consult his local service station for specialist attention. If after long use the liners are not removable by hand an extractor such as that shown in **FIG 1:20** may be used. Carefully clean the cylinder block and all the dismantled components. Inspect all parts and renew all which are outside the permitted tolerances. When refitting the liners, fit a new rubber seal to each liner and insert the liners in their housings so that the reference marks face the camshaft side. The liner protrusion above the cylinder block should be between 0 and 0.7 mm. Liners are available for renewal in four grades identified by I, II, III and IIII with corresponding grades of pistons A, B, C and D. The diameter of a piston is measured at right angles to the gudgeon pin and 48 mm from the lower edge of the lowest piston ring groove towards the bottom of the piston.

In the event of liner/piston renewal, remove the gudgeon pins from the new pistons, paired with the liners, lubricate them and reassemble the piston/connecting rod assemblies by hand. Ensure the correct

FIG 1:17 Removing the clutch

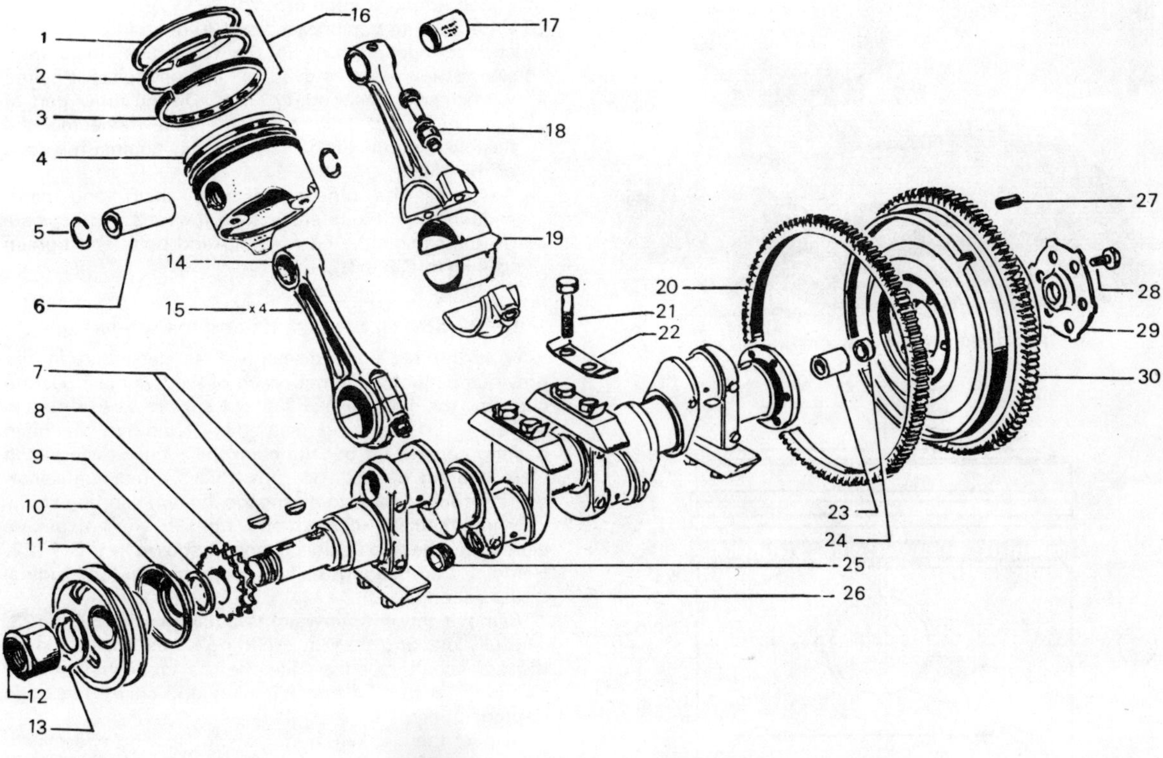

FIG 1:18 An exploded view of the crankshaft, connecting rods and pistons

Key to Fig 1:18 1 Upper compression ring 2 Lower compression ring 3 Scraper ring 4 Piston assembly 5 Circlip 6 Gudgeon pin 7 Woodruff keys 8 Crankshaft sprocket 9 Thrust washer 10 Oil thrower 11 Pulley 12 Nut 13 Tab washer 14 Bush 15 Connecting rod 16 Piston ring assembly 17 Small end bush 18 Big end bolt assembly 19 Big end bush 20 Starter ring 21 Bolt 22 Tab washer 23 Locating bush 24 Seal 25 Crankpin plug 26 Counterweight 27 Dowel 28 Screw 29 Locking plate 30 Flywheel assembly

FIG 1:19 Withdrawing a piston and connecting rod assembly with the liner retaining screws inserted

FIG 1:20 Removing a cylinder liner

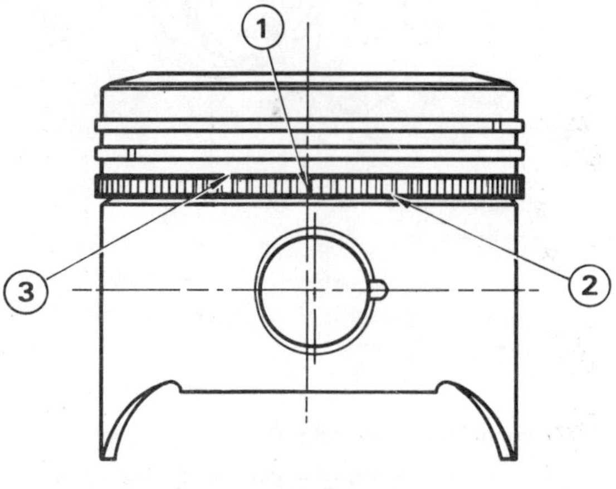

FIG 1:21 Piston rings

Key to Fig 1:21 1 Expander 2 and 3 Flexible rings

positioning of the pistons. A piston is stamped on the top with the mark 'AV' and an arrow, which must point towards the front of the engine when the piston is assembled.

Each piston is fitted with two compression rings and one 'Perfect Circle' oil scraper ring, the top compression ring being chrome plated. If the existing pistons continue to be employed, decarbonize the ring grooves and fit the rings as follows:

1 Locate the expander section of the oil control ring in the lowest piston groove. Referring to **FIG 1:21**, position the gap in the expander 1 along the axis of the gudgeon pin.
2 Working from the piston head, fit one flexible ring on top of the expander section, first engaging the end of the flexible ring over the expander end. Fit the other flexible ring over the bottom face of the expander section similarly. The gaps of the flexible rings 2 and 3 should be located 20 to 50 mm from the gap in the expander. The length of the expander must never be altered.
3 Check the ring gaps by locating the piston ring in the unworn portion of the cylinder liner and measuring the gap, which should be .4 mm for both compression and oil control rings.
4 Fit the compression rings to the pistons with the reference marks facing upwards and the chrome plated ring in the top groove.
5 With the ring gaps spaced at 120 deg., fit the pistons and connecting rods in the respective liners from which they were removed, or keep new pistons paired with their corresponding liners. Oil the inner part of the liners and take care to avoid damaging the flexible sections of the scraper rings against the edge of the liners.
6 Assemble the big-end bearing shells and caps, ensuring that the references on the rods and caps are on the same side. Fit new big-end bolts and tighten to 4 kg m (29 lb ft).

1:12 Removing crankshaft and main bearings

With the big-ends dismantled as described in the previous Section, first mark each of the five main bearing caps and the crankcase so that the caps can be refitted in the same positions on reassembly. Remove the main bearing caps to lift out the crankshaft, unscrewing each main bearing cap bolt in turn. Pull the rear crankshaft bearing cap upwards to disengage the two centring studs. The intermediate, central and front bearing caps are centred by the two flexible bushes 1 shown in **FIG 1:22**. Remove the bearing half-shells and the longitudinal thrust bearings.

Remove the counterweights as shown in **FIG 1:23**, carefully marking them for refitting so as not to disturb the crankshaft balance. Remove the crankshaft sludge trap plugs with a 14 mm Allen key and clear the sludge trap chambers.

Inspect the crankshaft journals for scoring and ovality in comparison with the specified main bearing journal diameter. Measure the diameters of the bearing journals and crankpins in order to fit the corresponding shells. Parts showing evidence of wear should be renewed. Clean the crankshaft oilways thoroughly, particularly if any bearings have run. Renew the bearing shells if they show signs of scoring or breaking away. All parts should be lubricated with engine oil before refitting.

Prepare the crankshaft for refitting by installing new plugs, coated with Festinol, in the sludge traps of each crankshaft journal. Tighten the plugs to a torque of 5.5 kg m (39.7 lb ft) and lock them by centre punching several times. Position the counterweights as dismantled, tighten the bolts to a torque of 6.75 kg m (48.8 lb ft) and lock them.

To reassemble, position the bearing half-shells of the crankshaft in the corresponding cylinder block housings. Lubricate the bearings and carefully locate the crankshaft in place. Insert the thrust half bearings (see **FIG 1:24**) in their original positions on either side of the rear bearing, with the lubrication grooves facing the crankshaft.

Fit the rear bearing cap, with the half-shell in place, without the lateral seals. Then fit the remaining bearing caps with their shells, the centre bearing cap having 2 embossments towards the rear, the front 1, the intermediate rear 2 and the intermediate front 1. Tighten the bearing cap bolts to a torque of 7.5 kg m (54.7 lb ft) and turn the crankshaft to ensure that there are no tight spots.

Check the longitudinal end play with the aid of a dial gauge. Fix the gauge support in a suitable position (see **FIG 1:25**) and bring the gauge sender to rest on the end of the crankshaft. Push the crankshaft fully forward when the gauge will indicate the amount of play. This should be within .08 and .20 mm. Should the end float be outside this tolerance fit oversize thrust washers which are available for service.

Remove the rear bearing cap and install the rubber side joints on each side of the bearing cap. Fit the special tool No. 8.0110X to compress the joints as shown in **FIG 1:26.** Oil the assembly and locate it in position on the block. Fit the bearing cap bolts finger tight, withdraw the assembly tool and tighten the cap bolts to a torque of 7.5 kg m (54.7 lb ft). Finally cut off the rubber side seals .5 mm above the machined surface of the cylinder block. A shim plate 8.0110D is available to cut the seals to the required level.

1:13 Reassembling stripped engine

Much of the work of reassembling a stripped engine has already been described in previous Sections, where it has been convenient to include it with other details concerning particular assemblies. The refitting of the crankshaft has been described in **Section 1:12,** which is followed by refitting the flywheel on the crankshaft flange. Carefully clean the crankshaft flange and the mating surface of the flywheel, then locate the flywheel, use a new lockwasher and tighten the retaining bolts to a torque of 6.75 kg m (49 lb ft). The clutch assembly, except where automatic transmission is used, may now be reassembled on the flywheel. Position the clutch plate according to the locating marks made when dismantling and with the flexible hub facing the gearbox. Before tightening the clutch cover attaching bolts insert a clutch disc aligning tool 8.0207 through the disc hub until it engages the spigot bearing in the crankshaft. Tighten the cover attaching bolts evenly by diagonal selection to a torque of 1.5 kg m (11 lb ft) after refitting the Onduflex washers and remove the clutch disc locator.

Refitting of the piston and connecting rod assemblies is described in **Section 1:11,** the sump and oil pump in

FIG 1:22 Removing the main bearing caps

FIG 1:23 Removing the crankshaft counterweights

FIG 1:24 Fitting thrust half bearings on each side of the rear main bearing

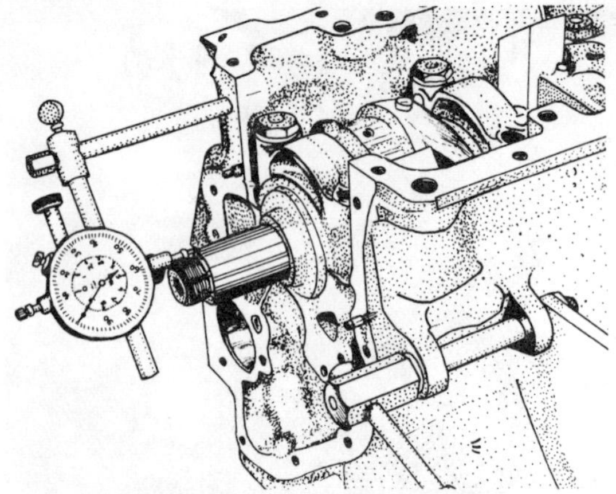

FIG 1:25 Checking the end float or longitudinal play of the crankshaft

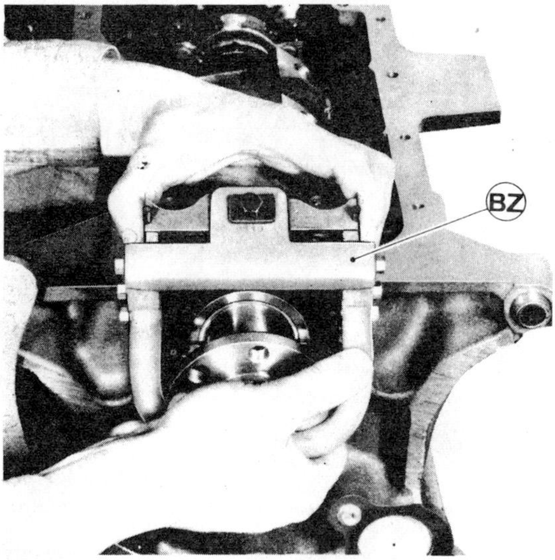

FIG 1:26 Fitting rear main bearing cap seal with the aid of the assembly tool 8.0110X indicated by BZ

Section 1:8, the camshaft and timing gear in **Section 1:7,** the valve tappets, pushrods, valves, rocker shaft assembly and cylinder head in **Section 1:5.** Fitting the distributor and details of ignition timing are dealt with in **Chapter 3.** The alternator and starter motor may be refitted at this stage or left until the engine is in the car.

1:14 Refitting engine in car

Take the weight of the engine on suitable lifting tackle and lower the engine into position opposite the gearbox mainshaft. Engage a gear and couple the two components together whilst turning the crankshaft with a 35 mm open-ended spanner. Check the engine/gearbox alignment and do not force the components together to avoid the risk of distorting the clutch plate.

Automatic transmission:

When reassembling the engine to an automatic transmission, first secure the converter housing to the cylinder block then bring one of the openings in the flywheel to the bottom.

Rotate the converter (using a screwdriver engaged in the cooling fins) to line up one of the threaded holes with the coupling plate on the flywheel.

Tighten the bolts to 16 lb ft.

Restore the engine auxiliary equipment and connections by proceeding in the reverse order of their removal. Use new flat and locking washers and renew all hoses and rubber unions which are worn.

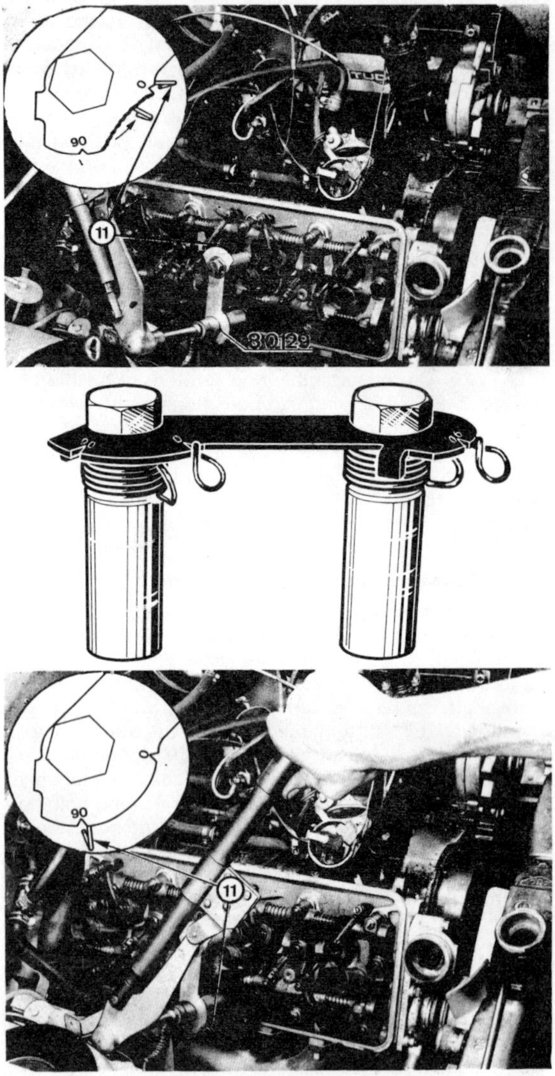

FIG 1:27 Tightening the cylinder head bolts when compressed liners are installed

Refill the radiator with coolant and check for leaks. Refill the engine and transmission with the correct grade of lubricating oil. Refit the bonnet and check its alignment. After a final inspection to ensure that all components have been properly connected, run the engine and carry out any minor adjustments which may be necessary, including attention to any oil or water leaks and the operation of the alternator, the brake servo and the oil pressure and choke warning lights. After the car has travelled 1000 km (600 miles) retighten the cylinder head bolts and adjust the rockers to their normal gap as described in **Section 1 :5**.

1 :15 Fault diagnosis

(a) Engine will not start

1 Defective coil
2 Faulty distributor capacitor
3 Dirty, pitted or incorrectly set contact breaker points
4 Ignition wires loose or insulation faulty
5 Water on sparking plug leads
6 Corrosion of battery terminals or discharged condition
7 Faulty or jammed starter
8 Sparking plug leads wrongly connected
9 Vapour lock in fuel pipes
10 Defective fuel pump
11 Overchoking
12 Underchoking
13 Blocked petrol filter or carburetter jets
14 Leaking valves
15 Sticking valves
16 Valve timing incorrect
17 Ignition timing incorrect

(b) Engine stalls

Check 1, 2, 3, 4, 10, 11, 12, 13, 14 and 15 in (a)
1 Sparking plugs defective or gap incorrect
2 Retarded ignition
3 Mixture too weak
4 Water in fuel system
5 Petrol tank breather choked
6 Incorrect valve clearance

(c) Engine idles badly

Check 1 and 6 in (b)
1 Air leak in manifold joints
2 Slow-running jet blocked or out of adjustment
3 Air leak in carburetter
4 Over-rich mixture
5 Worn piston rings
6 Worn valve stems or guides
7 Weak exhaust valve springs

(d) Engine misfires

Check 1, 2, 3, 4, 5, 8, 10, 13, 14, 15, 16 and 17 in (a); and 1, 2, 3 and 6 in (b)
1 Weak or broken valve springs

(e) Engine overheats (see **Chapter 4**)

(f) Compression low

Check 14 and 15 in (a); 5 and 6 in (c); and 1 in (d)
1 Worn piston ring grooves
2 Scored or worn cylinder bores

(g) Engine lacks power

Check 3, 10, 11, 13, 14, 15 and 16 in (a); 1, 2, 3 and 6 in (b); 5 and 6 in (c); and 1 in (d). Also check (e) and (f).
1 Leaking joint washers
2 Fouled sparking plugs
3 Automatic advance not operating

(h) Burnt valves or seats

Check 14 and 15 in (a); 6 in (b); and 1 in (d). Also check (e)
1 Excessive carbon around valve seat and head

(j) Sticking valves

Check 1 in (d)
1 Bent valve stem
2 Scored valve stem or guide
3 Incorrect valve clearance

(k) Excessive cylinder wear

Check 11 in (a); and check (c)
1 Lack of oil
2 Dirty oil
3 Piston rings gummed up or broken
4 Badly fitting piston rings
5 Connecting rods bent

(l) Excessive oil consumption

Check 5 and 6 in (c); and check (k)
1 Ring gaps too wide
2 Oil return holes in piston choked with carbon
3 Scored cylinders
4 Oil level too high
5 External oil leaks
6 Ineffective valve stem oil seals

(m) Crankshaft and connecting rod failure

Check 1 in (k)
1 Restricted oilways
2 Worn journals or crankpins
3 Loose bearing caps
4 Extremely low oil pressure
5 Bent connecting rod

(n) Internal water leakage (see **Chapter 4**)

(o) Poor circulation (see **Chapter 4**)

(p) Corrosion (see **Chapter 4**)

(q) High fuel consumption (see **Chapter 2**)

(r) Engine vibration

1 Loose generator bolts
2 Fan blades out of balance
3 Incorrect clearance for front engine mounting rubbers
4 Exhaust pipe mountings too tight

NOTES

CHAPTER 2

THE FUEL SYSTEM

2:1 The fuel system

Fuel is supplied from a tank of 56 litre (12 gallons) capacity situated under the floor of the luggage compartment. From the tank, pipe and hose connections carry the fuel to a Guiot YY type mechanical fuel pump on the lefthand side of the crankcase. The pump feeds the Solex carburetter, either a single choke 34 PBICA unit or a twin choke type 32-35 SEIEA. Some U.S. market cars have two single choke units. The carburetter draws air through a Lautrette air cleaner.

To obtain a better power output, improved combustion and reduction of hydrocarbon emission from the exhaust, an optional alternative to a carburetter is provided by a Kugelfischer fuel injection unit. With this system mechanically metered and timed charges of fuel, according to both speed and load requirements, are injected into the engine inlet valve ports.

FUEL PUMP

2:2 Operating principles

The fuel pump is operated from an eccentric on the camshaft through a spring-loaded rocker arm (see **FIG 2:1**). The arm or lever moves a flexible diaphragm against a spring to create a partial vacuum in the pump, which enables the atmospheric pressure in the tank to send fuel through the connecting pipe to the pump. The return

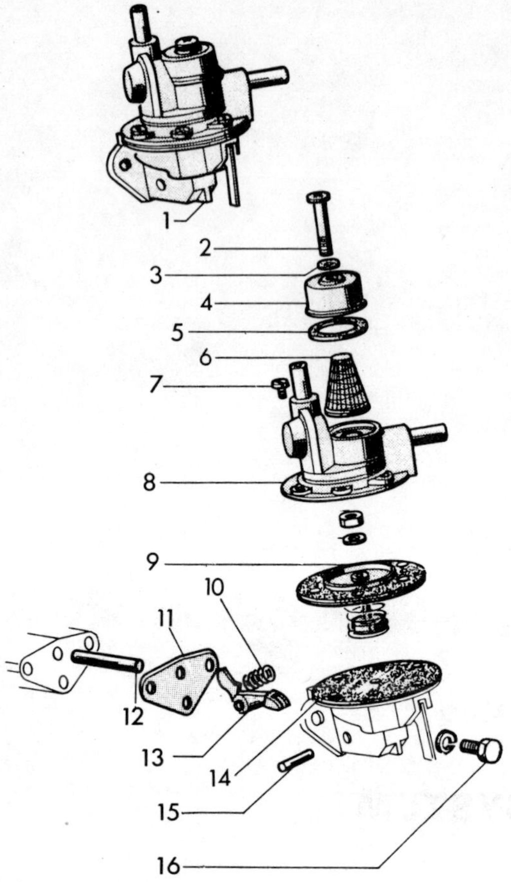

FIG 2:1 The fuel pump and main components

Key to Fig 2:1 1 Assembled pump 2 Upper cover retaining screw 3 Joint 4 Upper cover 5 Joint 6 Filter screen 7 Screw 8 Housing 9 Upper diaphragm assembly 10 Rocker arm spring 11 Joint 12 Spindle 13 Rocker arm 14 Lower diaphragm assembly 15 Pin 16 Retaining bolt

action of the spring then pushes the diaphragm upwards to deliver the fuel to the carburetter float chamber. When the bowl is full the float closes a needle valve, preventing further supply from the pump until the carburetter requires more fuel and the needle valve opens. In the meantime the pump rocker arm is given an idling movement.

With the fuel injection system, the fuel is supplied to the mechanical injection pump by a constant delivery electric pump fitted between the tank and the injection pump. In some cases a return pipe is connected to the tank by which any fuel surplus to the engine requirements is passed back to the tank. There may be a filter fitted in the pump outlet.

2:3 Routine maintenance and testing

Action of the pump is automatic and normally no maintenance is required. If trouble is experienced with the fuel supply the first approach should be to ensure that there are no leaks or obstructions in the fuel line. The pump filter gauze should be removed periodically for examination and cleaning. Detach the main fuel pipe from the pump and plug it to avoid loss of fuel. Remove the upper cover to obtain access to the filter, which should be washed in paraffin and allowed to dry. After refitting the filter and cover but with the fuel line disconnected a rough flow test can be made by rotating the engine a few times with the starter motor, when the pump should show an ample delivery of fuel. **Do not, however, carry out this test with a hot engine.** If the flow is still insufficient, remove the pump for examination.

2:4 Removal, dismantling and refitting

To remove a fuel pump, disconnect the inlet and outlet pipes, remove the retaining nuts and withdraw the pump and its gasket.

Remove the upper cover and filter as previously described, then mark across the flanges of the diaphragm housing cover and the pump body to ensure correct relationship when reassembling. Disengage the diaphragm assembly and the pushrod.

Inspect the rocker arm and components for wear. It is not necessary to remove the rocker arm unless excessive wear of the assembly is evident. The seats of the inlet and outlet valves are set in the cover of the pump. If the valves are ineffective it will be necessary to renew the pump. Examine the diaphragms for hardness or cracks, refit them dry on reassembly, and ensure that the screw holes in the diaphragms correspond with the threaded holes in the pump body. Reassemble in the reverse order of the dismantling operations and refit the pump with a new gasket. Prime the pump with the lever.

CARBURETTER

2:5 Operating principles

A choke control on the dashboard provides means for adjusting the mixture strength for starting from cold, slow-running from cold and driving away. With the control fully pulled out the mixture is enriched and is gradually weakened by progressively releasing the dashboard control. A half-way position is used when the engine is just warm, either after having run in the previous position or when the engine has not become quite cold after stopping.

A diagrammatic view of the main features of the carburetter is shown in **FIG 2:2** and an exploded view of the component parts in **FIG 2:3.** When the engine has reached normal temperature, slow-running is obtained through the jet 'gN' (see **FIG 2:2**). For adjustment, a throttle adjustment screw allows the speed of the engine to be varied and a volume control screw 'w' corrects the richness of the mixture. Emulsifying air is supplied through a calibrated orifice 'u¹' in the body of the carburetter located in an annular space beneath the choke tube 'K'. For normal running the fuel is provided by the main jet 'Gg' and the air through the choke tube. The correct balance is automatically ensured by air entering through and calibrated by the correction jet 'a'. Underneath the correction jet is an emulsion tube 's' with lateral holes. The calibration of this component should not be altered.

Acceleration is assisted by an accelerating pump injecting a small amount of supplementary fuel when accelerating action is applied. When the throttle is in the idling position the diaphragm M is connected to the accelerator by means of a lever on the throttle spindle. As soon as the throttle is opened, movement of the diaphragm forces petrol from the reserve into the injector 'i' discharging into the choke tube. Replacement accelerator pumps have a nut and locknut (163 and 164 in **FIG 2:3**) which enable the pump stroke to be adjusted, but in complete carburetters the adjustment is pre-set with one nut which is peened over.

For cold weather conditions, to prevent stalling of the engine if ice forms in the carburetter, a connection 'R' is provided for the circulation of water from the car heating system.

2:6 Routine maintenance, tuning for slow-running

Normal maintenance work which can be undertaken without extensive dismantling includes periodic cleaning of the float chamber and jets. After removing the float chamber cover the float arm and float are lifted out and the chamber swilled in clean petrol to remove all sediment. The jets should also be occasionally removed and cleared, preferably using a compressed air supply. **Never use wire or anything which may enlarge the jets.** Every 3000 km or 2000 miles clean the gauze around the pump valve H in **FIG 2:2.**

Before adjusting for slow-running it should be noted that satisfactory adjustment is impossible if there are air leaks in the intake system, incorrect fuel level or fouled sparking plugs. The engine must also be run until warmed up to the normal working temperature and operating with the fan engaged. Referring to **FIG 2:4,** adjustment is made as follows:

1 Adjust the idling or throttle screw 1 until the engine is running at a fairly fast idling speed of approximately 820 rev/min.
2 Find the maximum engine speed using the mixture screw 2.
3 Slacken the screw 1 progressively to bring the engine speed down to approximately 820 rev/min.
4 Tighten the mixture screw 2 until the engine speed drops abruptly, then slacken it the minimum amount necessary to obtain an engine speed of approximately 800 rev/min.

In cars fitted with automatic transmission, ensure that the handbrake is applied and the selector lever in the P or N position for adjustment of the idling speed. If the lever is in any other position the car may move with increase in engine speed. After adjusting the idling speed, move the selector lever to the No. 3 or drive position and check that the adjustment made provides smooth idling consistent with minimum creep. Ensure that the engine is not unduly speeded up during this operation.

2:7 Dismantling and reassembly

To remove a carburetter, remove the clip retaining the air cleaner hose and then disconnect the throttle spindle, the fuel pipe, the distributor vacuum advance suction pipe and the water circulation pipes. Remove the carburetter flange attaching nuts and lift away the carburetter and gasket. Referring to **FIG 2:3,** dismantling procedure is as follows:

1 Remove the three float chamber cover screws 126 and the spring washers 18 and lift off the cover 109 and the gasket 65.
2 Remove the starter valve assembly 23 and the starter fuel jet 75.
3 Remove the emulsion tube 81 and the air correction jet above it. From inside the float chamber remove the toggle spindle 66 and the float assembly 62.

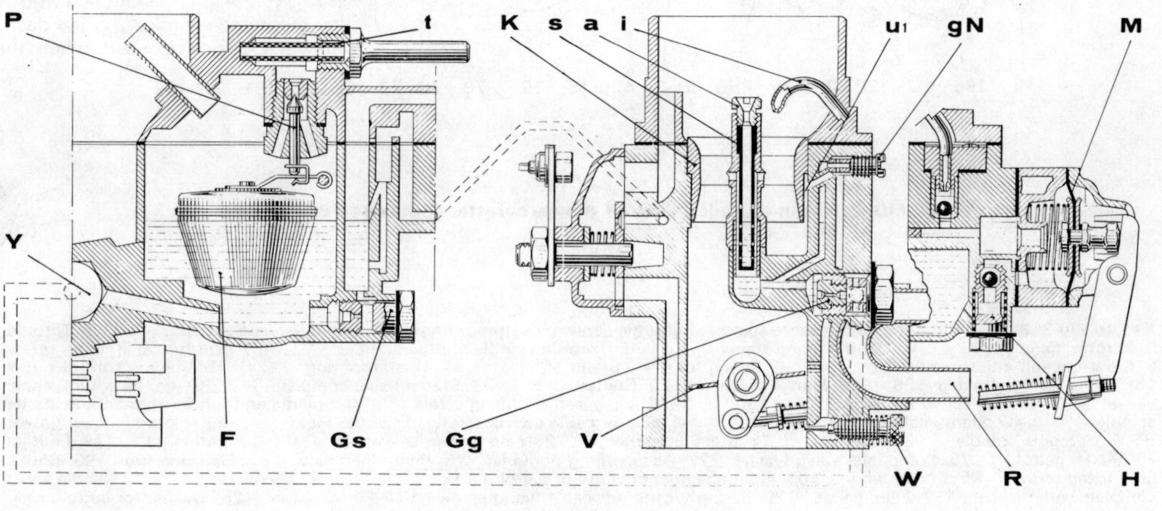

FIG 2:2 Sectional views of the carburetter

Key to Fig 2:2 **a** Correction jet **F** Float **Gg** Main jet **Gs** Starter petrol jet **gN** Pilot jet **H** Pump valve **i** Pump injector **K** Choke tube **M** Pump membrane **P** Needle valve **R** Water circuit connection **s** Emulsion tube **t** Filter element **u**[1] Calibrated orifice for idling air bleed **V** Throttle **W** Volume control screw **Y** Main jet carrier

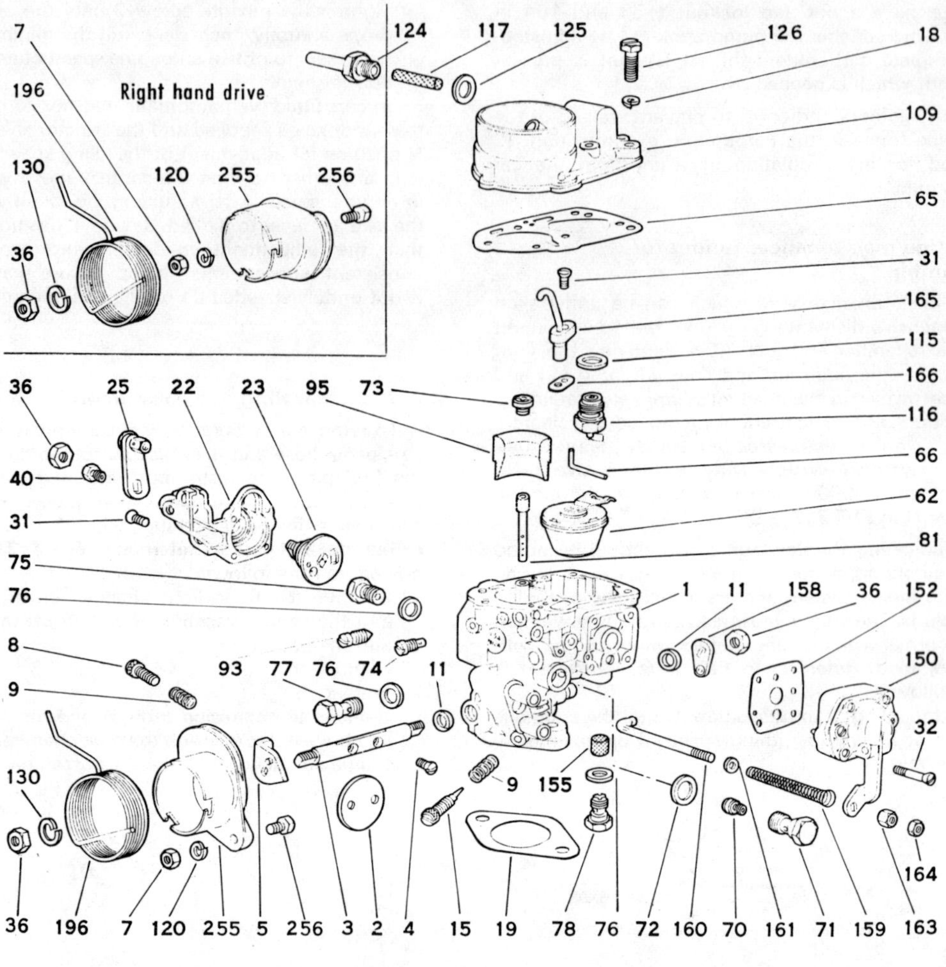

FIG 2:3 An exploded view of the carburetter (Solex 34 PBICA 5)

Key to Fig 2:3 1 Body with throttle spindle, butterfly, screws, dustproof rings and suction advance drilling 2 Throttle 3 Throttle spindle 4 Throttle fixing screw 5 Throttle spindle abutment plate 7 Nut for cable fixing screw 8 Slow-running adjustment screw 9 Spring for items 8 and 15 11 Dustproof ring 15 Volume control screw 18 Spring washer for item 126 19 Flange washer 22 Starter cover 23 Starter valve complete 25 Starter lever with cable swivel 31 Fixing screw for items 22 and 165 32 Pump assembly fixing screw 36 Spindle end nut for throttle and starter spindles 40 Starter cable locking screw 41 Starter cable swivel screw 62 Float 65 Float chamber gasket 66 Float toggle spindle 70 Main jet 71 Main jet carrier 72 Main jet carrier washer 73 Correction jet 74 Pilot jet 75 Starter petrol jet 76 Pump inlet valve washer 77 Accelerating pump jet 78 Pump inlet valve 81 Emulsion tube 93 Choke tube fixing screw 95 Choke tube 109 Float chamber cover with petrol union 115 Needle valve washer 116 Needle valve complete with washer 117 Filter gauze 120 Spring washer for cable fixing screw 124 Petrol union 125 Washer for petrol union 126 Float chamber assembly screw 130 Spring washer for item 3 150 Accelerating pump 152 Pump body gasket 155 Pump filter gauze 158 Pump intermediate actuating lever 159 Pump control rod spring 160 Pump control rod 161 Pump control rod retaining washer 163 Pump control rod adjustment nut 164 Adjustment nut locknut 165 Pump injector assembly 166 Pump injector support gasket 196 Throttle control return spring 255 Throttle control 256 Cable fixing screw for throttle control

4 Take out the four screws 32 holding the accelerating pump assembly and disconnect the pump from the control rod 160.

5 Detach the main jet 70 and carrier, then remove the volume control screw 15 and the pump inlet valve 78. Also remove the accelerating pump jet 77 and the pilot jet 74.

Check the jet sizes against those given in the Technical Data Section. Ensure that all drillings and jet orifices are unobstructed. Blow through the jets and never use wire or anything which may enlarge the orifices. Renew the accelerator pump diaphragm if its condition is doubtful and test the one-way operation of the pump check valve.

Reassemble as dismantled but in reverse order of operations. Fit new gaskets and note that a kit is available for carburetter overhaul, containing new parts to replace those which wear the most as well as a complete set of gaskets. Refit the carburetter to the engine with a new gasket and ensure that the mating faces are clean.

AIR CLEANER

2:8 Routine maintenance

The Lautrette air cleaner fitted is of the dry type and is retained in position by clips at each end. The filter

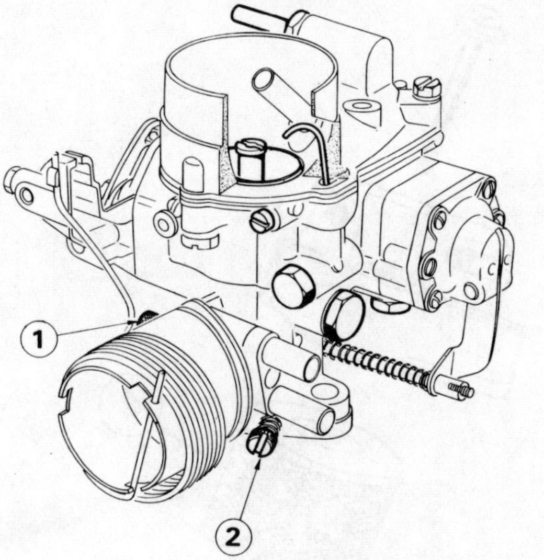

FIG 2:4 Adjustments for slow-running

Key to Fig 2:4 1 Idling screw 2 Mixture screw

Feed circuit

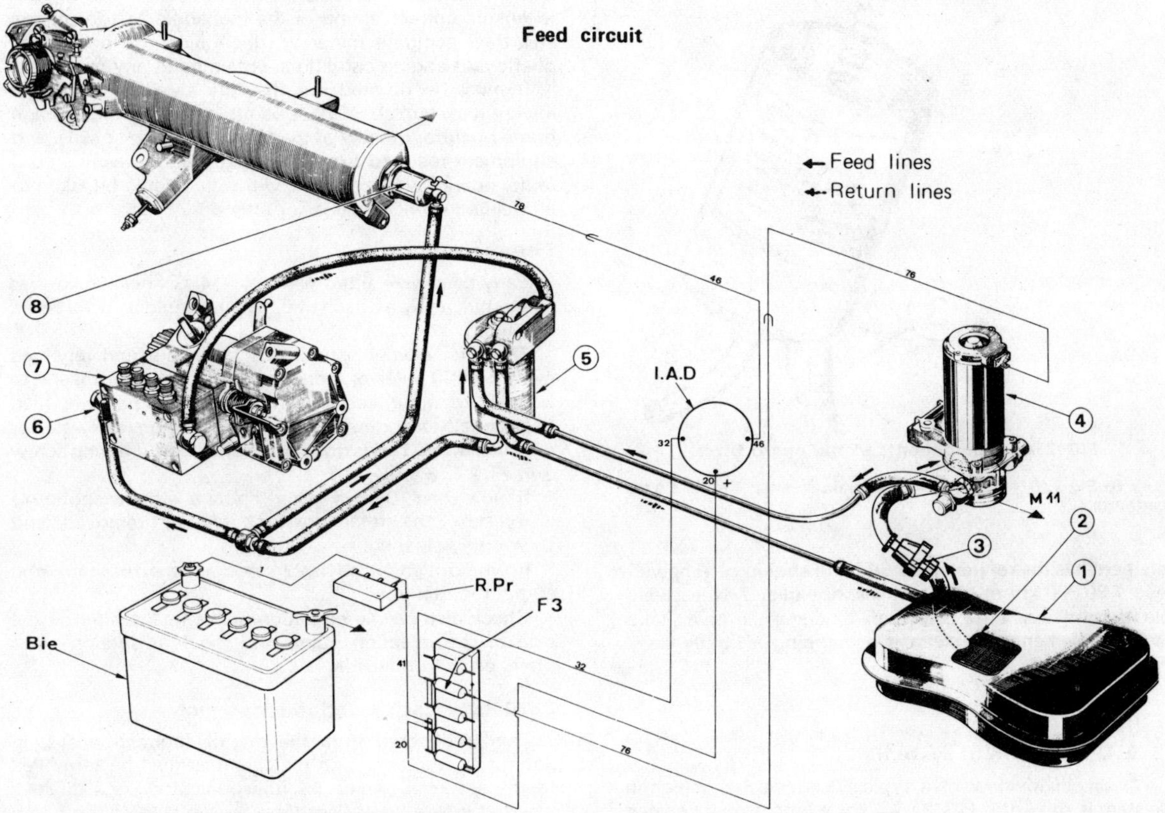

FIG 2:5 A typical Kugelfischer fuel injection system Peugeot 504, engine type KF6

Key to Fig 2:5 1 Fuel tank 2 Fuel strainer 3 Pre-filter 4 Electric fuel lift pump 5 Micro filter and water trap 6 Injection pump filter 7 Injection pump 8 Electro valve (starter) **Biè** Battery **R.pr** Relay **F3** Fuse **I.A.D.** Ignition switch

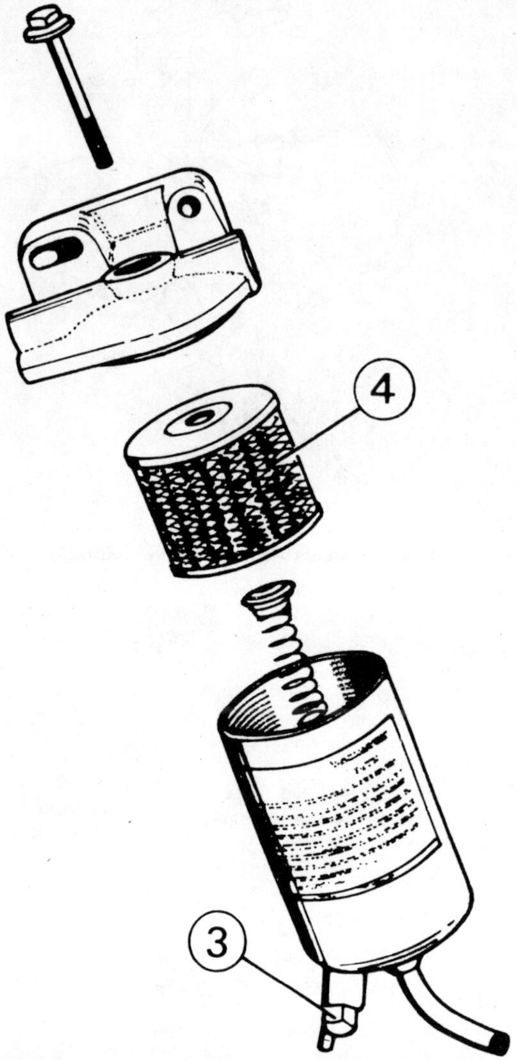

FIG 2:6 Components of the micro filter

Key to Fig 2:6 3 Bleeding or drain screw 4 C113 filter cartridge

element has the reference EL.697 and should be renewed every 20,000 km or 12,000 miles, or earlier if excessively dusty conditions have been experienced. At intervals take out the element and clean it by tapping it lightly on a firm surface.

FUEL INJECTION

2:9 Description of system

A simplified view of a typical Kugelfischer injection system is shown in **FIG 2:5**, from which it may be seen that the fuel is drawn from the tank 1 through the coarse strainer 2 and the pre-filter 3 to the electric lift pump 4. The fuel is then pumped through the microfilter and water trap 5 to the injection pump 7, which also includes a further filter element 6 in the intake union, and distributed to the four cylinders in the engine. A number of mixture control devices are included in the system in order to ensure correct timing of the individual fuel injections and their accurate metering, depending on the atmospheric and engine conditions obtaining at any moment.

It must be pointed out that the servicing of a fuel injection system should not be attempted by the average home operator in view of the highly specialized skills and equipment required to ensure a satisfactory result, and if faulty operation is experienced the car should be taken to a qualified service station for attention.

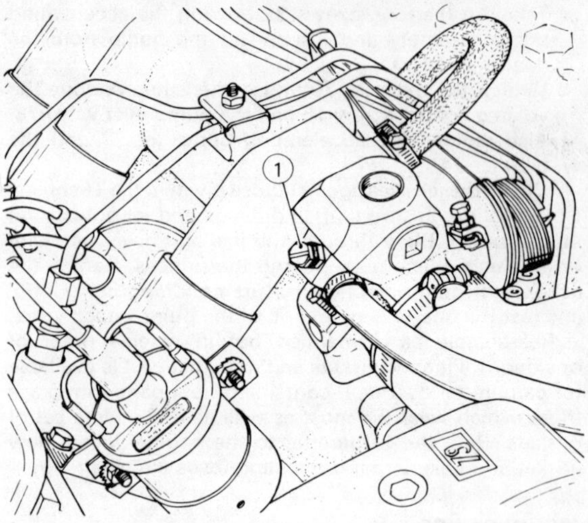

FIG 2:7 Showing the air bleed screw on the manifold

Filters:

Early cars were fitted with an AMFG filter which was later replaced by a Bosch unit, which should be used when renewing.

The filter element should be taken out and renewed every 10,000 miles or more frequently if there is reason to suspect contaminated fuel. The filter should also be bled occasionally to drain off any accumulations of water or dirty sediment. This is done by means of the draining screw 3 in **FIG 2:6**.

If more than 10 cc of water (about a large teaspoonful) is present, the filter bowl should be removed and thoroughly cleaned.

It would also be advisable to drain the fuel tank and empty the fuel lines.

Check also on the condition of the intake filter on the side of the injection pump and the four suction valve filters on the underside.

2:10 Lubrication and maintenance

This is effected from the engine lubrication system and for correct operation the chamber must be kept filled to the set level, which is either indicated on a dipstick inserted in the large filler tube on the side of the pump or by a level indicating hole on the front of the pump. If necessary, top up with clean engine oil to the dipstick mark or until it flows from the level hole. Refit the hexagon headed plug and the filler plug.

Slow running adjustment:

The correct idling speed for these engines is 850 rev/min and is set by adjustment of the air bleed screw, 1 in **FIG 2:7**, to meter the air and the enrichener stop screw, 2 in **FIG 2:8**, to meter the petrol. Note that turning the screw 2 inwards richens the mixture, unscrewing it weakens the mixture.

Bring the engine up to full working temperature and then disconnect the cable from the EXC terminal on the alternator. Adjust the air bleed screw to obtain an engine speed of 850 rev/min.

Insert a 3 mm Allen key in the screw 2 and very carefully raise the enrichener lever. The engine speed should increase to between 950 and 970 rev/min.

If the speed is over 970 rev/min the mixture is too lean and the stop should be screwed in by a quarter-of-a-turn. If the engine speed is less than 950 rev/min the mixture is too rich and the stop screw should be turned out by a quarter-of-a-turn.

After each adjustment of the stop screw 2 the correct idling speed must be reset by acting on screw 1 and then

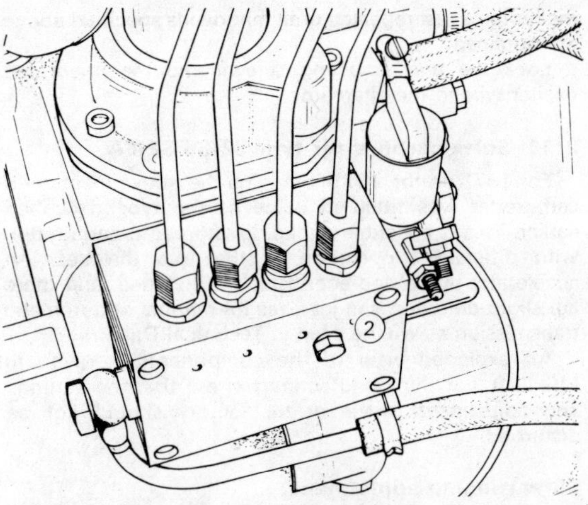

FIG 2:8 The enrichener stop screw. The hexagon headed plug seals the oil level indicator hole

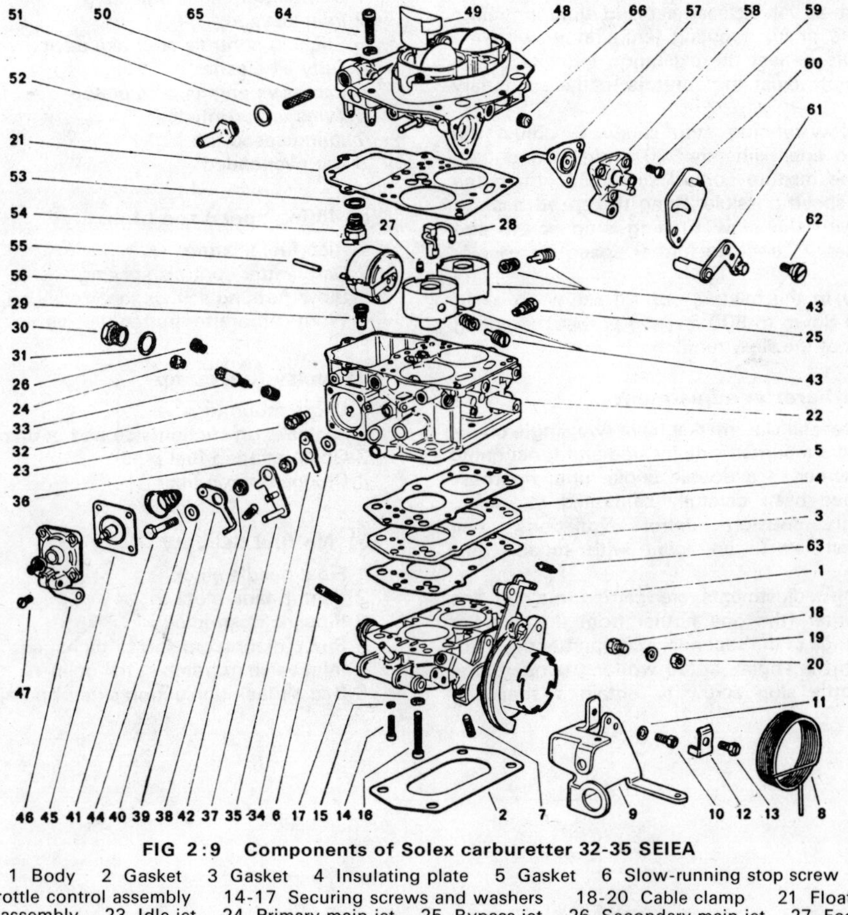

FIG 2:9 Components of Solex carburetter 32-35 SEIEA

Key to Fig 2:9 1 Body 2 Gasket 3 Gasket 4 Insulating plate 5 Gasket 6 Slow-running stop screw 7 Throttle stop screw 8-13 Throttle control assembly 14-17 Securing screws and washers 18-20 Cable clamp 21 Float chamber gasket 22 Float chamber assembly 23 Idle jet 24 Primary main jet 25 Bypass jet 26 Secondary main jet 27 Econostat calibrator 28 Pump injector 29 Ball valve 30 Plug 31 Washer 32-33 Mixture control screw 34-42 Throttle interconnecting linkage 43 Venturi assemblies 44-47 Accelerator pump 48 Float chamber cover assembly 49 Cover 50 Filter 51 Washer 52 Fuel inlet 53 Washer 54 Needle valve 55 Spindle 56 Float 57-62 Choke operating mechanism 63 Spring 64 Screw 65 Washer 66 Plug the richness test repeated until the speeds specified above are obtained.

Lock the two adjusting screws and reconnect the exciter wire to the alternator.

2:11 Solex carburetter type 32-35 SEIEA

For 1971 on the 1971 cc engine the above mentioned carburetter was fitted in place of the type described earlier. This is a double choke downdraught carburetter, with differential operation of the two throttles. An accelerator pump and econostat are included, and there are slight differences in jet sizes for manual or automatic transmission as will be seen in Technical Data.

An exploded view of the components is given in **FIG 2:9**, but the manufacturers stress that the settings and adjustments made at the factory should not be disturbed.

Slow running adjustment:

Before commencing to adjust the slow running settings it is important to ensure that the other engine components and accessories are in good order and adjustment, such as valve clearances and ignition timing. Have the engine at full working temperature with the fan engaged. Disconnect the excitation terminal of the alternator. Do not adjust the controls to the secondary throttle.

Using the slow-running stop screw 6, adjust the engine speed to approximately 840 rev/min, and then by means of the mixture control screw 33 obtain the highest engine speed possible. Bring the speed back to 840 rev/min with the slow running stop screw and repeat the procedure until no further speed increase is obtained.

Finally screw in the mixture control screw so as to bring the speed down to 800 rev/min without affecting the smoothness of the slow running.

2:12 Twin carburetter adjustment

Recent cars for the U.S. market have two single choke Solex carburetters mounted side by side and functioning in a similar manner to a double choke unit. As these carburetters have been carefully calibrated to ensure conformity with emission control regulations, their servicing is best left to an agent with suitable test equipment.

Slow running adjustments are carried out on the primary carburetter (the one further from the cylinder head). The settings of the secondary carburetter must not be altered. With the engine at full working temperature, adjust the throttle stop screw to obtain a speed of 820 rev/min for 1972 models, 800 rev/min for 1973 models. Unscrew the idle mixture adjuster just above the manifold until the engine is running steadily. Then turn the throttle stop screw again to obtain a speed of 870 rev/min (1972) or 830 to 880 rev/min (1973). Finally screw in the mixture adjuster to set the speed to 800 rev/min for 1972 models, 800 to 850 rev/min for 1973 models.

2:13 Fault diagnosis

(a) Leakage or insufficient fuel delivered

1 Air vent in tank restricted
2 Petrol pipes blocked
3 Air leaks at pipe connections
4 Pump or carburetter filters blocked
5 Pump gaskets faulty
6 Pump diaphragm defective
7 Pump valves sticking or seating badly
8 Fuel vaporizing in pipelines due to heat

(b) Excessive fuel consumption

1 Carburetter needs adjusting
2 Fuel leakage
3 Sticking controls or choke device
4 Dirty air cleaner
5 Excessive engine temperature
6 Tyres under-inflated
7 Idling speed too high
8 Car overloaded

(c) Idling speed too high

1 Rich fuel mixture
2 Carburetter controls sticking
3 Slow-running screws incorrectly adjusted
4 Worn carburetter butterfly valve

(d) Noisy fuel pump

1 Loose mountings
2 Air leaks on suction side and at diaphragm
3 Obstruction in fuel pipe
4 Clogged pump filter

(e) No fuel delivery

1 Float needle stuck
2 Vent in tank blocked
3 Pipeline obstructed
4 Pump diaphragm stiff or damaged
5 Inlet valve in pump stuck open
6 Bad air leak on suction side of pump

CHAPTER 3

THE IGNITION SYSTEM

3:1 Operating principles of automatic timing controls

The main elements in the ignition system providing high-tension current to the sparking plugs are the battery, the ignition coil, the contact breaker and the distributor. Distributors are of the Ducellier 4161 B or SEV-Marchal NA4C types on carburetter engines and a Ducellier 4218 A on fuel injection engines. The firing order is 1–3–4–2, counting from the flywheel end of the engine.

The distributor is mounted on the lefthand side of the crankcase and is driven clockwise at half engine speed by a skew gear on the crankshaft through the oil pump driving gear, which engages a driving sleeve secured to the lower end of the distributor mainshaft. Ignition advance is mechanically controlled according to engine speed by governor weights inside the distributor body and according to engine load by vacuum control acting directly on the contact breaker plate (see **FIG 3:1**), which is movable in relation to the distributor body. The governor mechanism consists of two weights pivoted so that they move outwards from the distributor shaft as the engine speed increases, turning the cam on the shaft assembly H and so advancing the firing point. The weights are restrained by springs to give a progressive advance action. The vacuum mechanism includes a spring-loaded diaphragm in a circular metal housing connected to the carburetter by a suction pipe. Manifold depression thus gives correct spark advance corresponding to the load on the engine. Models for U.S. use have no vacuum control unit.

3:2 Distributor maintenance, contact point adjustment

The distributor must always be kept clean and dry, neglect of which is sometimes the cause of difficult starting. Maintenance of the distributor is chiefly concerned with occasional lubrication of the moving parts. Unclip the cap, lift out the rotor (see **FIG 3:1**) and apply two drops of engine oil to the felt pad in the centre of the cam. At the same time the cam faces should be very lightly smeared with petroleum jelly. Only a film of oil should be applied to the breaker arm pivot, ensuring that no trace is allowed to contaminate the distributor points, resulting in burning and difficult starting.

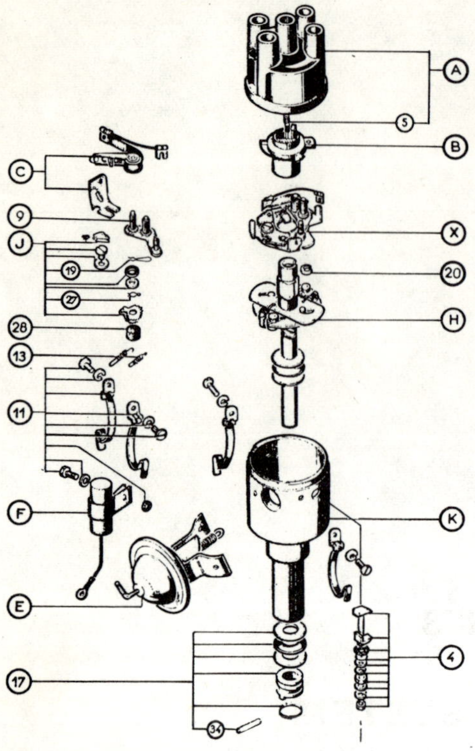

FIG 3:1 An exploded view of the Ducellier distributor No. 4161

Key to Fig 3:1 **A** Cap **B** Rotor **C** Contact set **E** Vacuum unit **F** Condenser **H** Shaft assembly **J** Contact breaker mounting **K** Housing **X** Breaker assembly 4 Terminal assembly 5 Carbon brush 9 Spark control lever 11 Retaining clips 13 Weight springs 17 Driving dog 19 Breaker clip 20 Circlip 27 Vacuum unit clip 28 Cam felt 34 Locking pin

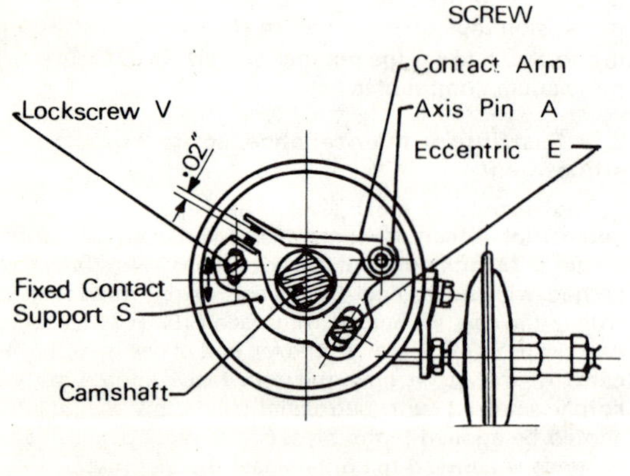

FIG 3:2 Contact breaker gap adjustment

To adjust the contact breaker points, remove the distributor cap and rotor and slacken the locking screw V in **FIG 3:2.** Move the eccentric E in the appropriate direction to obtain the correct gap through the displacement of the support S, which pivots about the axis pin A. Set the gap to .4 mm (.016 inch), except for Marchal 'cassette' type points where the gap is .3 mm (.012 inch).

Retighten the screw V, and recheck the gap. The gap must be set and measured when the cam peak is centralized on the contact arm.

If the contact breaker points are dirty or pitted they must be cleaned by polishing them with a fine carborundum stone, taking care to keep the faces flat and square. Afterwards, wipe away all traces of dust with a non-fluffy cloth moistened in fuel. Renew badly worn or pitted contacts.

If the engine runs unevenly, set it to idle at a fast speed. Taking care not to touch any metal part of the sparking plug leads, pull up the insulator sleeves and short each plug in turn, using a screwdriver with an insulated handle. Connect the screwdriver between the plug top and the cylinder head. Shorting a plug in a cylinder which is not firing will make no difference.

Having located the faulty cylinder, stop the engine and remove the plug lead. Start the engine and hold the lead carefully to avoid shocks, so that the metal end is about $\frac{3}{16}$ inch or 5 mm away from the cylinder head. A strong regular spark shows that the fault probably lies with the plug. Remove and clean the plug or, alternatively, substitute a new plug.

If the spark is weak and irregular, check that the lead is not perished or cracked. If it appears to be defective, renew it and try another test. If there is no improvement, remove the distributor cap and wipe the inside clean and dry. Examine the carbon button for wear and the segments for burning. Inspect the cap for cracks and tracking burns. Tracking will be indicated by a thin black line between the segments, and this can be cured only by fitting a new cap.

3:3 Distributor removal, servicing and refitting

Removal of the distributor is performed by firstly disconnecting the high-tension leads from the sparking plugs. Then disconnect both the high-tension and low-tension leads from the coil, followed by disconnecting the vacuum line from the distributor. Unscrew the bolt retaining the distributor to the engine when the distributor may be carefully withdrawn. **FIG 3:3** shows the oil pump drive shaft and machined face of the distributor support after removal of the distributor, with the groove in the shaft in line with the pushrod orifice 'a' when the No. 1 piston is at TDC or point of ignition.

To dismantle the distributor, the usual sequence of operations for units of this type is as follows:

1 Mark the radial position of the rotor arm on the distributor housing and remove the arm.
2 Withdraw the circuit breaker assembly and remove the contacts and capacitor.
3 Detach the vacuum control, circuit breaker plate assembly, earth wire and the LT lead. Lift away the vacuum control unit.
4 Check that the circuit breaker upper plate rotates smoothly on the lower plate. If unserviceable, renew the assembly. Check the mainshaft for its fit in the housing.

5 Examine the contact breaker points for wear. They need only be renewed if badly worn or burnt. Contacts showing a greyish colour and only slight signs of pitting need not be renewed. Clean as described in **Section 3:2.**
6 Refit the components in the reverse order of removal. A short-circuit in the capacitor will cause ignition failure, but precise testing requires specialized equipment. The simplest test for a suspected capacitor is by substitution. Wipe the distributor cap inside and out with a clean dry cloth and examine for cracks and tracking burns.
7 If the engine has not been turned since the distributor was removed, refit the distributor by lining up the rotor with the mark previously made on the housing and engaging the slot in the driving sleeve with the dogs on the oil pump gear. Coat the machined surface of the distributor support (see **FIG 3:3**) with Festinol and secure the distributor on the cylinder block. Adjustment of contacts and the fitting of new parts will affect the timing, which should be finally checked as desribed in **Section 3:4.**

3:4 Retiming ignition

If an engine has been turned after the distributor has been removed, the timing should be set as follows:

1 With the engine on compression stroke for No. 1 cylinder, insert an 8 mm diameter bar in the timing hole on the top righthand side of the clutch housing (see **FIG 3:4**).
2 Holding light inward pressure on the end of the bar, rotate the crankshaft until the bar drops into the timing recess in the flywheel. This is the firing point for No. 1 cylinder.
3 Fit the distributor, correctly adjusted, into the distributor support in its approximate position, and pressing down on the distributor body, turn the rotor to engage the driving slot in the drive spindle. Connect the vacuum advance pipe and the low-tension terminal to the coil.
4 Connect a timing light between the low-tension terminal on the distributor and earth. Switch on the ignition.
5 Rotate the distributor to the right until the light goes out, then turn the distributor slowly in the opposite direction until the light just lights. Tighten the support collar bolt. Check that the distributor rotor is pointing to the position of No. 1 sparking plug terminal in the distributor cap when the cap is in position. Remove the 8 mm bar.

This procedure provides a basic setting when the timing has been completely lost and also the correct final setting for engines with no timing plate. Where a timing plate is fitted above the crankshaft pulley, turn the crankshaft clockwise until the mark on the pulley is aligned with the appropriate graduation on the plate and then set the distributor as in items 4 and 5 in the sequence already described. Correct settings (for engines with a timing plate)are as follows:

0 deg. (TDC) for U.S. 1971 standards.
5 deg. BTDC for 1971 cc engines and U.S. 1970, 1972 and 1973 standards.
10 deg. BTDC for 1796 cc engines (post-July 1970) and U.S. 1969 standards.

FIG 3:3 Distributor removed from engine, showing oil pump drive shaft slot in line with pushrod orifice 'a' with No. 1 piston at TDC

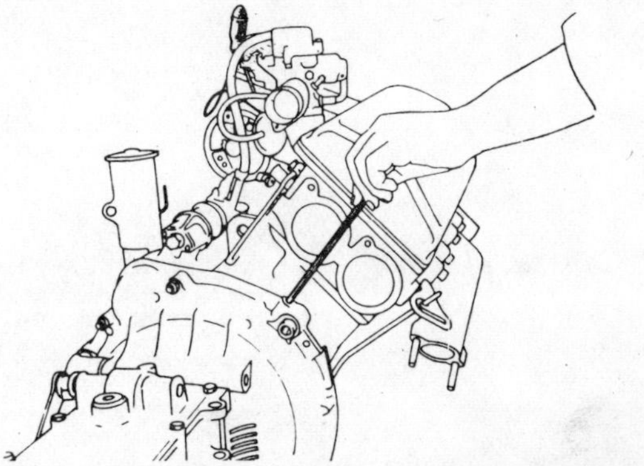

FIG 3:4 Method of finding the crankshaft position for correct ignition timing

Stroboscopic timing:

The timing settings mentioned above are applicable, but it is important that the engine speed should not be allowed to exceed 850 rev/min.

3:5 Sparking plugs

Examine deposits on the firing end to check on working conditions. The normal condition will be for a plug which is of the correct grade used for a mixed period of high and low-speed driving. This leaves a deposit which is from brown to greyish tan in colour. White to yellowish powdery deposits indicate long periods of constant-speed driving or much low-speed city driving. Neither of these deposits will affect performance if the plugs are cleaned on a blasting machine and the gaps reset.

Wet black deposits can be traced to oil fouling, due mainly to cylinder bore wear, or worn pistons, rings and valve stems. Dry, fluffy black deposits are caused by rich mixture or misfiring. Excessive idling or low speeds will also keep plug temperatures so low that normal deposits are not burned off.

A white blistered appearance of the insulator nose, and badly eroded electrodes, indicate overheating. This can be caused by weak mixture, poor cooling, incorrect ignition timing or sustained high speeds and heavy loads.

After cleaning, which should include the sparking plug threads, set the gap between the electrodes to .6 mm (.024 inch). Refit the plugs, using new gaskets, and tighten to a torque of 2.25 kg m (16.4 lb ft).

3:6 Fault diagnosis

(a) Engine will not fire

1 Battery discharged
2 Distributor points dirty, pitted or out of adjustment
3 Distributor cap dirty, cracked or 'tracking'
4 Carbon brush inside distributor cap not in contact with rotor
5 Faulty cable or loose connection in low-tension circuit
6 Distributor rotor arm cracked
7 Faulty coil
8 Broken contact breaker spring
9 Contact points stuck open

(b) Engine misfires

1 Check 2, 3, 5, and 7 in (a)
2 Weak contact spring
3 High-tension plug and coil leads cracked or perished
4 Sparking plug loose
5 Sparking plug insulation cracked
6 Sparking plug gap incorrect
7 Ignition timing too far advanced

CHAPTER 4

THE COOLING SYSTEM

4:1 Principle of system

The engine is watercooled by water circulating through the tube and corrugated fin radiator and through the water passages in the cylinder block. The system works under slight pressure, maintained by the spring loading of the radiator cap, which enables a higher temperature to prevail before the water boils. Circulation of the water is by thermosyphon action assisted by a centrifugal water pump, with a thermostat in the water outlet to give an initially reduced circulation for rapidly warming up the engine from cold. A disengageable fan of plastic material, shown with other components in **FIG 4:1**, is provided to maintain engine optimum temperature through an electromagnetic clutch controlled by a thermoswitch fitted in the radiator.

The fan is loose on the water pump shaft and the electro-magnet housed in the pump pulley. The magnet is energized to engage or release the fan at appropriate water temperatures as described in **Section 4:4**.

4:2 Maintenance, flushing, antifreeze, belt tension

Service attention required is mainly to ensure that the radiator is kept clear of sediment, that the coolant level is topped up as necessary to about 5 cm from the top of the filling orifice and that the correct tension of the fan belt is maintained. Do not overfill the radiator, otherwise the surplus will overflow.

The system should be flushed out about once a year. To drain the system the car should be standing on level ground, the radiator cap removed and the two drain taps opened. One of the taps is on the radiator bottom tank (see **FIG 4:1**) and the other on the rear righthand side of the cylinder block. Do not remove the radiator cap immediately after stopping the engine when it is hot. Always allow the coolant temperature to drop below its normal boiling point. Then turn the cap slightly to loosen it on the filler neck, to relieve any excess pressure in the system before completely removing the cap. If the coolant contains an antifreeze preparation, a clean dry tray should be positioned under the radiator and the coolant retained.

Internal cleaning of the radiator is undertaken by inserting a hose from a freshwater tap into the filler neck and allowing water to flush through the system with the drain taps open. Flushing is continued until the water comes out clear. Additionally, reverse flushing may give improved results and is performed by applying water under pressure through the bottom hose connection. Refill the system on completion, first ensuring that the taps on the cylinder block and the radiator are correctly closed.

An antifreeze solution should be used during winter months to prevent damage to the engine due to frozen coolant. For this purpose an ethylene glycol type is preferable to an alcohol type having a tendency to evaporate rapidly at the high temperature at which the engine operates. The amount of antifreeze to be added to the system depends upon the degree of protection required. With a cooling system capacity of 7.8 litre (including heater) the manufacturer's recommendations are as follows:

Antifreeze to be added (litre)	*Protection given*
1	Down to —5°C
2	Down to —12°C
3	Down to —21°C
4	Down to —34°C

Adjustment of the fan belt is undertaken as shown in **FIG 4:2.** Slacken the belt by releasing the alternator on its mounting and then draw two pencil lines on the top surface of the belt 100 mm apart. Then refit the alternator

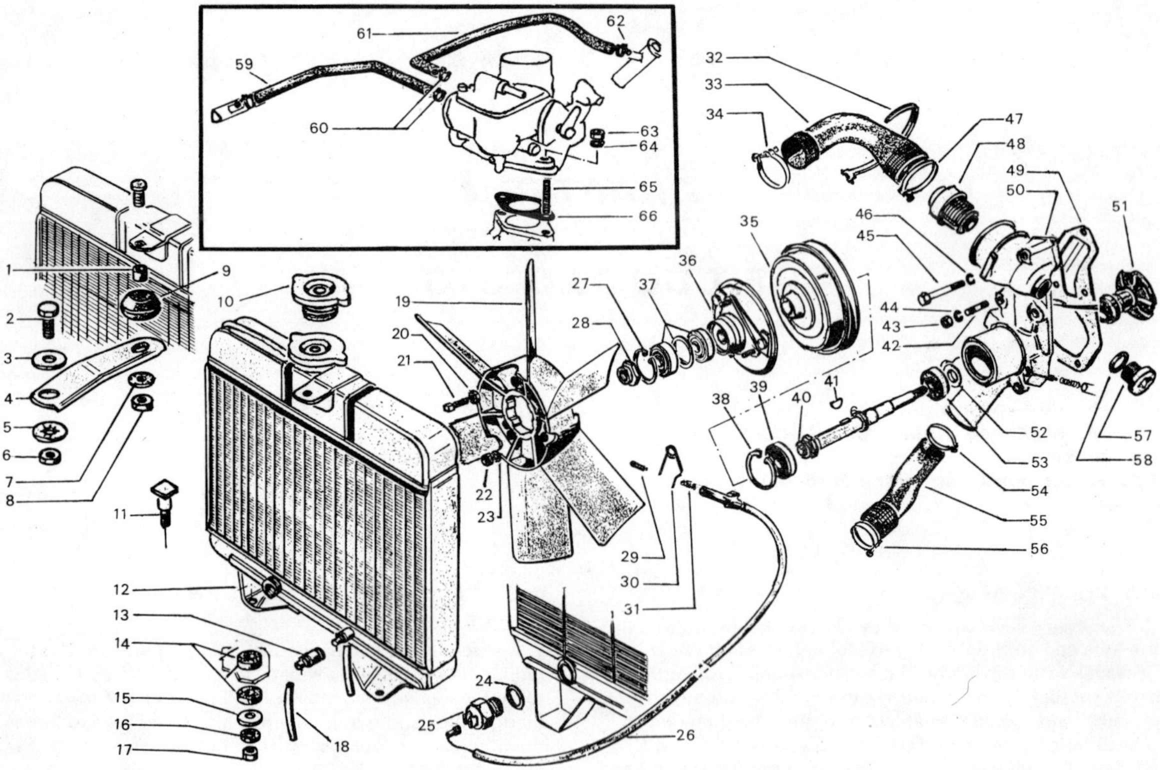

FIG 4:1 An exploded view of the radiator, fan and water pump components

Key to Fig 4:1 1 Distance piece 2 Bolt 3 Washer 4 Bracket 5 Lock washer 6 Nut 7 Shakeproof washer 8 Nut 9 Vibration mounting 10 Radiator cap 11 Square-headed bolt 12 Radiator assembly 13 Drain cock 14 Rubber rings 15 Washer 16 Shakeproof washer 17 Nut 18 Drain pipe 19 Fan 20 Nut 21 Adjusting screw 22 Nut 23 Shakeproof washer 24 Reinforced asbestos ring 25 Temperature sender unit 26 Lead to pulley 27 Circlip 28 Nut 29 Carbon brush 30 Spring clip 31 Spring 32 Clip 33 Upper radiator hose 34 Clip 35 Electro magnetic pulley 36 Fan coupling 37 Bearing assembly 38 Circlip 39 Bearing 40 Water pump spindle 41 Woodruff key 42 Stud 43 Nut 44 Spring washer 45 Bolt 46 Spring washer 47 Clip 48 Thermostat 49 Gasket 50 Water pump housing 51 Impeller 52 Sealing washer 53 Ballbearing 54 Clip 55 Lower radiator hose 56 Clip 57 Plug 58 Reinforced asbestos washer 59 Carburetter heater pipe 60 Clips 61 Carburetter heater pipe 62 Clip 63 Nut 64 Lockwasher 65 Stud 66 Gasket slide lug and adjust the tension of the fan belt so that the two marks 100 mm apart when the belt is slack are 102 to 103 mm apart when the belt is adjusted. Tighten the alternator retaining bolts in this position. The tension of the belt should be periodically checked as a loose fan belt will cause it to slip on the pulleys, resulting in engine overheating and possibly the failure of the alternator to charge the battery. Removal and renewal of a belt is undertaken by pivoting the alternator towards the engine as far as possible. Then if necessary rotate the engine by using a wrench applied to the crankshaft pulley bolt and slip the belt over the edge of the alternator pulley. Do not pull on the fan blades. Fit the new belt and adjust to the tension previously described. Recheck the tension when the car has run 1000 miles or 1500 km.

FIG 4:2 Fan belt tension adjustment

4:3 Water pump removal and dismantling

To remove the water pump, proceed as follows:

1 Drain the cooling system and disconnect the battery.
2 Remove the radiator, the top hose and the fan belt.
3 Disconnect the lower hose, the water pump heater union and the self-disengaging fan brush holder, if fitted.
4 Disengage the four securing nuts and remove the pump complete with fan and pulley.
5 For the dismantling of the pump, service practice is to use special tools made up in the workshop to the dimensions shown in **FIG 4:3** and also a water pump tool kit No. 8/0107.Y comprising shaped jaws for locking the pulley in a vice, an impeller extractor and a seal extractor. It may therefore be more appropriate for the work to be undertaken by a suitably equipped service agent. Operations, however, are as follows:
6 Hold the pulley in a vice with soft jaws and remove the hub nut. Then hold the pulley by hand and tap the end of a shaft with a mallet to disengage the pump body. Do not rest the pulley on the bronze collector ring. Withdraw the key from the shaft.
7 With the pump again in the vice, remove the impeller and seal assembly with the aid of a suitable extractor (see **FIG 4:4**). A special extractor is included in the tool kit mentioned in Operation 5 to remove the seal if it has remained in place.
8 Withdraw the front bearing circlip and immerse the pump body in boiling water. Withdraw the shaft and its bearings with the aid of a press and a drift of 12 mm diameter pressing on the spacer D in **FIG 4:3.**
9 If necessary, withdraw the front and rear bearings, using the plate E and the spacer D in conjunction with a press. Check the condition of the bearings, the seal and the bearing surface in the pump body. Renew any parts which appear unserviceable.
10 Test the electro-magnet winding as shown in **FIG 4:5** with the aid of an ammeter and a 12-volt battery. Connect one of the leads on the interior slip ring so as not to scratch the brush bearing surface and the other on the body of the pulley. No reading on the ammeter will indicate that the winding is broken. A reading of .8 indicates that the winding is serviceable and a higher reading shows that the winding is earthed. Renew the pulley assembly if found to be unserviceable.

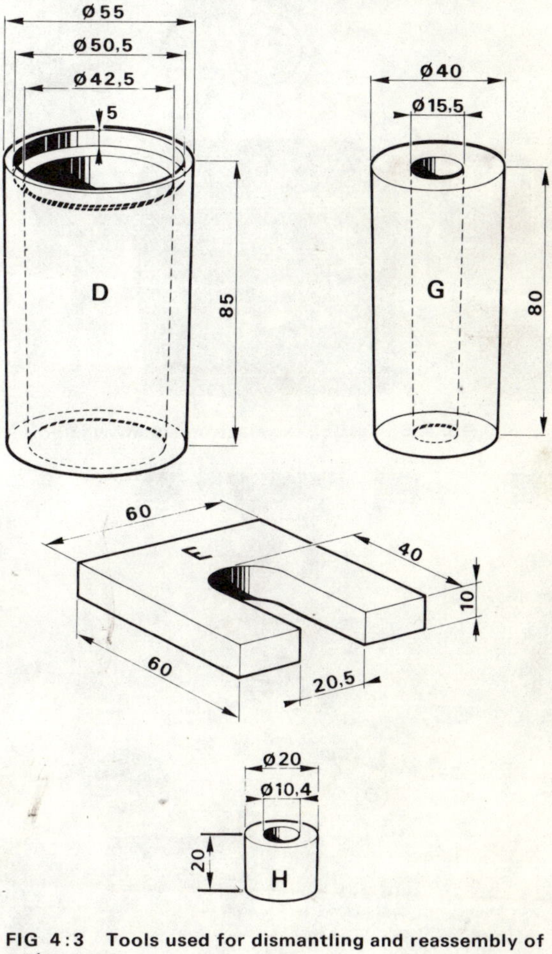

FIG 4:3 Tools used for dismantling and reassembly of water pump

Key to Fig 4:3 **D** Spacer **E** Plate **G** Bushing **H** Bushing

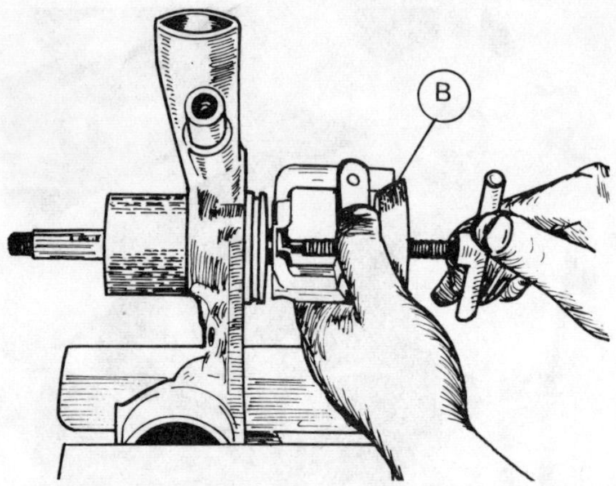

FIG 4:4 Removing the impeller assembly with the aid of the extractor **B**

FIG 4:5 Testing the electromagnet winding

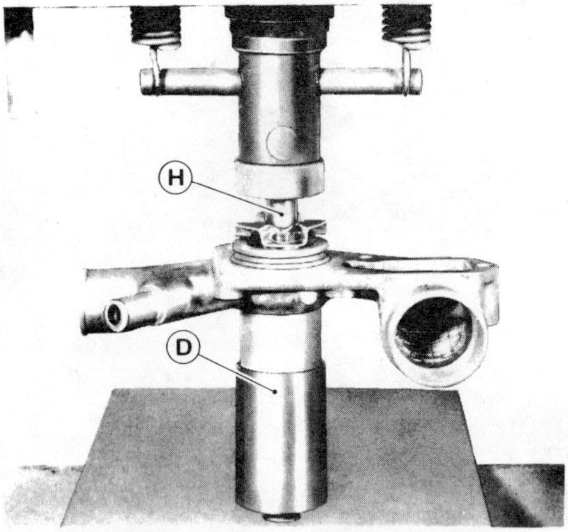

FIG 4:6 Refitting the seal and impeller assembly, using the bushing **H** and pressing on the spacer **D**

4:4 Water pump reassembly and refitting

1 Grease the ballbearings with multi-purpose grease and press them on the shaft with the aid of a press and the plate E. The open sides of the bearings should face each other. Fill the space between the bearings with grease.

2 Heat the pump body in boiling water for several minutes and press the shaft and bearings into the body, with the aid of the bushing G located between the press and the front bearing.

3 Fit the retaining circlip in the recess in the front of the pump body. Circlips of thicknesses of 1.75, 1.80, 1.85, 1.90 and 1.95 mm are available, of which the maximum size should be selected to eliminate axial play on the shaft.

4 Grease the rear end of the shaft and the seal bearing surface.

5 Locate the seal-impeller assembly on the shaft so that the splines of the impeller correspond to those on the shaft. Insert the assembly with a press (see **FIG 4:6**), with the aid of the bushing H and the spacer D.

6 Check and adjust if necessary the clearance between the front face of the impeller and the rear face of the pump (see **FIG 4:7**). The impeller should turn freely with a maximum gap of 1 mm between the impeller blades and the pump flange.

7 Renew if necessary the two hub bearings of the fan with the washer 1 (see **FIG 4:8**) and the circlips 2. Circlips of thicknesses increasing by .5 mm are available between 1.50 and 1.85 mm, of which the thickest possible should be used to eliminate the play.

8 Fit the key in the shaft, the fan pulley and hub nut, tightening the nut to a torque of 3.5 kg m (25 lb ft).

9 Check the gap between the fan and the electromagnet, which should be between .35 and .40 mm. Adjustment is made by the three square-headed bolts 3 in **FIG 4:9**.

10 Check the operation of the fan by connecting the brush holder wire to the + terminal and the water pump body to the negative terminal of a battery.

11 Refit the water pump in the reverse order of the removal operations, ensuring that the mating surfaces are clean and using a new dry gasket. Adjust the fan belt as described in **Section 4:2** and refill the cooling system.

12 Start the engine and allow it to reach its normal operating temperature. With a thermometer placed in the radiator check that the fan takes up the drive at a water temperature of 87±3°C and disengages when the temperature falls to 79±3°C. If the fan fails to engage at the specified temperature, check the fuse F3. If the fuse is in order, bridge the terminals of the thermo-switch located at the bottom of the radiator. If the fan now engages the thermo-switch is faulty and should be renewed, employing a tightening torque of 4 kg m (29 lb ft). As a temporary measure, the fan may be kept in permanent engagement by tightening fully the three adjusting bolts mentioned in Operation 9.

4:5 Thermostat removal and testing

A thermostat of the Calorstat type is situated in the outlet connection of the water pump and can be removed after the water in the cooling system has been drained to a level below the bottom of the housing. The instrument is designed to restrict the circulation of the coolant until the engine warms up sufficiently to heat the coolant to a temperature which will open the thermostat valve.

Testing of the thermostat is carried out by suspending it in water which is gradually heated, the temperature being taken at intervals with a thermometer. Neither the thermostat nor the thermometer must touch the bottom of the container holding the water. The thermostat valve should commence to open at a temperature of 74°C to 76°C and should be fully open at a temperature of 87°C with a maximum valve lift of 7.5 mm. The height of the thermostat with the valve closed is 53 mm.

If the thermostat does not function properly, do not attempt any adjustment but replace with a new unit. Refit the water outlet connection, refill the cooling system and check the connection for leakage.

FIG 4:7 Measuring the clearance of the impeller blades

4:6 Fault diagnosis

(a) Internal water leakage

1 Cracked cylinder wall
2 Loose cylinder head nuts
3 Cracked cylinder head
4 Faulty head gasket (see **Chapter 1**)

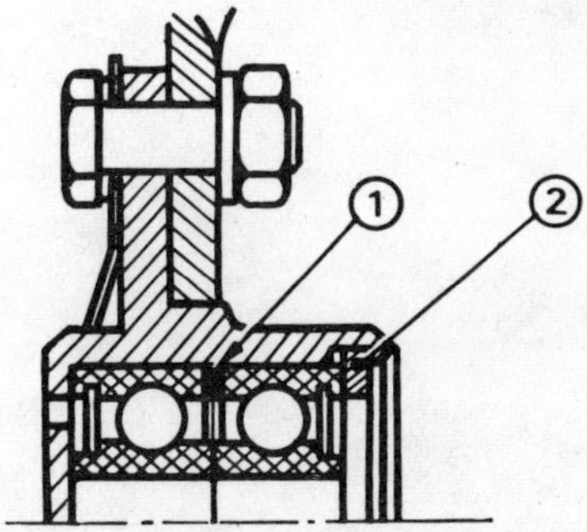

FIG 4:8 Fan bearings showing **1** Washer, **2** Circlips

(b) Poor circulation

1 Radiator core blocked
2 Engine water passages restricted
3 Low water level
4 Loose fan belt
5 Defective thermostat
6 Perished or collapsed radiator hoses

(c) Corrosion

1 Impurities in the water
2 Infrequent draining and flushing

(d) Overheating

1 Check (b)
2 Sludge in crankcase
3 Faulty ignition timing (see **Chapter 3**)
4 Low oil level in sump
5 Tight engine
6 Choked exhaust system
7 Binding brakes
8 Slipping clutch (see **Chapter 5**)
9 Incorrect valve timing (see **Chapter 1**)
10 Retarded ignition (see **Chapter 3**)
11 Mixture too weak (see **Chapter 2**)

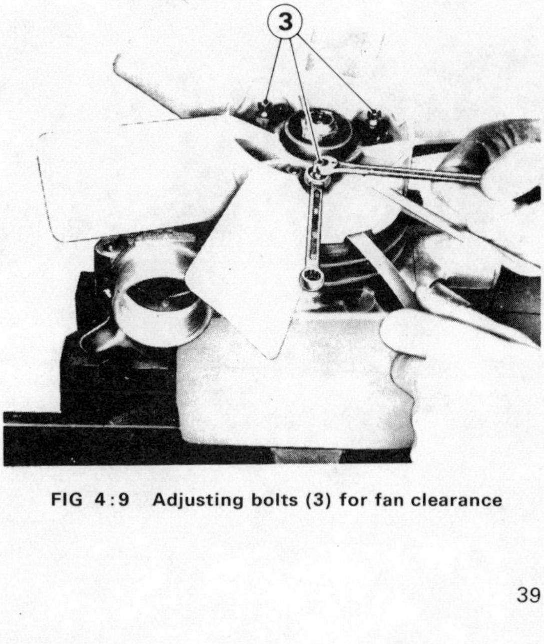

FIG 4:9 Adjusting bolts (3) for fan clearance

NOTES

CHAPTER 5

THE CLUTCH

5:1 Construction and operation

The clutch is of the diaphragm spring type, details of the construction of which are shown in **FIG 5:1**. The assembly is enclosed in the housing 1 and bolted to engine flywheel. It incorporates a single dry plate disc 3, the clutch pressure plate 4a, the diaphragm spring 4c fitted between the pressure plate and the cover 4b and a thrust or release ballbearing 5.

The disc has riveted friction linings and drives the gearbox main drive pinion through a splined hub which slides on the splines of the transmission pinion. The diaphragm spring consists of a series of radial sectors (see **FIG 5:4**) to give the spring its necessary flexibility for deflection. When the clutch pedal is depressed for disengaging the clutch, the clutch fork 7 moves forward and the thrust bearing exerts pressure on the centre of the diaphragm spring towards the flywheel. The diaphragm then takes up a dished form and its outer edge deflects towards the gearbox, releasing the clutch pressure exerted on the flywheel by the disc.

The operation of the clutch fork by the clutch pedal is undertaken hydraulically by means of the clutch master cylinder 1 and the operating or slave cylinder 2 shown in **FIG 5:2**, receiving hydraulic fluid from the fluid reservoir which serves both clutch and brake systems. The clutch pedal is linked by a pushrod to the piston in the master cylinder, so that when the pedal is depressed the piston moves forward and puts the fluid in the system under high pressure. The pressure is transmitted to the slave cylinder, causing the piston in the slave cylinder to operate the clutch release lever. When the clutch pedal is released the movements are reversed. A backing spring (see **FIG 5:10**) at the rear of the clutch fork and the pedal return spring (see **FIG 5:3**) operate to push the slave cylinder piston back to the end of its travel, causing the fluid thus expelled from the slave cylinder to flow back into the master cylinder. Details of the master and slave cylinders are shown in the sectional views in **FIGS 5:11** and **5:12**, also in the exploded view of the system in **FIG 5:3**.

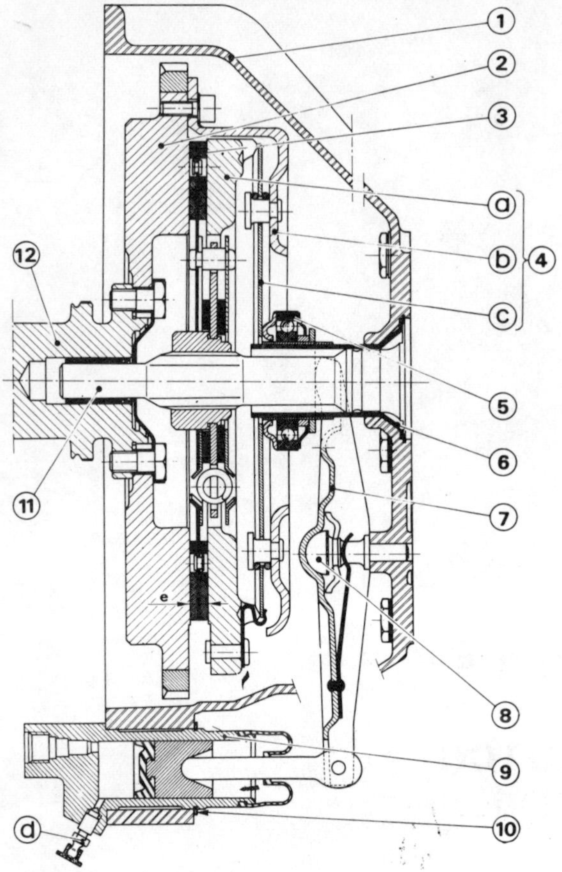

FIG 5:1 A sectional view of the clutch mechanism

Key to Fig 5:1 1 Clutch housing 2 Flywheel 3 Clutch disc 4a Pressure plate 4b Clutch cover 4c Diaphragm spring 5 Thrust ballbearing 6 Guide bush 7 Clutch fork 8 Fork-thrust ball 9 Operating or slave cylinder 10 Cylinder retaining ring 11 Drive shaft 12 Crankshaft **d** Bleed screw **e** Disc thickness

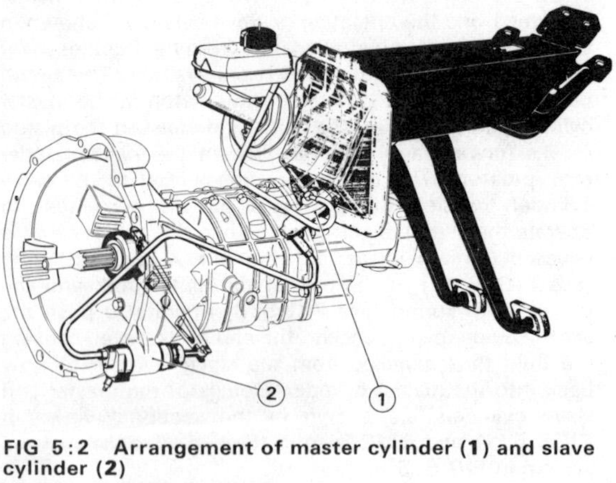

FIG 5:2 Arrangement of master cylinder (1) and slave cylinder (2)

5:2 Maintenance and adjustments

The level of clutch fluid in the master cylinder reservoir shown in **FIG 5:2** should be regularly inspected and maintained at the correct level. An excessively low level will be signified by the warning lamp on the dashboard. If the lamp operates the hydraulic circuit should be examined for leakages. When topping up the reservoir the cap should be wiped with a cloth before removal and care should be taken that no foreign matter enters. Use only the hydraulic fluid recommended by the manufacturers, i.e. Lockheed 55.

Adjustment of pedal free travel has been eliminated by provision being made for the thrust bearing to remain constantly in contact with the clutch mechanism. Two methods have been used, which are described in **Section 5:7.**

5:3 Servicing the hydraulic system

All hydraulic parts should be cleaned by washing in the approved Lockheed 55 hydraulic fluid. Mineral oils, or fluids with a mineral oil base, should never be used, as they cause the rubber seals or cups to swell and become ineffective. The slightest trace of mineral oil could render the clutch inoperative. Always inspect the seals, including new ones, carefully before fitting and reject any which show the slightest imperfection. All pistons and housings must be carefully inspected and rejected if any scores or blemishes are present. Prior to assembly, immerse all hydraulic components in clean approved fluid to facilitate fitting and to provide initial lubrication for working surfaces.

To remove the master cylinder, disconnect the pipe from the reservoir and empty the fluid into a waste container. Referring to **FIG 5:3** disconnect the hydraulic union to the slave cylinder and the piston from the clutch pedal. Remove the retaining bolts and withdraw the master cylinder. Dismantle the cylinder by extracting the circlip and the piston stop washer from the cylinder bore, when the piston assembly, main and secondary cups and return spring may be withdrawn. Keep all the components in order for reassembly if serviceable. A similar procedure is followed for removing and dismantling the slave cylinder after removing the cylinder retaining ring shown in **FIG 5:1.**

All parts should be cleaned, using no other liquid than brake fluid. Inspect the parts carefully for damage or wear as described previously in this Section. Particular attention should be given to the lips on the piston seals, but do not distort the seals when examining. After dipping in hydraulic fluid, also smearing the cylinder bore surface with fluid, the parts can be inserted in the cylinder in the reverse order of their removal. Particular care must be taken not to damage the lips of the main and secondary cups when assembling. Refit the retaining circlip and then the cylinders as removed. Tighten the fluid pipes firmly but not sufficiently to damage the threads. The reservoir must finally be refilled with approved fluid and the system bled as described in **Section 5:6.**

5:4 Clutch removal and dismantling

The removal of the clutch after removal of the engine leaving the gearbox in position was described in **Chapter 1, Section 1:9**. When refitting the clutch disc locator tool No. 8.0207 must be used to centre the disc

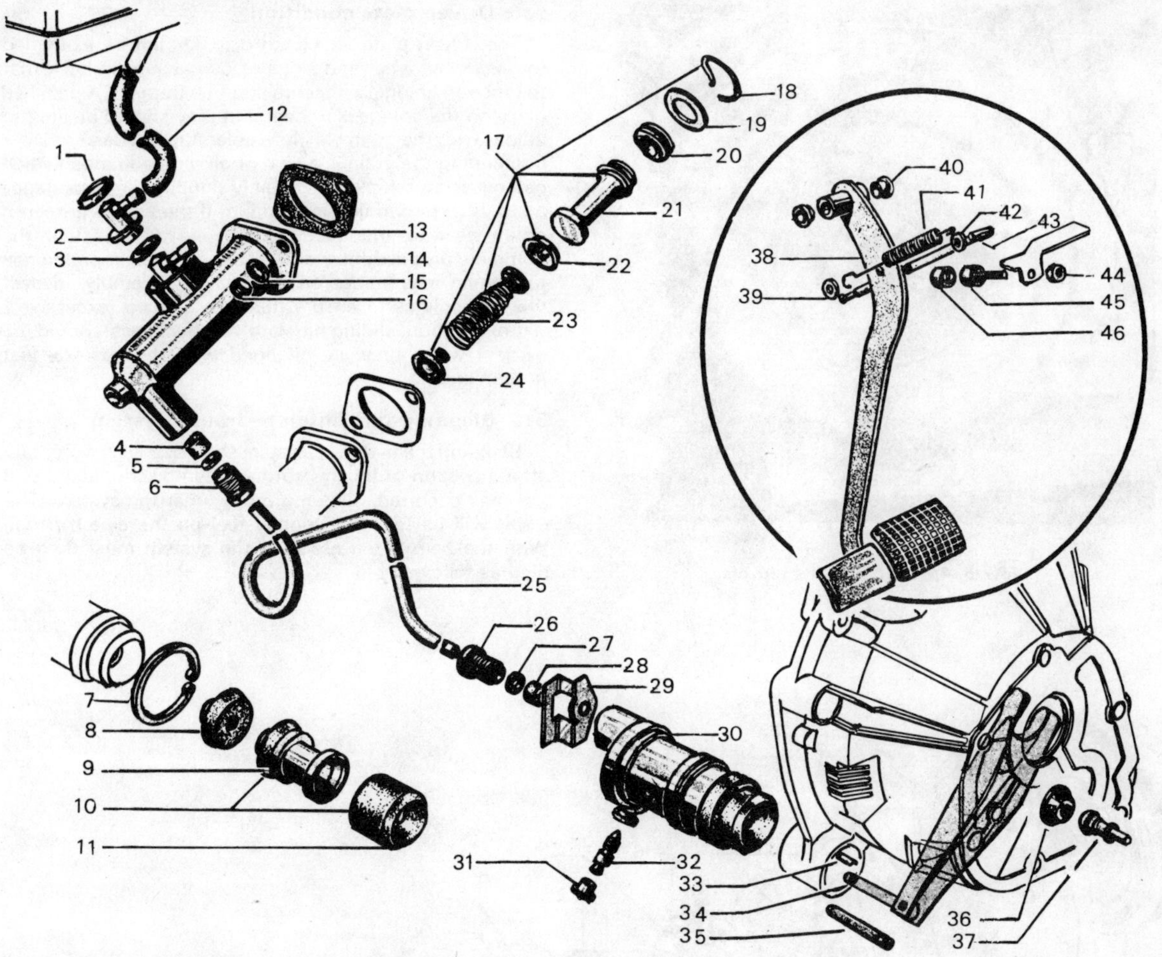

FIG 5:3 An exploded view of the hydraulic system and clutch pedal assembly

Key to Fig 5:3 1 Ring nut 2 Nylon union 3 Seal 4 Rubber ring 5 Washer 6 Union 7 Circlip 8 Cup 9 Piston assembly 10 Repair kit 11 Rubber boot 12 Flexible pipe 13 Gasket 14 Clutch master cylinder 15 Shakeproof washer 16 Nut 17 Repair kit complete 18 Circlip 19 Thrust washer 20 Secondary cup 21 Piston 22 Primary cup 23 Spring 24 Valve 25 Nylon pipe 26 Union 27 Washer 28 Rubber ring 29 Locking plate 30 Clutch cylinder 31 Rubber cap 32 Bleed valve 33, 34 and 35 Types of pushrod fitted 36 Rubber shroud 37 Ball pivot 38 Clutch pedal 39 Washer 40 Bush 41 Spring 42 Washer 43 Pushrod 44 Nut 45 Stop 46 Cap

correctly with the flexible hub towards the gearbox, as shown in **FIG 5:4.** The bolts with Onduflex washers are tightened to a torque of 1.5 kg m (11 lb ft).

An exploded view of the clutch components is shown in **FIG 5:5.** Inspect the thrust bearing (see **FIG 5:6**) for condition and renew it if necessary, releasing the retaining clip and removing the bearing by rotating it anticlockwise. Smear the guide sleeve with lubricant, then engage the new bearing by positioning the retaining jaw (1 in **FIG 5:7**) towards the starter motor housing. Engage the thrust bearing with the clutch release fork by rotating the bearing clockwise and refit the retaining clip. If required, the guide sleeve may be renewed with the aid of a press for its extraction and the use of a specially designed installing ring No. 8.0310 for its insertion, for which it may be desirable to enlist the facilities of a service agent.

Check the bearing surface of the disc on the flywheel. Referring to **FIG 5:8,** the bearing surface 'a' may be trued up on a lathe, but note that it will be necessary for the same metal thickness to be removed from part 'b' of the flywheel receiving the mechanism in order not to alter the diaphragm tension.

The clutch release fork and the thrust bearing may be removed by working from inside the housing. Referring to **FIG 5:9,** remove the rubber cup 1 and the ball head thrust 2. Renew the rubber cup if unserviceable. To refit (see **FIG 5:10**), pack the rubber cup with grease and slide the release fork 3 from the inside towards the outside of the housing. Use a screwdriver to raise the clutch release fork backing spring 4 and engage the fork on the ball head, with the spring backed against the rubber cup. Then fit the thrust ballbearing.

FIG 5:4 Refitting the clutch

5:5 Driven plate condition

The driven plate, or clutch disc, should be examined for excessive wear and signs of overheating. Check that the friction linings are secure and free from oil. A polished glaze on the linings is normal, but they should be light in colour with the grain clearly visible. A much darker colour obliterating the grain is a sign of oil on the linings, which can cause clutch slip or possibly difficulty in disengagement. If this condition is found, or if the linings are worn down near to the rivet heads, it is advised that the complete disc assembly should be renewed in preference to riveting new linings on the existing assembly. Inspect the hub splines to ensure that they are not excessively worn. A good sliding fit with no slackness should be evident when they are engaged with the gearbox first motion shaft.

5:6 Bleeding the clutch hydraulic system

Bleeding the hydraulic system should only be necessary after a section of the system has been disconnected or a leak has occurred, allowing air to enter the system. The result will be felt as a spongy feel on the clutch pedal. With the help of an assistant the system must then be bled as follows:

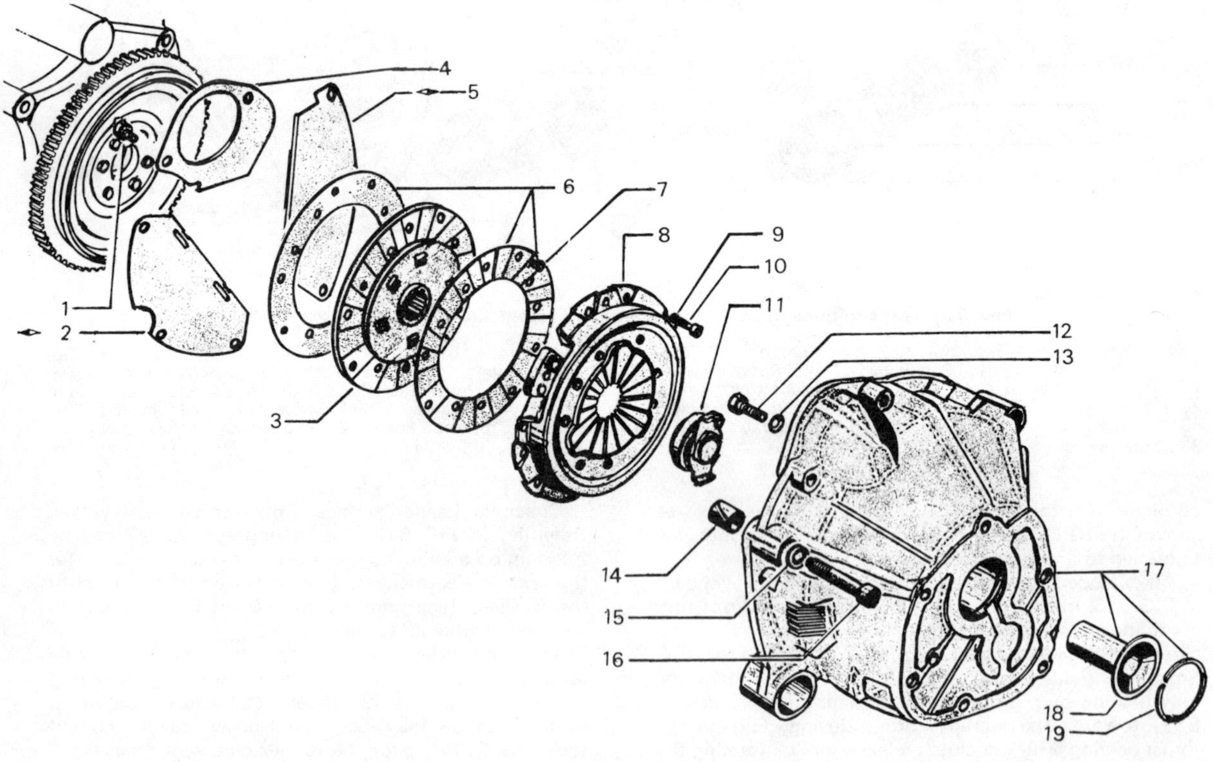

FIG 5:5 An exploded view of the clutch components

Key to Fig 5:5 1 Screw 2, 4 and 5 Backplates 3 Clutch disc assembly 6 Repair kit 7 Rivet 8 Pressure plate assembly 9 Spring washer 10 Bolt 11 Release bearing 12 Bolt 13 Washer 14 Split bush 15 Spring washer 16 Bolt 17 Bell housing 18 Release bearing bush 19 Circlip

1 Clean the bleeder screw 'd' in **FIG 5:1** on the slave cylinder and attach a rubber or transparent plastic tube to the screw, allowing the other end to hang into a glass jar filled with sufficient brake fluid for immersion of the tube end. Keep the end of the tube below the fluid level throughout the operations.

2 Slacken the bleeder screw half to one complete turn. Top up the level of the fluid in the reservoir to about $\frac{1}{4}$ inch or 6 mm below the bottom of the filler aperture. Use only the recommended brake fluid.

3 As the assistant depresses the clutch pedal slowly, tighten the bleeder screw before the pedal reaches the end of its travel. Allow the pedal to return unassisted.

4 Repeat this operation until all air bubbles cease to emerge from the tube and keep the fluid level topped up during and after the process of bleeding.

5 Ensure that the filler cap vent is clear, refit the cap and check the clutch for correct operation with the engine running. Fluid bled from the system should be discarded.

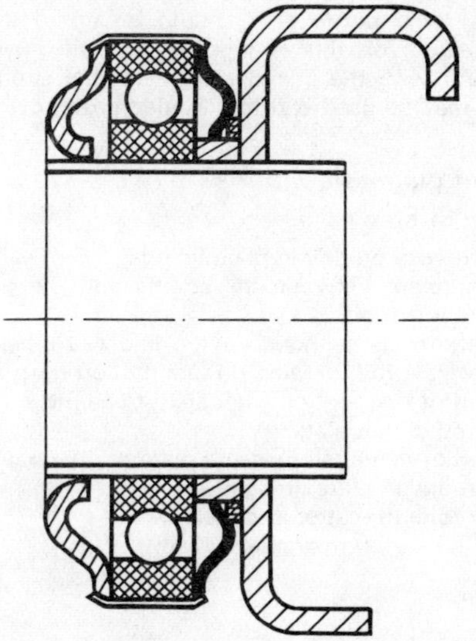

FIG 5:6 Clutch thrust bearing

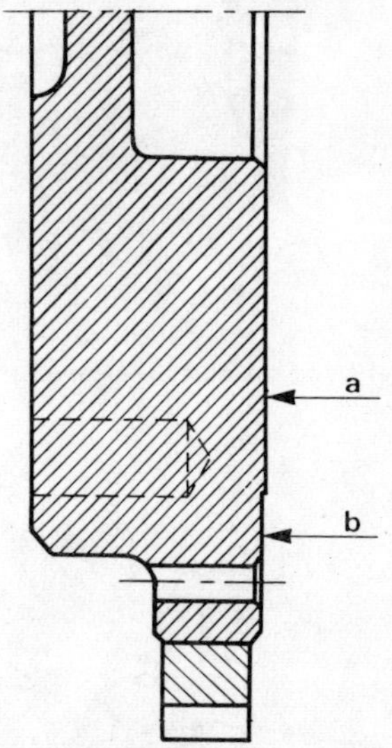

FIG 5:8 Flywheel bearing surface. References to a and b are made in the text

FIG 5:7 Refitting the thrust bearing, showing position of retaining jaw 1

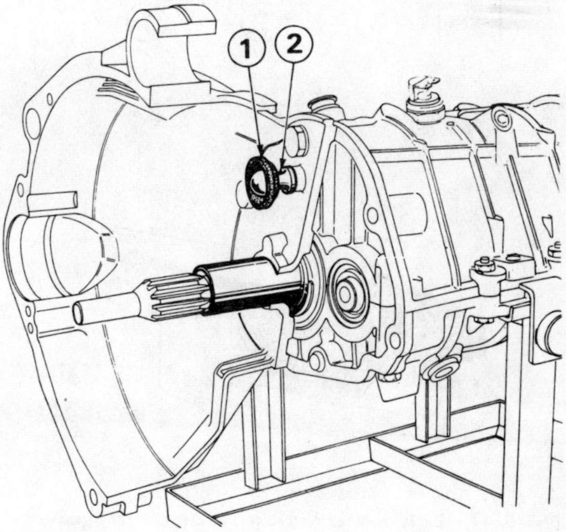

FIG 5:9 Rubber cup (1) and fork thrust ball (2)

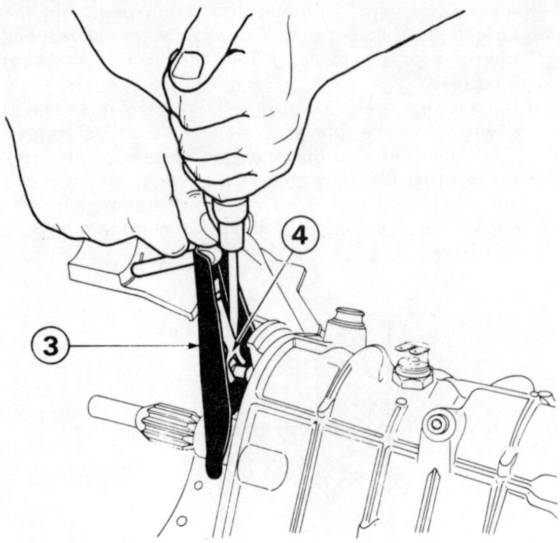

FIG 5:10 Refitting the clutch release fork 3 on backing spring 4

5:7 Modifications

In cars up to serial numbers 504.A01/1014917 and 504.A02/1012919 a residual pressure valve 3 (see **FIG 5:11**) with a special spring 2 was fitted to the master cylinder 1 to give a residual pressure of .8 kg/sq cm with the purpose of ensuring a constant contact of the thrust bearing on the clutch mechanism. The clutch slave cylinder 4 incorporated a special cup 5.

In later cars in the 504.A01 and A02 series and from the beginning of the 504.B02 and C02 series, the residual pressure valve and special spring in the master cylinder were discontinued and the slave cylinder was fitted with an internal spring 6 (see **FIG 5:12**) against the cup 5 to serve the same purpose. It should be noted that the master cylinder on this arrangement should always be fitted along with the cylinder with internal spring, but the latter may be used with the former master cylinder.

5:8 Fault diagnosis

(a) Drag or spin

1 Oil or grease on driven plate linings
2 Misalignment between the engine and the gearbox first motion shaft
3 Leaking master cylinder, slave cylinder or pipeline
4 Driven plate hub binding on first motion shaft splines
5 Binding of first motion shaft spigot bearing
6 Distorted clutch plate
7 Warped or damaged pressure plate or clutch cover
8 Broken driven plate linings
9 Dirt or foreign matter in clutch
10 Air in the clutch hydraulic system

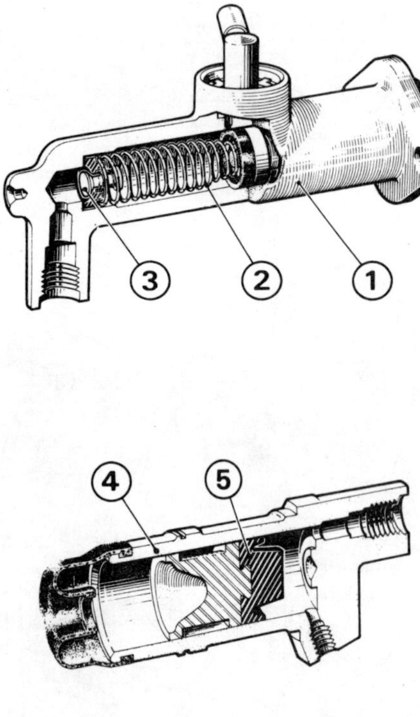

FIG 5:11 Early master and slave cylinder arrangements

Key to Fig 5:11 1 Master cylinder 2 Spring 3 Residual pressure valve 4 Slave cylinder 5 Cup

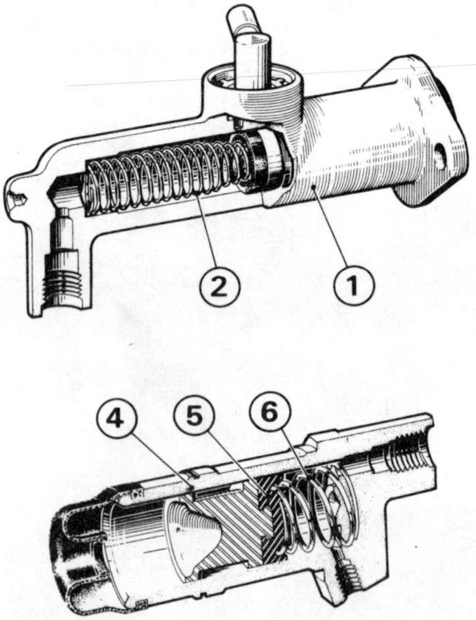

FIG 5:12 Later master and slave cylinder arrangements

Key to Fig 5:12 1 Master cylinder 2 Spring 4 Slave cylinder 5 Cup 6 Internal spring

(b) Fierceness or snatch

1 Check 1, 2 and 3 in (a)
2 Worn clutch linings

(c) Slip

1 Check 1 and 2 in (a)
2 Check 2 in (b)
3 Seized piston in clutch slave cylinder

(d) Judder

1 Check 1 and 2 in (a)
2 Pressure plate not parallel with flywheel face
3 Contact area of driven plate linings not evenly distributed
4 Bent first motion shaft
5 Buckled driven plate
6 Loose propeller shaft bolts

(e) Rattle

1 Broken springs in driven plate
2 Worn release mechanism
3 Excessive backlash in transmission
4 Wear in transmission bearings
5 Release bearing loose

(f) Tick or knock

1 Worn first motion shaft spigot or bearing
2 Badly worn splines in driven plate hub
3 Release plate out of line
4 Faulty Bendix drive on starter motor
5 Loose flywheel

(g) Driven plate fracture

1 Check 2 in (a)
2 Drag and distortion due to hanging gearbox in plate hub

NOTES

CHAPTER 6

THE GEARBOX (OR TRANSMISSION)

6:1 Construction

The gearbox consists of a two-piece ribbed casing with front and rear sections as shown in **FIG 6:1,** incorporating four fully synchronized forward gears and a reverse gear. Gearchange is by remote control from a gearlever below the steering wheel. Automatic transmission (see **Chapter 7**) may optionally be provided.

A cutaway and a sectional view of the construction of the gearbox are shown in **FIGS 6:2** and **6:3.** The primary or first motion shaft has one fixed pinion. Washers to adjust lateral play are available in various thicknesses in steps of .05 mm from .15 to .35 mm. The secondary or main shaft in line with the primary shaft carries the first, second, third and reverse gear pinions, with adjusting washers available for the first gear pinion in thicknesses of .25, .30, .35, .40 and .60 mm. An intermediate or layshaft has four fixed pinions and a reverse gear pinion secured by a circlip. Shims are available for adjusting lateral play of thicknesses in steps of .05 mm between 2.25 to 3.40 mm. The reverse shaft has a bushed pinion with helical teeth. Gear ratios are as follows:

First	*Second*	*Third*	*Fourth*	*Reverse*
3.663:1	2.169:1	1.409:1	1.000:1	3.747:1

6:2 Maintenance

The gearbox oil level should be checked every 5000 km or 3000 miles and topped up as necessary with an approved lubricant, for which the makers recommend Esso Extra motor oil 20.W 30/40. A combined oil level and filler plug is situated on the side of the gearbox as shown in **FIG 6:1.** All dirt should be cleaned away from around the plug before removing it and the oil should be maintained level with the bottom of the filler plug hole. Every 10,000 km or 6000 miles the oil in the gearbox should be drained by removing the magnetic plug on the underside of the gearbox, preferably whilst the oil is warm after running the engine. Clean the plug carefully to remove any metal particles, then refit it with a new washer and refill the gearbox to the correct level as previously described. The oil capacity of the gearbox is 1.15 litre and both plugs should be tightened to a torque of 2.75 kg m (20 lb ft).

6:3 Gearbox removal

To remove the gearbox the car should preferably be situated on a lift or over a pit for convenience of access. Preliminary operations are to disconnect the battery and drain the gearbox as described in the previous Section.

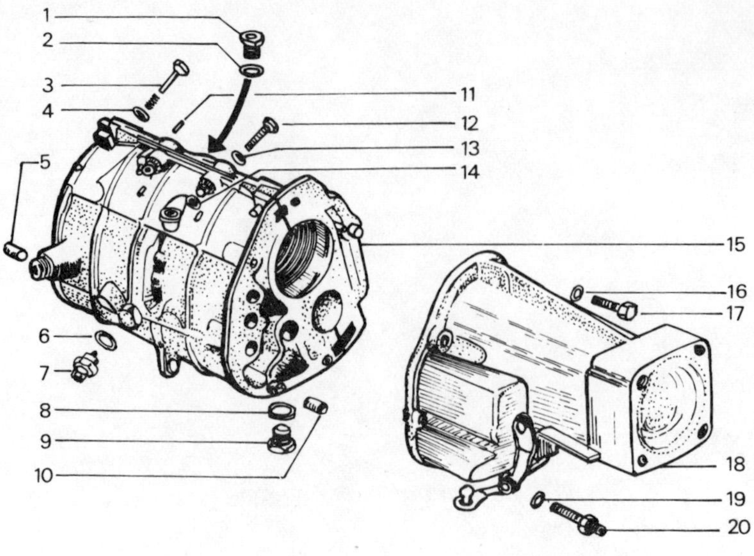

FIG 6:1 Gearbox casing front and rear sections

Key to Fig 6:1 1 Filler and level plug 2 Washer 3 Screw 4 Washer 5 Split bush 6 Washer 7 Reversing light switch 8 Washer 9 Drain plug 10 Dowel 11 Pin 12 Bolt 13 Washer 14 Nut 15 Gearbox casing 16 Washer 17 Bolt 18 Rear casing 19 Washer 20 Stud

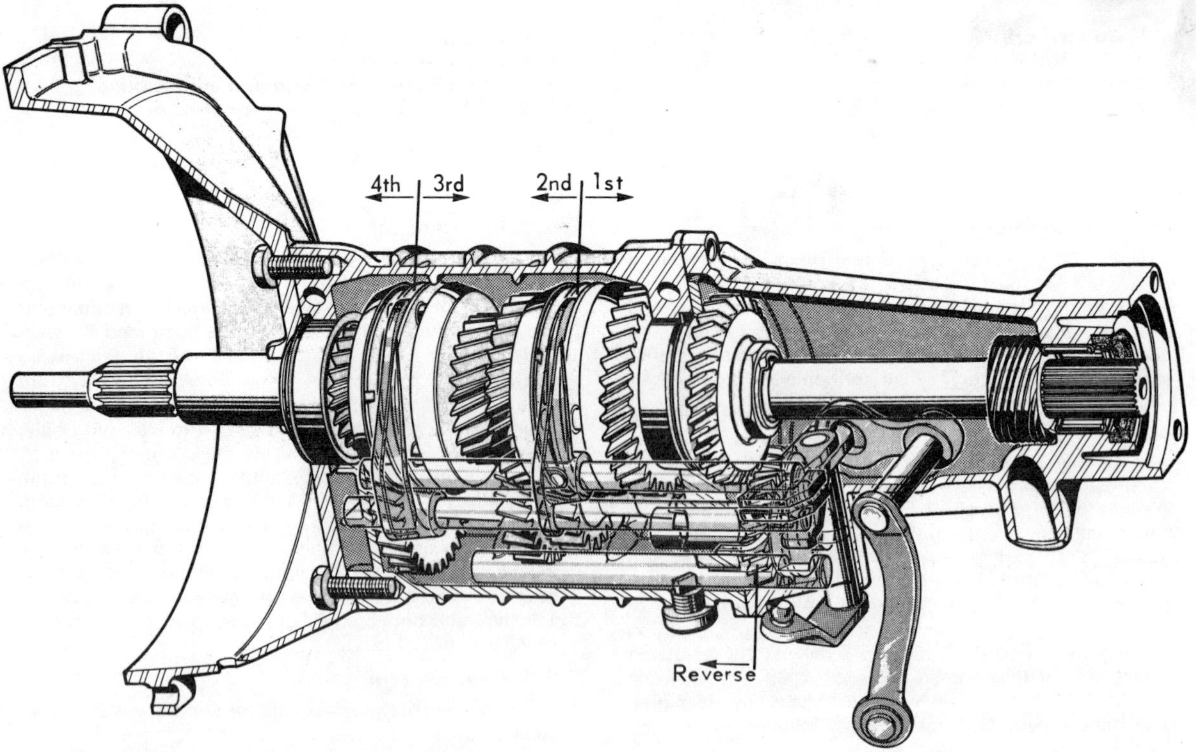

FIG 6:2 A cutaway view of the gearbox

Procedure is then as follows:

1 Remove the ignition coil, the radiator upper mounting and both bolts of the radiator lower mounting on the front crossmember. There is no need to drain the cooling system.

2 Remove the securing bolts to free the starter motor without disconnecting it. Withdraw the closure plate.

3 Remove the air cleaner to avoid damage to the regulator cover.

4 On engines employing fuel injection, disconnect the electro-valve supply pipe and the air cleaner to air distribution chamber union.

5 Remove the engine oil filler plug without disconnecting the vapour circulating connections.

6 Remove (a) the three nuts retaining the exhaust pipe to the manifold (b) the nut retaining the front silencer on the connecting tube (c) the upper nut on the rear attachment to the tube (d) the rear attachment from the body. Remove the heat dissipation plate.

7 Support the clutch housing by a jack placed below it. Remove the three assembling bolts 1 (see **FIG 6:4**) on the connecting tube to the gearbox housing. The illustration shows the use of a 'Facom' tool with articulated extension. Slacken the fourth bolt as in **FIG 6:5** with a shouldered Allen key of 8 mm across the flats, but do not unscrew completely.

8 Remove both bolts attaching the differential under the suspension crossmember. Where fuel injection is used, the electric supply pump should be detached in order to move the differential backwards.

9 Separate the torque tube from the gearbox by about 20 mm and insert the holding plate 8.0403S as shown in **FIG 6:6.** Secure the plate on the lower part of the tube with two bolts and remove the propeller shaft assembly from the gearbox.

10 Release the clutch hydraulic cylinder without disconnecting the pipe.

11 Disengage the counter lever 2 (see **FIG 6:7**) with its connecting rods 3.

12 Disconnect the reversing light switch leads 4, the earth lead 5 on the gearbox and the speedometer cable 6.

13 Remove the flector clamp bolt and the steering gear housing securing bolts, then lower the housing without disconnecting the ball joints. Remove the clutch housing closure plates.

14 Remove the three Allen bolts (see **FIG 6:8**) retaining the gearbox and clutch housing to the engine. Lower the jack but do not allow the weight of the gearbox to hang on the main drive pinion.

15 Take the weight of the engine on suitable hoisting apparatus (see **FIG 6:9**) and rotate the engine on its rubber mountings as far as possible to disengage the gearbox under the tunnel. Use a wooden block to prevent the radiator weight damaging the hoses.

16 Release and withdraw the gearbox assembly by rotating it a quarter of a turn clockwise to allow the starter motor boss to clear the tunnel, as shown in **FIG 6:10.**

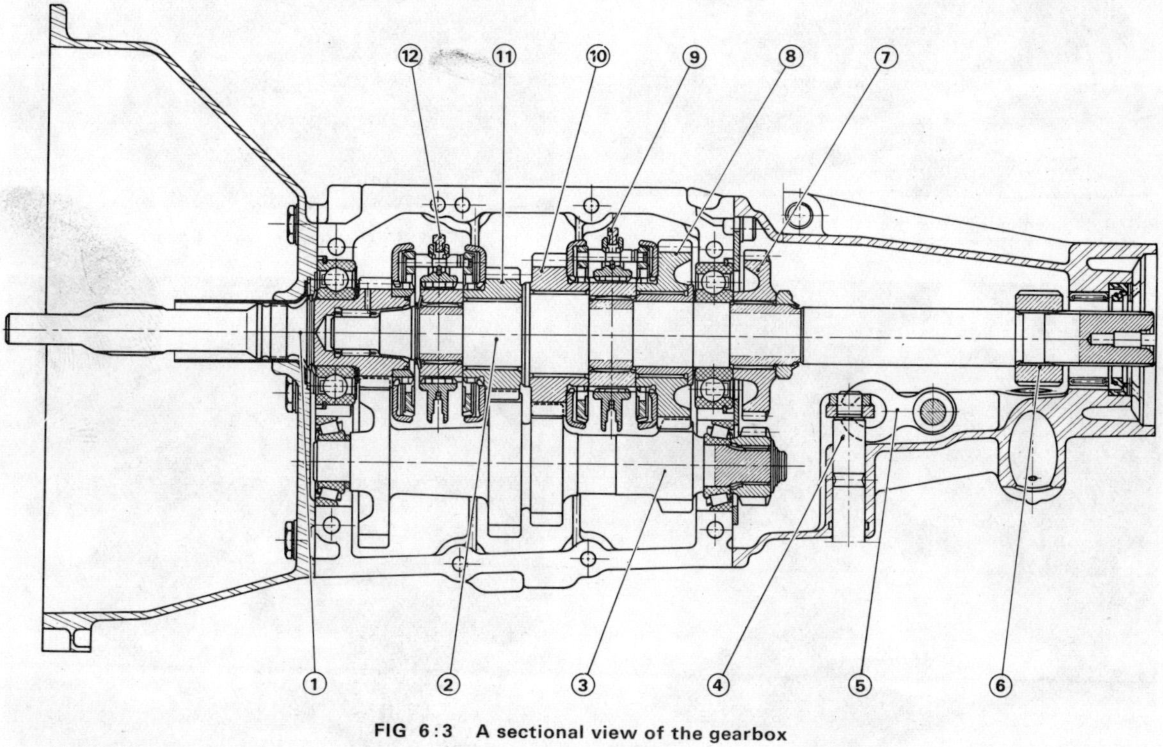

FIG 6:3 A sectional view of the gearbox

Key to Fig 6:3 1 Drive shaft 2 Mainshaft 3 Layshaft or intermediate shaft 4 Gearchange control 5 Gear selector control 6 Speedometer drive 7 Reverse pinion 8 First gear pinion 9 First and second gear synchromesh cones 10 Second gear pinion 11 Third gear pinion 12 Third and fourth gear synchromesh cones

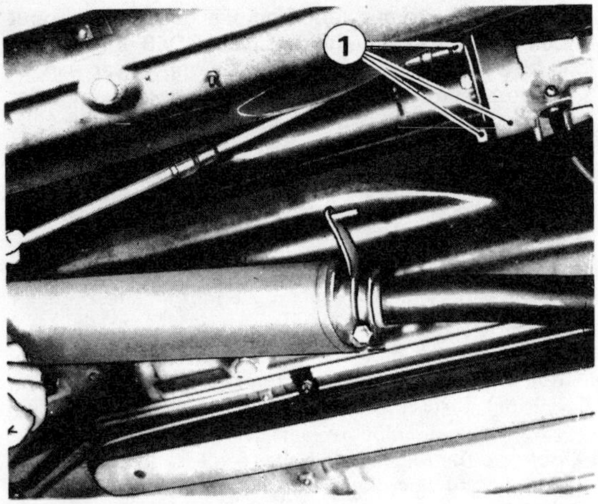

FIG 6:4 Removing the three bolts 1 securing the torque tube to the gearbox housing

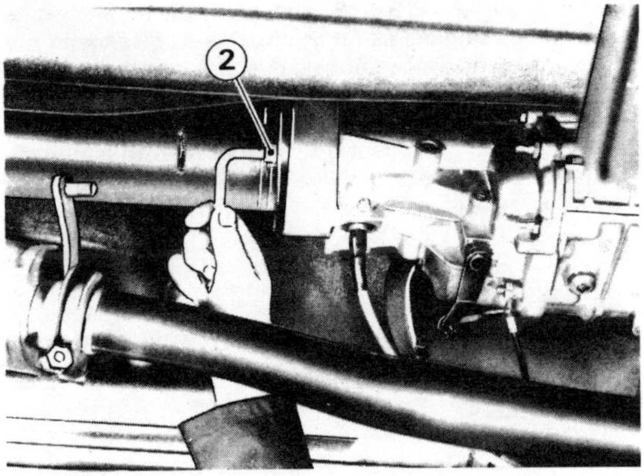

FIG 6:5 Removing the fourth bolt 2 securing the torque tube to the gearbox housing

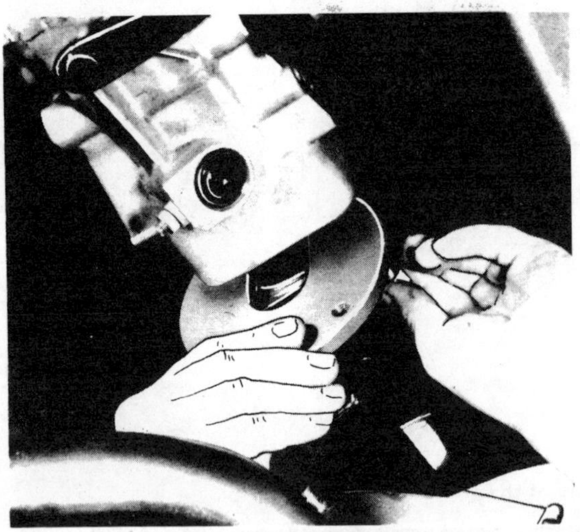

FIG 6:6 Inserting the propeller shaft holding plate between the torque tube and the gearbox

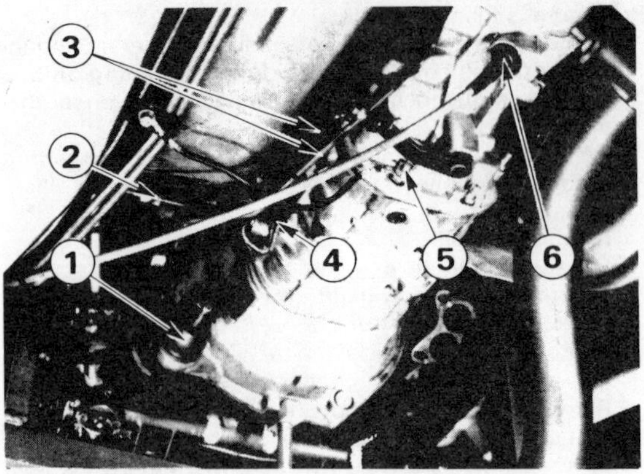

FIG 6:7 Gearbox supplementary items

Key to Fig 6:7 1 Clutch slave cylinder 2 Counter lever 3 Rods 4 Reversing light switch leads 5 Earth lead 6 Speedometer cable

FIG 6:8 Disconnecting the gearbox

FIG 6:9 Supporting the engine

6:4 Gearbox dismantling

The operations concerned with the dismantling of the gearbox can be conveniently undertaken if the unit is mounted on a suitable stand. Another method is to attach it to a fixture which can be secured in a vice. Complete dismantling and reassembly of the gearbox requires the use of a hydraulic press for the removal of the gears as well as special tools and gauging equipment for reassembly, for which the assistance of a service agent will normally be required. If extensive repairs are necessary it may be more economical to fit a replacement gearbox on an exchange basis. The components, however, can be removed for inspection as follows:

1 Remove the clutch release fork and the clutch housing as described in **Chapter 5.** Then remove the reversing lights switch, the speedometer drive socket stop screw 5 (see **FIG 6:11**) and the socket 6 with the aid of the pliers as shown.

2 Reverse the position of the gearbox, set the control lever 1 (see **FIG 6:12**) at neutral and pull the selector lever 2 fully to the rear. Then remove the seven housing retaining bolts, for which a wrench of the Facom J.13.L type may be used with a 13 mm socket extension.

3 Remove the rear housing, using a mallet if necessary. Proceed to remove the four screws 3 (see **FIG 6:13**) with a 6 mm Allen key, then the eight assembly screws from the half housings and finally the upper housing. Lift off and remove the gear and pinion assembly as shown in **FIG 6:14.** An exploded view of the gearbox components is to be seen in **FIG 6:15.**

To dismantle the striking forks and locking devices, operations are as follows:

1 Engage second gear and remove the pin from the first and second gear striking fork as shown in **FIG 6:16.** Engage fourth gear and remove the pin from the third and fourth gear striking fork 3.

2 Referring to **FIG 6:17,** remove the locking plug with a 5 mm Allen key and withdraw the first and second gear fork shaft 2 and the third and fourth gear shaft 4.

3 Remove the locking plug 6 (see **FIG 6:18**) on the side of the gearbox to remove the reverse striking fork 7 with the countershaft pinion.

4 Remove the three locking springs, four balls and the locking finger from the passage shown in **FIG 6:19.** If the balls are difficult to extract, use a 7 mm diameter rod to free them.

5 Remove the locking needle (see **FIG 6:20**) from the third and fourth speed fork shaft.

6 Drive out the pin 2 (see **FIG 6:21**) from the reverse pinion shaft 3 and force this shaft towards the inside of the housing.

6:5 Gearbox reassembly

Before reassembling ensure that all parts are clean and that oil drillings are free from obstruction. Oil the components with the recommended gear oil during the assembly. Examine splines and gear teeth for wear, for which a comparative check with new parts will be helpful. Misshapen teeth on the synchronizing rings will cause baulking trouble. It is essential that the friction surfaces of the rings are in good condition, otherwise faulty synchromesh operation will result.

FIG 6:10 Releasing the gearbox

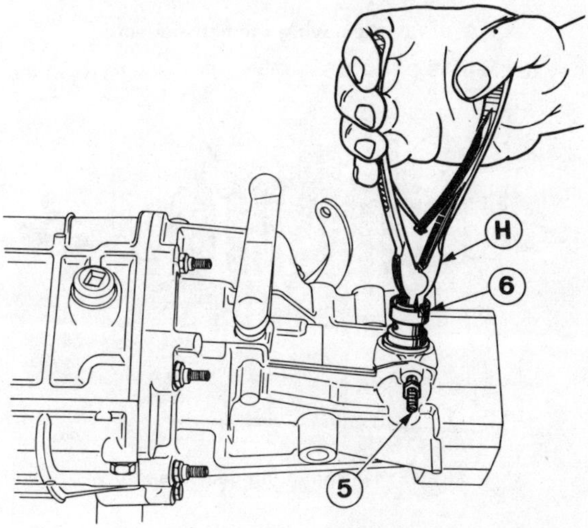

FIG 6:11 Removing the speedometer drive socket

Key to Fig 6:11 5 Stop screw 6 Drive socket H Pliers

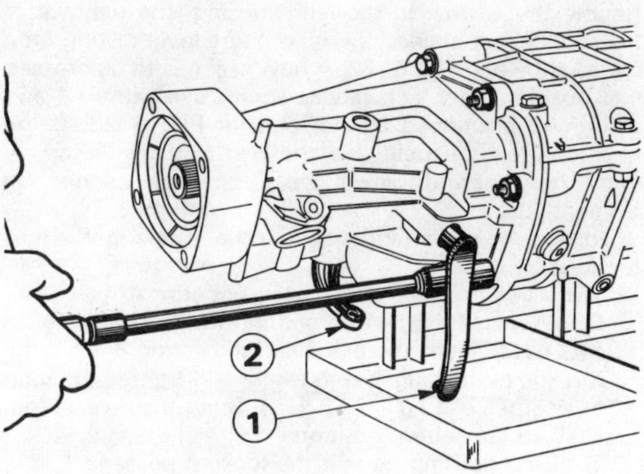

FIG 6:12 Removing the rear housing

Key to Fig 6:12 1 Control lever 2 Selector lever

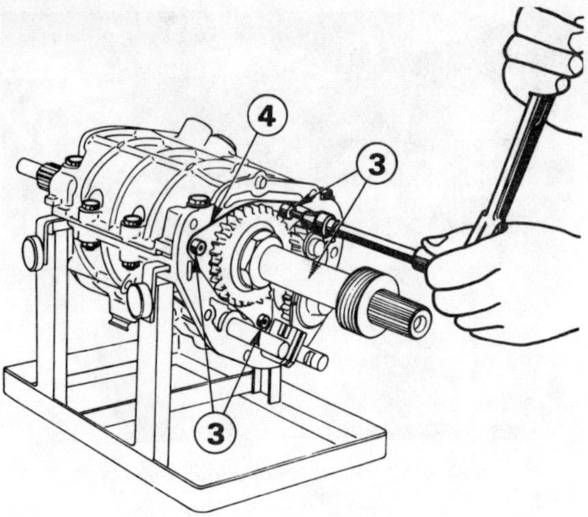

FIG 6:13 Removing the half housing

Key to Fig 6:13 3 Allen screws 4 Bearing lockplate

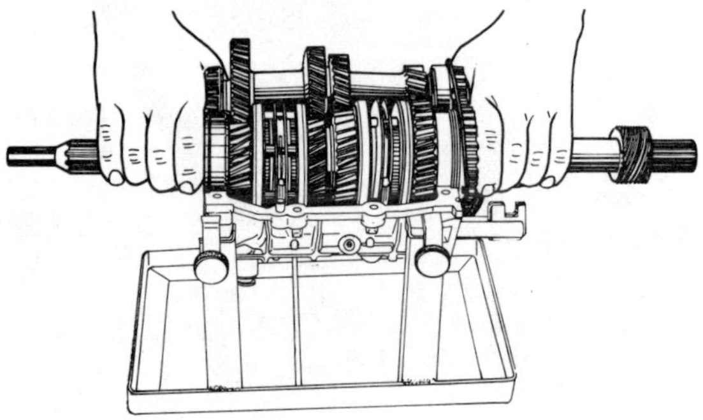

FIG 6:14 Removing gear assembly

Renew any defective parts, with the assistance of a service agent if necessary. Snap rings used on shafts, springs and striking fork pins should always be renewed. Renew the oil seal in the rear housing, the removal of the seal being obtained by using a tyre lever resting on a bar as shown in **FIG 6:22.** A new seal has to be pressed into position, for which service agents use a drift A1 and a ring A2 positioned as indicated in **FIG 6:23.** If the gear controls are defective the rear housing assembly must be renewed, since these controls cannot be dismantled.

To refit the gearchange mechanism, operations are as follows:

1 With the gearbox drain hole uppermost (see **FIG 6:24**) install the reverse shifting fork 4. Referring to **FIG 6:25,** insert the ball 7 and the spring 8. Coat the threads of the plug 9 with sealer and tighten the plug to a torque of 1 kg m (7.2 lb ft). Bring the reverse fork shaft to the neutral position.

2 Turn the housing so that the locking passage 1 is in the vertical position as shown in **FIG 6:26.** Fit the third and fourth and reverse locking finger 2.

3 Referring to **FIG 6:27,** smear the locking needle 3 with tallow and insert it in its housing in the third and fourth gearchange fork shaft 4.

4 With the gearbox upright as shown in **FIG 6:28,** fit the first and second gearchange fork 5, the larger one, and the third and fourth gearchange fork 6. Locate the fork shaft 4 until it is flush with the ball lock hole 7.

5 Insert the spring and one locking ball in the passage 1 shown in **FIG 6:29.** Press the ball against the spring with a drift and then remove the drift whilst pressing the shaft inwards.

6 Set the shaft 2 in **FIG 6:30** at the neutral position and secure the third and fourth gearchange fork 3 with a new pin.

7 With the housing resting on its righthand side as shown in **FIG 6:31,** insert a locking ball into the passage 4 to contact the third and fourth gear shaft 2.

8 Insert the first and second gear shaft 5 up to the neutral position. Fit the locking ball 6 and spring 7 into the passage 4.

9 Coat the plug 8 with sealer and tighten to a torque of 1 kg m (7.2 lb ft). Secure the first and second striking fork 9 with a new pin.

Before refitting the gear assembly, place the clutch housing on a flat surface to check the parallelism of the front and rear faces of housing, using a dial gauge as indicated in **FIG 6:32.** The housing must be renewed if the faces are out of line by more than .1 mm.

Refit the gear assembly in the lefthand housing as shown in **FIG 6:33.** Care must be taken that the striking forks correctly engage the synchronizer rings. Fit the intermediate gearshaft front bearing outer race if it has been removed. Then lightly smear the mating surfaces of the half housings with a good sealing compound and refit the lefthand half housing.

Referring to **FIG 6:34,** insert the four housing bolts and tighten them to a torque of .5 kg m (3.6 lb ft). Continue by lightly smearing the rear face of the clutch housing with the sealer and securing this housing with six bolts tightened to a torque of 2.75 kg m (20 lb ft). Secure the rear backing plate by four Allen screws tightened to a torque of 1 kg m (7.2 lb ft). Then loosen the four housing bolts (see **FIG 6:35**) and strike the half housings with a mallet whilst turning the drive shaft. Retighten the bolts to a torque of 1.5 kg m (11 lb ft).

The half housings at their rear mating surfaces must not be out of line by more than .02 mm. A dial indicator with the support F shown in **FIG 6:36** is used to check this requirement.

Smear the mating surface of the rear housing with a good sealer and fit the housing. Referring to **FIG 6:37,** engage the three double-thread studs 1 and the four retaining bolts 2. Pull the selector lever 3 fully backwards and tighten the seven bolts and studs to a torque of 1.5 kg m (11 lb ft). Oil the bearing in the rear housing.

Refit the speedometer drive socket (see **FIG 6:11**) with a new O-ring smeared with tallow and position the parts by rotating them. Also refit the drive socket stop screw with its locknut. The clutch release fork should now be refitted as described in **Chapter 5,** inserting the rubber cup filled with grease in the groove behind the ball thrust. Refit the reverse lights switch with a new seal. Switches with copper bodies and metallo-plastic gaskets should be tightened to 1.25 kg m (9 lb ft) and switches with steel bodies and copper gaskets tightened to 2.75 kg m (20 lb ft).

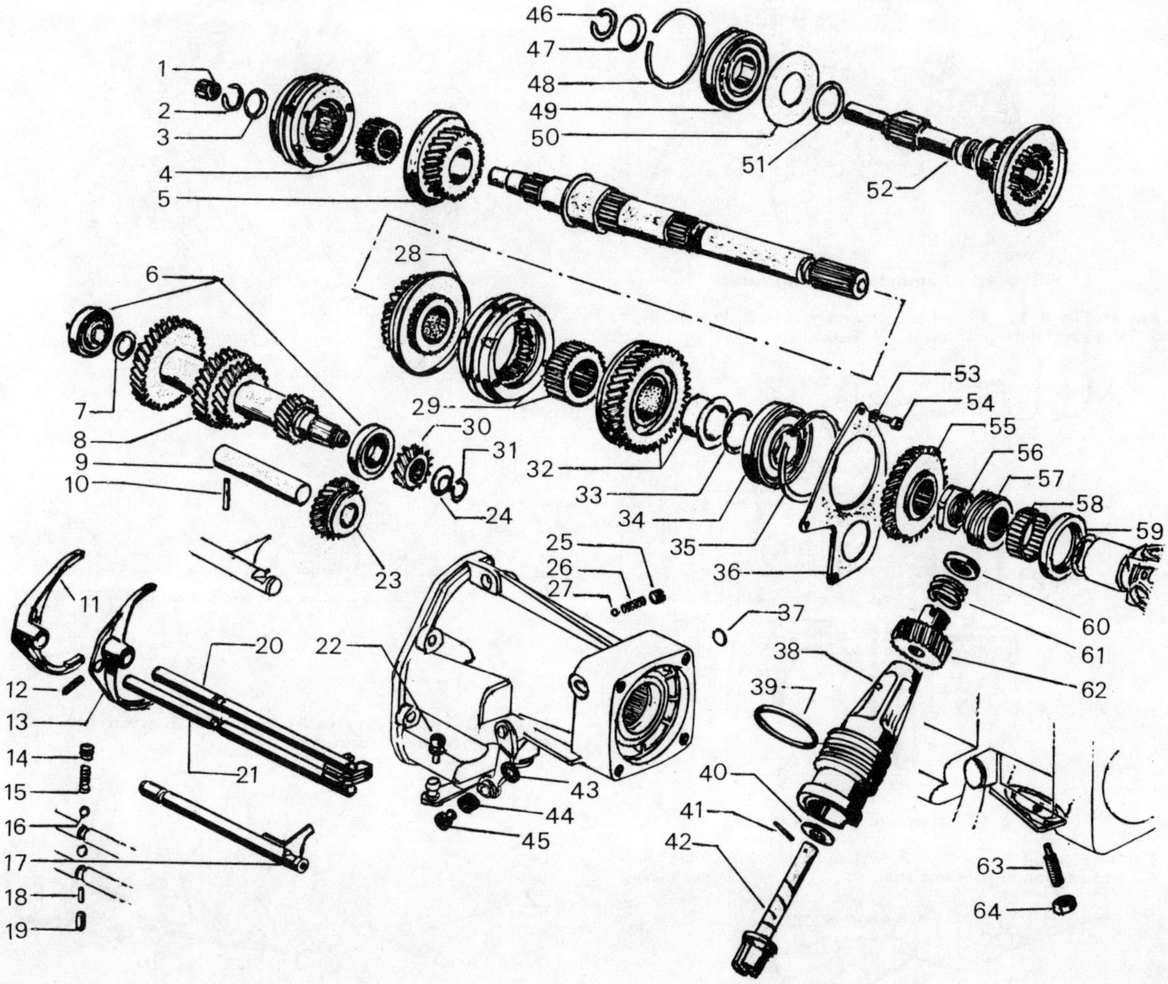

FIG 6:15 An exploded view of the gearbox components

Key to Fig 6:15 1 Needle roller bearing 2 Circlip 3 Belleville washer 4 Synchronizer sleeve and hub 5 1st gear wheel 6 Bearings 7 Washer 8 Countershaft 9 Reverse gearshaft 10 Pin 11 3rd/4th selection fork 12 Pin 13 1st/2nd selection fork 14 Plug 15 Spring 16 Ball 17 Reverse gear selection shaft 18 Pin 19 Plug 20 1st/2nd selection shaft 21 3rd/4th selection shaft 22 Ball end 23 Reverse idler gear 24 Belleville washer 25 Plug 26 Spring 27 Ball 28 2nd gearwheel 29 Synchronizer sleeve and nut 30 Reverse drive gearwheel 31 Circlip 32 1st gearwheel, needle roller bearing and distance sleeve 33 Shims 34 Ballbearing 35 Circlip 36 Bearing retaining plate 37 Ring 38 Speedometer housing 39 Seal 40 Thrust washer 41 Pin 42 Drive shaft 43 Washer 44 Clamp 45 Spindle 46 Circlip 47 Bellville washer 48 Circlip 49 Ballbearing 50 Oil slinger 51 Shim 52 First motion shaft 53 Spring washer 54 Stud and nut 55 Reverse driven gear 56 Nut 57 Speedometer drive gear 58 Needle roller bearing 59 Oil seal 60 Spring retainer 61 Spring 62 Speedometer driven gear 63 Locating screw 64 Nut

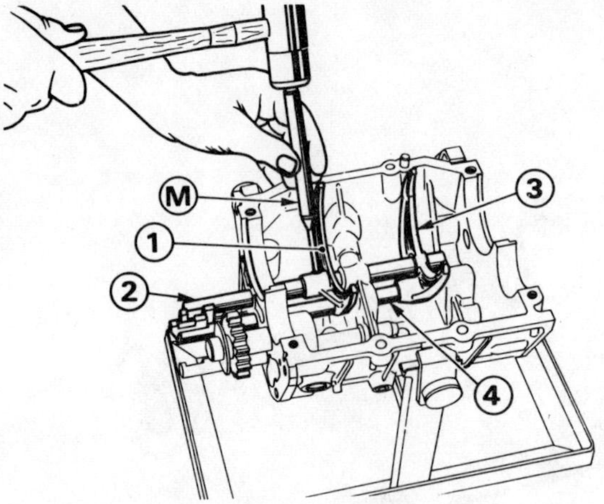

FIG 6:16 Removing striking forks

Key to Fig 6:16 1 First and second gear fork 2 Fork shaft 3 Third and fourth gear fork 4 Fork shaft M Drift

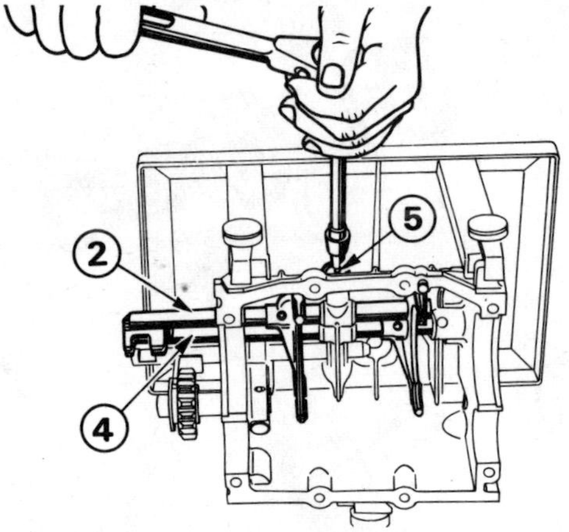

FIG 6:17 Removing locking plug

Key to Fig 6:17 2 First and second gear fork shaft 4 Third and fourth gear fork shaft 5 Locking plug

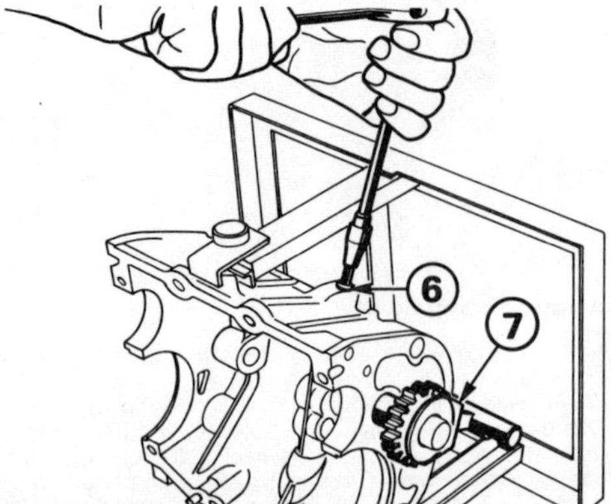

FIG 6:18 Removing locking plug **6** and reverse striking fork **7**

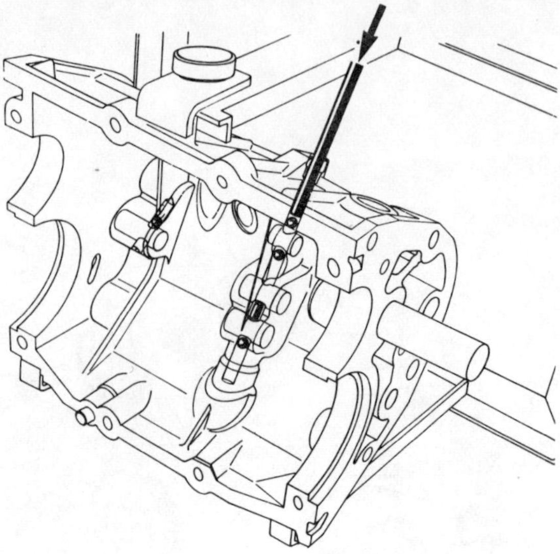

FIG 6:19 Locking springs and balls

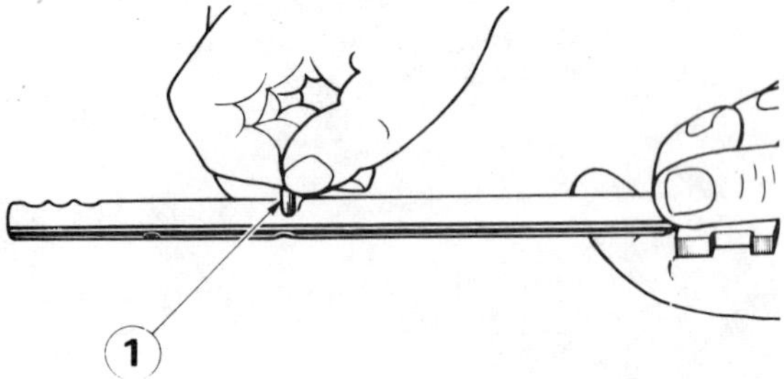

FIG 6:20 Removing locking needle **1** from the third and fourth-speed fork shaft

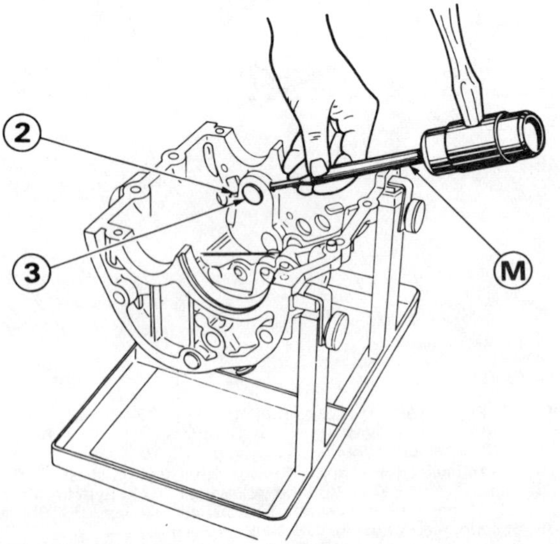

FIG 6:21 Removing pin **2** from reverse pinion shaft **3** with the drift **M**

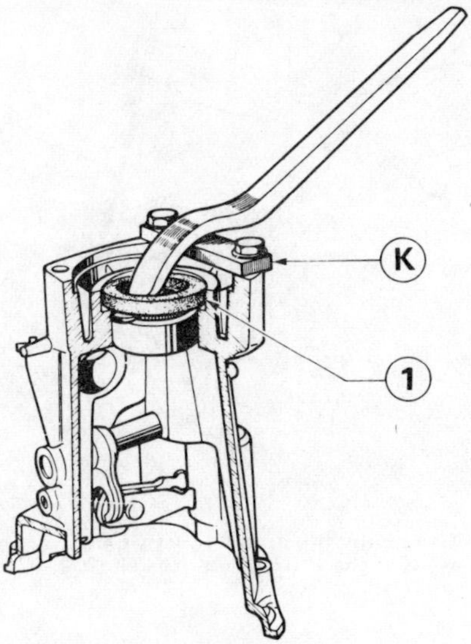

FIG 6:22 Method of removing the rear oil seal **1** with a safety bar **K** and a tyre lever

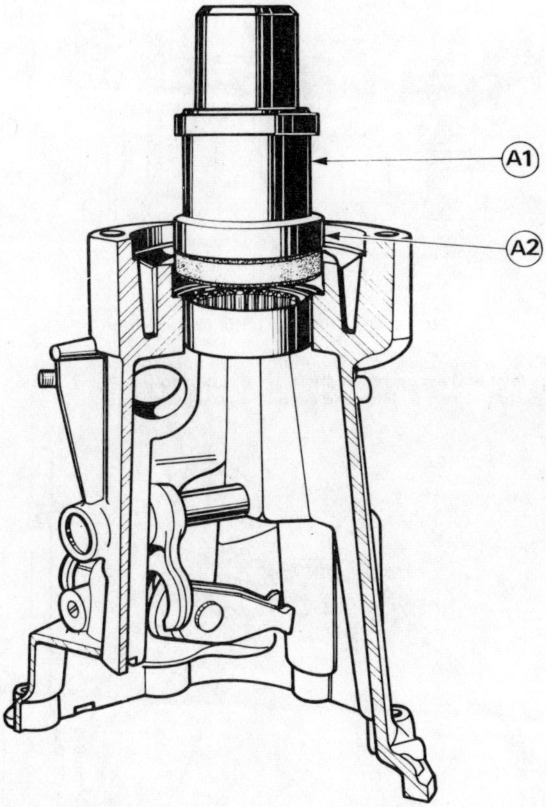

FIG 6:23 Installing the rear oil seal with the drift **A1** and the seal fitting ring **A2** (tool set No. 8.0310.Z)

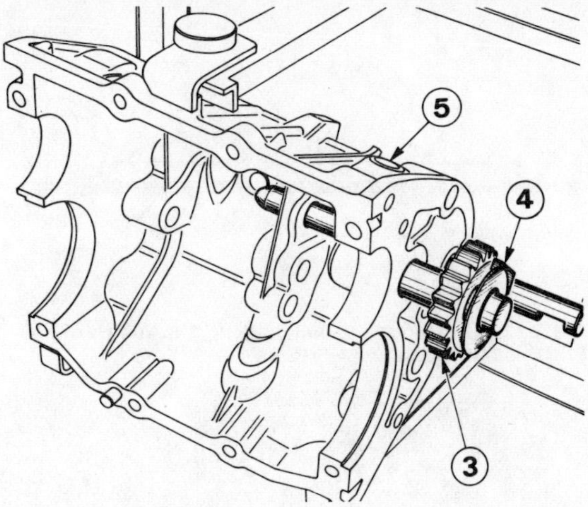

FIG 6:24 Fitting the reverse pinion **3** and the striking fork **4** with the drain hole **5** upwards

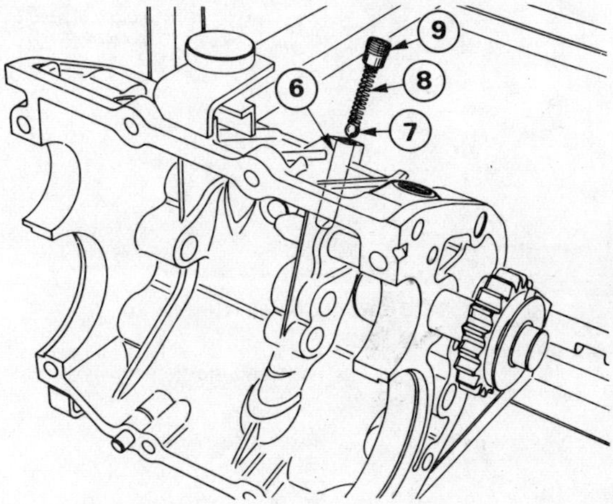

FIG 6:25 Inserting the ball **7** and the spring **8** into the locking passage **6** with the plug **9**

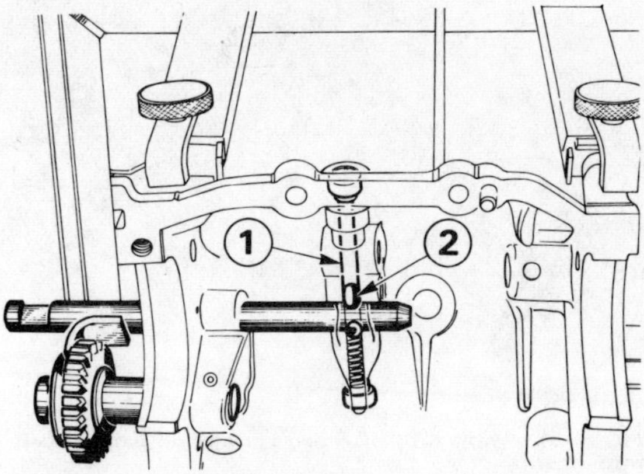

FIG 6:26 Fitting the third and fourth and reverse locking finger **2** with the locking passage **1** situated vertically

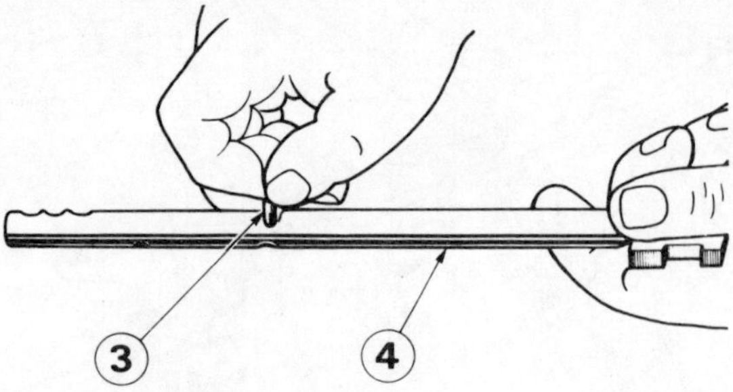

FIG 6:27 Fitting the locking needle 3 in the third and fourth gearchange fork shaft 4

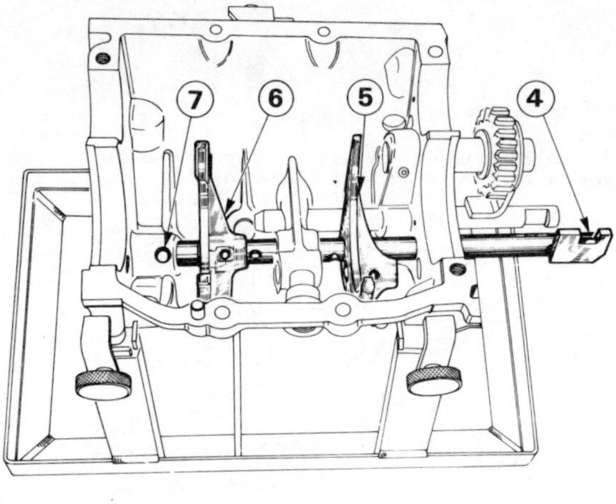

FIG 6:28 Refitting striking forks

Key to Fig 6:28 4 Fork shaft 5 First and second gearchange fork 6 Third and fourth gearchange fork 7 Ball lock hole

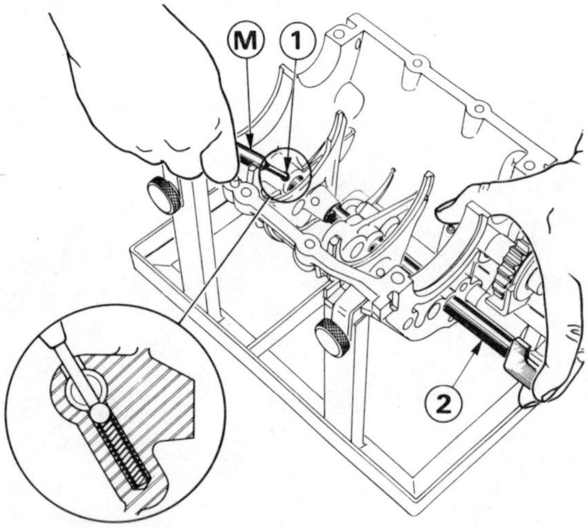

FIG 6:29 Method of inserting spring and locking ball into location

Key to Fig 6:29 1 Passage for spring and ball (see inset) 2 Shaft **M** Drift

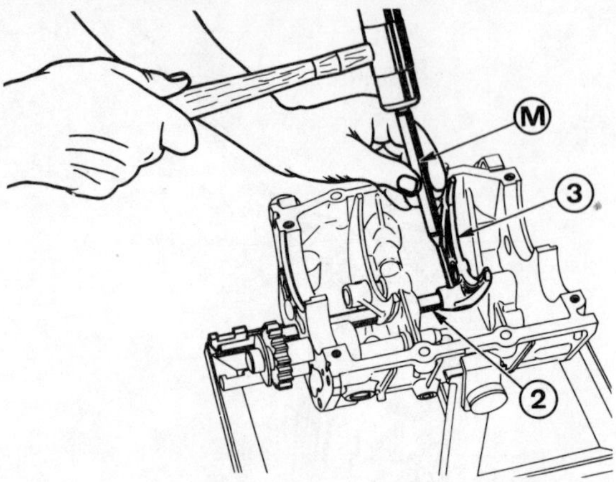

FIG 6:30 Fitting third and fourth gearchange fork 3 with a new pin, the drift M and the shaft 2 at neutral

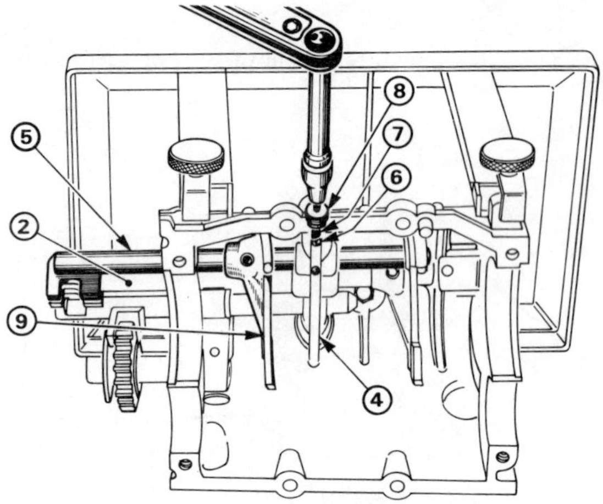

FIG 6:31 Fitting balls and springs

Key to Fig 6:31 2 Third and fourth gear shaft 4 Passage 5 First and second gear shaft 6 Locking ball 7 Spring 8 Plug 9 First and second gear striking fork

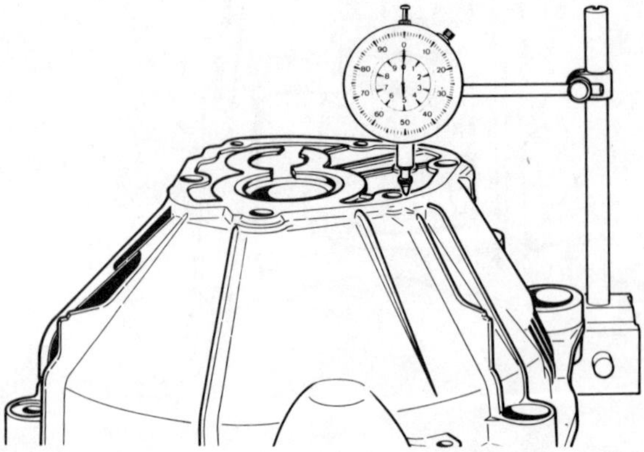

FIG 6:32 Checking accuracy of clutch housing faces

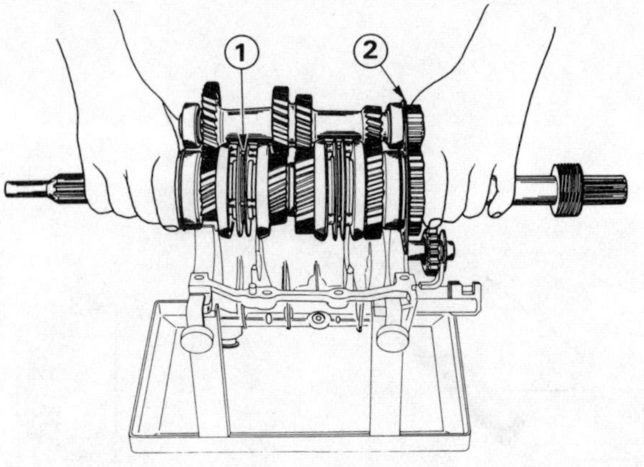

FIG 6:33 Refitting gear assembly

Key to Fig 6:33 1 Third and fourth gear 2 Backing plate

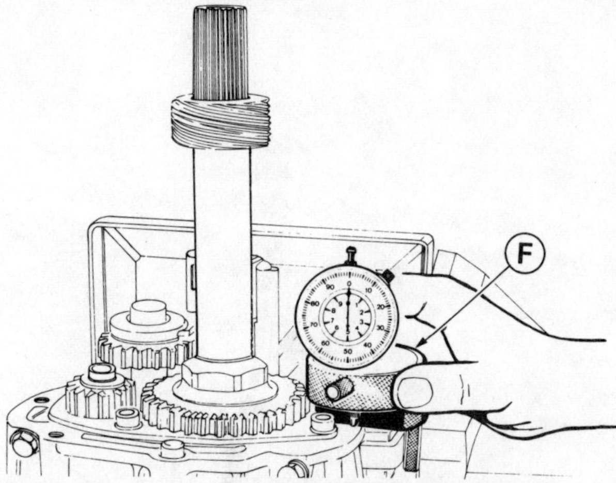

FIG 6:36 Checking the accuracy of fit of the half housings, using a dial indicator with support F (tool set No. 8.0310.Z)

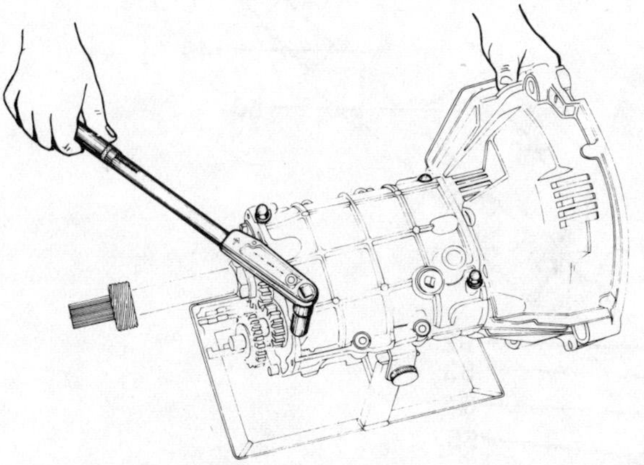

FIG 6:34 Securing the bolts and the clutch housing

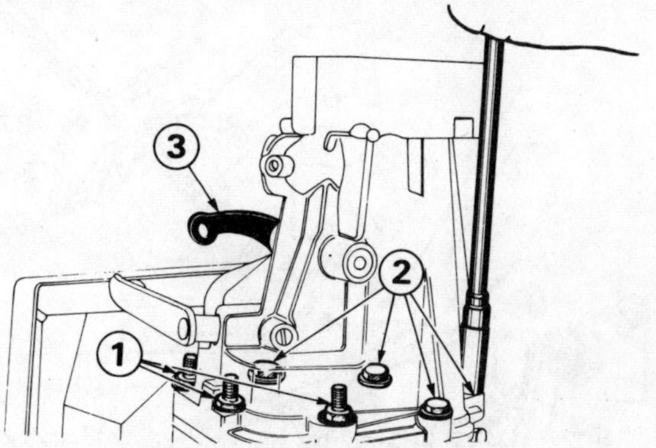

FIG 6:37 Fitting the rear housing

Key to Fig 6:37 1 Three double-thread studs 2 Four securing bolts 3 Selector lever

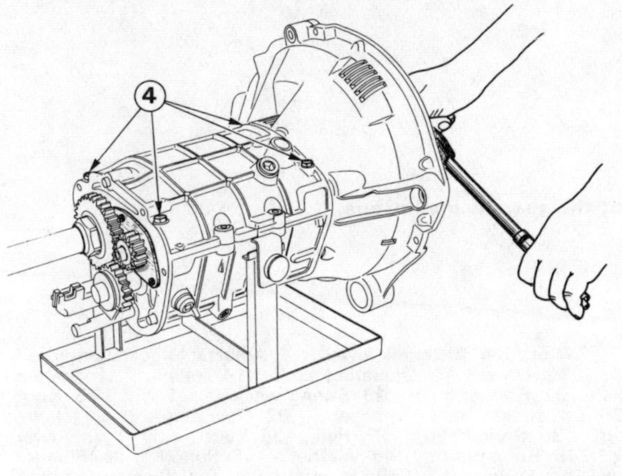

FIG 6:35 Final fitting of housing bolts 4

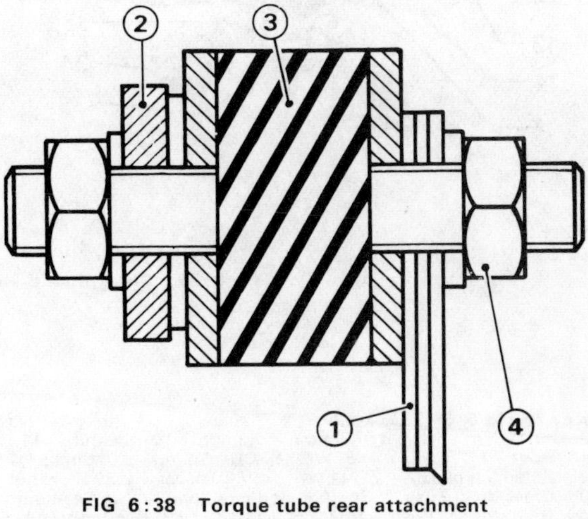

FIG 6:38 Torque tube rear attachment

Key to Fig 6:38 1 Rear attachment 2 Torque tube lug 3 Rubber ring 4 Securing nut

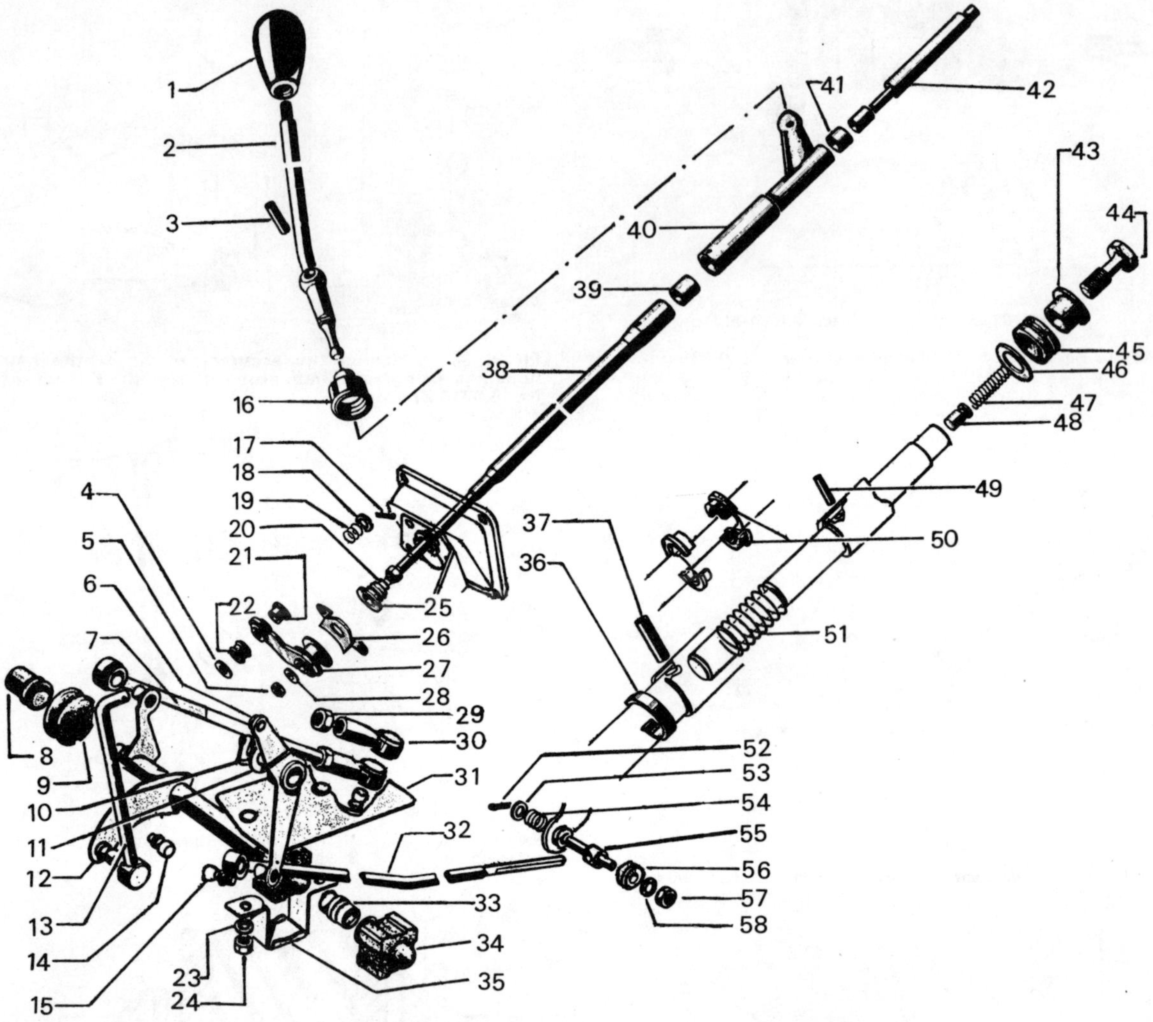

FIG 6:39 An exploded view of the gearchange linkage

Key to Fig 6:39 1 Knob 2 Gearlever 3 Pin 4 Washer 5 Nut 6 Bellcrank lever 7 Adjustable gearchange rod 8 Cross-shaft bush 9 Vibration mounting 10 Splitpin 11 Washer 12 Lever 13 Operating shaft 14 Ballpin 15 Ballpin 16 Boot 17 Splitpin 18 Washer 19 Spring 20 Circlip 21 Bush 22 Rubber bush 23 Spring washer 24 Nut 25 Boot 26 Retaining plate 27 Lever 28 Washer 29 Locknut 30 Ball socket 31 Bracket 32 Operating rod, adjustable 33 Cross-shaft bush 34 Vibration mounting 35 Securing bracket 36 Spring clip 37 Pin 38 Tube 39 Bush, lower 40 Guide 41 Bush, upper 42 Shaft 43 Bearing 44 Screw 45 Rubber ring 46 Washer 47 Spring 48 Plunger 49 Pin 50 Split bearing ring 51 Spring 52 Splitpin 53 Washer 54 Spring 55 Spindle with guide 56 Clamp 57 Nut 58 Shakeproof washer

6:6 Gearbox refitting

Refitting operations are in general the reverse of those followed for removal and are undertaken as follows:

1 With the engine supported on the hoisting apparatus used in removal, lightly smear the front part of the engine drive shaft as well as the interior of the thrust ballbearing guide sleeve with a recommended grease.

2 Check that the mating faces of clutch housing and engine are clean and free from burrs. Position the gearbox and engage the engine drive shaft with the clutch disc without using excessive force. **Do not allow the weight of the transmission to hang on the main drive pinion after it has entered the hub of the clutch disc.**

3 Secure the gearbox (see **FIG 6:8**) with the three Allen screws equipped with new washers and tightened to a torque of 5.5 kg m (40 lb ft). Remove the block placed under the radiator (see **Section 6:3**) and lower the hoisting apparatus.

4 Place a jack under the clutch housing and align the engine-gearbox assembly with the propeller shaft. Lightly smear a recommended grease on the propeller shaft splines.

5 Engage the propeller shaft splined sleeve with the drive shaft, then remove the shaft holding plate 8.0403.S. Check the final engagement of the propeller shaft with the gearbox and refit the four Allen screws indicated in **FIGS 6:4** and **6:5.**

6 Reconnect the earth lead to the gearbox, the reversing lights switch leads and the speedometer drive cable. The drive worm should just be engaged on the pinion and only the locknut should be tightened.

7 Refit the gearchange extension and connecting rods, also the drain plug with a new seal and tightened to a torque of 2.75 kg m (20 lb ft).

8 Refit the clutch housing closure plates, the clutch cylinder and the steering gear housing (see **Chapter 10**). Secure the radiator to the front crossmember and tighten the bolts to a torque of 1 kg m (7.2 lb ft).

9 Attach the heat dissipation plate under the car floor and refit the exhaust pipe assembly with a new metalloplastic gasket. Referring to **FIG 6:38,** fit the rear attachment 1 to the connecting tube lug and ensure that the rubber ring 3 does not turn whilst tightening the nut 4.

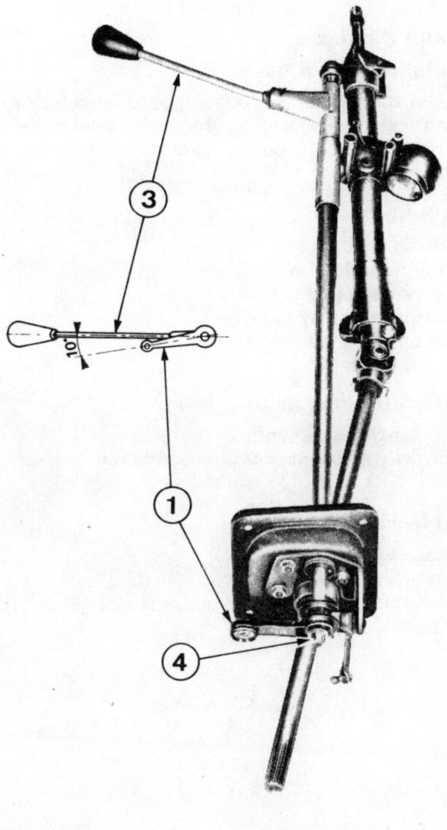

FIG 6:40 Gearlever mechanism

Key to Fig 6:40 1 Lower lever 3 Gearchange lever 4 'Nylstop' nut

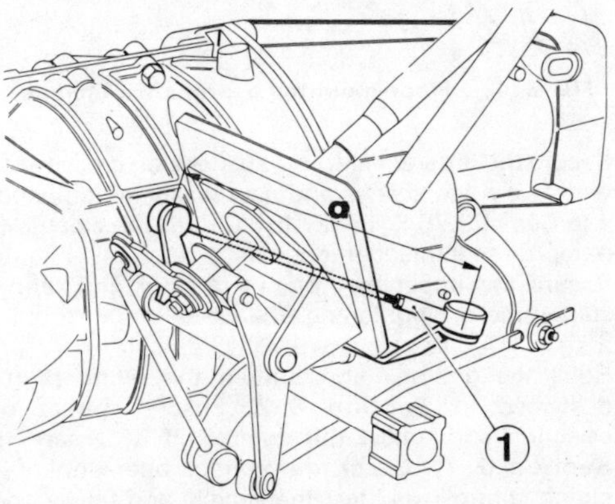

FIG 6:41 Gear selector control link (1) a=248±1 mm

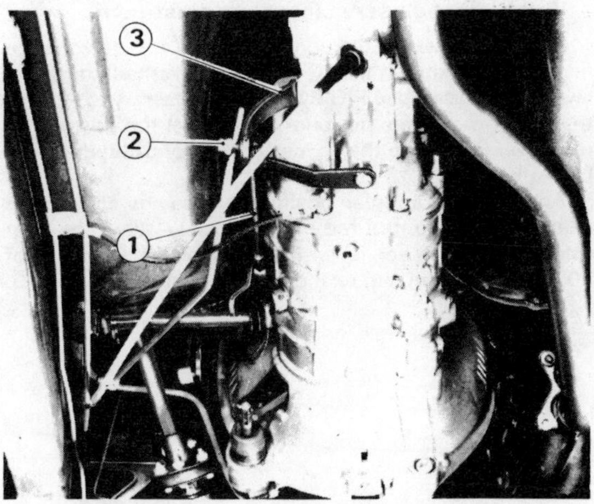

FIG 6:42 Adjusting selector control

Key to Fig 6:42 1 Selector control link 2 Nut 3 Selector lever

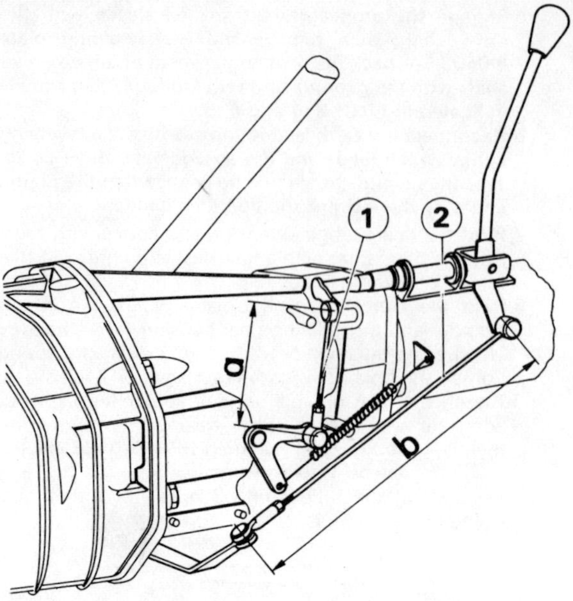

FIG 6:43 Floor-mounted gearchange linkage

10 Secure the differential to the suspension crossmember with two Allen screws and new washers tightened to a torque of 3.75 kg m (27 lb ft). Refit the electric fuel pump on fuel injection engines.
11 Secure the upper part of the radiator and refit the starter motor, tightening the bolts to a torque of 2 kg m (14.5 lb ft).
12 Refill the gearbox and tighten the filling plug as described in **Section 6:2.** Ensure correct gear selection and adjust the controls if necessary (see **Section 6:7**). Check the correct operation of the clutch control, road test the vehicle and finally check the housings and the gearbox plugs for leaks.

6:7 Gearchange servicing and adjustment

A general view of the components of the gearchange mechanism is shown in **FIG 6:39.** To overhaul the gear-lever mechanism (see **FIG 6:40**) it is necessary to remove the steering column, but prior to removal the position of the lower lever 1 on the splines of the control rod should be marked.

An incorrect angular position of the lower lever in relation to the control rod may adversely affect the gear selection. The lower lever 1 should be at an angle of 10 deg. downwards in relation to the gearchange lever 3. If this is not the case, remove the 'Nylstop' nut 4 and the flat washer, disengage the lever 1 and reposition correctly.

The gear selector control link should have a length of 248±1 mm as indicated at 'a' in **FIG 6:41.** For its adjustment on the car, referring to **FIG 6:42,** fit the selector control link set at the specified length. Inside the car, place the gearchange lever in the neutral position, then from under the car proceed as follows:

1 Unscrew the nut 2 and ensure that the selector lever 3 is in the neutral position.
2 Mark the maximum free play positions permitted by the selector lever 3.
3 Place the selector lever in the midway position and retighten the nut 2.
4 Check the correct gear selection in all gears.

Floor mounted gearchange:

FIG 6:43 shows the linkage of the alternative, floor-mounted gearchange. To adjust the linkage, disconnect the control links **1** and **2**, loosen the locknuts and turn the threaded end fittings so that dimension **a** is 89 mm and dimension **b** is 290 mm. Tighten the locknuts and refit the links.

6:8 Fault diagnosis

(a) Jumping out of gear

1 Broken springs behind locating balls for selector rods
2 Excessively worn locating grooves in selector rods
3 Fork retaining pins loose or broken

(b) Noisy gearbox

1 Insufficient oil
2 Incorrect grade of oil
3 Worn or damaged bearings
4 Excessive end play in laygear
5 Worn or damaged gear teeth

(c) Difficulty in engaging gear

1 Worn synchromesh cones
2 Incorrectly adjusted or worn gearchange linkage

(d) Oil leaks

1 Damaged joint washers
2 Worn or damaged oil seals
3 Front and rear gearbox casings loose or faces damaged

CHAPTER 7

THE AUTOMATIC TRANSMISSION

7:1 Construction and operation

The ZF (Zahnradfabrik Friedrischafen) automatic transmission shown in **FIGS 7:1** and **7:2** is available as an alternative to the manual gearbox on Peugeot 504 cars. The main features of the transmission are a hydraulic torque converter, a gearbox and an automatic control unit. The torque converter is driven by the engine crankshaft and automatic operation is then obtained by the converter transmitting its hydrokinetic energy to the propeller shaft through an epicyclic gear, also hydraulically controlled. The fluid drive is directly employed in all transmission stages and hence the automatic selection of forward low and high gear ranges takes place with a smooth and continuously variable torque output governed by road speed and the position of the accelerator pedal. Reverse gear engagement is again hydraulically performed when selected.

The gearbox provides three ratios plus reverse which are driven by two concentric planetary pinions connected by three pairs of planet gears, as at 8 in **FIG 7:2.** An epicyclic or planetary gear system is one in which a central sun wheel has smaller planet pinions rotating around it in the manner of the solar system, the planet wheels themselves meshing with an internally-toothed ring gear which surrounds the assembly. The drive through an epicyclic gear can give varied output ratios depending on which elements of the gear set are either driven or held stationary. The gear used in the ZF automatic transmission system is known as a compound or Ravignaux planetary gear set (see **FIG 7:3**) which combines two sets of planetary pinions and two sun gears. Gear changes are carried out by the locking of satellite gears by disc brakes and two multiplate clutches, which require no upkeep. The automatic control unit is located inside the oil pan or sump below the gear assembly and controls the operation of the multiplate clutches through a number of valves.

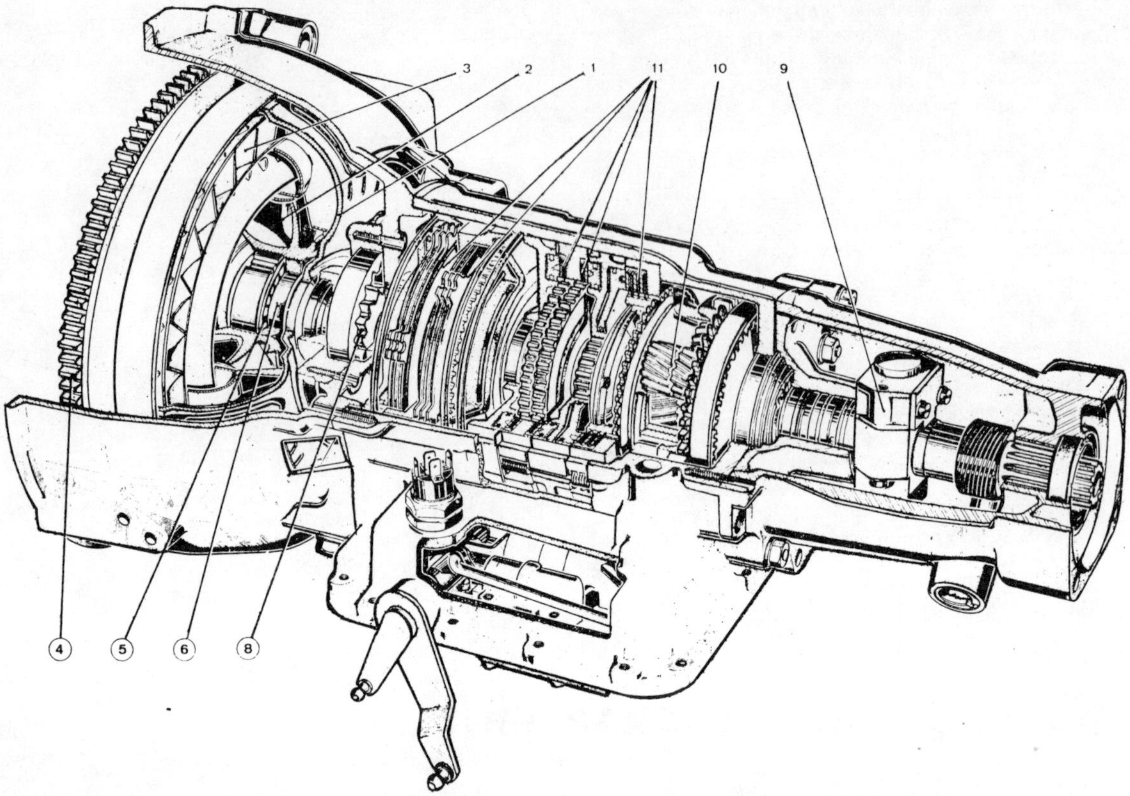

FIG 7:1 A cutaway view of the ZF automatic transmission unit

Key to Fig 7:1 1 Impeller 2 Stator 3 Turbine 4 Ring gear 5 Uni-directional clutch 6 Input shaft 8 Pump 9 Governor 10 Epicyclic gear set 11 Clutches

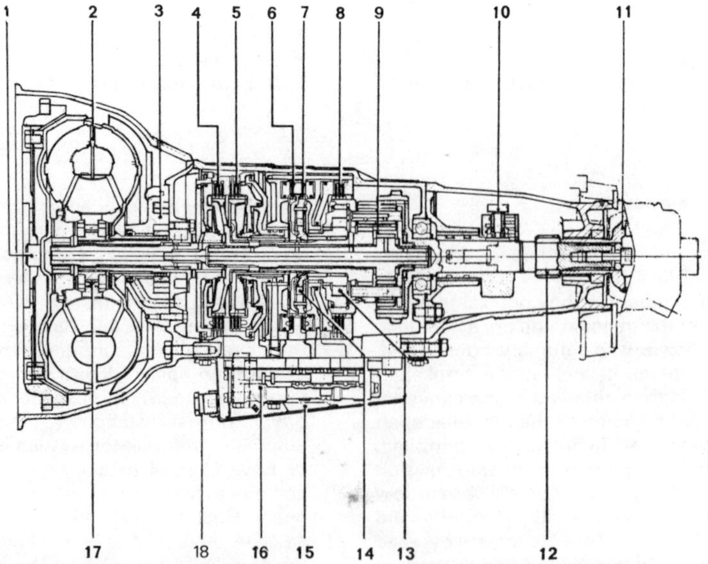

FIG 7:2 A sectional view of the transmission unit

Key to Fig 7:2 1 Input shaft 2 Torque converter 3 Pump 4 Clutch A (see text) 5 Clutch B (see text) 6 and 7 Disc brake C 8 Brake D 9 Epicyclic gear train 10 Governor 11 Output shaft 12 Speedometer drive gear 13 Freewheel 14 Freewheel 15 Strainer 16 Valve block 17 Freewheel 18 Drain plug

The torque converter filled with oil has three main elements: an impeller driven by the engine, a turbine or rotor attached to the gearbox input shaft and a stator (or torque multiplier) mounted on a free-wheel or uni-directional clutch between the impeller and the turbine (see **FIG 7:2**). The freewheel is incorporated so that the stator can only revolve in the same direction as the impeller. When the impeller is rotated by the engine, the fluid with which the converter is kept charged is thrown outwards by centrifugal force through the impeller vanes and is directed into the turbine, causing the turbine to rotate as well. The fluid passes through the turbine vanes and is directed backwards into the stator, which remains stationary as it cannot revolve in the reverse direction against the one-way clutch. The direction of the fluid passing through the stator vanes is changed, so that on re-entering the impeller the fluid assists in driving it and thus provides a torque multiplication.

Six operating ranges are provided and selected by the floor mounted selector lever. The ranges are shown by the letters and numbers on the indicator plate on the central console in the following order:

P—Parking. In this position, when at rest, the rear drive wheels are locked by a safety mechanical device which is independent of the handbrake.

R—Reverse. A safety notch prevents any misengagement.

N—Neutral, with drive wheels not locked.

3—Fully automatic drive for general use in town and country. Starting in first gear with subsequent gearchanges dependent upon accelerator position.

2—Allows use of first two gear ratios without passing into third. Convenient for fast overtaking and braking when descending steep hills.

1—Uses first gear only without passing into second. Gives maximum engine braking effort for descending very steep slopes such as mountain passes.

A diagrammatic representation of how the various changes are effected is given in **FIG 7:4.**

7:2 Routine maintenance

Every 5000 miles (8000 km) the transmission fluid level should be checked with the car on a level surface with the handbrake applied and the gearbox at normal operating temperature, as reached after approximately 5 miles (8 km) of driving. Select N and allow the engine to idle for two or three minutes. With the engine still idling in N, withdraw the dipstick and examine the oil level. If necessary, add sufficient fluid to bring the level to the full mark, for which the manufacturers recommend Esso Automatic Transmission Fluid type A-AQATF 2974.A. The difference between the MINI and MAXI marks on the dipstick is approximately .25 litre. Oil cooling is by a heat exchanger located in the engine radiator and the total capacity of the system is 5.5 litre.

The transmission fluid level should be maintained with care. An incorrect level may be one cause among others of slip or judder in starting, and overheating may arise due to a high fluid level during sustained high speeds.

The gearbox should be drained and refilled at intervals of 1000, 5000, 15,000, 30,000 and 45,000 km following, under the same conditions as when topping up. After draining and refitting the drain plug, add 2 litre of the approved fluid, run the engine and then complete the filling process until the MAXI level on the dipstick is reached. Check the tightness of the drain plug. At the 1000 km stage the converter oil should also be drained and renewed.

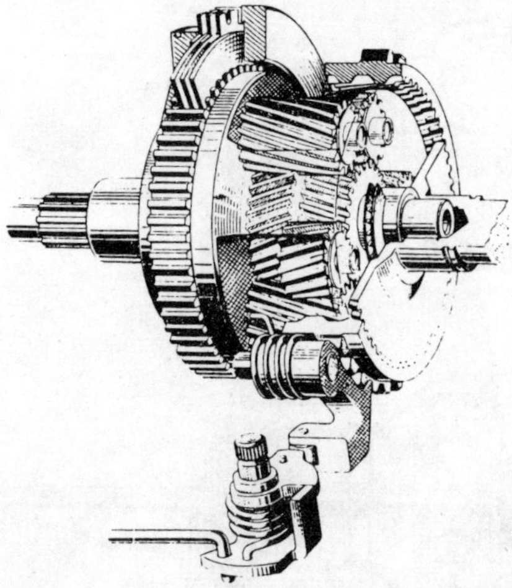

FIG 7:3 A sectional view of the Ravigneaux compound planetary gear set

7:3 Removing and refitting automatic gearbox

To remove and refit the gearbox, operations are as follows:

1 Remove the exhaust downpipe and the exhaust support bolts.

2 Remove the speedometer drive securing screw located at the rear end of the transmission casing and carefully lift away the speedometer drive. Detach the propeller shaft at the gearbox drive flange and place the propeller shaft as far away as possible from the rear of the gear casing.

3 Disconnect the manual selector lever from the lever on the transmission housing, also the starter cable.

4 Take the weight of the power unit on a garage hydraulic crane or an overhead hoist and slacken the bolts retaining the engine to the torque converter. Withdraw the oil filler pipe from the gearbox and plug the hole immediately to prevent excessive loss of oil.

5 Remove the lower torque converter housing cover-plate bolts. Remove the four diaphragm securing bolts which may be reached through the hole in the flywheel, turning the crankshaft a little at a time.

6 Carefully ease the engine upwards and towards the front as far as movement of the rubber engine mountings will allow. Remove the previously slackened gearbox-to-engine mounting bolts and take the weight of the gearbox using a garage hydraulic jack with a suitable cradle fitted to the saddle. Take care that the torque converter remains on the transmission and does not slip forward, bearing in mind that it is filled with oil. Push back the converter with a screwdriver through the holes in the flywheel as the gearbox is withdrawn.

FIG 7:4 Diagrams showing the power flow for engagement of gears

Key to Fig 7:4 1 Engine crankshaft 2 Torque converter 3 Clutch A 4 Clutch B 5 Disc brake C1 6 Disc brake C 7 Disc brake D 8 Planetary gear train Z1 to Z5 9 Output shaft 10 Freewheel 11 Freewheel 12 Freewheel **P** Impeller **L** Stator **T** Turbine

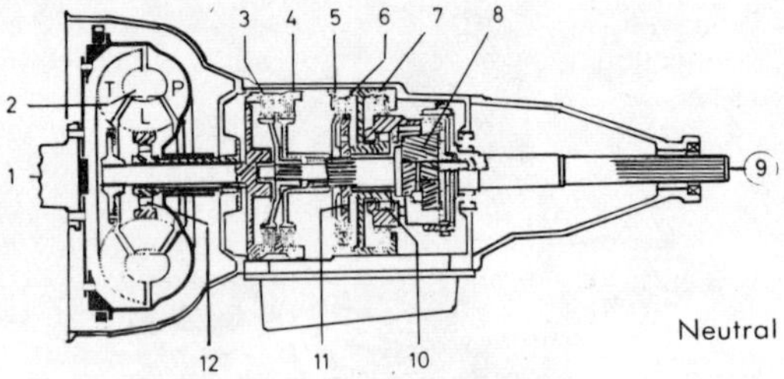

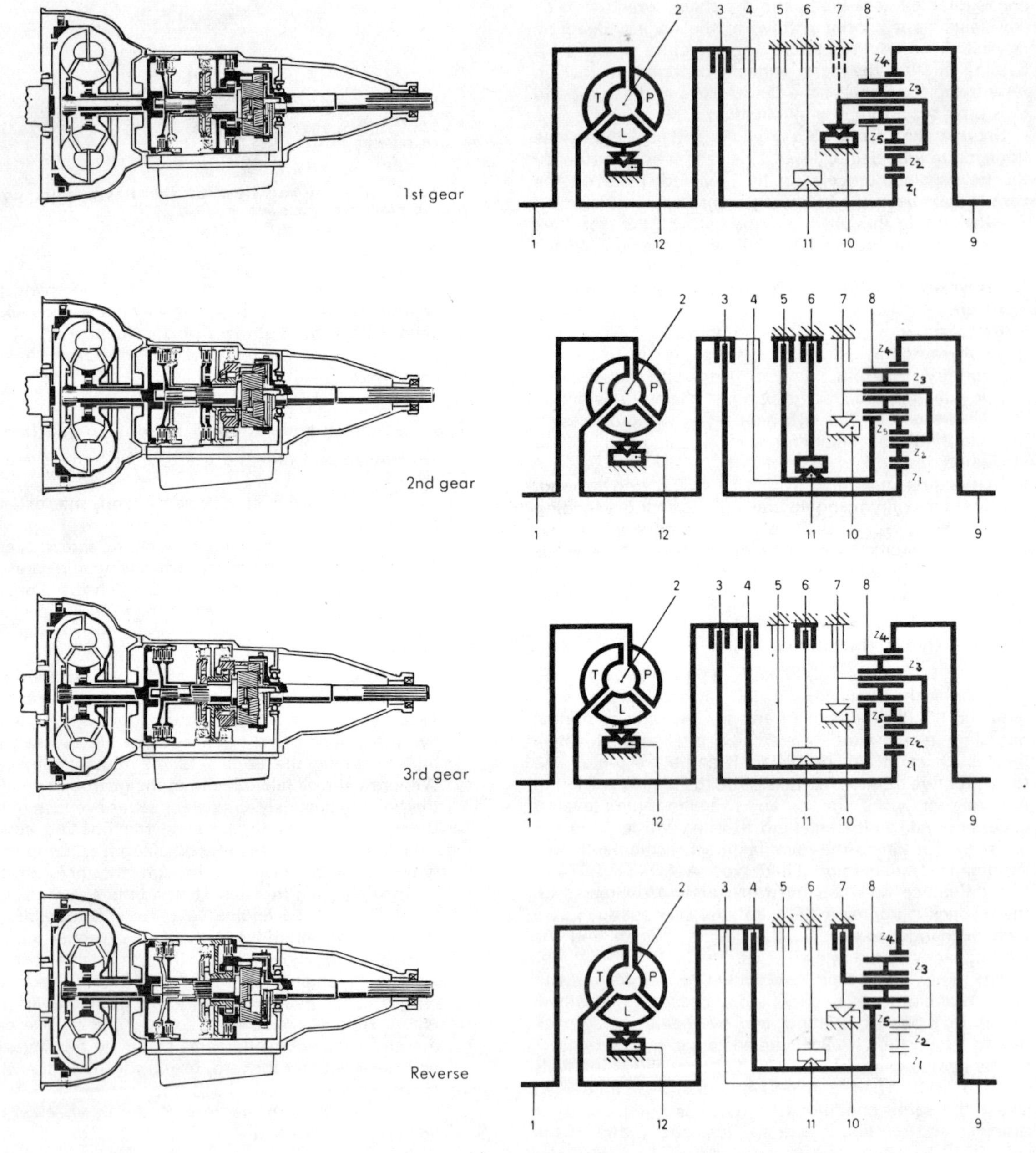

Further dismantling of the transmission is not generally undertaken in normal service operations and if serious trouble is experienced the manufacturers provide a complete transmission assembly in exchange. Road testing and pressure tests, however, can be carried out as described later, which can be of assistance in identifying any faults which may be experienced and possibly remedied without the need for extensive dismantling.

Refitting is undertaken in the reverse order of the removal of the transmission, giving due regard to the following items:

1 Particular attention should be given to the two dowel sleeves located in the front face of the converter housing, especially if a standard exchange assembly is being fitted. A defective sleeve could cause serious damage to the converter and driving disc.

2 Secure the four diaphragm securing bolts that are located through the hole in the flywheel to a torque of 1.6 to 2.3 kg m (11.6 to 17.4 lb ft).

3 When reassembling the cables to the starter lock and reversing lamps switch as shown in **FIG 7:5** the two opposed pins furthest apart (8 and 9) should be connected to cables coloured green/black and green/white. The two pins closer together should be connected to cables brown/black and brown.

4 When reassembling the exhaust manifold to downpipe connection coat the threaded studs with a good sealer.

7:4 Testing

Quality of engine performance can greatly influence the effective operation of an automatic transmission and affect the designed ranges of shift change applicable to an engine in good running order. Various factors have to be considered in the transmission itself when assessing the nature of a fault, but it is important first to ensure that:

1 The throttle butterfly opens fully and is not prevented from doing so by the throttle fixing screw. If the throttle stop adjustment is incorrectly made, preventing full movement of the accelerator pedal, the carburetter butterfly will not open fully, resulting in poor performance.

2 There is no free play in the accelerator linkage.

3 The transmission fluid level is correct and the engine and automatic transmission are at their normal working temperatures, as described in **Section 7:2.**

The vehicle should be road tested using all ranges, noting any discrepancies in operation. The following table of shift speeds shows the ranges in which the gear changes should occur under various conditions:

Throttle opening	*Gearchanges*							
	Upshifts				*Downshifts*			
	1st to 2nd		*2nd to 3rd*		*3rd to 2nd*		*2nd to 1st*	
	km/hr	*mile/hr*	*km/hr*	*mile/hr*	*km/hr*	*mile/hr*	*km/hr*	*mile/hr*
$\frac{1}{4}$ open	15	9	25	16	23	14	12	7
$\frac{1}{2}$ open	17	11	27	17	25	16	15	9
$\frac{3}{4}$ open	31	19	89	55	60	37	25	16
Fully open	38	24	92	57	62	38	30	19
Kick-down	60	37	100	62	97	60	53	33
					112*	70*	68**	42**

*Maximum speed for change down to 2nd when selecting 2nd
**Maximum speed for change down to 1st when selecting 1st

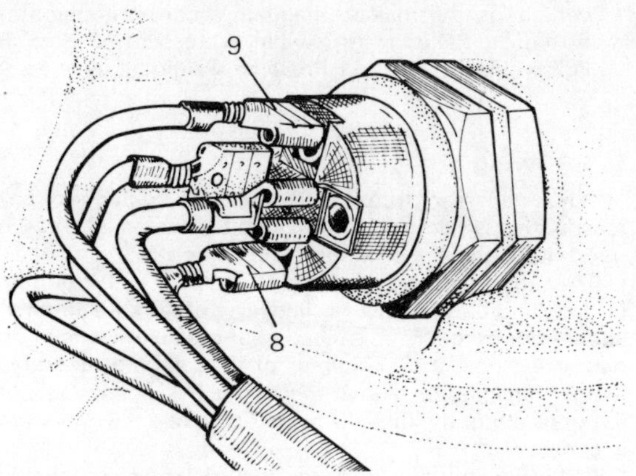

FIG 7:5 Starting lock and reversing switch connections

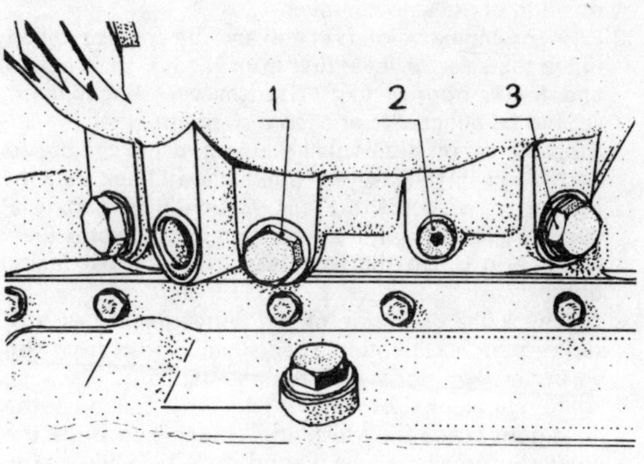

FIG 7:6 Pressure test connecting points

Key to Fig 7:6 1 Converter pressure 2 Clutch A pressure 3 Main pressure

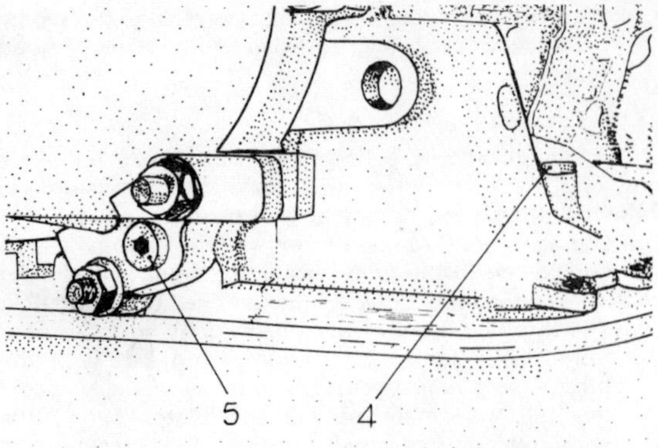

FIG 7:7 Pressure test connecting points

Key to Fig 7:7 4 Gearchange throttle valve pressure
5 Governor pressure

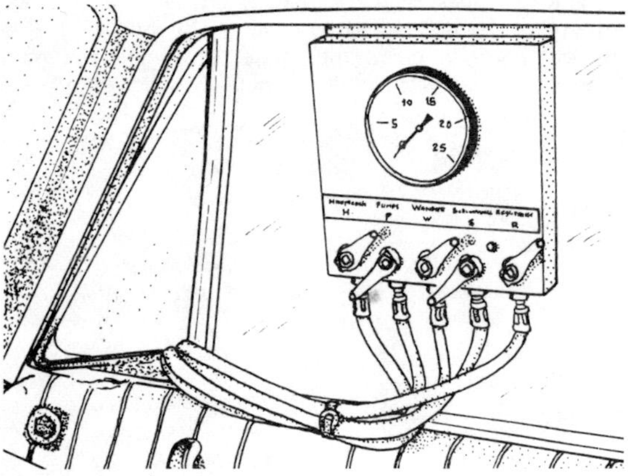

FIG 7:8 Checking the line pressure

Other tests which may be undertaken are:

1 Test that the starter operation is confined to the P or N position of the selector lever.

2 With the engine at idling speed and the brakes applied, move the selector lever first from N to 3, then N to 1 and finally from N to R. Transmission engagement should be noticeable at each movement.

3 Stop the car on a downhill gradient, using the brakes and select P. Release the brakes and check that the parking pawl holds the car. Before disengaging P apply the brakes and ensure that the selector lever remains in P. Do the same test with the car facing uphill.

4 To check the operation of the converter in cases of slip or poor acceleration, special stall speed tests can be undertaken, for which the assistance of a service agent should be obtained. The stall speed is the maximum speed at which the engine can drive the converter impeller whilst the turbine is held stationary. A high stall speed will indicate that the converter is not receiving its required fluid supply or that slip is occurring in the gearbox clutches.

The main procedure for identifying faults is to check the line pressures in the various hydraulic circuits, for which a tachometer or revolution indicator and an oil pressure gauge accurately calibrated up to 10 kg/sq cm or 150 lb/sq in. The test points at which the gauge is connected into the system are shown in **FIGS 7:6** and **7:7.** The maker's standard test equipment is shown in **FIG 7:8,** which consists of a pressure gauge complete with hoses and the required adaptors to fit the check points. Testing is carried out as follows:

1 To test the converter oil pressure the gauge is connected to the test point 1 in **FIG 7:6.** With the selector lever in the N position, the accelerator linkage detached and the engine speed adjusted to 1000 rev/min, the gauge should read 1.6 kg/sq cm (22.76 lb/sq in). Place the accelerator linkage in the kick-down position by hand, when the gauge should indicate 3.5 kg/sq cm (49.78 lb/sq in).

2 To test the clutch A (see **FIG 7:4**) the test point 2 in **FIG 7:6** is used. Move the selector lever into position 3, with the accelerator linkage disconnected, the handbrake on and the footbrake firmly applied by an assistant in the car. At an engine speed of 1000 rev/min the fluid pressure should be between 5.0 and 5.3 kg/sq cm (71.12 and 75.38 lb/sq in). With the accelerator linkage in the kick-down position as in Operation 1, the gauge should indicate between 7.0 and 7.3 kg/sq cm (99.56 and 103.83 lb/sq in).

3 To test the main pressure the test point 3 in **FIG 7:6** is used. Place the selector lever at N with the accelerator linkage disconnected. With an engine speed of 1000 rev/min a pressure of 5.0 kg/sq cm (71.12 lb/sq in) should be obtained. In the accelerator kick-down position the gauge should indicate 7.0 kg/sq cm (99.56 lb/sq in).

4 To test the gearchange throttle valve pressure the test point 4 in **FIG 7:7** is used. Place the selector lever at N with the accelerator disconnected. With an engine speed of 1000 rev/min a gauge reading of 0.9 to 1.2 kg/sq cm (12.80 to 17.07 lb/sq in) should be obtained. In the accelerator kick-down position the indicated pressure should be between 3.5 and 3.7 kg/sq cm (49.78 and 52.63 lb/sq in).

5 To test the governor pressure, test point 5 in **FIG 7:7** is used, with the selector lever in position 3. Drive the vehicle on the road to maintain a constant speed of 50 km/hr (31 mile/hr), when a pressure of .3 to .5 kg/sq cm (4.27 to 7.11 lb/sq in) should be registered.

7:5 Towing

If it is necessary to tow the vehicle to a garage for any reason, this is permissible provided the transmission is in good order and the selector is in position N.

Towing should be carried out at speeds of less than 50 km/hr (30 mile/hr) and distances of 40 km (25 mile) should not normally be exceeded. If greater distances are necessary, one litre (1¾ pints) of fluid should be added to the transmission above the normal full mark. Do not forget to return the oil level to normal when the operation is concluded.

If the transmission is in any way defective or longer/faster tows are intended, the rear end of the car should be raised and the vehicle towed on the front wheels.

With this type of transmission it is not possible to start the engine by means of towing, or pushing, the car. In the event of the battery being unable to operate the starter, an external battery should be connected in parallel by means of 'jumper' leads.

7:6 Fault diagnosis

(a) Gearchange points too high

1 Accelerator linkage incorrectly adjusted
2 Leakage in governor inlet line
3 Leakage past governor piston rings
4 Governor bush jammed

(b) Gearchange points too low

1 Accelerator linkage incorrectly adjusted
2 Governor bush jammed
3 Throttle pressure too low

(c) Accelerator kick-down not available

1 Accelerator linkage incorrectly adjusted
2 Throttle pressure valve sticking

(d) Selector lever cannot be moved to P position

1 Selector linkage incorrectly adjusted
2 Parking lock mechanism defective

(e) Selector lever cannot be moved to R position

1 Selector linkage incorrectly adjusted

(f) Vehicle will not move forwards or backwards

1 Selector linkage incorrectly adjusted
2 Oil level too low
3 Oil pressure too low
4 No drive to oil pump
5 Reducing passage in input shaft blocked

(g) Vehicle remains in 1st gear

1 Selector valve 1 to 2 jammed
2 Selector piston 1 to 2 jammed
3 Governor bush jammed

(h) Vehicle remains in 1st and 2nd gears

1 Selector valve 2 to 3 jammed
2 Selector piston 2 to 3 jammed
3 Latched sealing ring for clutch B (see **FIG 7:4**) leaking

(i) Vehicle remains in 2nd gear

1 Selector 1 to 2 and 2 to 3 jammed
2 Selector piston 1 to 2 and 2 to 3 jammed

(j) Vehicle remains in 3rd gear

1 Selector valves 1 to 2 and 2 to 3 jammed
2 Selector pistons 1 to 2 and 2 to 3 jammed
3 Governor bush jammed

(k) No reverse gear available

1 Forward/reverse locking valve jammed
2 Excessive end play on latched sealing ring for clutch B
3 Clutch B defective
4 Selector linkage incorrectly adjusted

(l) Slipping at gearchange points

1 Accelerator linkage disconnected
2 Oil pressure too low

(m) Slipping at 1st/2nd gearchange point

1 Brakes C and C1 (see **FIG 7:4**) slipping
2 Oil pressure too low
3 Oil inlet lines blocked
4 Freewheel at C defective

(n) Slipping at 2nd/3rd gearchange point

1 Excessive end float at latched sealing ring for clutch B
2 Oil pressure too low
3 Oil inlet lines blocked
4 Clutch B defective

(o) Slipping in 3rd gear

1 Excessive end float at latched sealing ring for clutch B
2 Oil pressure too low
3 Clutch B defective

(p) With selector lever in position A, 1st gear not receiving power from engine

1 Auxiliary freewheel defective

(q) With lever in position 2, very violent change from 2nd/1st gear

1 Excessive clutch overlap between C1, C and D
2 Pressure reducing valve jammed

(r) With lever in position 1 or 2, no braking effect in 1st gear

1 Brake D defective
2 Pressure reducing valve jammed

(s) No braking effect in 2nd gear

1 Brake C defective

(t) Whining sound at gearbox output, varying with speed and load

1 Squeaking from propeller shaft centre bearing

(u) Whining varying with speed and load change

1 Centre bearing of propeller shaft defective

(v) High-pitched whistling noise in neutral, disappears on accelerating

1 Torque converter plate whistling—hydraulic flow noise

(w) Knocking noise in neutral

1 Follower plate broken
2 Fixing eyelet on converter broken off

(x) Rattling noise in neutral, disappears when a gear is engaged or when the engine is revved up in the neutral position

1 Valve rattle in change mechanism
2 Oil level not correct

(y) Whistling noise dependent on gear engaged

1 Planet wheel assembly noisy

(z) Torque converter bellhousing oily

1 Shaft sealing ring defective
2 O-ring on pump housing missing or defective
3 Torque converter leaking at weld seams

(aa) Oil loss occurs at shift lever or accelerator pedal

1 Shaft sealing ring in shift lever or O-ring on shift lever defective

(bb) Speedometer drive leaking

1 O-ring or sealing ring damaged

(cc) Inspection or drain plugs leaking

1 Sealing ring damaged

(dd) Driven flange oily

1 Shaft sealing ring defective

(ee) Oil leaking at filler neck

1 O-ring defective or missing

(ff) Oil leaks at breather

1 Incorrect oil level

CHAPTER 8

PROPELLER SHAFT, REAR AXLE, REAR SUSPENSION

8:1 Description and construction

The propeller shaft in Peugeot 504 cars is completely enclosed in a rigid torque tube bolted at one end to the gearbox and at the other end to the differential housing, as shown in **FIG 8:1**. The ends of the propeller shaft itself are internally splined to transmit the drive from the gearbox mainshaft to the differential pinion. As shown in the details of the assembly in **FIG 8:2**, the shaft is supported at the centre by a needle bearing in the torque tube.

Independent suspension is provided on all four wheels. At the rear it comprises the trailing arms 2 (see **FIG 8:1**) the helical springs 6 and the telescopic double-acting dampers 7. An anti-roll bar 8 is fitted, of slightly less diameter than the similar one provided in front.

The complete final drive and rear suspension assembly is supported by the two fabricated steel crossmembers 1 and 9, forming a sub-frame which is attached to the main structure through resilient silentbloc mountings. The front crossmember retains the trailing arms carrying the coil springs and the dampers, which are restrained at their upper ends by the rear crossmember situated at a higher level.

The rear axle incorporates a hypoid final drive in which the pinion is located below the axis of the gear, the assembly being contained in a housing which is suspended from the rear crossmember. The outcome is that the rear axle is rigidly connected to the gearbox with resilient silentblocs incorporated in the mounting of the engine/transmission unit on the body structure.

Details of the final drive and differential unit are given in **FIGS 8:3** and **8:4**, which show the drive shafts extending from each side of the differential unit to each rear wheel. Constant velocity Glaenzer-Spicer pot joints are incorporated at both ends of each shaft. The design includes a roller spline sliding mechanism to allow for shaft lateral movement to compensate for road surface inequalities.

8:2 Routine maintenance

The hypoid gear and pinion in the rear axle require a special extreme pressure gear oil, for which Esso Gear Oil GP.90 is recommended by the manufacturers. The plugs sealing the filling orifice and the drain hole at the rear of the housing are indicated by the arrows in **FIG 8:5**. The oil capacity is 1.2 litre (2.1 pints) and the level

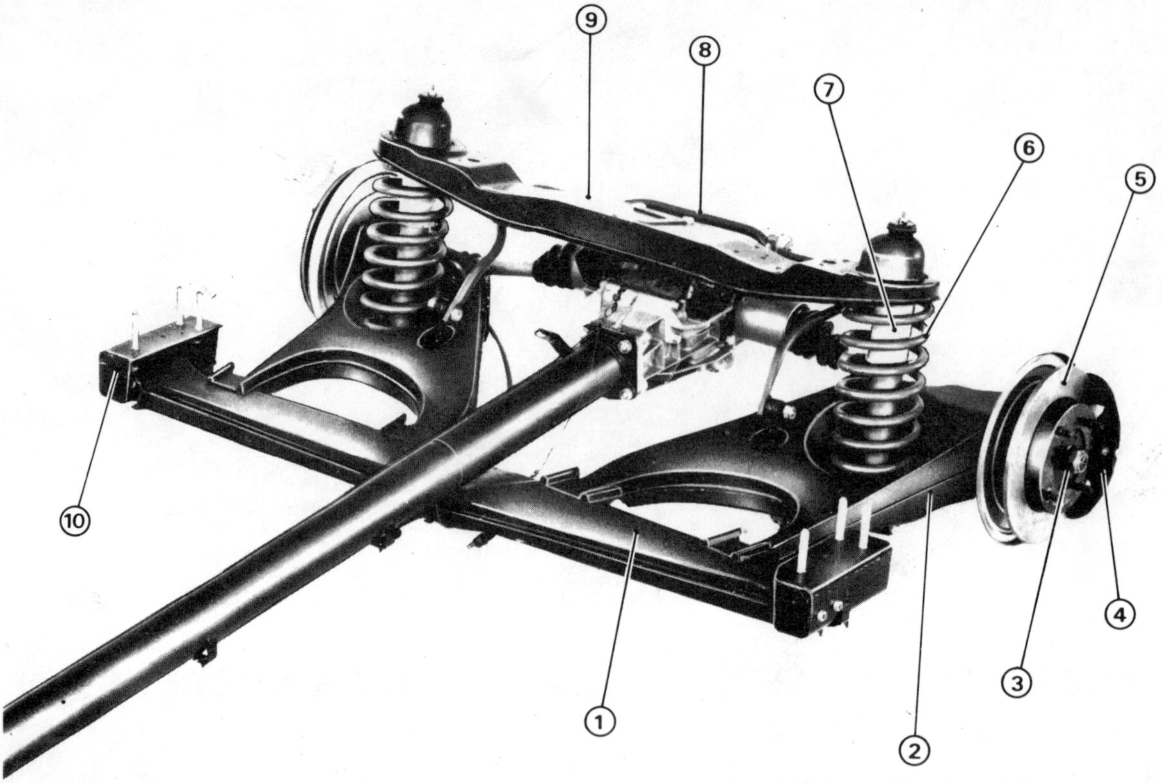

FIG 8:1 A view of the rear axle and suspension

Key to Fig 8:1 1 Rear crossmember 2 Rear arm 3 Rear hub 4 Brake caliper 5 Brake disc 6 Suspension spring 7 Rear damper 8 Anti-roll bar 9 Rear suspension crossmember 10 Rear crossmember support

of oil in the axle should be maintained at the bottom of the filler plug hole. Clean around the plug when removing it and make sure that the plug is clean when refitting it. The axle should be drained and refilled with the recommended oil after the first 1000 km or 600 miles and then every 15,000 km or 9000 miles. At other times check the level every 5000 km or 3000 miles.

The centre bearing of the propeller shaft requires lubrication every 5000 km or 3000 miles. Esso Multipurpose Grease H is recommended by the manufacturers and should be applied to the grease nipple on the side of the torque tube as shown in **FIG 8:6.** At the same time examine the condition of the gaiters protecting the drive shaft joints. It is essential that they should fully prevent any possibility of the entry of water or dust, which would seriously damage the drive shaft journals and bearing packs.

8:3 Propeller shaft removal and refitting

For removing and refitting the propeller shaft the two guide rods and bars 8.0906 shown in **FIG 8:7** are used, together with the propeller shaft holding plate shown in **FIG 6:6** in **Chapter 6.** Operations are as follows:

1 With the car positioned on a garage lift or over a pit, remove the exhaust pipe assembly. Rest it at the rear on the crossmember and at the front on a suitable support. Remove the heat dissipation plate.

2 Remove both Allen screws from the rear axle housing. Rest the torque tube on the rear crossmember. Position a jack under the crossmember lefthand support.

3 Remove the rear seat cushion and slacken all three crossmember securing nuts. Remove the front nut.

4 Remove the plastic plug from the guide hole and insert the guide rod. Tighten and lock it with the bar (see **FIG 8:8**).

5 **Leave the rod in the guide hole** and remove the crossmember rear securing nuts and thrust washers. Lower the crossmember until the bar bears against the floor. Repeat these operations on the righthand side.

6 Separate the differential from the torque tube (see **FIG 8:9**), move the differential rearwards and rest it on a wooden block. Remove the spring located inside the propeller shaft (see **FIG 8:2**). In order to be able to move the car freely, the differential can be secured to the suspension crossmember by two 204 cylinder head bolts.

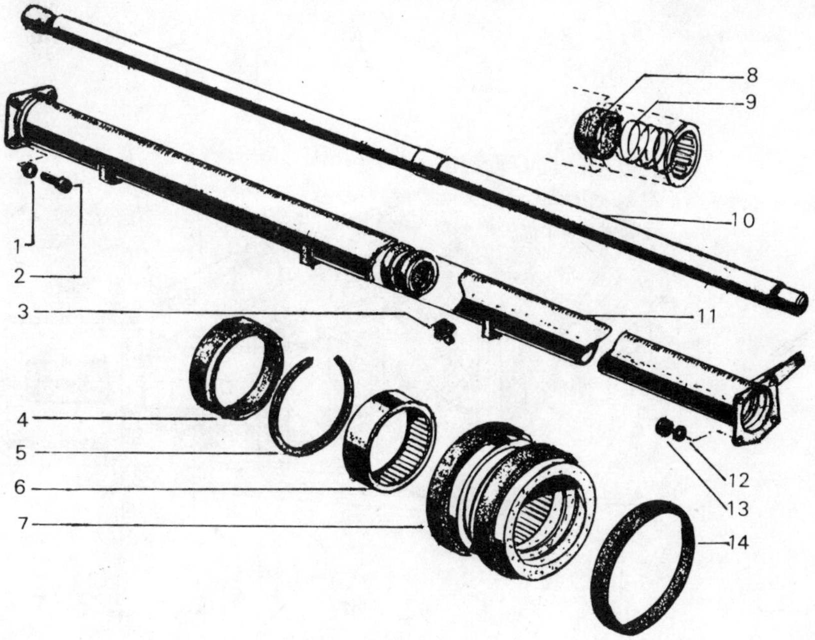

FIG 8:2 An exploded view of the torque tube and propeller shaft

Key to Fig 8:2 1 Nut 2 Bolt 3 Grease nipple 4 Bearing retainer 5 Retaining ring 6 Needle roller bearing 7 Centre bearing assembly 8 Spring seat 9 Spring 10 Propeller shaft 11 Torque tube 12 Washer 13 Nut 14 Support ring

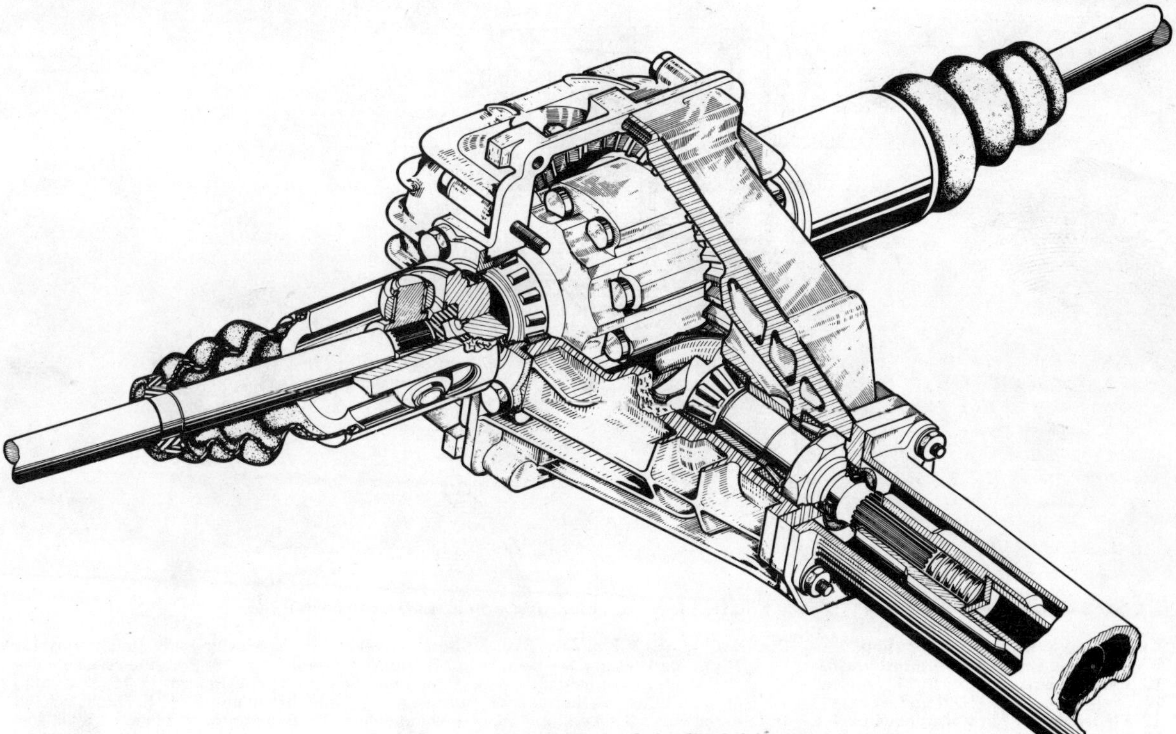

FIG 8:3 A sectional view of the final drive gear

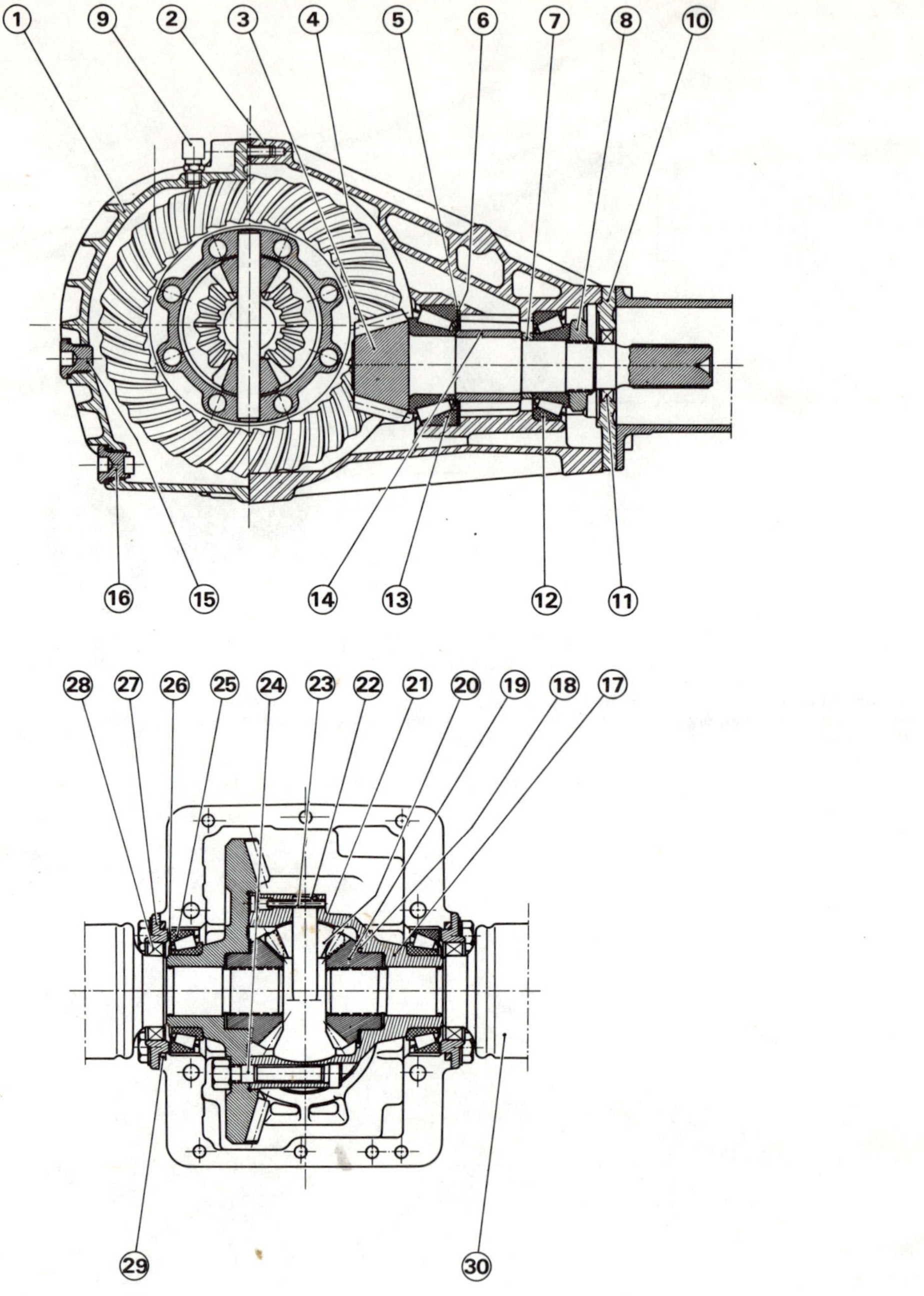

FIG 8:4 Diagrammatic views of the crownwheel and differential gear

Key to Fig 8:4 1 Housing 2 Cover 3 Pinion 4 Crownwheel 5 Meshing adjustment washers 6 Drive pinion rear bearing thrust washer 7 Pre-load setting washers 8 Tightening nut 9 Pressure release valve 10 Front oil seal support 11 Front oil seal 12 Pinion front bearing 13 Pinion rear bearing 14 Spacer 15 Filler plug 16 Drain plug 17 Differential case 18 Sun gear thrust washer 19 Sun gear 20 Planet pinion 21 Thrust washer 22 Planet shaft 23 Mecanindus pin 24 Differential bolt 25 Bearing 26 Adjusting shim 27 Bearing thrust plate 28 Oil seal 29 Thrust plate O-ring 30 Halfshaft or drive shaft

7 Remove the four Allen screws and separate the torque tube from the gearbox by approximately 20 mm. Insert the propeller shaft holding plate as described in **Chapter 6,** securing it with two Allen screws.

8 Lower the exhaust pipe downwards at the front, separate the propeller shaft from the gearbox and bring the assembled shaft and tube forward to withdraw it (see **FIG 8:10**).

To renew the centre bearing a special tool No. 8.0403.U has been designed to remove and refit the bearing. The apparatus consists of a rod with an impact puller at one end and a rocking lever at the other end to grip the bearing for its extraction, together with a spacer plate and guide ring to ensure the correct reassembly of a bearing. For this work, therefore, it is advisable to obtain the assistance of a service agent with the necessary equipment.

Refitting the propeller shaft follows the removal procedure in reverse order as follows:

1 Make sure that the tube, gearbox and differential surfaces are perfectly clean. Smear Multipurpose Grease H on the front part of the propeller shaft splines and press the propeller shaft front part against the tube, using the holding plate as shown in **FIG 8:11.**

2 Support the tube on the rear crossmember, engage the shaft sleeve with the gearbox output shaft and remove the holding plate. Refit the four Allen screws (see **FIGS 8:12** and **8:13**) with new Blocfor washers and tighten to a torque of 6 kg m (43.5 lb ft).

3 Fit the spring inside the other end of the tube, grease the shaft splines and couple the shaft with the differential. Fit new Blocfor washers on the assembling studs and tighten the nuts to 6 kg m (43.5 lb ft) as shown in **FIG 8:14.**

4 Refit the differential to the suspension crossmember (see **FIG 8:15**) and tighten the screws to a torque of 3.75 kg m (27 lb ft). Refit the heat dissipation plate and the exhaust pipe assembly.

5 With a jack under the righthand support, raise the crossmember up to the floor and remove the guide. Close the hole with the plastic plug. Install the flat washers and new tab locks on the studs and tighten the nuts (see **FIG 8:16**) to a torque of either 4 kg m (29 lb ft) or 6.5 kg m (47 lb ft) according to whether the serial numbers are respectively below or from any of the numbers 504.A01.1005546, 504.A02.1003649, 504.A03 (beginning of series), 504.B02.1032357 or 504.C02.1009769. Bend the tab tongues over the nut to lock in position.

6 Carry out the same operations on the lefthand side to secure the rear crossmember. Refit the seat cushion, grease the propeller shaft centre bearing (see **Section 8:2**) and check the gearbox oil level.

FIG 8:6 Lubricating propeller shaft centre bearing

FIG 8:5 Rear axle filling and draining plugs

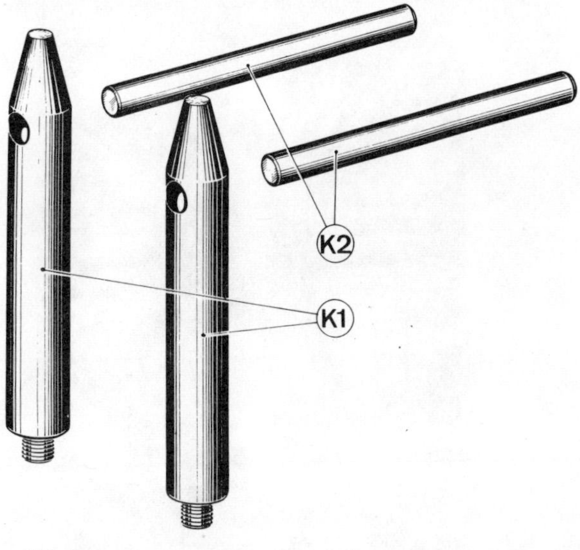

FIG 8:7 Tools used for dismantling propeller shaft

Key to Fig 8:7 **K1** Rear crossmember guide rods **K2** Bars

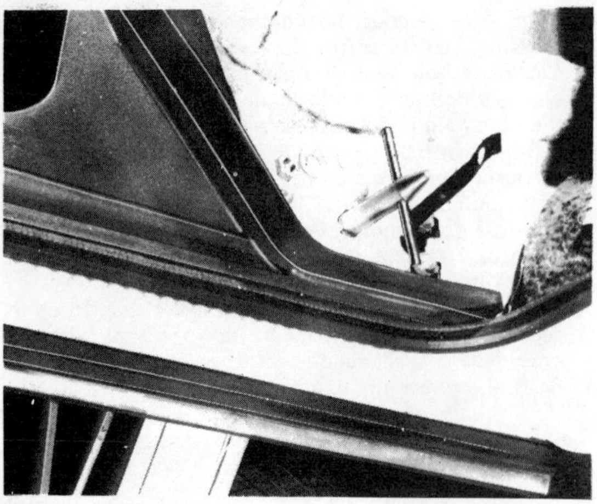

FIG 8:8 Locating guide rod

FIG 8:9 Separating the torque tube from the differential housing

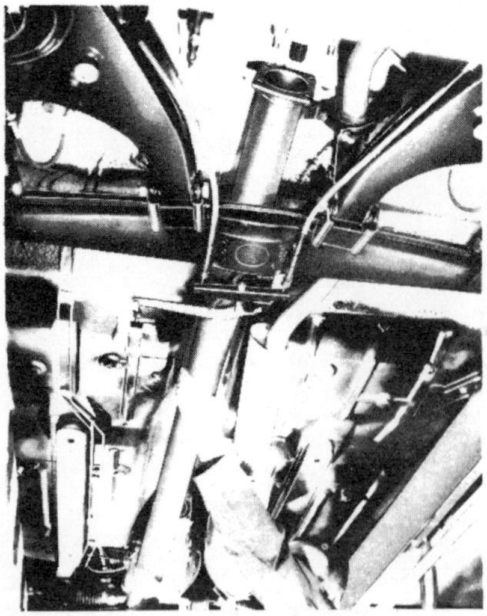

FIG 8:10 Withdrawing the torque tube assembly

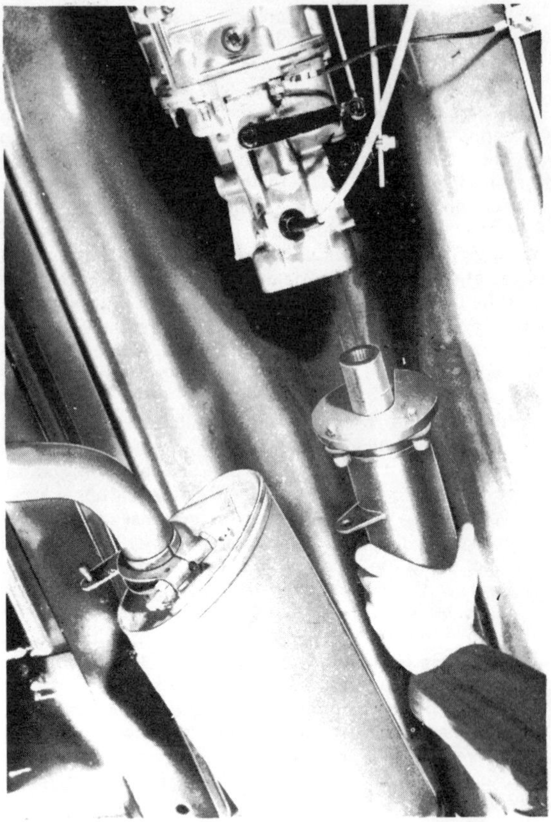

FIG 8:11 Refitting the torque tube assembly

FIG 8:12 Fitting three of the Allen assembling screws **1**

FIG 8:13 Fitting the fourth assembly screw **2**

FIG 8:14 Coupling the differential with the torque tube assembly

FIG 8:15 Securing the differential to the suspension crossmember

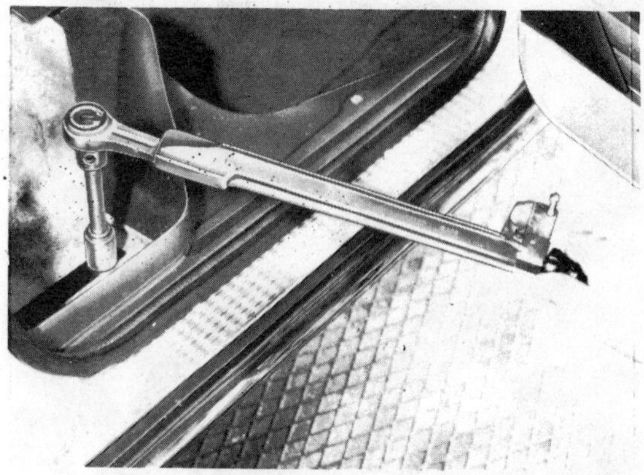

FIG 8:16 Securing the rear crossmember

FIG 8:17 Slackening the hub nut using the holding tool **A**

FIG 8:18 Rear brake caliper, showing the thrust spring **1**, the retaining fork **2** and the brake pads **3**

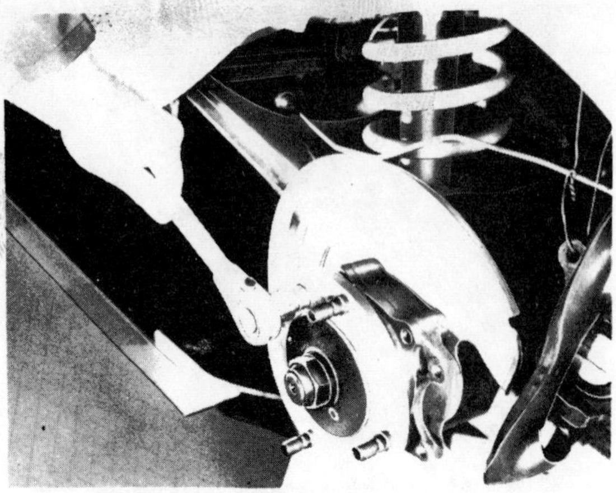

FIG 8:19 Removing the four Allen screws securing the knuckle to the suspension arm

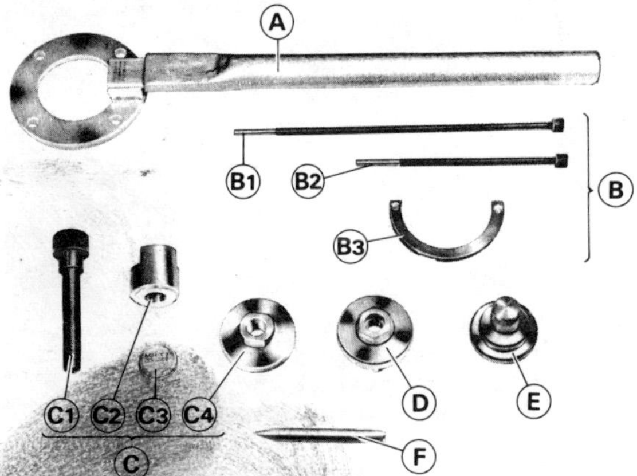

FIG 8:20 Tools No. 8.0521.Z for overhaul of rear hubs

Key to Fig 8:20 **A** Holding tool **B** Hub carrier extractor, including **B1** long bolt, **B2** short bolt and **B3** thrust plate **C** Tools for dismantling and reassembling hub and bearing, including **C1** bolt, **C2** nut, **C3** thrust pad and **C4** extractor **D** Spanner head for carrier nut **E** Drift for fitting hub seal **F** Punch

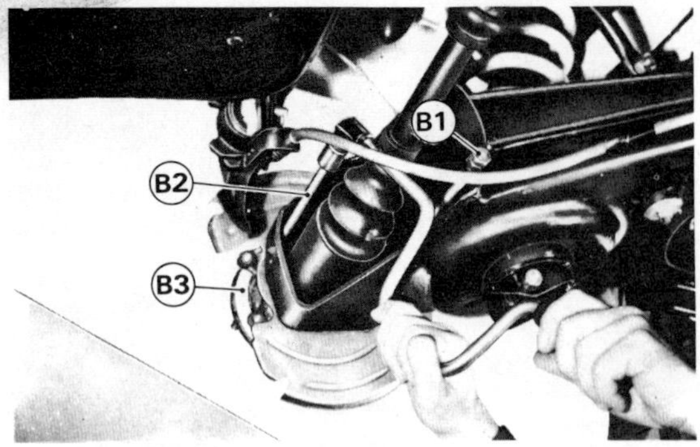

FIG 8:21 Removing drive shaft assembly, using screws **B1** and **B2** bearing against plate **B3**

8:4 Drive shafts removal and refitting

Removal of a drive shaft is undertaken as follows:

1 Raise the rear of the car and chock it under the suspension arm as shown in **FIG 8:17.** Fit the hub holding tool A (see **FIG 8:20**) on the hub and slacken the hub nut without removing it.

2 Detach the holding tool, then remove the brake pad anti-squeal spring 1 (see **FIG 8:18**), the retaining fork 2 and the brake pads 3.

3 Open the brake hose retaining clip on the rear arm. Remove the brake caliper retaining bolts with the aid of an 8 mm Allen socket. Withdraw the caliper and suspend it from the bodywork, bending the hose as little as possible.

4 Remove the crosshead screws securing the brake disc to the hub and mark their positions on the disc. Remove the disc.

5 Remove the four Allen screws securing the hub carrier or knuckle to the rear arm (see **FIG 8:19**). Use a socket spanner in the hole provided in the hub.

6 Withdraw the hub carrier and drive shaft assembly using the bolts B1 and B2 (see **FIGS 8:20** and **8:21**) positioned diagonally and the thrust plate B3 on the hub. Tighten alternately the two bolts in contact with the plate, removing the carrier from the rear arm. Remove the tools.

7 Remove the hub nut and washer, then disengage the drive shaft from the hub carrier, for which the use of a press may be necessary.

8 The renewal of the double ballbearing in the carrier may be undertaken at this stage if required. Clamp the carrier in a vice with soft jaws, unlock the carrier nut and place the spanner head D (see **FIG 8:20**) on the nut, locking D with the bolt C1 (see **FIG 8:22**). Use an open-end spanner and an extension to unscrew the carrier nut. Place the thrust pad C3 inside the hub and screw the extractor C4 into the carrier body, also the bolt C1 into C4. Tighten C1 to withdraw the hub. Remove C4 and C3 to extract the bearing with the nut C2, if necessary using a press. Turn the carrier over and remove the outer oil seal with a tyre lever.

9 Grease a new bearing with Esso Multipurpose Grease H. Refitting operations are generally the dismantling operations in reverse. Renew the carrier nut with its two-lipped oil seal and the outer oil seal, for which the drift E is used. Insert the bearing and reassemble using the tools previously described. Tighten the carrier nut to a final torque of 25 kgm (181 lbft). The punch F is used to lock the carrier nut in the notches provided.

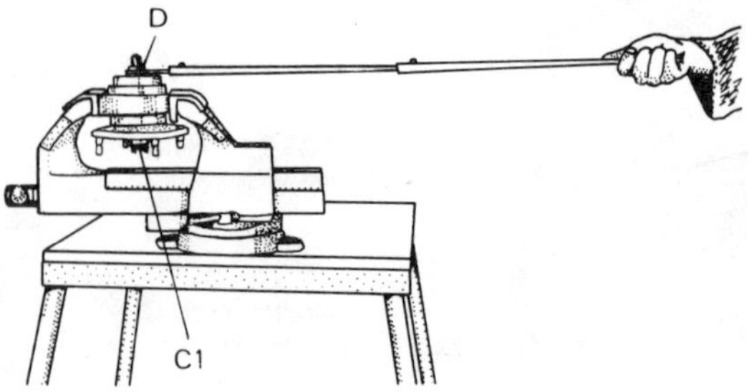

FIG 8:22 Removing the carrier nut, using the spanner head **D** and the bolt **C1**

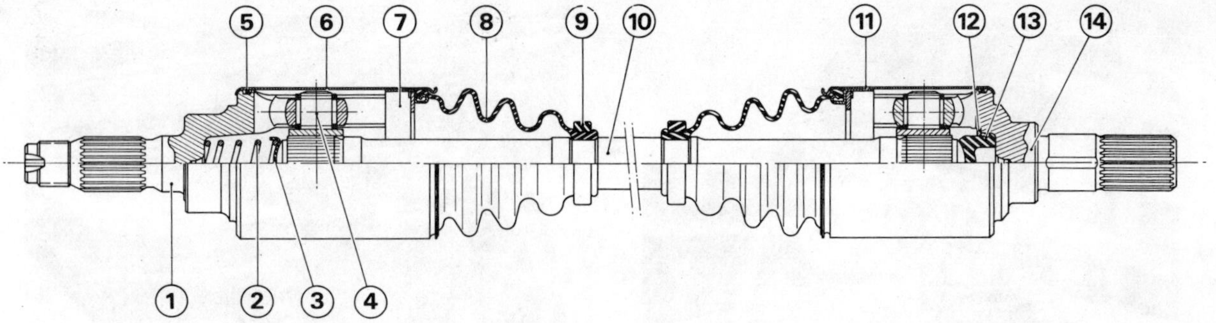

FIG 8 : 23 A sectional view of the drive shafts

Key to Fig 8 : 23 Wheel side: 1 Tulip 2 Spring 3 Cup 4 Journal and bearing pack 5 O-ring 6 Cover 7 Spacer 8 Gaiter 9 Retaining ring 10 Shaft
Differential side: 11 Cover 12 Thrust washer 13 Stop 14 Tulip

A sectional view of a drive shaft is given in **FIG 8 : 23** and external fittings together with the journal and bearing pack are shown in **FIG 8 : 24.** The journal and bearing pack, including a tripod, rollers and needle bearings, is renewable only as a complete unit. The dismantling of a drive shaft involves the use of a hydraulic press and special tools to be made up in a workshop for removing and refitting the journal and bearing pack, for which a service agents assistance will normally be required.

To refit the hub carrier and drive shaft on the car, proceed as follows:

1 Ensure that the parts are thoroughly clean and free from defects. Hold the carrier in a vice as shown in **FIG 8 : 25.** Lubricate the drive shaft splines on the wheel side (the makers recommend Molykote 321) and engage the drive shaft into the hub. Fit the washer 2 and a new hub unit 3.

2 Check that the differential housing lateral seal ring 4 in **FIG 8 : 26** is in good condition. Smear the gap between the seal lips with tallow or grease and also grease the drive shaft splines.

3 Engage the assembly in its housing on the suspension arm (see **FIG 8 : 27**) and carefully insert the drive shaft splines into the differential housing. Use new Blocfor washers and secure the carrier to the suspension arm. Tighten the Allen screws to a torque of 4 kg m (29 lb ft).

4 Refit the brake disc according to marks made when removing it and reassemble the brake caliper with new Blocfor washers. Tighten the screws to a torque of 4.25 kg m (31 lb ft).

5 Fit the brake pads and the holding fork. Tighten the bolt to a torque of 1.75 kg m (13 lb ft). Install the thrust spring in the brake pads with the arrow pointing in the direction of rotation of the disc.

6 Refit the brake pipe on the suspension arm. Using the holding tool A (see **FIG 8 : 20**), tighten the drive shaft nut to a torque of 25 kg m (189 lb ft) by the method shown in **FIG 8 : 17.**

7 Remove the holding tool, refit the wheel and tighten the nuts to a torque of 6 kg m (43.5 lb ft). Fit the wheel trim and check the oil level in the rear axle. Top up if necessary with the approved oil.

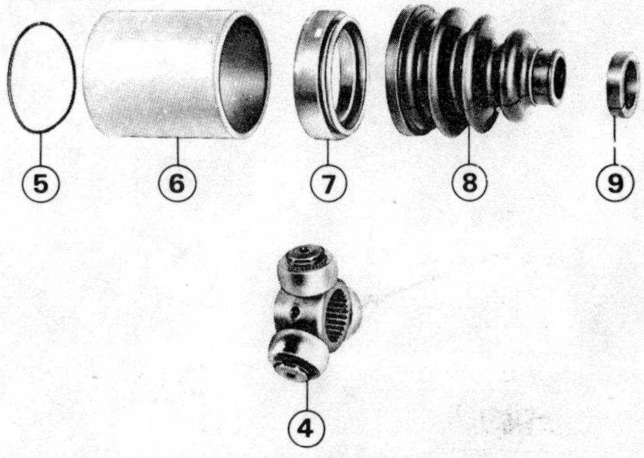

FIG 8 : 24 Drive shaft components

Key to Fig 8 : 24 4 Journal and bearing pack 5 O-ring 6 Cover 7 Spacer 8 Gaiter 9 Retaining ring

FIG 8 : 25 Securing the drive shaft into the hub

Key to Fig 8 : 25 1 Carrier 2 Washer 3 Hub nut

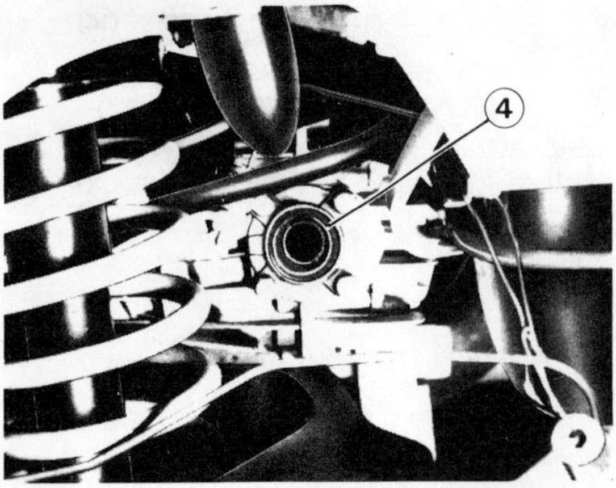

FIG 8:26 Lateral seal ring (**4**) in differential housing

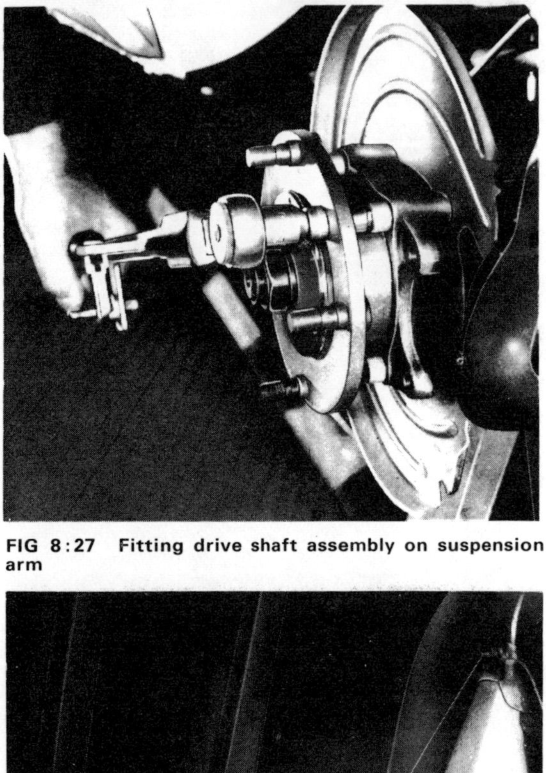

FIG 8:27 Fitting drive shaft assembly on suspension arm

FIG 8:28 Removing rear damper upper attachment

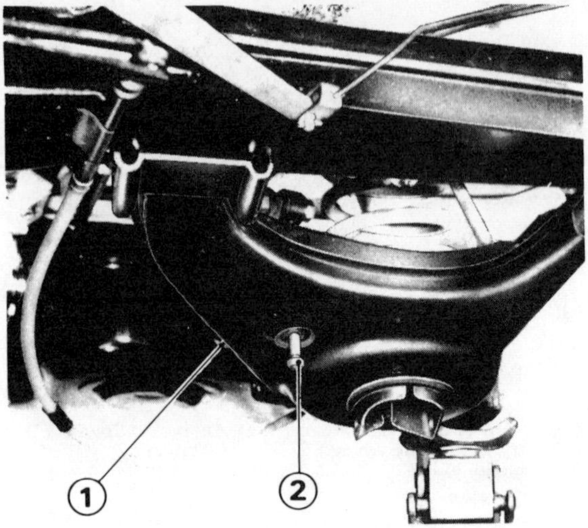

FIG 8:29 Rear arm, showing handbrake cable mounting **1** and anti-roll bar attachment **2**

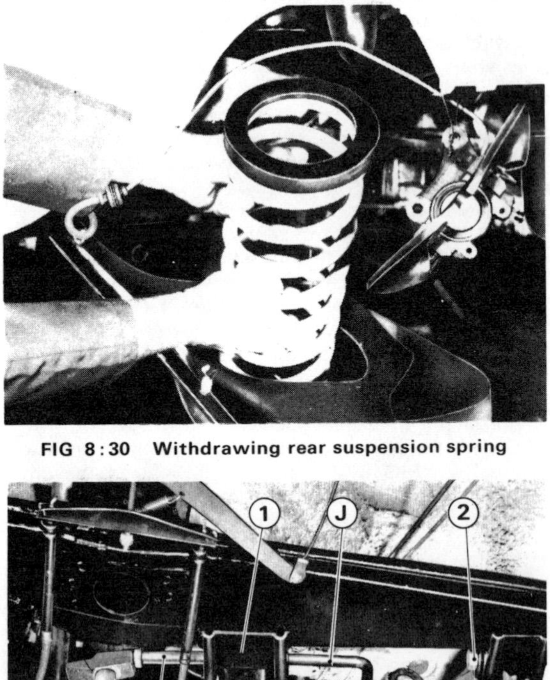

FIG 8:30 Withdrawing rear suspension spring

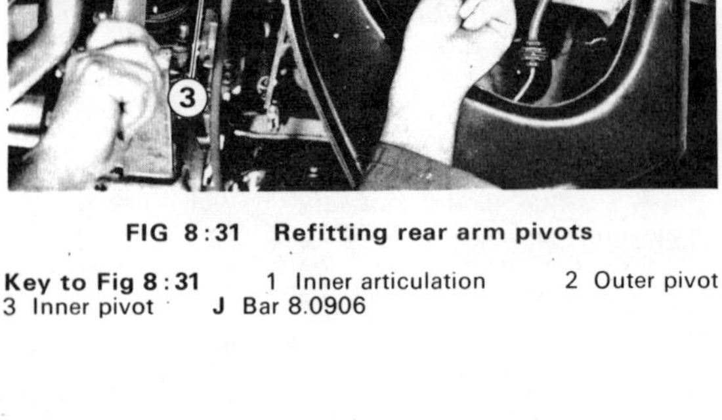

FIG 8:31 Refitting rear arm pivots

Key to Fig 8:31 1 Inner articulation 2 Outer pivot 3 Inner pivot **J** Bar 8.0906

8:5 Rear arms and suspension removal and refitting

To remove a rear arm it is necessary first to remove the drive shaft as described in **Section 8:4.** Then raise the rear of the car and chock it under each crossmember support. Referring to **FIG 8:1,** position a jack under the rear arm 2 and raise the arm so that the damper is not extended. It remains to remove the damper, the spring and the arm itself. The rear springs are held compressed between the arms and the crossmember by the dampers and **removal of damper must never be attempted without first compressing the spring.** Operations are as follows:

1 From the inside of the boot (see **FIG 8:28**) slacken the damper upper Nylstop bolt whilst holding the damper on the flat surface using a 5 mm open-ended spanner. Remove the upper sheet metal cup and the rubber washer.
2 On the rear arm remove the lower securing pivot and withdraw the damper from the hole provided in the rear arm.
3 Remove the flexible hose from the lug on the rear arm by slackening the nut on the hose.
4 Referring to **FIG 8:29,** unclip the handbrake mounting 1 on the rear arm.
5 Remove the nut 2 securing the anti-roll bar link under the rear arm. Withdraw the metal cup and the rubber washer, then refit the nut 2 immediately to prevent the upper parts falling inside the rear arm.
6 Unscrew the rear arm pivot nuts, then lower the jack carefully until the suspension spring is fully extended.
7 Remove the spring and its upper rubber cup as shown in **FIG 8:30.** Withdraw the rear arm pivots and remove the rear arm.
8 Check closely the condition of the rear arm rubber bushes and renew them if any doubt exists as to their serviceability. To extract a bush a special cutter is used in a hand-drill to remove the shoulder of the bush, in order to avoid damaging the arm with adverse effect on the suspension. Special drifts and a hydraulic press are also employed, which will normally require the facilities provided by a suitably equipped service agent.
9 Renewal of the damper flexible bushes if required is undertaken with the same tools and following the same procedure as described for the steering rack silentblocs in **Section 10:6** of **Chapter 10.**

Refitting operations are undertaken as follows:

1 Locate the rear arm in the corresponding yokes on the crossmember.
2 Referring to **FIG 8:31,** retain the inner articulation 1 by means of the bar J (tool No. 8.0906) and insert the outer pivot 2 in its housing. Then insert the pivot 3 in its correct direction and attach new Nylstop nuts without tightening them.

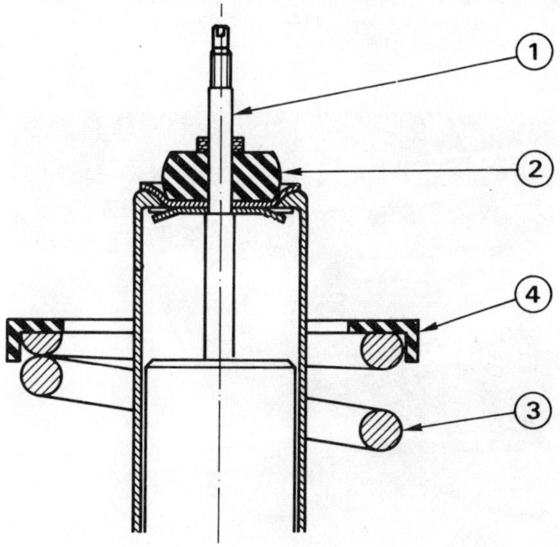

FIG 8:33 A sectional view of a rear damper

Key to Fig 8:33 1 Damper rod 2 Rubber washer 3 Suspension spring 4 Rubber cup

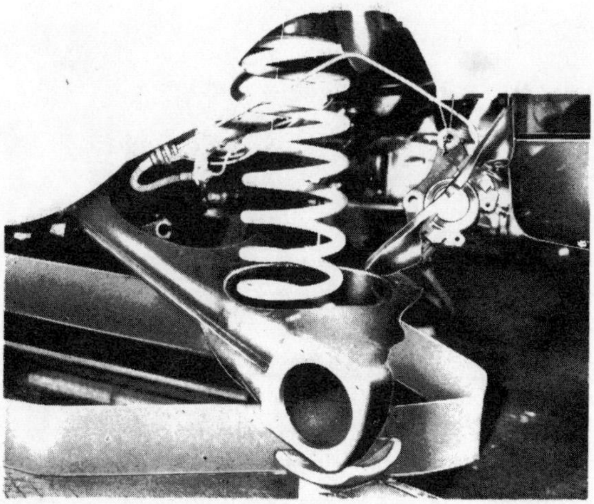

FIG 8:32 Locating a rear spring for refitting

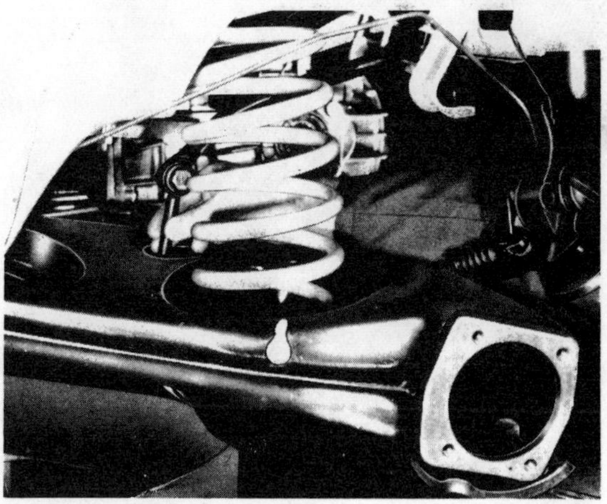

FIG 8:34 Raising the rear arm with spring in position

3 Place a jack under the rear part of the arm as shown in **FIG 8:32**, then proceed to coat the upper rubber spring cup (4 in **FIG 8:33**) with Teepol to facilitate its positioning. If this cup is to be renewed, check that the correct type is used by reference to **Section 8:6**.

4 Locate the spring between its upper and lower mountings, then raise the arm as shown in **FIG 8:34**, ensuring that the spring centres correctly. At the same time guide the anti-roll bar connecting link into its location in the rear arm.

5 Referring to **FIG 8:33**, fully extend the damper rod 1, fit a new rubber washer 2 and ensure that the parts are correctly assembled on the rod.

6 Renew the metal cup (see **FIG 8:28**) and the damper upper securing nut. Fit the damper without tightening the lower securing nut but tighten the upper nut to a torque of 1.25 kg m (9 lb ft). Lower and remove the jack.

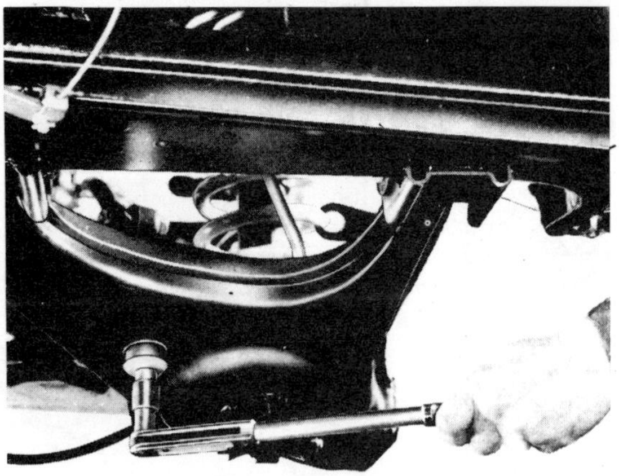

FIG 8:35 Reconnecting the anti-roll bar

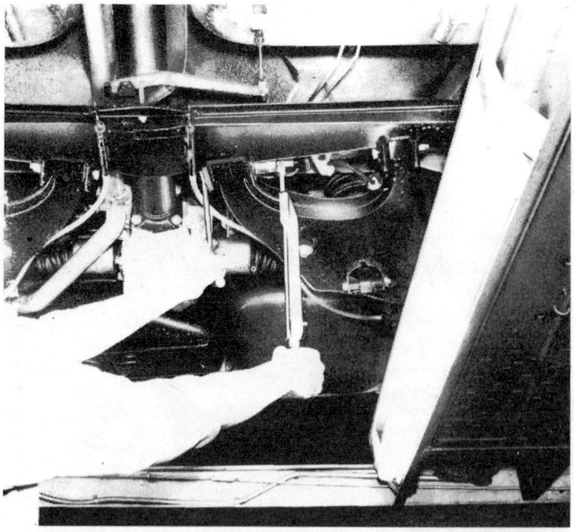

FIG 8:36 Tightening the rear arm pivot nuts

7 Refit the anti-roll bar connecting link with rubber washer and metal cup, tightening the nut (see **FIG 8:35**) to a torque of 1.25 kg m (9 lb ft). Refit the rear brake flexible hose and the handbrake cable and then the drive shaft as described in **Section 8:4**.

8 Fit the wheel, lower the car and tighten the wheel nuts to a torque of 6 kg m (43.5 lb ft). Fit the wheel trim.

9 Seat two persons in the rear of the car to position the flexible bushes in the neutral position, then tighten the rear arm pivot nuts (see **FIG 8:36**) to a torque of 6.5 kg m (47 lb ft) and the lower damper nut to 4.5 kg m (33 lb ft).

10 Check the oil level in the differential and top up if necessary with the approved oil.

8:6 Modifications

The damper securing cups 'a' in **FIG 8:37** in cars up to serial numbers 504.A01.1007476 and 504.A02. 1004862 are welded at the lower part of the suspension crossmember 1. The suspension crossmember spacer 2 has a total height of 37 mm and the rubber seating cup 3 a total height of 15 mm. In later cars the cups are welded at the upper part of the crossmember, so that the spacer 2 and the seating cup 3 have heights of 34.5 mm and 17.5 mm respectively.

The parts of the later fitting can be mounted as an assembly on cars manufactured prior to the modification, but they are not interchangeable separately with parts of the former fitting.

A further modification is the rigid rear axle fitted to estate cars and commercial vehicles. This type of axle, which is also used on Peugot 504L models where they are available, is described in **Section 8:7**.

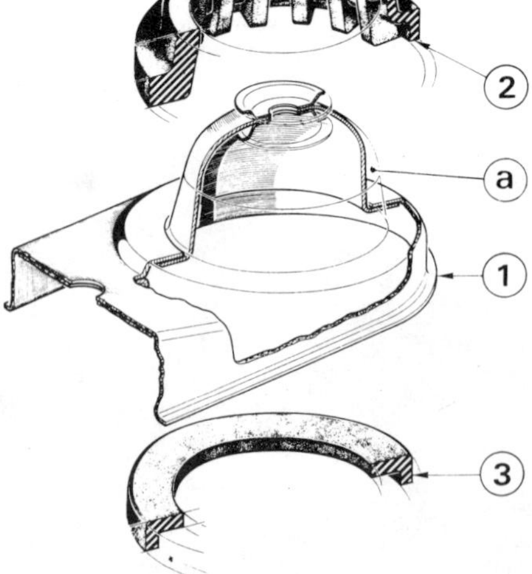

FIG 8:37 Crossmember damper cup and components

Key to Fig 8:37 1 Suspension crossmember 2 Spacer 3 Rubber seating cup **a** Damper securing cup

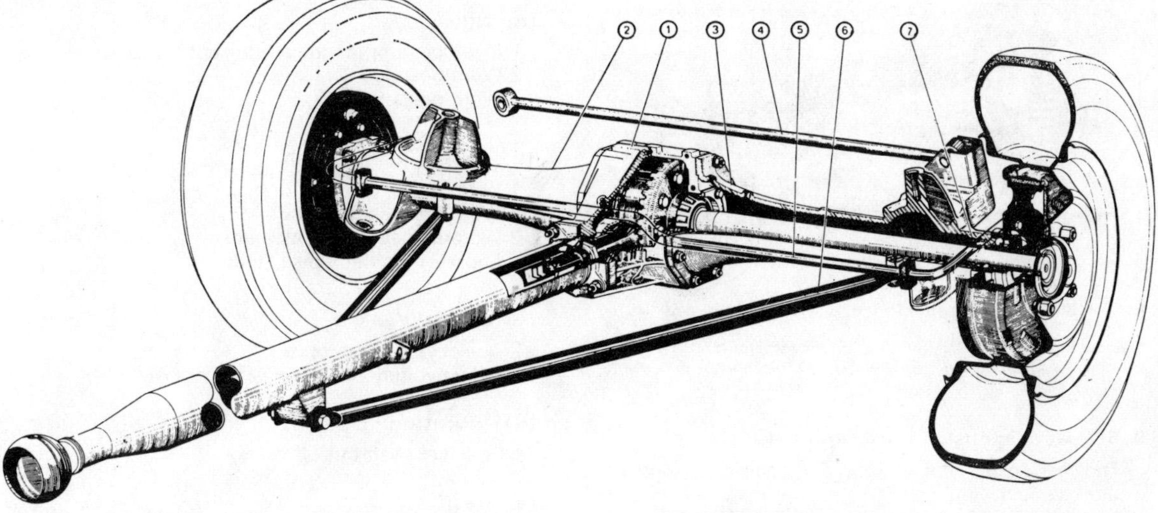

FIG 8:38 Cutaway view of the rigid axle assembly

Key to Fig 8:38 1 Axle housing 2 Righthand axle tube 3 Lefthand axle tube 4 Panhard rod 5 Anti-roll bar 6 Axle locating arms 7 Oil seal

8:7 The rigid rear axle

This type of axle assembly is shown in the cutaway drawing of **FIG 8:38**. Fore and aft location is ensured by using two triangulated arms 6 at the extremities of the axle, and sideways movement is controlled by the Panhard rod 4, attached to a mounting bracket on the lefthand side of the axle casing as shown.

The method of suspension used with this axle on estate and commercial vehicles employs double coil springs while the 504L saloon has single coil springs on each side and an anti-roll bar. It will also be noted that drum brakes of the leading/trailing shoe type are used instead of the disc brakes fitted to the standard saloon models.

Removing the axle:

Disconnect the dampers from the axle and also the Panhard rod. Release the spring of the brake compensator from the rod but do not unscrew the nut.

Disconnect the anti-roll bar (when fitted) from its connecting rods, the sheaths for the handbrake cables from the floor and the brake hydraulic hoses, not forgetting to seal off the delivery side to prevent fluid spillage.

Disconnect the operating cables for the rear brakes from the operating lever and then remove the lever to the rear.

Raise the rear end of the body so as to free the coil springs, then remove the exhaust pipe clamps from the manifold and the gearbox housing.

It is now necessary to support the engine and transmission. This is best carried out with the special engine support bracket 8.0103-Z, which has an adjustable support applied under the clutch housing.

Unscrew the upper and lower bolts securing the engine rear mounting and carefully lower the engine supporting tool until the rear of the gearbox has dropped about 45 mm ($1\frac{3}{4}$ inch). It is important at this time to ensure that the underside of the engine is not allowed to rest on the steering gear.

Unscrew the four securing bolts from the torque tube ball joint cover and then withdraw the axle while supporting the torque tube and replace the rear engine support.

Raise the car body sufficiently to allow the axle and road wheels to be removed.

Re-installation of the axle is a reversal of the removal procedure, but pay attention to the following points:

To ensure that the rear engine mounting is secure, see that it is thoroughly cleaned but do not use a solvent such as trichlorethylene for this purpose. The two joint faces should be coated with a sealer such as Hermetite.

When fitting the coil springs, see that the end of the bottom spiral is towards the rear of the car.

Use new Nylstop self-locking nuts on the damper mountings.

Bleed the braking system as described in **Chapter 11:12**.

Removing the axle halfshafts:

Jack up and support the rear of the car and remove the appropriate road wheel.

Remove the countersunk screws and lift off the brake drum.

Disconnect the bearing retaining flanges from the rear axle tube.

Use a suitable puller, such as 8.0601, attached to the wheel mounting studs to extract the halfshaft.

When refitting the halfshaft, fit a paper joint smeared with a sealing compound on each side of the brake plate.

Ensure that the oil vent hole in the flange is in line with the hole in the axle tube and reverse the removal procedure.

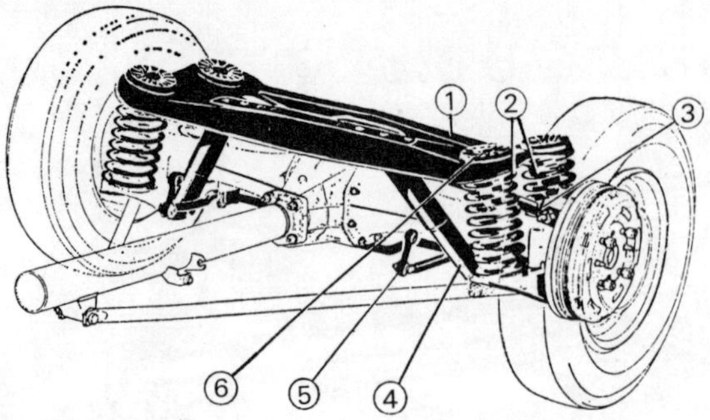

FIG 8:39 Rear suspension used with rigid rear axle

Key to Fig 8:39 1 Suspension crossmember 2 Coil springs 3 Drum brake 4 Damper 5 Stabilizer 6 Spring seat

8:8 Rear suspension with rigid axle

The rear suspension employed on vehicles such as estate cars and vans equipped with a rigid rear axle is shown in **FIG 8:39**, which shows clearly the method of mounting the four coil springs on the suspension crossmember.

The suspension for the 504L is similar but uses only one coil spring on each side.

8:9 Fault diagnosis

(a) Noisy axle

1 Insufficient or incorrect lubricant
2 Worn bearings
3 Worn gears

(b) Excessive backlash

1 Worn gears, bearings or bearing housings
2 Worn drive shaft splines
3 Worn constant velocity joints
4 Loose or broken wheel studs

(c) Oil leakage

1 Defective seals in hubs
2 Defective differential housing oil seal

(d) Vibration

1 Propeller shaft out of balance

(e) Rattles

1 Defective damper mountings

(f) 'Settling'

1 Weak or broken springs

CHAPTER 9

FRONT SUSPENSION AND HUBS

9:1 Description of system

Independent front suspension arrangements are provided on each side of the car, with coil springs and double-acting telescopic dampers operating in conjunction with Macpherson struts and an anti-roll bar. A general view of the front suspension is shown in **FIG 9:1** and details of the various units in **FIG 9:2.** Referring to **FIG 9:1,** a main cast steel crossmember 8 supports the engine and the rack and pinion steering gear. Transverse suspension links pivot on this member and connect it to the tubular stub axles 9 through resilient mountings or 'silentblocs'. A fabricated crossmember 12 in front of the main crossmember is connected by trailing locating links or radius arms to the latter, also with silentbloc bushes. The anti-roll bar 6 is mounted on the front crossmember and connected to the transverse arms by the link 7. The front crossmember also carries the radiator and is provided at the centre with a jack guide.

The two helical springs are mounted vertically and rest on the telescopic damper cylinders which are integral with the stub axles. The Peugeot dampers can be dismantled for overhaul if required. Each suspension unit is guided at the bottom by a transversal arm and a radius arm, the two units being connected by the anti-roll bar. At the top the suspension units are anchored to the body in the wheel arches on each side.

9:2 Routine maintenance, lubrication points

Every 20,000 km or 12,000 miles the hub nut caps (see **FIG 9:9**) should be removed and cleaned and refitted after inserting a small amount of approved grease, about the size of a walnut, in the bottoms of the caps. Esso Multipurpose Grease H is recommended by the manufacturers. Do not pack the hub with grease as this may result in the grease working out on to the brake friction surfaces. Opportunity may be taken at the same time to clean the brake disc, degreasing it if necessary with a cloth soaked in trichlorethylene. At intervening periods some idea of the degree of end float and wear of the bearings can be obtained by jacking up the car, grasping the wheel horizontally, rocking it and noting the amount of movement obtained. If there is excessive slackness or roughness in the bearings or if there is any sign of contamination of the grease by water or grit, it is essential to remove the hub for examination of the bearings.

Two lubrication nipples are provided on each side of the car on the ball joints connecting the suspension linkage. These should be lubricated at intervals of 5000 km or 3000 miles with an approved grease. Before injecting the grease clean and examine the nipples for damage and if necessary renew them.

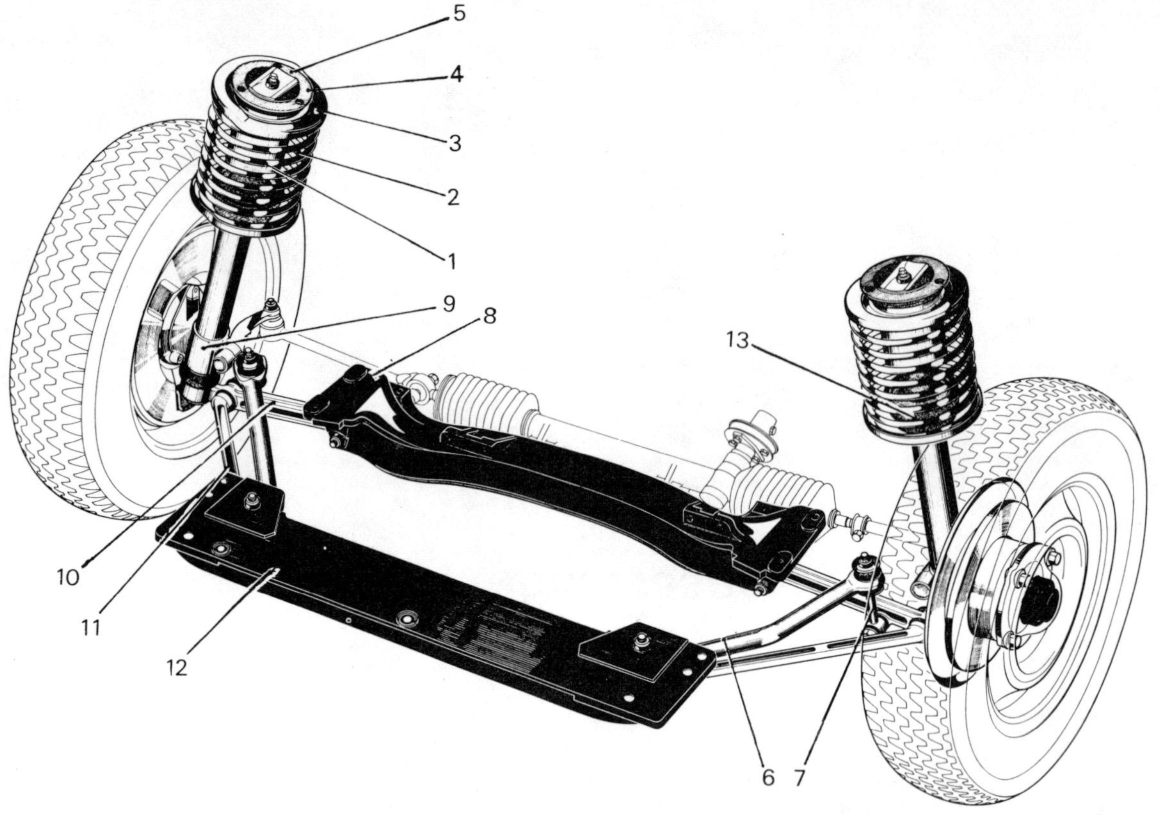

FIG 9:1 A view of the front suspension

Key to Fig 9:1 1 Damper 2 Suspension spring 3 Spring upper seating cup 4 Upper flexible mounting 5 Safety cup 6 Anti-roll bar (Not on commercial models) 7 Anti-roll bar connecting link 8 Main crossmember 9 Stub axle 10 Triangle rear arm 11 Triangle front arm 12 Front crossmember 13 Rebound block

9:3 Front hub removal and refitting

Removal of a front hub is commenced by raising the front of the car, chocking it on firm supports under the front crossmember and removing the wheel. Then detach the bolts retaining the brake caliper and hang it from the bodywork (see **FIG 9:3**), without removing the brake hose. Remove the hub cap and the nut, then remove the hub.

For renewal of the bearings a number of special tools are made to close limits in service workshops as they are not available from the manufacturers. They include:

A A thrust plate for removing the outer race of the extractor bearing.

B A thrust plate for removing the outer race of the inner bearing.

C A drift used with the thrust plates for removing the outer bearing race.

D A hub thrust block with thrust faces for the hub exterior and interior respectively.

E A drift for positioning the outer wheel bearing.

F A drift for positioning the inner wheel bearing.

The tools are used as follows:

1 Remove the hub nut cap O-ring and clean the surplus grease from the hub.
2 To remove the inner bearing (see **FIG 9:4**), insert the plate B in the hub, located on the outer race. Place the hub on the block D on the side with the larger diameter. Using the drift C, remove the bearing and oil seal, preferably in a press.
3 To remove the outer bearing (see **FIG 9:5**), insert the plate A in the hub, turn over the block D and place the hub on the block. Remove the race with the drift C.
4 Clean and dry the components for reassembling, but new bearings should be fitted without degreasing. Grease the hub and bearings with approved grease and check that the outer races are inserted in the correct direction (see **FIG 9:6**). Note that the inner and outer bearing races, as well as the ball cages, are paired and the pairing must not be altered.
5 Insert the complete outer bearing in the hub (see **FIG 9:7**) using the block D, the drift E and a press. Withdraw the inner race.

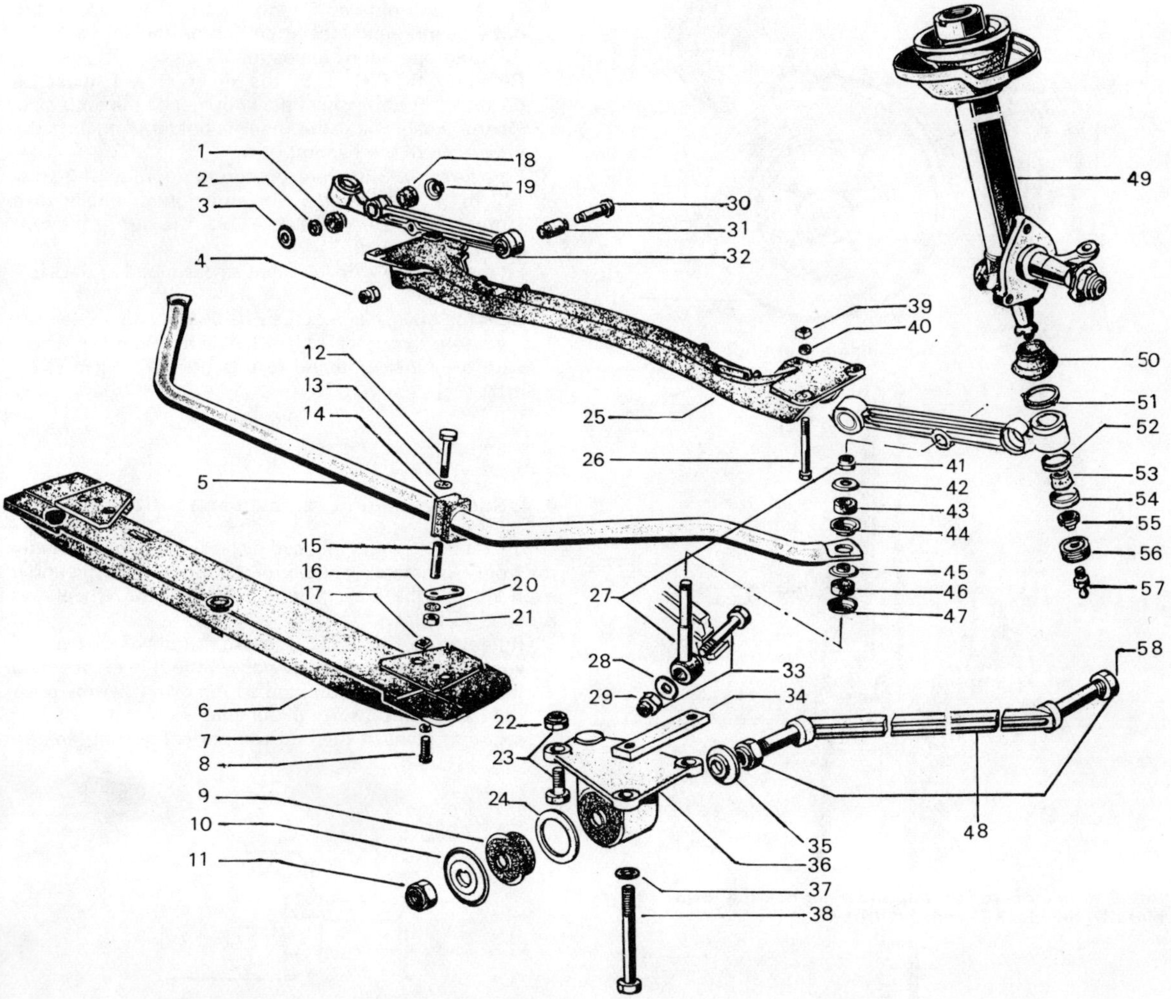

FIG 9:2 An exploded view of the front suspension

Key to Fig 9:2 1 Rubber bush 2 Washer 3 Dished washer 4 Nut 5 Anti-roll bar 6 Front crossmember 7 Washer 8 Bolt 9 Rubber bush 10 Washer 11 Nut 12 Bolt 13 Shakeproof washer 14 Rubber bush 15 Distance tube 16 Shackle 17 Nut 18 Rubber bush 19 Dished washer 20 Shakeproof washer 21 Nut 22 Nut 23 Bolt 24 Distance washer 25 Main crossmember 26 Bolt 27 Anti-roll bar attachment 28 Washer 29 Nut 30 Bolt 31 Silentbloc bush 32 Track control arm 33 Bolt 34 Shackle 35 Washer 36 Bracket 37 Washer 38 Bolt 39 Nut 40 Washer 41 Nut 42 Dished washer 43 Rubber bush 44 Dished washer 45 Dished washer 46 Rubber bush 47 Dished washer 48 Radius arm 49 Damper 50 Rubber boot 51 Clip 52 Upper ball joint cup 53 Steering swivel ball joint head 54 Lower ball joint cup 55 Ball joint nut 56 Screwed cap 57 Greaser 58 Nut

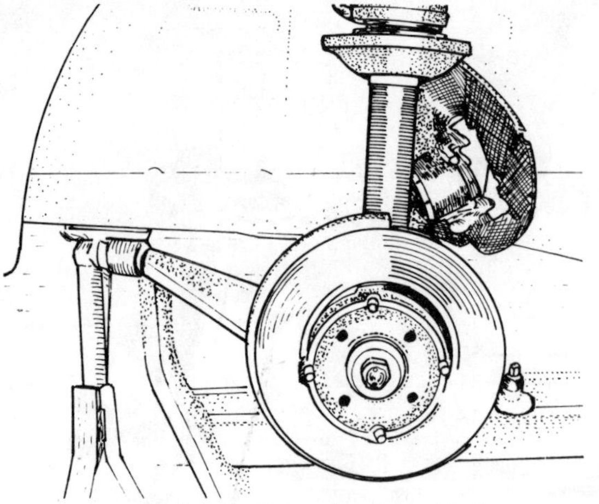

FIG 9:3 Removing a front hub

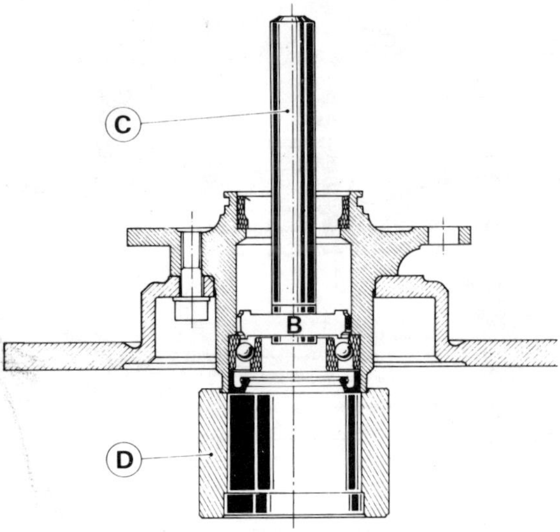

FIG 9:4 Removing a front hub inner bearing, using the plate **B**, the block **D** and the drift **C**

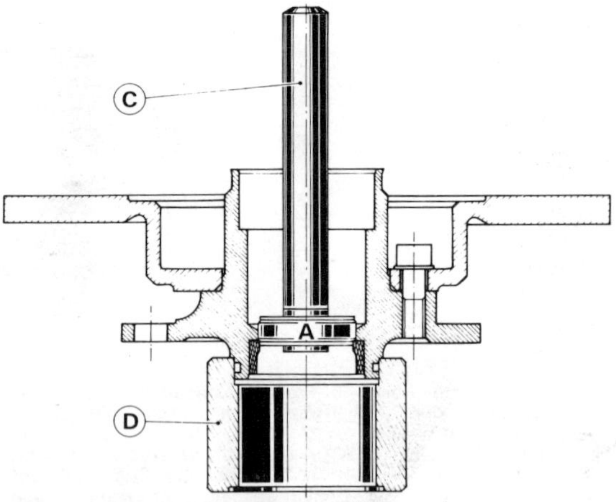

FIG 9:5 Removing a front hub outer bearing, using the plate **A**, the block **D** and the drift **C**

6 Insert the complete inner bearing in the hub (see **FIG 9:8**) using the block D turned over, the drift F and a press. Ensure that the races are completely and separately inserted.

7 Fit the oil seal, with its upper face flush with the hub, and the hub nut cap O-ring. Fit the inner race of the outer bearing and locate the hub on the stub axle.

Refitting operations are as follows:

1 Referring to **FIG 9:9,** the inner race 1 must be positioned tight against the shoulder of the stub axle.

2 Fit the washer and the inner shoulder 2 against the inner race of the bearing.

3 Fit a new nut 3 and pre-tighten to a torque of 3 kg m (22 lb ft). Slacken the nut and tighten finally to a torque of 1 kg m (7.2 lb ft). Lock the nut in the two grooves provided.

4 Fit the hub cap with lubricant as described in **Section 9:2.**

5 Refit the brake caliper (see **FIG 9:10**) and tighten the bolts to a torque of 7 kg m (51 lb ft). Refit the wheel with the nuts tightened to a torque of 6 kg m (43.5 lb ft).

9:4 Suspension unit removal and refitting

Operations are commenced by jacking up the car under the front crossmember and firmly supporting the car under each side of the crossmember. Remove the wheel and proceed as follows:

1 Referring to **FIG 9:11,** remove the brake caliper and suspend it from the bodywork without disconnecting the flexible hose. Continue by removing (a) the track rod ball joint using a suitable extractor, (b) the securing pivot of the anti-roll bar connecting link on

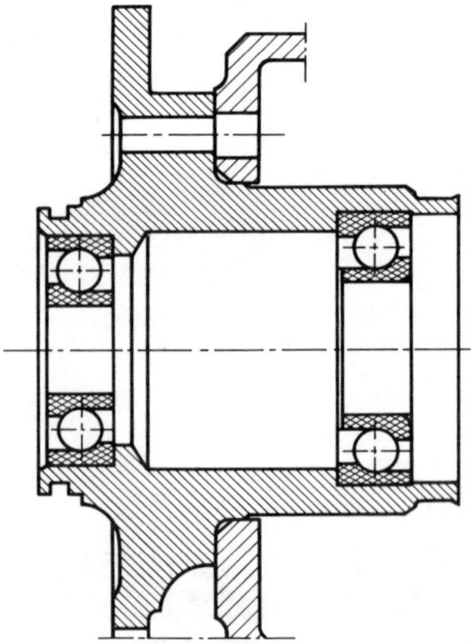

FIG 9:6 Correct location of bearings

the rear triangle arm, (c) the rear triangle arm pivot by tapping to disengage the splined part, and (d) the silentbloc nut securing the front arm to the rear arm.

2 Place a jack under the wheel hub and remove the three bolts securing the upper spring holder to the wing valance. Hold the spring on one of its coils (see **FIG 9:12**), lower the jack and remove the element from the car.

3 To refit the unit, position the upper holder so that the safety cup lies parallel with the car axis.

4 Place the element on a trolley jack fully lowered and position it under the front wing.

5 Raise the assembly, aligning the securing holes, and secure by using three bolts 1 (see **FIG 9:13**) equipped with new double toothed washers, tightening the bolts to a torque of 1 kg m (7.2 lb ft).

6 Remove the jack and fit in order on the front arm, the thrust washers, the cup and the half silentbloc.

7 Fit the arm thus equipped in the rear arm eye and mount in order the silentbloc second half and a new nylstop nut.

8 Engage the pivot 2 (see **FIG 9:14**) of the rear triangle arm, the head pointing rearwards and flush with the splines. Fit a new nylstop nut but do not tighten.

9 Refit the anti-roll bar connecting link on the rear arm by engaging the pivot with the top facing rearwards. Fit a washer and a nut without tightening.

10 Couple the track rod with the track arm, ensuring that the pin hole is perpendicular to the rod axis.

11 Tighten the ball joint nut (see **FIG 9:15**) equipped with a new Blocfor washer to a torque of 4.5 kg m (33 lb ft). Fit a new splitpin.

12 Refit the brake caliper (see **FIG 9:16**), using new Blocfor washers and tightening the bolts to a torque of 7 kg m (51 lb ft). Fit the rear articulation pivot 1 in **FIG 9:17.**

13 Referring to **FIG 9:18,** tighten the pivot nut 2 on the crossmember, the silentbloc nut 3 and the nut 4 securing the anti-roll bar connecting link to the rear arm, all to a torque of 4.5 kg m (33 lb ft).

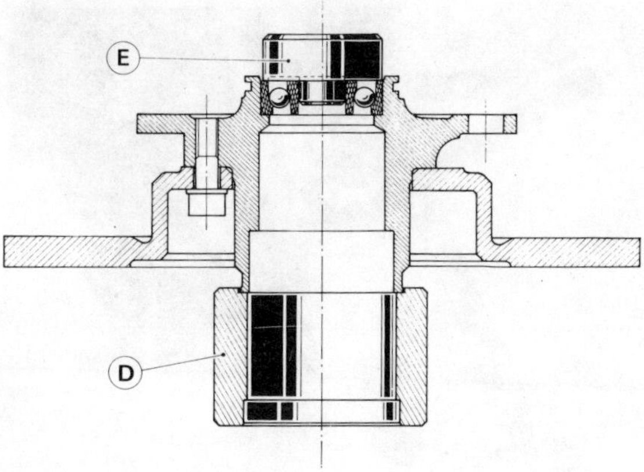

FIG 9:7 Fitting a front hub outer bearing using the block D and the drift E

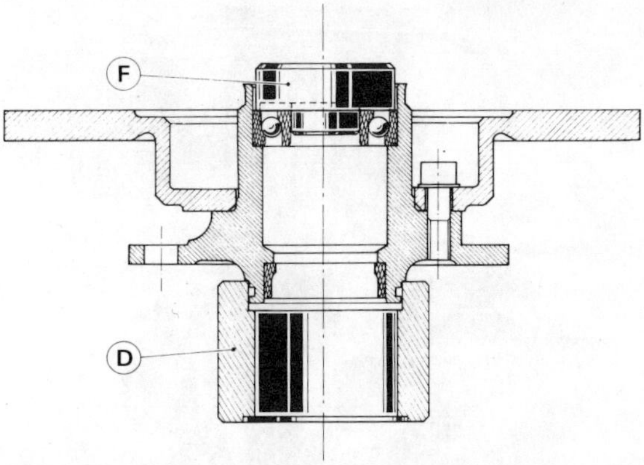

FIG 9:8 Fitting a front hub inner bearing using the block D and the drift E

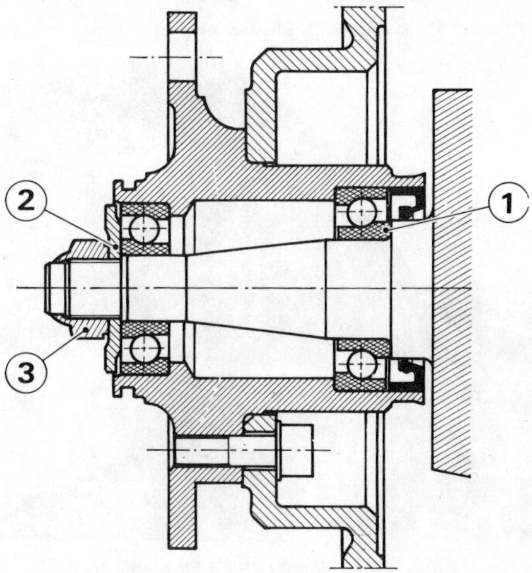

FIG 9:9 A sectional view of the front hub

Key to Fig 9:9 1 Inner race 2 Washer 3 Nut

FIG 9:10 Refitting the brake caliper

FIG 9:11 Dismantling lower end of a suspension unit

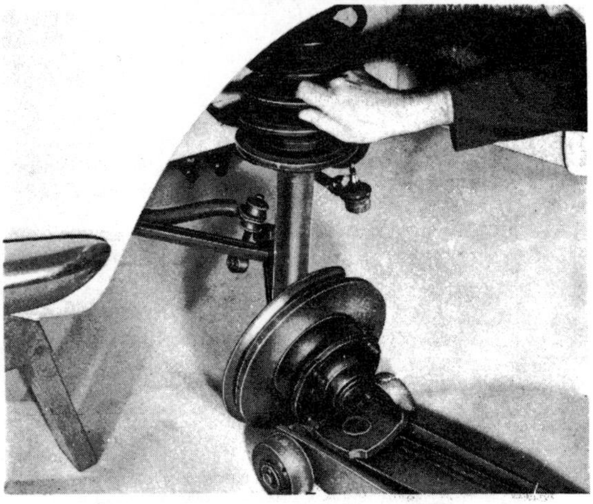

FIG 9:12 Removing a suspension unit

FIG 9:13 Securing a suspension unit with the three bolts **1**

FIG 9:14 Engagement of pivot **2** in the triangle rear arm

FIG 9:15 Securing the track rod ball joint

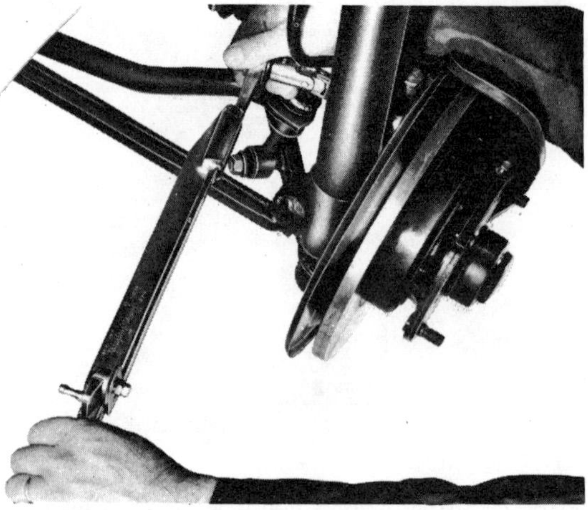

FIG 9:16 Refitting the front brake caliper

FIG 9:17 Refitting the rear articulation pivot **1**

FIG 9:18 Refitting the pivot nut **2** on the crossmember, the silentbloc nut **3** and the nut **4** securing the anti-roll bar connecting link to the rear arm

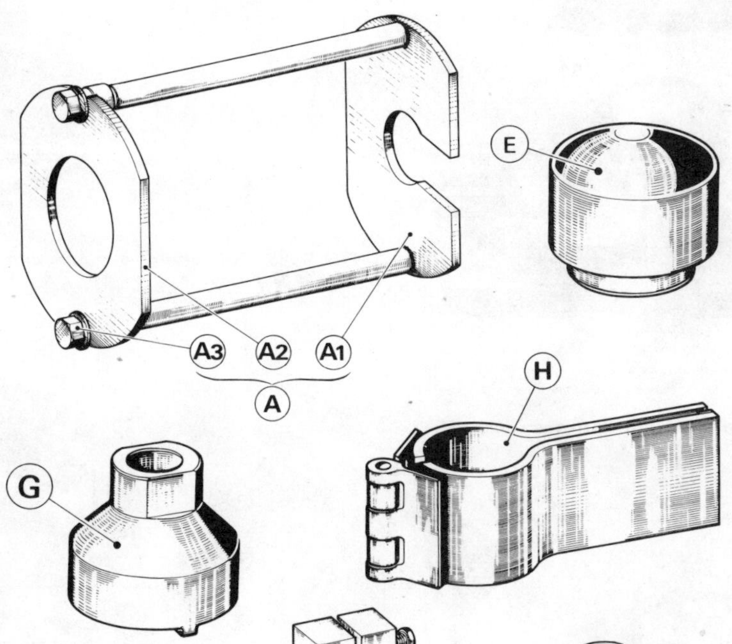

FIG 9:19 Tools for dismantling and reassembling a suspension unit

Key to Fig 9:19 **A** Compressor **A1** Lower clamp assembly **A2** Upper clamp **A3** Set of two operating screws **E** Lower needle bearing seal fitting drift **G** Front damper closing nut socket wrench **H** Holder **L** Front damper rod holding clamp **M** Front damper rod holding socket

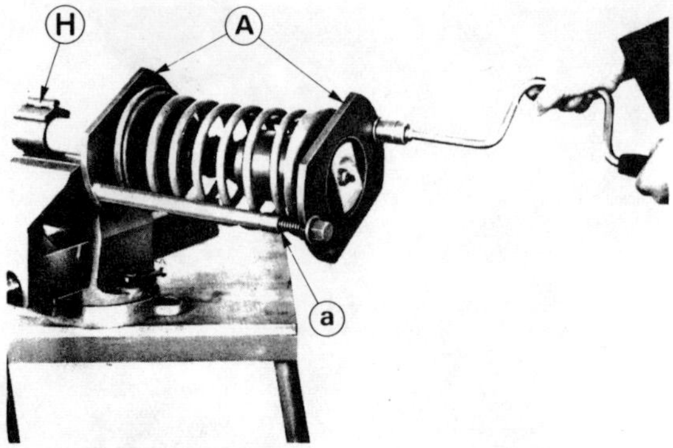

FIG 9:20 Compressing a suspension spring using the compressor A and holder H, until the spring upper holder meets the apparatus at 'a'

FIG 9:21 **Removing damper nut with the socket M**

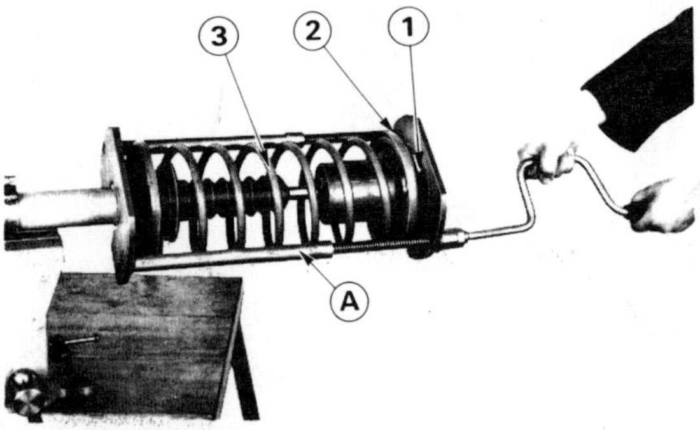

FIG 9:22 **Removing suspension spring**

Key to Fig 9:22 **A** Compressor 1 Upper holder 2 Spring upper cup 3 Suspension spring

9:5 Suspension unit dismantling and reassembly

The tools for dismantling a front suspension unit are shown in **FIG 9:19** and the method of their use is as follows:

1 Hold the suspension element horizontally in a vice using a holder H.
2 Fit the compressor A (see **FIG 9:20**) over the suspension spring and alternately tighten both operating screws until the spring upper holder comes into contact with the apparatus at 'a'.
3 Hold the damper rod using socket M (see **FIG 9:21**) and remove the nut.

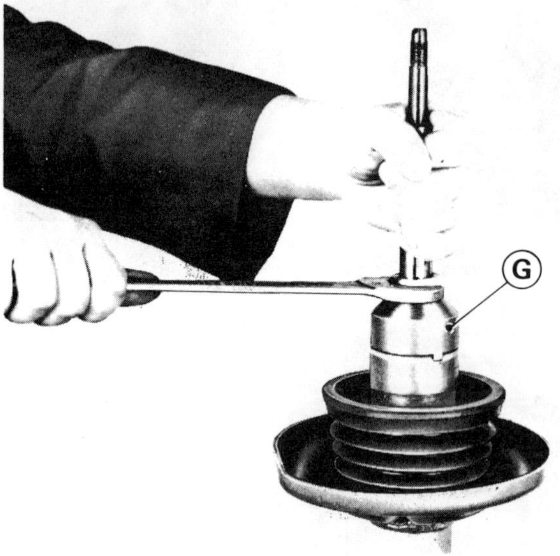

FIG 9:23 **Removing damper closing nut with the socket G**

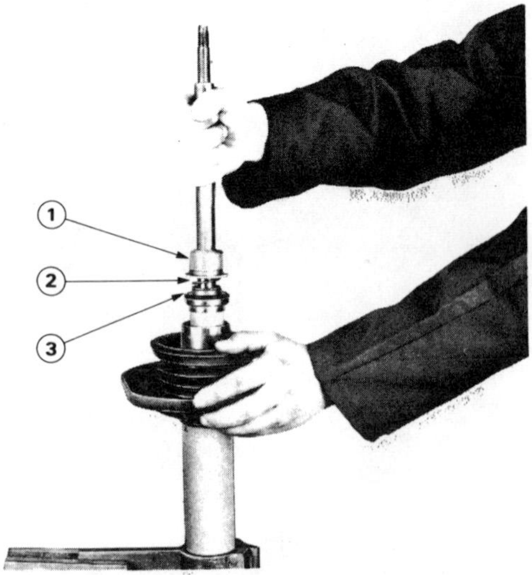

FIG 9:24 **Removing rod and piston assembly**

Key to Fig 9:24 1 Support cup with rod seal 2 Thrust washer and upper spring 3 Bushing and O-ring

4 Slacken both operating screws until the spring is fully extended. Remove the compressor A (see **FIG 9:22**), the upper holder 1, the spring upper cup 2 and the suspension spring 3.
5 Remove the damper rod rubber boot. Hold the suspension element vertically in a vice and remove the damper closing nut using the socket G and an open-ended spanner as shown in **FIG 9:23**.
6 Pull the rod slowly so that the oil does not splash and remove the rod and piston assembly as shown in **FIG 9:24**. Then remove the support cup with the rod seal 1, the thrust washer and upper spring 2 and the O-ring of the bushing 3.
7 Remove the rebound block using two tyre levers, in the manner shown in **FIG 9:25**.
8 Withdraw the damper from the vice and remove the oil from the damper body. Remove the compensator valve 2 (see **FIG 9:26**) from the damper cylinder.
9 When reassembling, examine the valve compensator 1 and the needle bearing 7 (see **FIG 9:27**) and renew them if their condition appears doubtful. Also renew the O-ring 2, the rod seal 3, the rubber boot 4, the nylstop nut 5, the lower rubber seal 6 and the needle bearing seal ring 8.

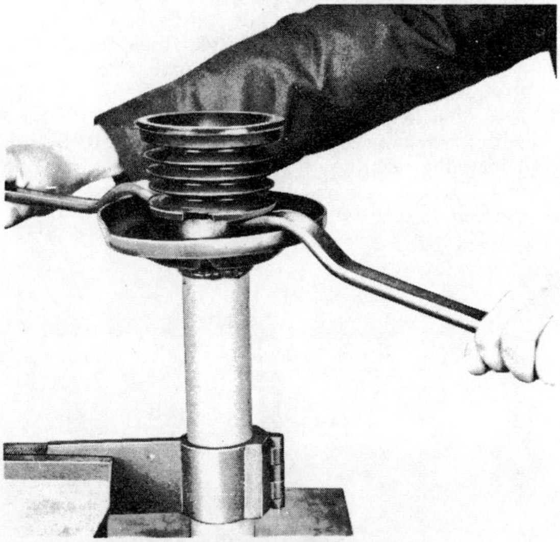

FIG 9:25 Removing rebound block

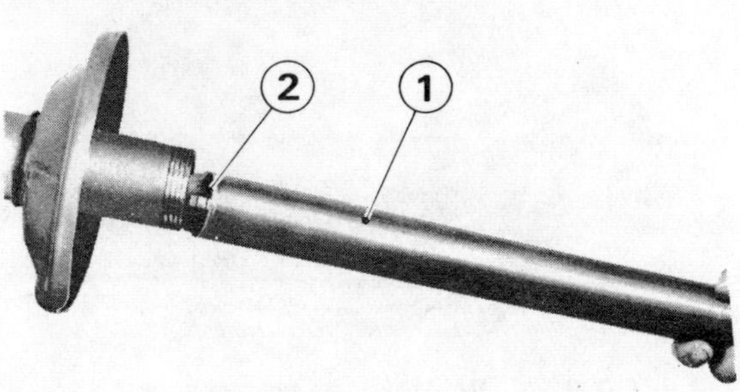

FIG 9:26 Damper cylinder (1) and compensator valve (2)

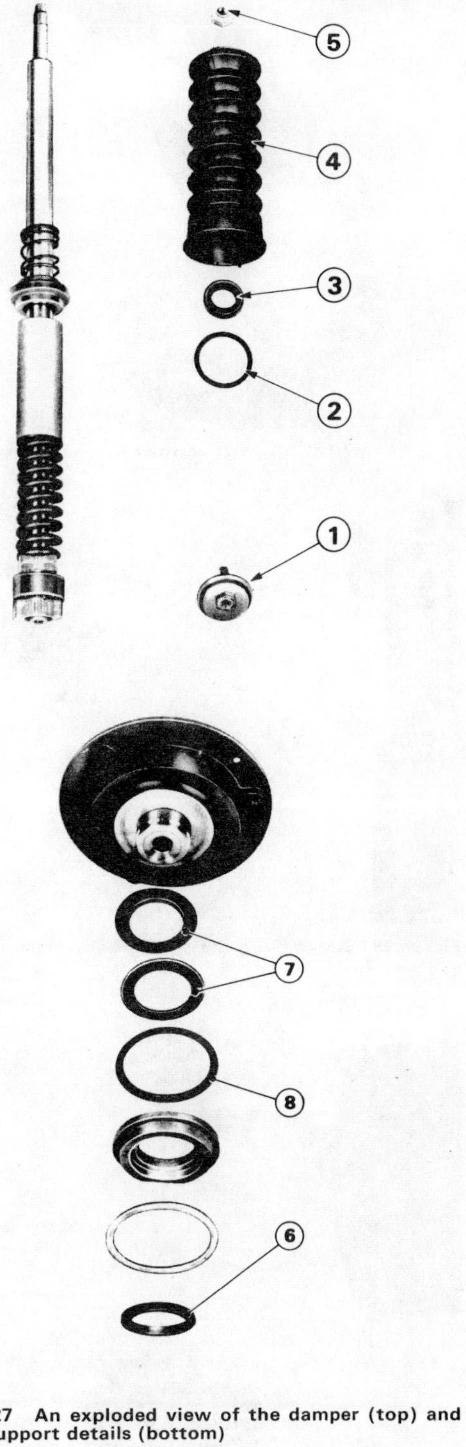

FIG 9:27 An exploded view of the damper (top) and upper support details (bottom)

Key to Fig 9:27 1 Valve compensator assembly 2 O-ring 3 Rod seal 4 Rubber boot 5 Nylstop nut 6 Lower rubber seal 7 Needle bearing 8 Seal ring of needle bearing

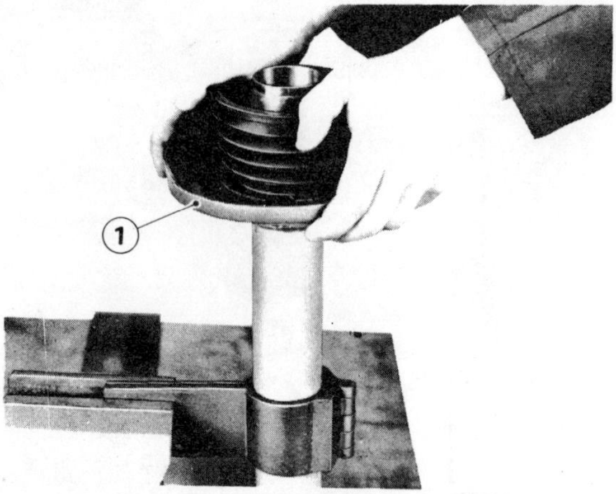

FIG 9:28 **Fitting the rebound block 1**

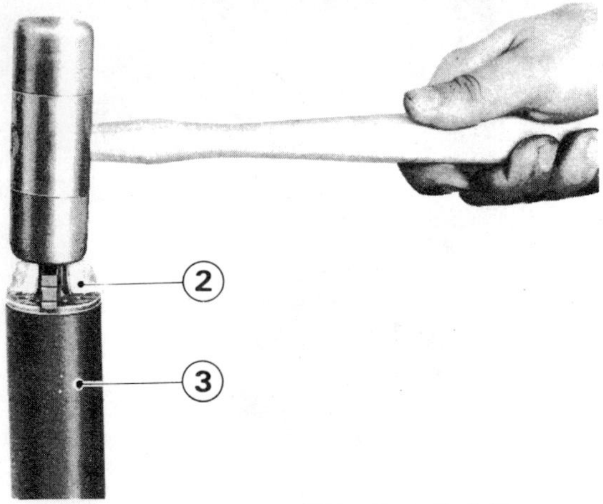

FIG 9:29 **Assembling the compensator valve 2 in the cylinder 3**

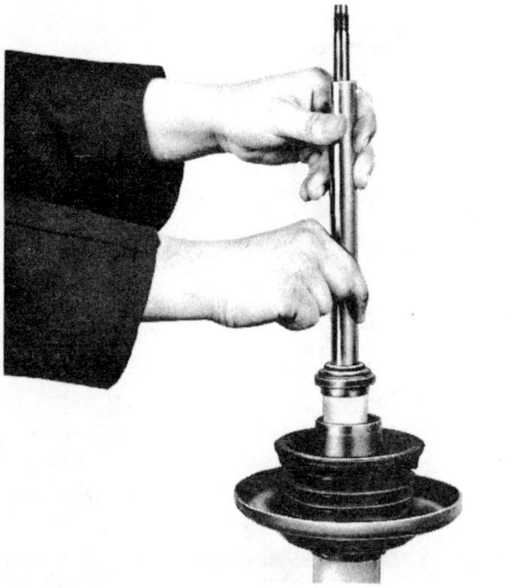

FIG 9:30 **Inserting the damper mechanism into the cylinder**

10 Hold the damper body vertically in a vice with the support H (see **FIG 9:28**). Smear tallow over the threads and the damper body upper part. Fit the rebound block 1.
11 Insert the compensator valve 2 (see **FIG 9:29**) in the cylinder 3 by tapping gently with a mallet. Blow out carefully these parts as well as the inner part of the damper body.
12 Place the cylinder assembly in the damper and fill the latter with 300 cc (.53 pint) of Esso Oleofluid 40X.
13 Gradually insert the mechanism into the cylinder to avoid any loss of oil, as shown in **FIG 9:30.**
14 Ensure the correct engagement of the upper bush 1 in **FIG 9:31.** The face 'a' must have a clearance of 3 mm from the damper body.
15 Fit a new O-ring 2 smeared with tallow. Locate the upper spring 3 and the thrust washer 4 with the domed side facing the spring, on the damper rod. Smear a new rod seal with tallow and insert the seal in the cup so that the edge 'b' shown in **FIG 9:32** is visible.
16 Carefully fit the cup equipped with its seal on the rod. Engage it until the thrust washer comes into contact with the spring. Fully tighten the closing nut on the body and tighten it, using socket G (see **FIGS 9:19** and **9:33**), to a torque of 8 kg m (58 lb ft). Check by hand the rod rotation and displacement.
17 Pull the damper rod fully out and fit the clamp L on the rod as shown in **FIG 9:34.** Hold the element horizontally in a vice and fit the rubber boot on the damper rod.
18 Place the rebound buffer thrust ring on a lead base with the seal recess facing upwards (see **FIG 9:35**). Locate the seal ring on the drift E, the lips of the ring being pressed against the drift, and fit the seal by tapping on the drift until the seal bottoms.

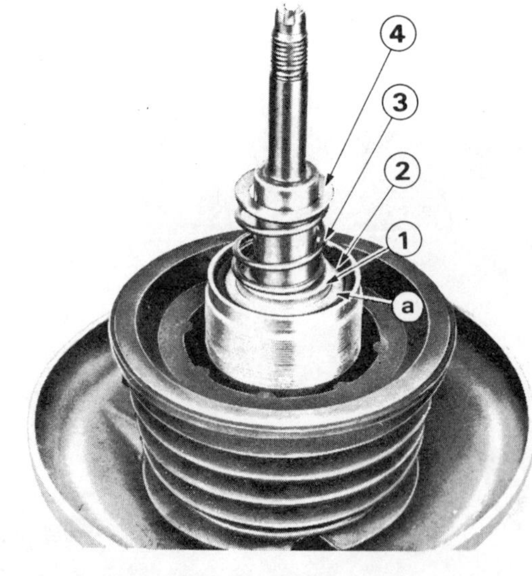

FIG 9:31 **Refitting damper components**

Key to Fig 9:31 1 Upper bush 2 O-ring 3 Upper spring 4 Thrust washer **a** Clearance of 3 mm

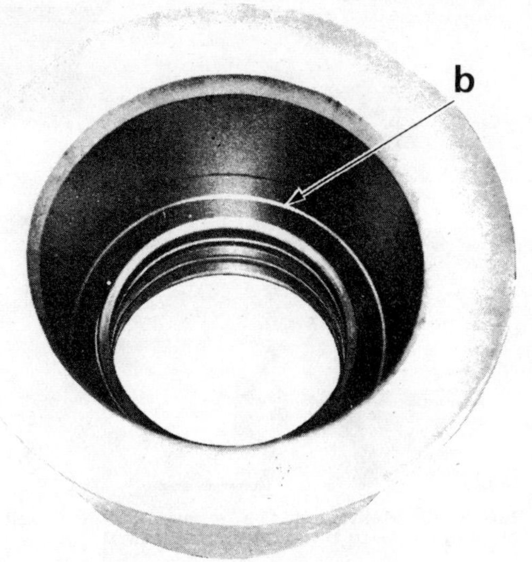

FIG 9:32 **Rod seal, showing edge b**

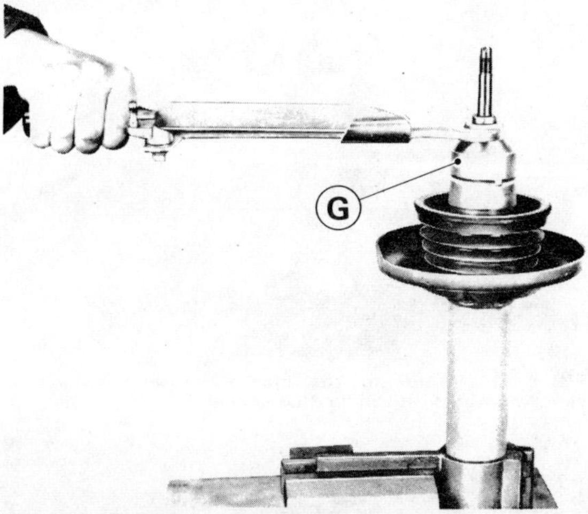

FIG 9:33 Fitting the cup and seal on the rod, using the socket G

FIG 9:34 Assembling the rubber boot, using the clamp L

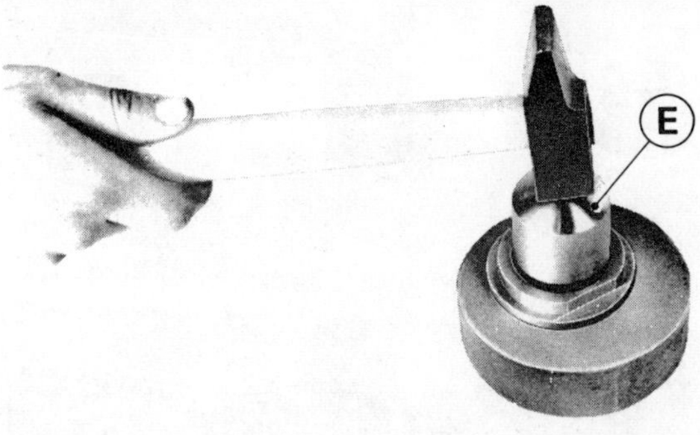

FIG 9:35 Fitting the seal with the drift E into the rebound buffer thrust ring

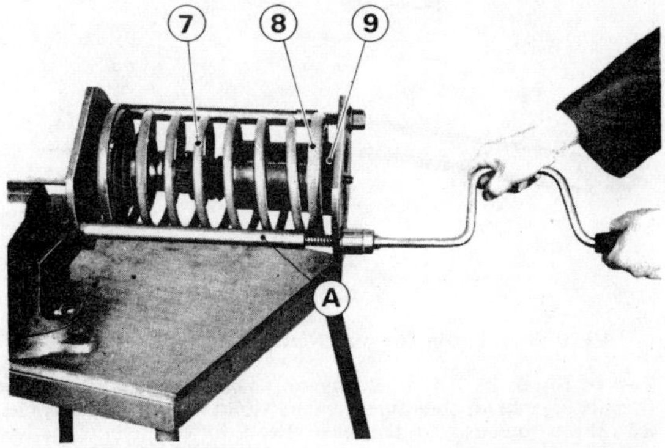

FIG 9:36 Compressing the spring for reassembly

Key to Fig 9:36 7 Suspension spring 8 Upper spring cup 9 Upper holder assembly **A** Compressor

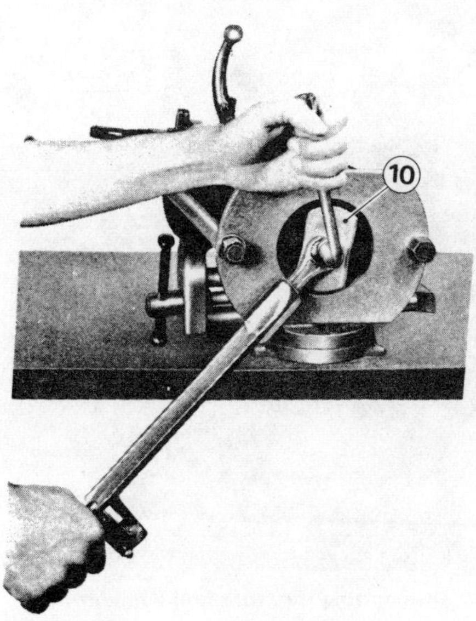

FIG 9:37 Fitting the safety cup 10

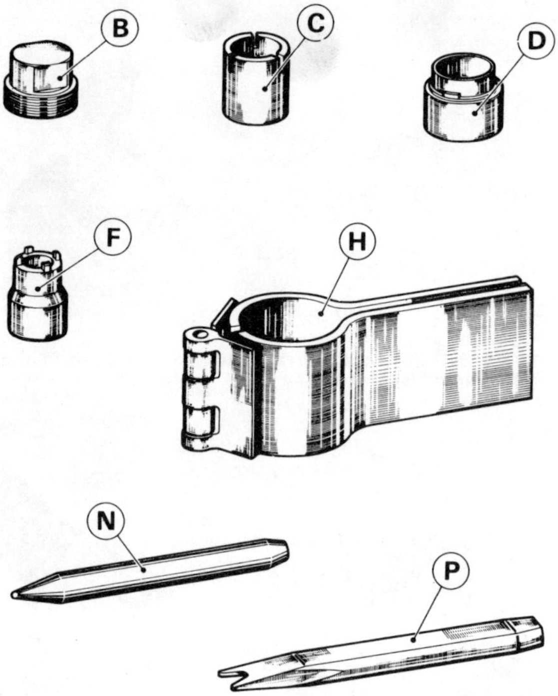

FIG 9:38 Tools for overhaul of triangle rear arm

Key to Fig 9:38 **B** Steering swivel ball joint extractor **C** Socket head for steering swivel ball joint housing closing nut, with three notches **D** Socket head, for the steering swivel ball joint housing closing nut, with three shoulders **F** Castled socket head for lower ball joint securing nut **H** Supporting clamp **N** Punch for locking the closing nut and the front hub nut **P** Punch for locking the steering swivel ball joint securing nut

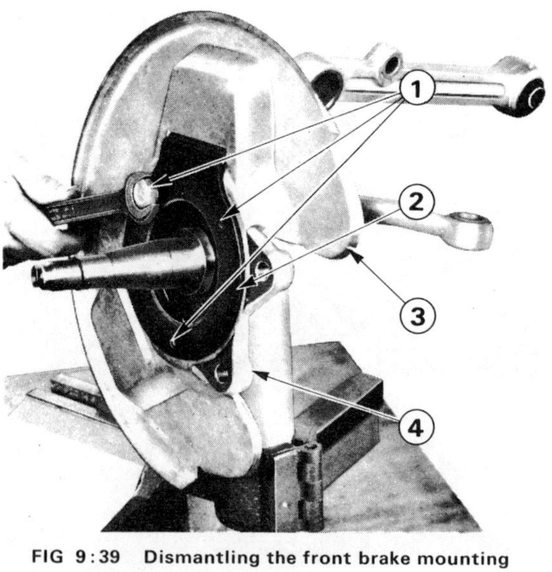

FIG 9:39 Dismantling the front brake mounting

Key to Fig 9:39 1 Three bolts 2 Grease nipple protector 3 Disc protector plate 4 Brake mounting

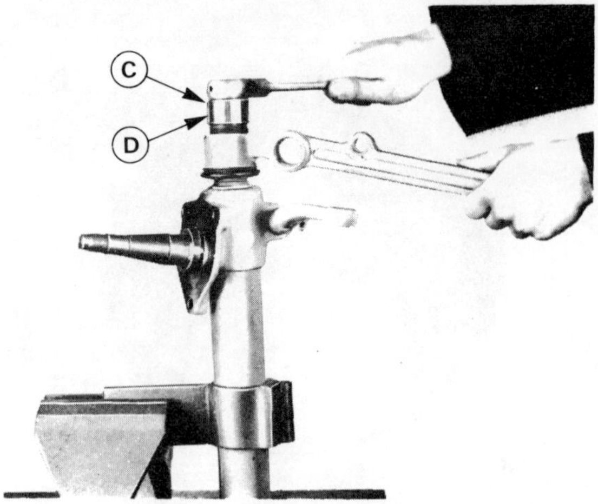

FIG 9:40 Removing the steering swivel ball joint closing nut with the socket head **C** or **D**

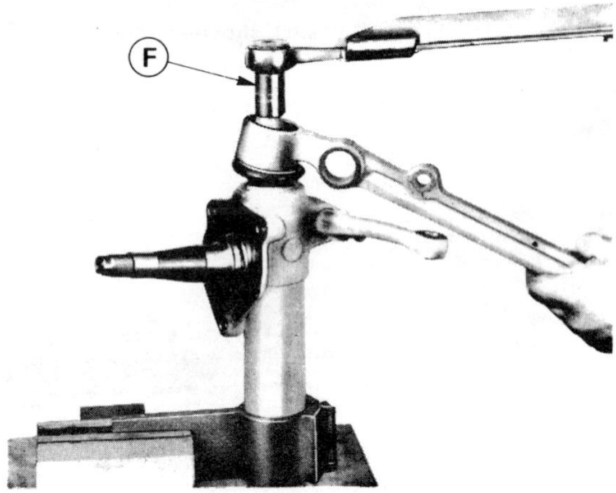

FIG 9:41 Removing the steering swivel ball joint securing nut with the castled socket **F**

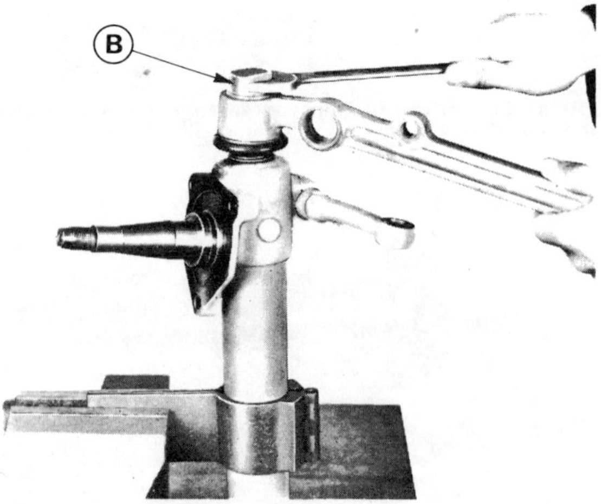

FIG 9:42 Removing the triangle rear arm with the extractor **B**

19 Referring to **FIG 9:27**, locate on the upper spring holder (a) the thrust plate with its collar facing downwards, (b) the needle bearing with the needles facings upwards and amply greased, (c) the bearing oil seal with the big lip pointing downwards, (d) the bearing thrust plate with its seal facing downwards and (e) the shim.
20 On the supporting element fit the suspension spring 7 (see **FIG 9:36**), the upper spring cup 8 and the upper holder assembly 9. Use the compressor A to compress the spring by tightening alternately both operating bolts. Ensure free engagement of the damper rod in the support recess.
21 Fit the safety cup 10 (see **FIG 9:37**) with its tab in the support groove. Fit a new Nylstop nut and tighten it to a torque of 4.5 kg m (33 lb ft) whilst holding the rod with the socket M. Remove the spring compressor and the rod holding clamp and engage the rubber boot over the closing nut.

9:6 Triangle rear arm removing and refitting

To remove and refit a triangle rear arm (see **FIG 9:1**), remove the suspension unit as described in **Section 9:4**, clamp the assembly in a vice with the aid of the support H (see **FIG 9:38**) and withdraw the hub and brake disc assembly. The tools employed in further operations are shown in **FIG 9:38** and procedure is as follows:

1 Remove the three bolts 1 (see **FIG 9:39**) and withdraw the grease nipple protector 2, the disc protector plate 3 and the brake mounting 4.
2 Unlock the steering swivel ball joint closing nut carefully and remove it using the socket head C or D as shown in **FIG 9:40**.
3 Remove the steering swivel ball joint securing nut with the castled socket F as shown in **FIG 9:41**.
4 Remove the triangle rear arm using the extractor B (see **FIG 9:42**) and withdraw the extractor B, the protector boot and its spring clip, the lower cup, the steering swivel ball joint and the upper cup.
5 When reassembling, renew the components 1, 2, 3, 5, 6 and 7 shown in **FIG 9:43**, also the steering swivel ball joint head 4 and the arm silentbloc 8 if necessary.
6 Fit the rubber protector 1 (see **FIG 9:44**) smeared with tallow on the arm and secure it with the spring clip 2. Fit the green upper cup 3 (8 mm thick) in its correct direction.
7 Grease the housing with Esso Multipurpose Grease H, then place the arm on the steering swivel ball joint cone and position the ball head. Tighten the ball head securing nut to a torque of 4.5 kg m (33 lb ft) using the castled socket F as shown in **FIG 9:45**.

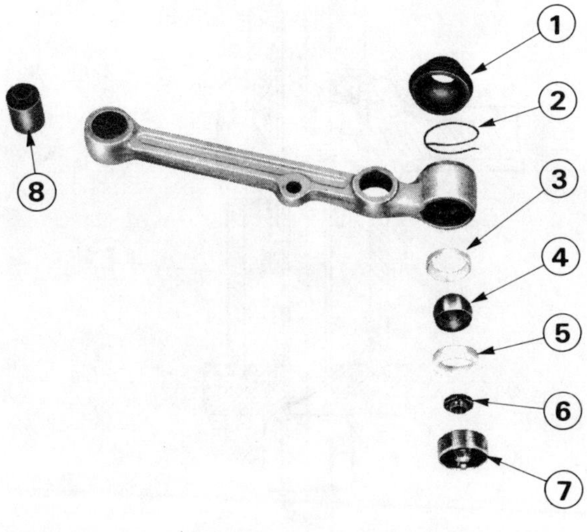

FIG 9:43 An exploded view of the triangle arm components

Key to Fig 9:43 1 The steering swivel ball joint stem rubber protector 2 Spring clip 3 Upper ball joint cup 4 Steering swivel ball joint head 5 Lower ball joint cup 6 Ball joint nut 7 Closing nut 8 Arm silentbloc

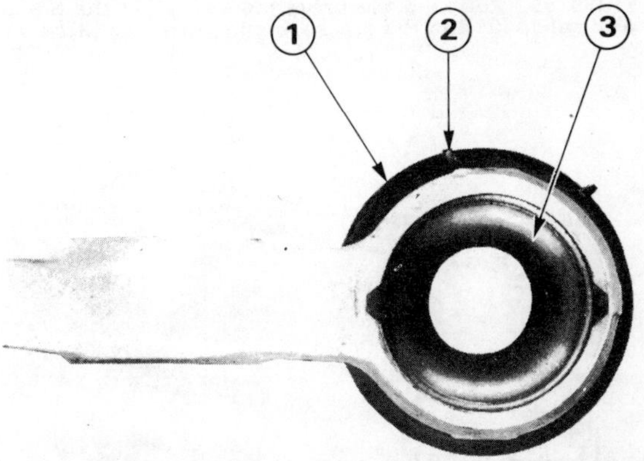

FIG 9:44 Fitting the upper cup 3 to the arm, with the rubber protector 1 secured with the spring clip 2

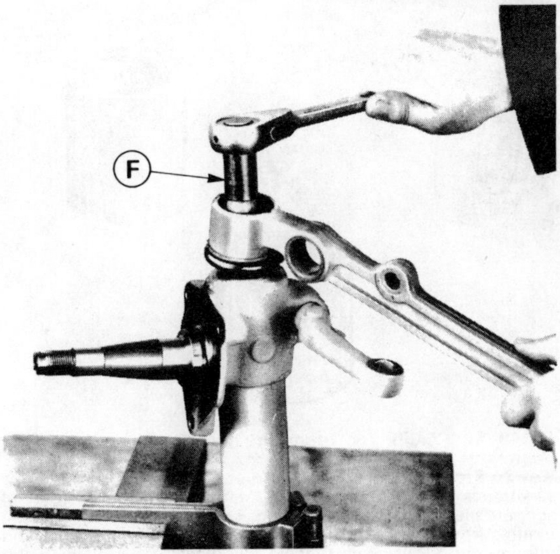

FIG 9:45 Assembling the ball head securing nut with the castled socket F

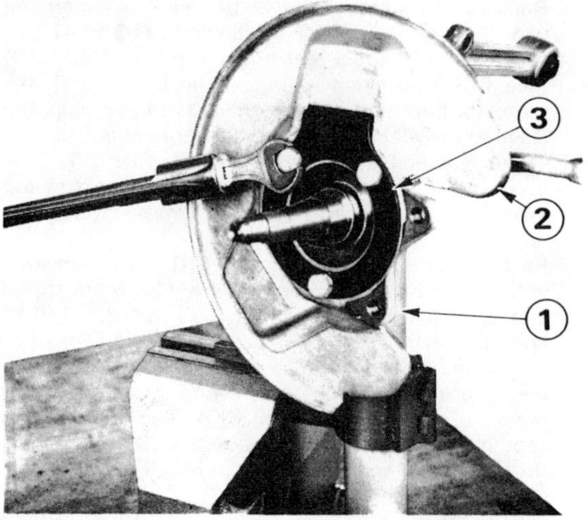

FIG 9:46 Refitting the brake mounting (1) the brake disc shield (2) and the grease nipple protector (3)

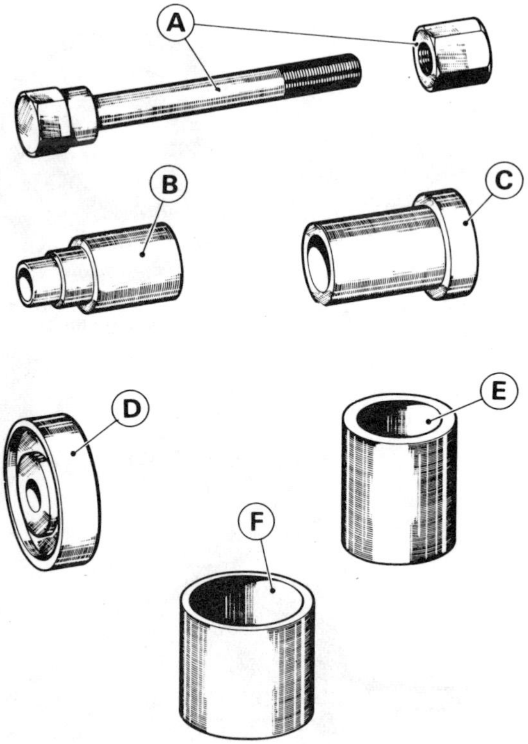

FIG 9:47 Tools for renewing front and rear flexible bushes

Key to Fig 9:47 **A** Nut and bolt for front triangle silentblocs **B** Removing and refitting drift for the bushing support silentbloc **C** Removing and refitting drift for the triangle front and rear arm silentblocs **D** Removing and refitting cup for the front triangle silentblocs **E** Removing and refitting ring for the front triangle rear arm silentbloc **F** Removing and refitting ring for the bushing support silentbloc

8 Lock the ball head securing nut using the punch P.

9 Position the lower nylon cup (white, 10 mm thick) on the ball head and fit a new closing nut. Tighten to a torque of 9.75 kg m (5.5 lb ft) using the socket head C or D. Move the arm around and retighten the nut to the specified torque until the two half cups are correctly positioned. Lock the nut using the punch N.

10 Locate on the steering swivel the brake mounting 1, with the securing points on the track arm side, the brake disc shield 2 and the grease nipple protector 3, as shown in **FIG 9:46.** Tighten the bolts equipped with new Blocfor washers to a torque of 5.5 kg m (40 lb ft). Lock the bolts with a punch mark on the threads protruding from the steering swivel.

9:7 Renewing flexible bushings

The apparatus shown in **FIG 9:47** is used for the renewal of front and rear flexible bushes, consisting of a special nut and bolt on which various cups and rings are fitted for the work in hand. To renew a flexible bush on a triangle rear arm, operations are as follows:

1 Assemble, in order, on the oiled bolt, the drift C as shown in **FIG 9:48,** the inner silentbloc ring 1 of the arm 2, the ring E, the cup D and the nut for the bolt A.

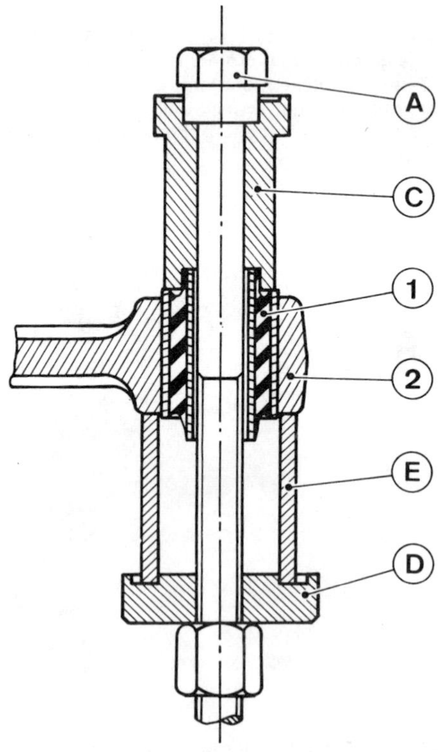

FIG 9:48 Removing a triangle rear arm silentbloc bush

Key to Fig 9:48 1 Inner silentbloc ring 2 Triangle arm **A** Bolt **C** Drift **D** Cup **E** Ring

2 Hold the nut and tighten the bolt until the silentbloc is withdrawn completely. Dismantle the apparatus and recover the silentbloc.
3 Smear with tallow the outer face of the new silentbloc and the bore of the triangle arm.
4 Place on the bolt A the drift C as shown in **FIG 9:49**, the silentbloc 1 with the chamfer facing downwards, the triangle arm 2, the ring E, the cup D and the nut for the bolt A.
5 Tighten until the drift C comes into contact with the arm 2. The correct position of the silentbloc in the arm is obtained through the shape of the drift C. Dismantle the apparatus.

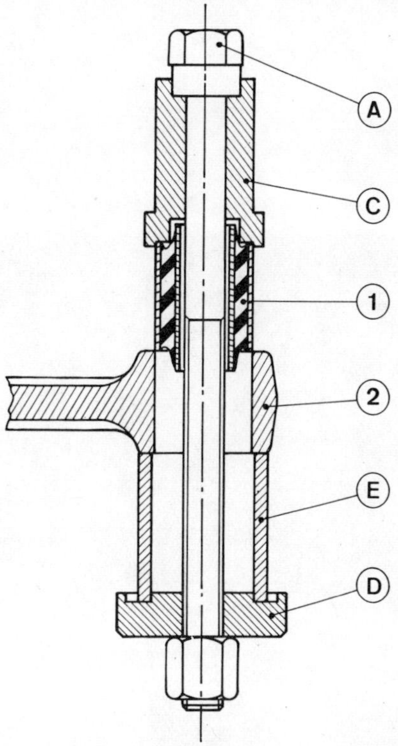

FIG 9:49 Fitting a triangle rear arm silentbloc bush

Key to Fig 9:49 1 Silentbloc 2 Triangle arm **A** Bolt **C** Drift **D** Cup **E** Ring

9:8 Suspension geometry

Suspension geometry includes the castor, camber and swivel pin or kingpin inclination angles. The castor angle, obtained by inclining the steering pivot, gives a self-centring action to the steering effort. Camber is an outward inclination of the top of the front wheels to facilitate cornering. Swivel pin inclination indicates that the swivel pins are inclined in the opposite direction, so that the line of the pin, if continued downwards, would meet the ground near the point of contact of the tyre.

The inclination angles are given in the Technical Data Section of the Appendix and all are set in manufacture. The angles may be checked, however, by using specially designed gauges and turntables of a proprietary nature, for which the assistance of a well-equipped service agent should be obtained.

9:9 Fault diagnosis

(a) Wheel wobble

1 Worn hub bearings
2 Uneven tyre wear
3 Loose suspension attachment
4 Loose wheel fixings

(b) Bottoming of suspension

1 Damper system not working

(c) Heavy steering

1 Front tyres under-inflated
2 Wrong suspension geometry

(d) Excessive tyre wear

1 Check 3 in (a), 1 in (b) and 2 in (c)

(e) Rattles

1 Worn triangle arm bushes
2 Loose connections on triangle arms
3 Loose suspension crossmember retaining bolts

NOTES

CHAPTER 10

THE STEERING GEAR

10 : 1 Operating principles and construction

The steering gear is of the rack and pinion type, the general arrangement of which is shown in **FIG 10 : 1** and details of the components in **FIG 10 : 2.** Referring to the former illustration, movement of the steering wheel 9 is transmitted by the steering shaft to a helically-toothed pinion 3 in the steering gearbox, which is mounted on the front crossmember. As a safety measure the steering shaft is constructed in two parts which are connected by the universal joint 6.

The pinion meshes with teeth machined at one end of the rack 2, which is contained in a tubular housing with gaiters firmly secured by clips at each end to maintain lubrication and to exclude road dirt. Rotary movement of the pinion engaging the teeth in the rack causes the latter to move transversely from side to side. To provide for relative movement within the steering linkage, universal joints at each end of the rack connect it to the track rods 4 and 5. Turning movement is then transmitted to the front wheels through the ball joints connecting the track rods to the steering arms in the front swivel hubs. The lefthand track rod 5 is adjustable for length. The turning radius between kerbs is 5.20 m (17 ft) and between walls 5.45 m (18 ft). An anti-theft steering lock 8 is provided on the steering shaft housing.

10 : 2 Routine maintenance

Maintenance attention is mainly concerned with the periodic lubrication of the steering gear. A grease nipple (see **FIG 10 : 7**) is fitted on the retaining plate of the rack plunger 11 in **FIG 10 : 1** and other grease nipples on each of the track rod ball joints (see **FIG 10 : 40**). Lubrication at these points with an approved lubricant, for which the manufacturers recommend Esso Multipurpose Grease H, should be given every 5000 km or 3000 miles. At the same time examine the steering gear bellows on each side for damage or wear. If any such signs are apparent the bellows should be renewed, referring to **Section 10 : 4** for details of attachment.

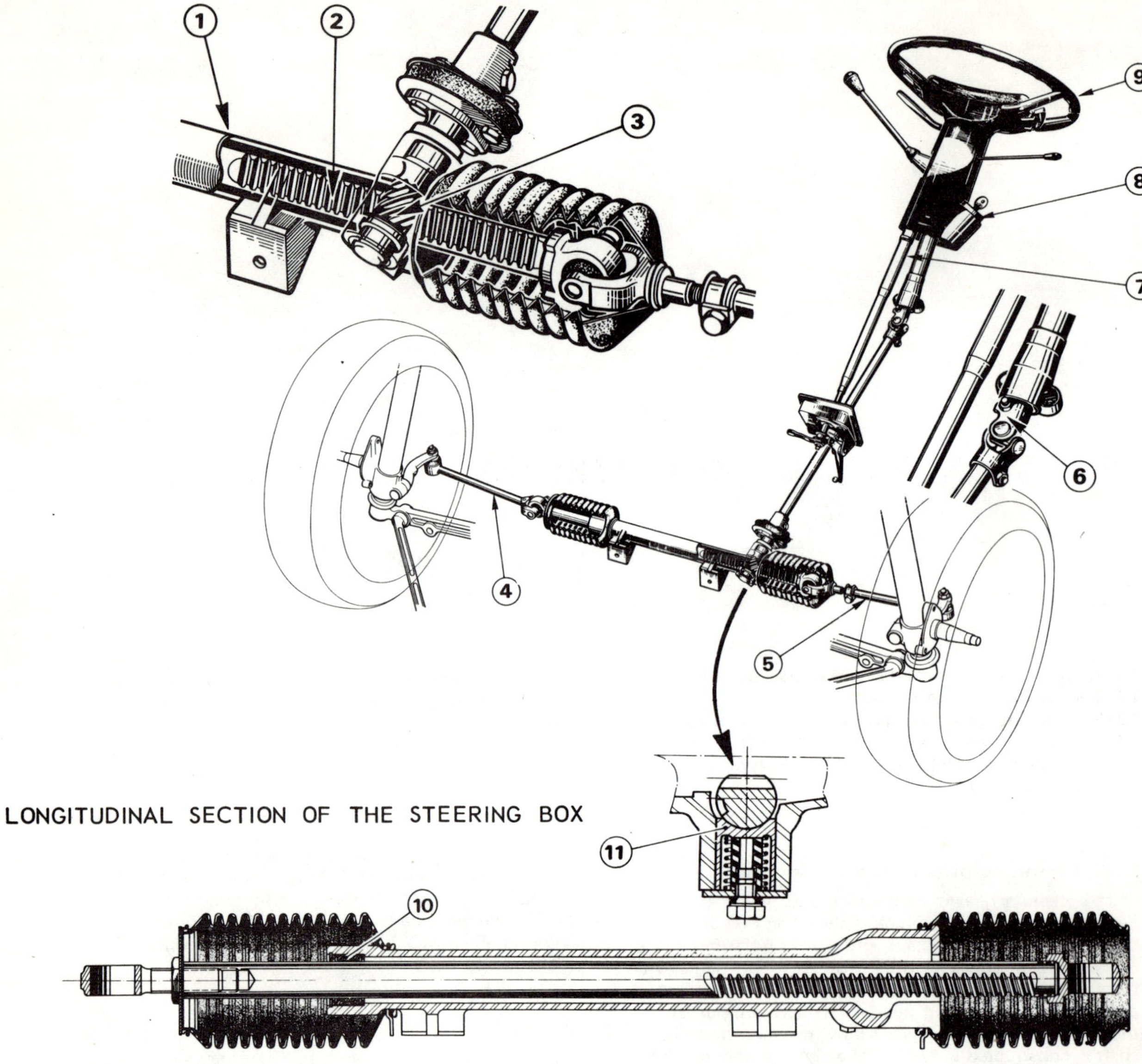

FIG 10:1 A view of the steering gear

Key to Fig 10:1 1 Steering box 2 Rack 3 Pinion 4 Righthand track rod 5 Lefthand track rod (adjustable in length) 6 Cardan-jointed steering column 7 Gearchange control arm 8 Anti-theft steering lock support 9 Steering wheel 10 Flexible guide bush for the rack 11 Rack plunger

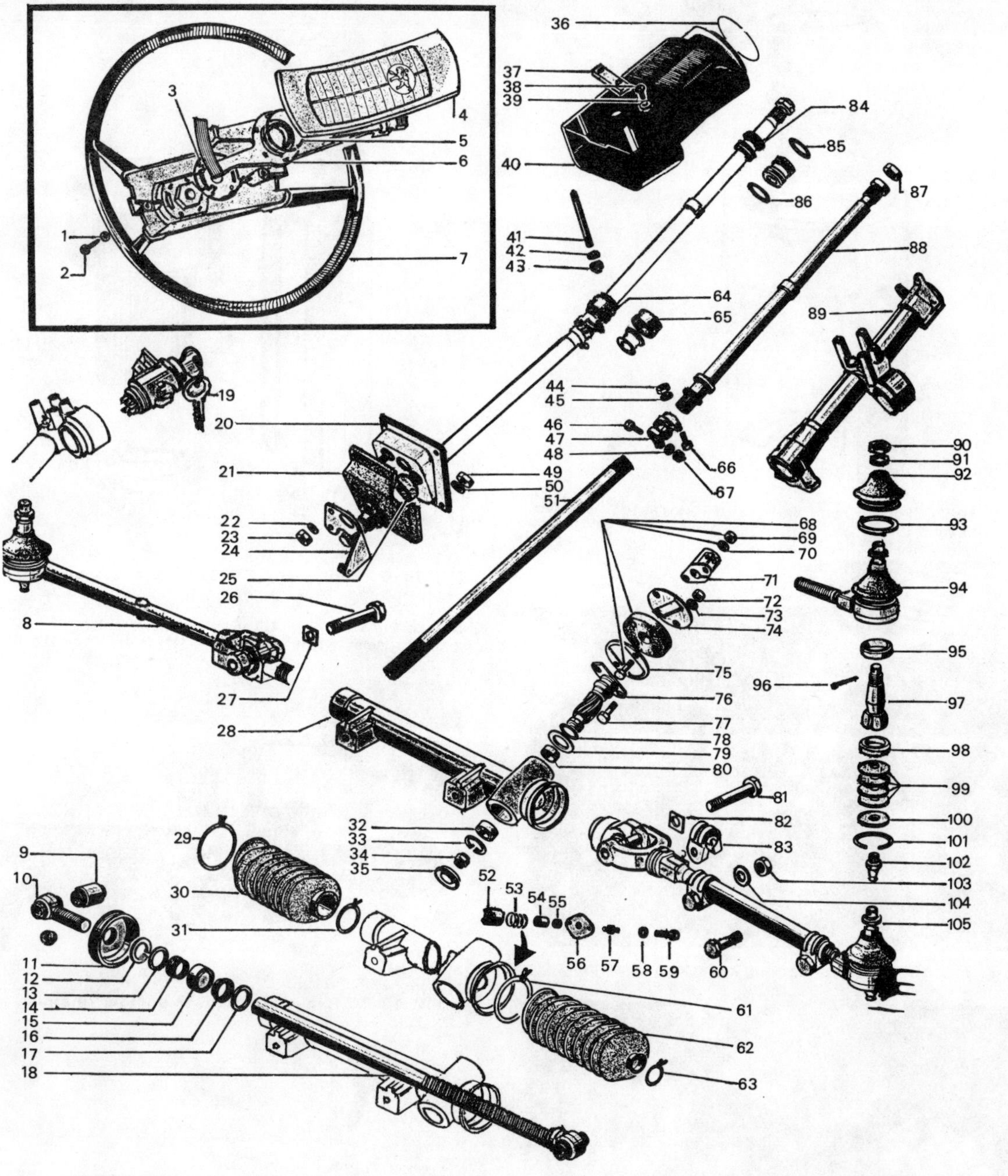

FIG 10:2 An exploded view of the steering gear

Key to Fig 10:2 1 Washer 2 Screw 3 Horn contact plate 4 Escutcheon 5 Spring 6 Horn push 7 Steering wheel 8 Track rod 9 Silentbloc bush 10 Rack eye end 11 Boot adaptor 12 Circlip 13 Washer 14 Flexible bush 15 Distance piece 16 Flexible bush 17 Washer 18 Rack 19 Steering lock assembly 20 Coverplate 21 Gasket 22 Washer 23 Nut 24 Bracket 25 Grommet 26 Bolt 27 Nut 28 Rack guide tube 29 Clip 30 Boot 31 Clip 32 Bearing 33 Circlip 34 Nut 35 Sealing cup 36 Circlip 37 Adaptor 38 Screw 39 Nut 40 Fairing 41 Stud 42 Shakeproof washer 43 Nut 44 Nut 45 Shakeproof washer 46 Bolt 47 Cardan joint 48 Shakeproof washer 49 Nut 50 Washer 51 Lower steering shaft 52 Plunger 53 Spring 54 Nylon stop 55 Shims 56 Retaining plate 57 Greaser 58 Washer 59 Screw 60 Bolt 61 Clip 62 Boot 63 Clip 64 Lower steering shaft bush assembly 65 Bush 66 Clamp bolt 67 Nut 68 Flector and bolt assembly 69 Nut 70 Washer 71 Flector to steering shaft clamp 72 Nut 73 Washer 74 Upper flector plate 75 Lower flector plate 76 Pinion 77 Bolt 78 O-ring 79 Thrust washer 80 Pinion bush 81 Bolt 82 Nut 83 Clamp 84 Upper steering shaft bush assembly 85 Locating ring 86 Locating ring 87 Nut 88 Upper steering shaft 89 Steering column 90 Nut 91 Washer 92 Boot 93 Clip 94 Ball joint assembly 95 Upper steel cup 96 Splitpin 97 Ball head 98 Lower nylon cup 99 Belleville washers 100 Ball joint cover 101 Circlip 102 Greaser 103 Nut 104 Washer 105 Adjustable track rod assembly

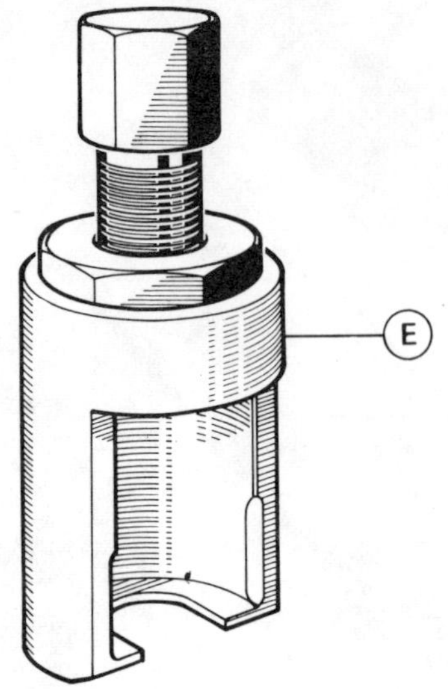

FIG 10:3 **Track rod ball joint extractor E, No. 8.0703.W**

FIG 10:4 **Disconnecting a track rod ball joint**

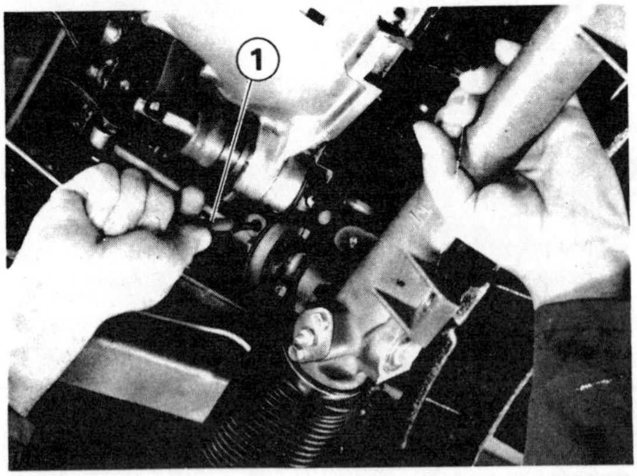

FIG 10:5 **Disengaging the steering column using a centre punch 1 in place of the flector bolt**

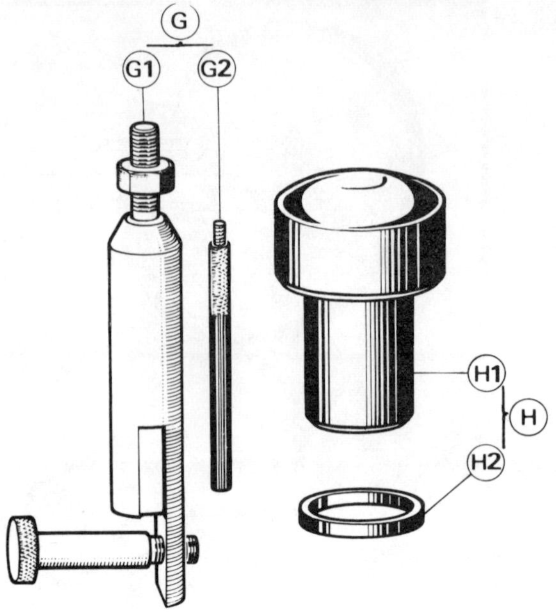

FIG 10:6 **Tools No. 8.0703.W for dismantling and reassembling steering gear**

Key to Fig 10:6 **G1** Dial indicator holder **G2** Dial indicator feeler extension **H1** Drift **H2** Spacer

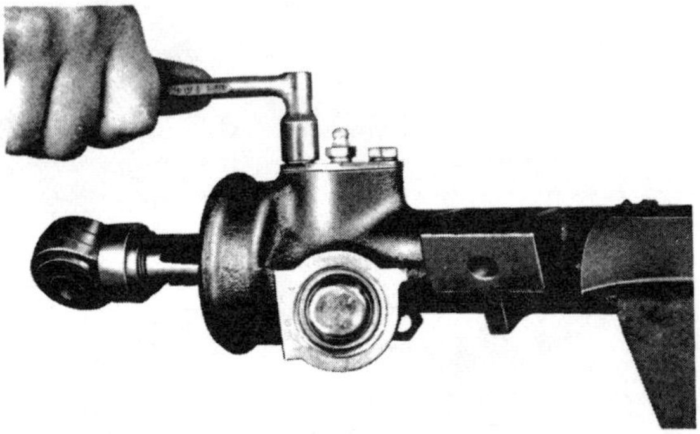

FIG 10:7 **Removing the rack plunger retaining plate**

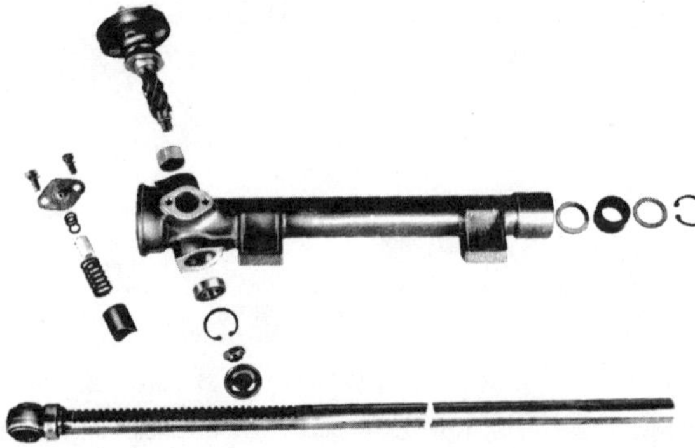

FIG 10:8 **An exploded view of the rack and pinion mechanism**

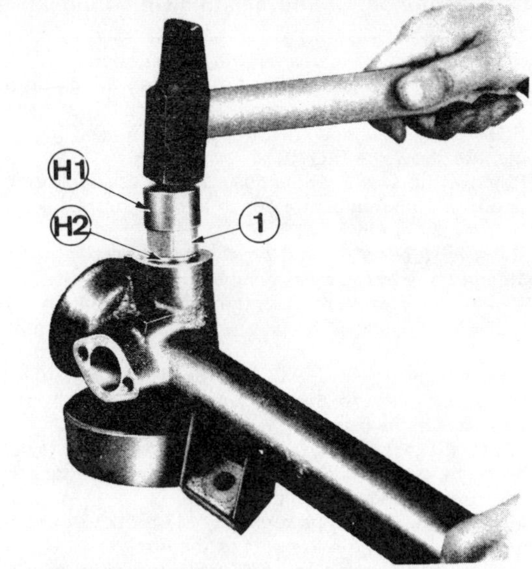

FIG 10:9 Renewing a pinion bush **1** with the aid of the drift **H1** and the spacer **H2**

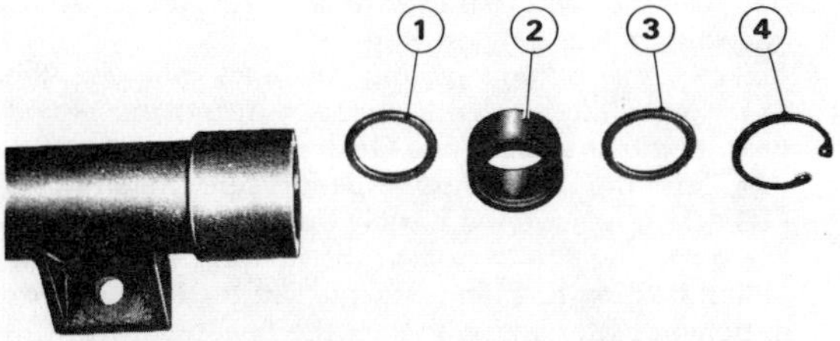

FIG 10:10 Rack housing details

Key to Fig 10:10 1 Inner thrust washer 2 Flexible bush 3 Outer thrust washer 4 Circlip

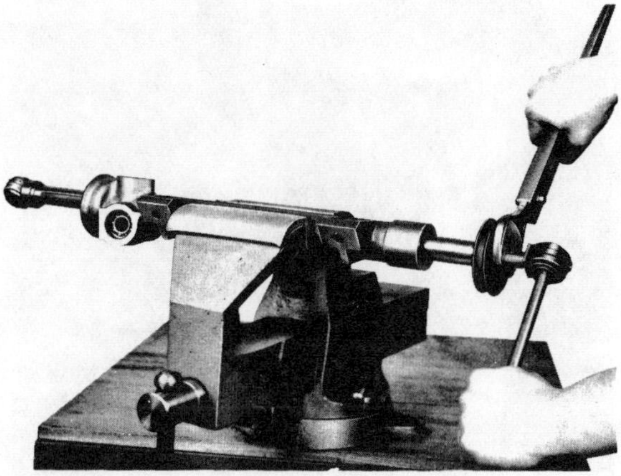

FIG 10:11 Locating the rack in the steering box

FIG 10:12 The locknut **5** positioned in contact with the steering box

FIG 10:13 Locating the pinion, with the nut locking groove **1** positioned as shown

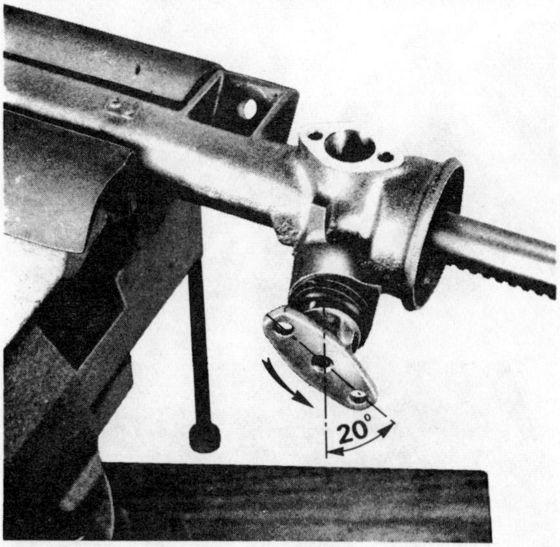

FIG 10:14 Pinion positioned at 20 deg. from the vertical

FIG 10:15 **Fitting the pinion, with the locknut 2 in contact with the steering box**

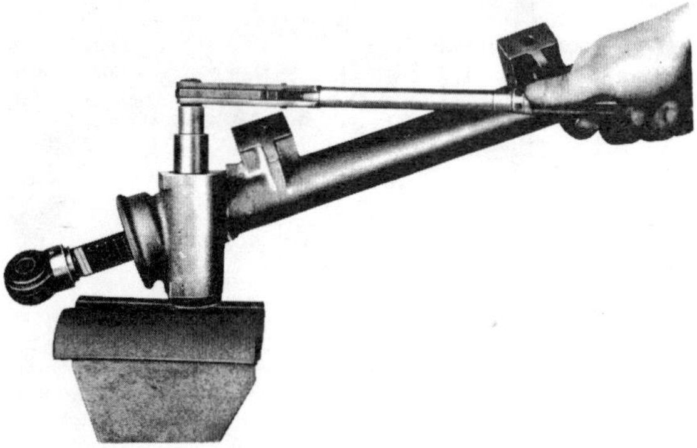

FIG 10:16 **Fitting a new pinion nut**

10:3 Steering gear removal and dismantling

To remove the steering gear proceed as follows:

1 Raise the front of the car and fit firm supports.
2 Disconnect the track rod ball joints with the aid of a suitable extractor. The service tool No. 8.0703E (see **FIG 10:3**) designed for the purpose is used in the manner shown in **FIG 10:4.**
3 Remove the steering column to flector assembly bolt and insert a 6 mm centre punch in place of the flector bolt, as shown in **FIG 10:5.**
4 Remove the two Allen-type screws securing the steering box to the crossmember.
5 Disengage and withdraw the steering column by rocking the flector slightly, using the centre punch as a lever.

The service tools No. 8.0703W used for dismantling and reassembly of the steering are shown in **FIG 10:6.** Procedure is as follows:

1 Clamp the steering box in a vice fitted with lead jaws. Mark the position of the flector collar with the rack in the straight-ahead position.
2 Remove the four clips retaining the rubber boots or bellows. Push the two boots to the right.
3 Unlock and remove the two track rod yoke pivots. Remove the two track rods.
4 Clamp the rack directly in the vice, fitted with aluminium jaws, to slacken the locknut, as shown in **FIG 10:7,** and remove the rack eye on the opposite side of the pinion.
5 Remove the rack plunger retaining plate, with its grease nipple and nylon stop.
6 Remove the plunger spring, the rack plunger, the bearing sealing cup, the pinion nut and the pinion with its thrust washer and O-ring.
7 Withdraw the rack from the pinion side. Referring to **FIG 10:8,** remove the flexible bush retaining circlips, the bush and the two steel thrust washers, also the pinion bearing retaining circlips. Dip the steering box in boiling water and withdraw the bearing.

FIG 10:17 **Locking the pinion nut**

FIG 10:18 **Fitting a new sealing cup**

8 Carefully clean the steering box and all the mechanical components. Inspect the rack and the pinion and renew these components if necessary. Note that the eye on the toothed end is part of the rack, but the silentbloc is renewable as described later in **Section 10:6.**

10:4 Steering gear reassembly and refitting

Procedure for reassembling and refitting the steering gear is as follows:

1 Renewal of the pinion nut, the bearing sealing cup and the Blocfor washers is advised as a matter of course during reassembly. Depending upon condition and wear, renew also the pinion bearing, the pinion bush, the flexible bush together with its rubber rings, the nylon plunger spacer and the rubber boots and clips.

2 To renew a pinion bush, place on the drift (see **FIG 10:9**) in order a new bush 1 and the spacer H2. Insert the drift in the old bush and tap the drift until it comes into contact with the steering box. From inside the steering box recover the used bush and the spacer H2.

3 Proceed to reassemble by greasing the bearing with Esso Multipurpose Grease H. Immerse the steering box in boiling water for a few minutes, then install the bearing in its housing, pressing on the outer race. Fit the circlip.

4 Insert in the housing, in the opposite end to the pinion, the inner thrust washer 1 (see **FIG 10:10**), the flexible bush equipped with its two rubber rings 2, the outer thrust washer 3 and the circlip 4.

5 Grease the rack and flexible bush, then insert the rack in the box, pinion side (see **FIG 10:11**). Thread temporarily the second eye on the rack together with its locknut, which should be tightened slightly.

6 Push the rack until the locknut 5 shown in **FIG 10:12** comes into contact with the steering box.

7 Grease the pinion, then locate in the machined pinion housing the O-ring followed by the thin metal thrust washer. Now locate the pinion in its bore, with the nut locking groove 1 (see **FIG 10:13**) facing away from the plunger housing.

8 Starting from the vertical position of the pinion flange, rotate it to the left through approximately 20 deg. as shown in **FIG 10:14.**

9 Push in the pinion until it abuts in the bearing. The pinion flange should be vertical (see **FIG 10:15**), with the locknut 2 still in contact with the extremity of the steering box.

10 Clamp the pinion flange in the vice fitted with soft jaws. Fit a new nut and tighten to 1.5 kg m (11 lb ft) as shown in **FIG 10:16.**

11 Lock the nut by tapping the nut collar into the groove on the pinion in the manner shown in **FIG 10:17.**

12 Grease the bearing housing with Esso Multipurpose Grease H. Fit the new sealing cup, tapping it into place with a mallet as shown in **FIG 10:18.**

13 The rack plunger must be assembled so that it has a free play of .10±.05 mm at the highest point of the rack, for which it is necessary to use a dial gauge. Commence by inserting the plunger in its housing, then place the spring inside the plunger.

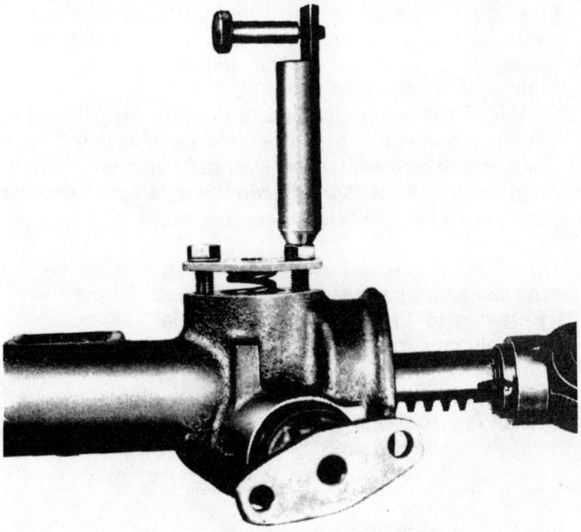

FIG 10:19 Assembly of thrust plate and dial indicator holder to measure the play in the plunger

FIG 10:20 Method of measuring vertical movement of rack during sideways movement

14 Attach the thrust plate by itself on the housing, securing it on one side with a 7 mm bolt and on the other side with a dial indicator holder 8.0703.G1 or similar fixture, as shown in **FIG 10:19.** Tighten the plate on the housing.

15 Referring to **FIG 10:20,** fit the extension feeler G2 to the dial indicator and position it in contact with the plunger through the threaded hole in the plate.

16 Slide the rack from one side to the other of the steering box using the pinion. The hands of the dial indicator will show the high spots in the vertical movement of the rack during its displacement.

17 Mark the highest point indicated by the hand towards the right. Set the dial at zero at this point.

18 Using a lever as shown in **FIG 10:21**, raise the rack without forcing it until it abuts. Check the degree of movement registered on the dial indicator and note the value for the time being.

19 Remove the dial indicator and the plunger. Place the nylon stop inside the plunger and position a flat steel rule or a square edge plate over the nylon stop, when there should be a gap between the nylon stop and the rule (see **FIG 10:22**).

20 Eliminate this gap by adjusting washers, using the smallest number of washers possible. Washers are available in thicknesses of .10, .20 and .50 mm.

21 Referring to **FIG 10:23**, for the final adjustment of the plunger to obtain the free play specified in Operation 13, subtract .10 mm from the value previously obtained. The thickness of shims required should be added to those which are used to eliminate the clearance between the plunger and the nylon stop.

FIG 10:21 Checking vertical movement of rack

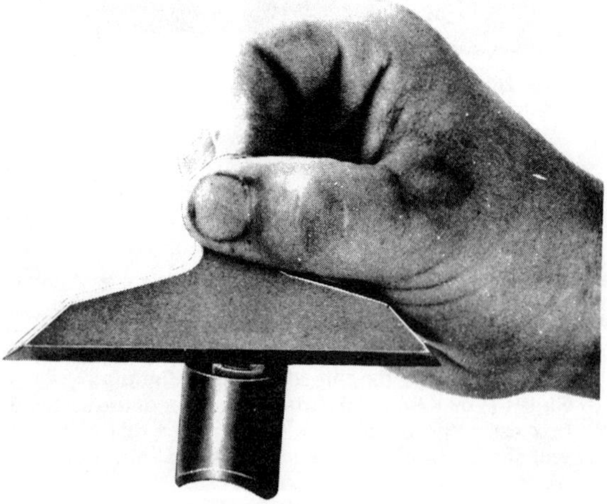

FIG 10:22 Examining clearance of nylon stop

22 Fit the grease nipple (see **FIG 10:24**) on the thrust plate and tighten it to a torque of 1 kg m (7.2 lb ft).

23 Assemble the shims determined in Operation 21 and the nylon stop. Locate the plunger and spring in their housing in the steering box.

24 Secure the thrust plate assembly (see **FIG 10:25**) with two 7 mm dia. bolts equipped with new Blocfor washers. Tighten the bolts to a torque of 1 kg m (7.2 lb ft). Grease the plunger with Esso Multipurpose Grease H.

25 Remove the eye from the rack on the opposite end to the pinion and fit the rubber boot. Refit and adjust the rack eye to obtain a clearance of 20 to 21 mm between the locknut and the shoulder of the eye, as shown in **FIG 10:26**.

26 Align the moveable eye with the fixed eye using two 12 mm diameter rods inserted in the inner rings of the silentblocs as shown in **FIG 10:27**. Tighten the locknut moderately to secure the eye.

27 Turn the pinion to disengage sufficiently the rack. Clamp the rack in a vice fitted with aluminium jaws. Tighten the locknut to a torque of 3.5 kg m (25 lb ft) to ensure the complete security of the eye as shown in **FIG 10:28**.

28 Locate the yoke of the track rod on the pinion side of the rack. Place the track rod in line with the track, with the head of the bolt on the same side as the pinion flange. Use a new tab washer and tighten the bolt (see **FIG 10:29**) to a torque of 4.5 kg m (33 lb ft). Bend the tab washer up around the bolt head.

29 Fit the rack boot on the pinion side so that the larger axis is perpendicular to the bearing faces of the mounting flanges on the steering box on the main crossmember. The prongs 1 on the clips (see **FIG 10:30**) must face the lower part of the steering box. Note that the prongs of the clips are shaped in such a way that they interlock easily using a pair of pliers. Do not attempt to bend them out of their original shape.

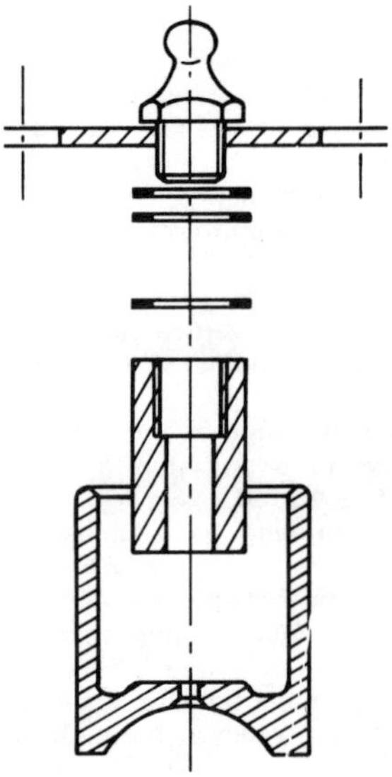

FIG 10:23 Diagram to show final adjustment of plunger

30 To obtain the necessary pre-adjustment of the pinion side track rod, adjust the distance between the shoulders of the yoke and ball joint housing to 180 mm as shown in **FIG 10 : 31.** Equalize the distance between the shoulders and the adjuster rod. The tightening of the two bolts 2 is effected with the steering gear in position on the car, after adjusting the toe-in of the front wheels (see **Section 10 : 8**).

31 Fit the rack boot on the opposite end to the pinion, following the instructions in Operation 29.

32 Fit the one-piece track rod to the rack, positioning the rod in line with the rack (see **FIG 10 : 32**). Fit a new tab lock and tighten the bolt to a torque of 4.5 kg m (33 lb ft). Bend the tab up around the bolt head.

33 To mount the flector (see **FIG 10 : 33**), fit four new Blocfor washers and bolts with the heads of the bolts towards the steering box. Position the plates on both sides of the flector with the holes forming a cross and secure the flector thus assembled to the pinion flange.

34 Centre the rack, in relation to the steering box, to the straight-ahead position, then fit the clamp to the flector using the reference mark made whilst dismantling.

35 Check that in the straight-ahead position the bore of the collar bolt hole is parallel to the rack and that the thrust faces of the pinion flange and the collar are in contact with the flector through the holes in the plates. Finally tighten the four retaining nuts to a torque of 1.75 kg m (13 lb ft) and lock the bolts (see **FIG 10 : 34**) by spreading the threads with a cold chisel.

FIG 10 : 25 Refitting the thrust plate assembly

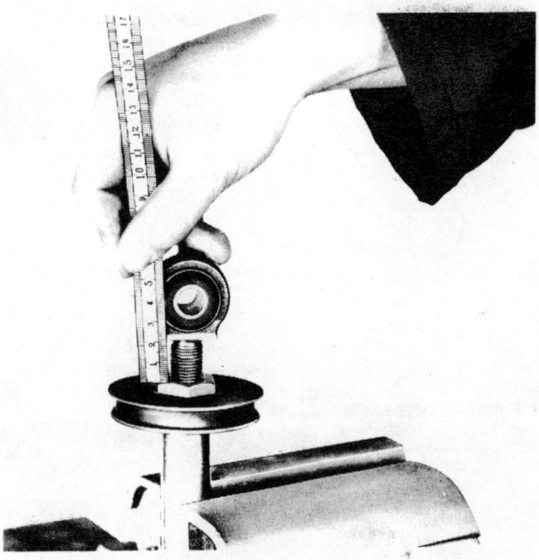

FIG 10 : 26 Adjusting the rack eye

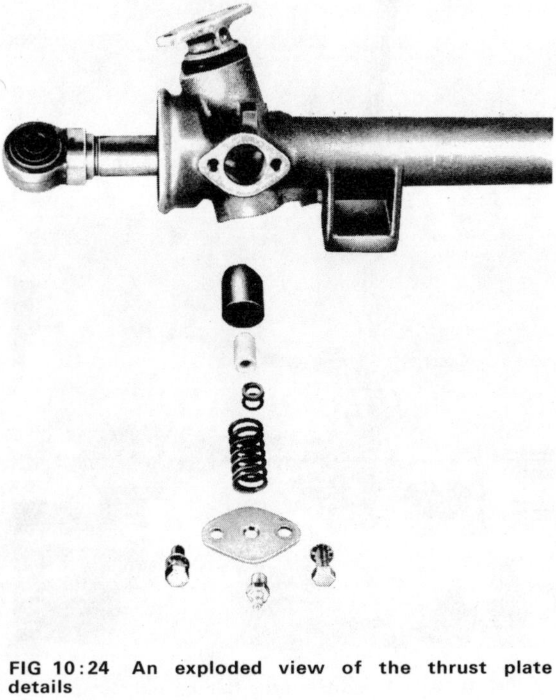

FIG 10 : 24 An exploded view of the thrust plate details

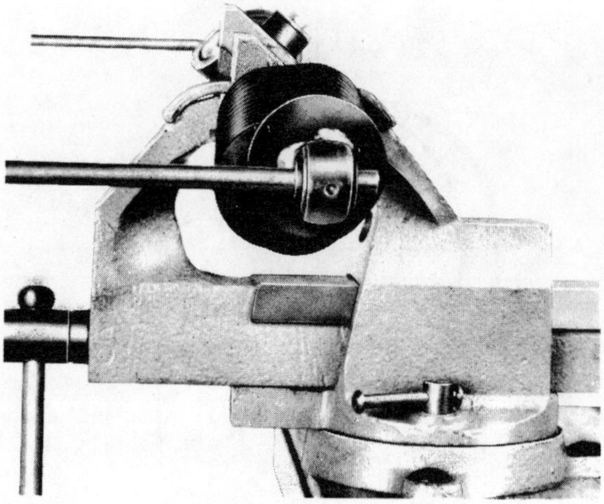

FIG 10 : 27 Aligning the movable eye

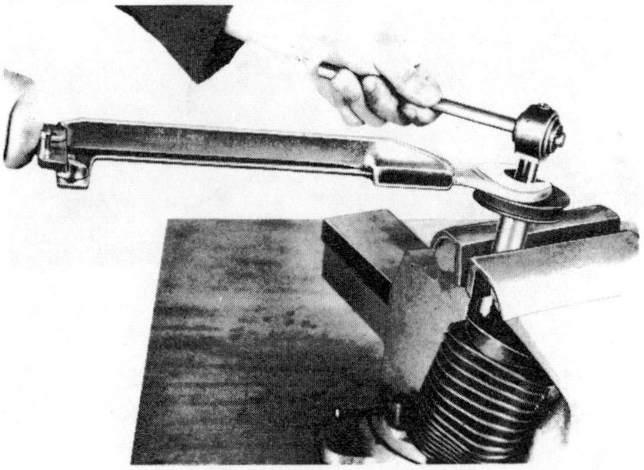

FIG 10:28 Tightening the eye locknut

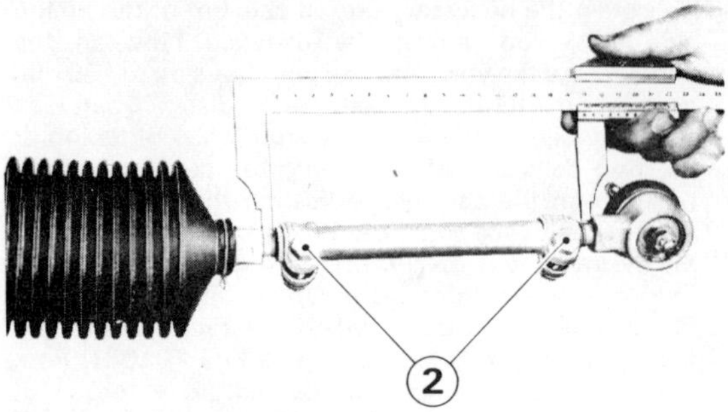

FIG 10:31 Pre-adjustment of the pinion side track rod, showing the clamp bolts **2**

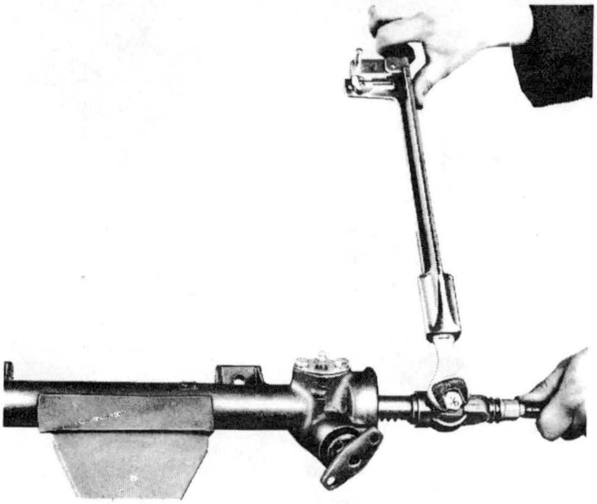

FIG 10:29 Reassembling a track rod

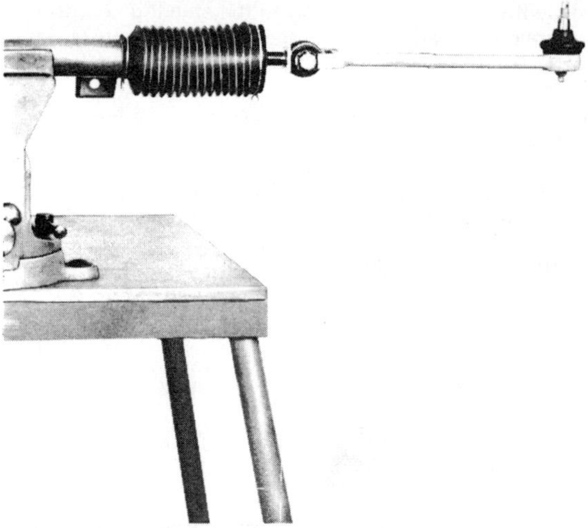

FIG 10:32 The one-piece track rod assembled to the rack

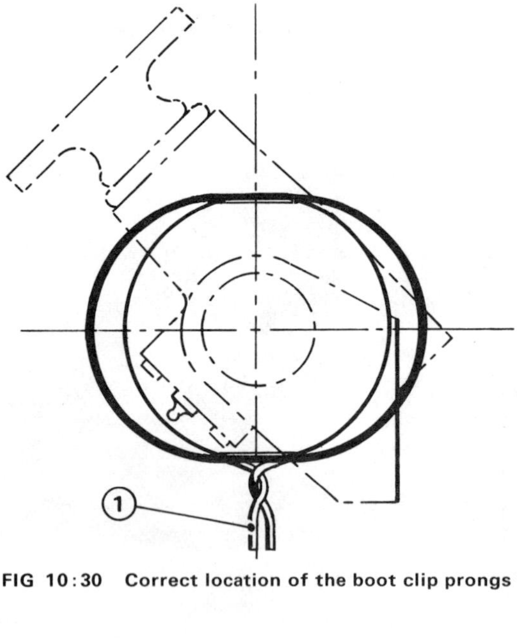

FIG 10:30 Correct location of the boot clip prongs **1**

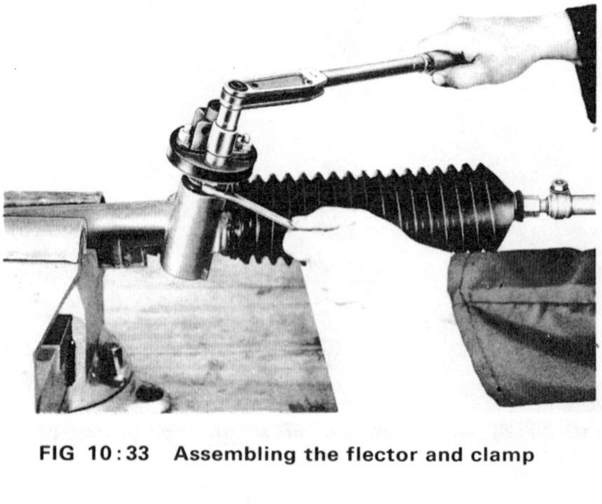

FIG 10:33 Assembling the flector and clamp

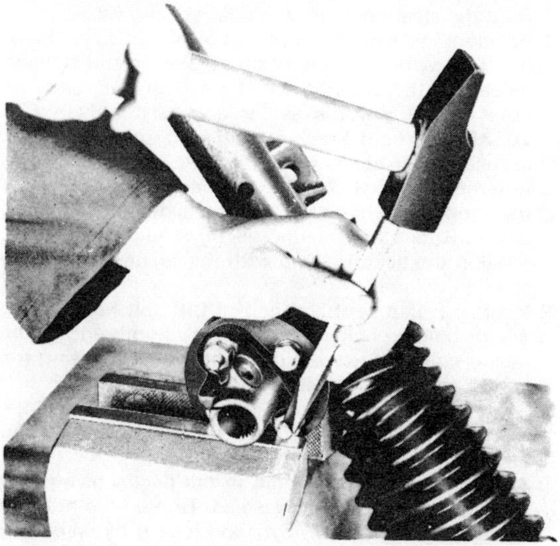

FIG 10:34 Locking the flector bolts

FIG 10:35 Front wheel positions for refitting the steering gear

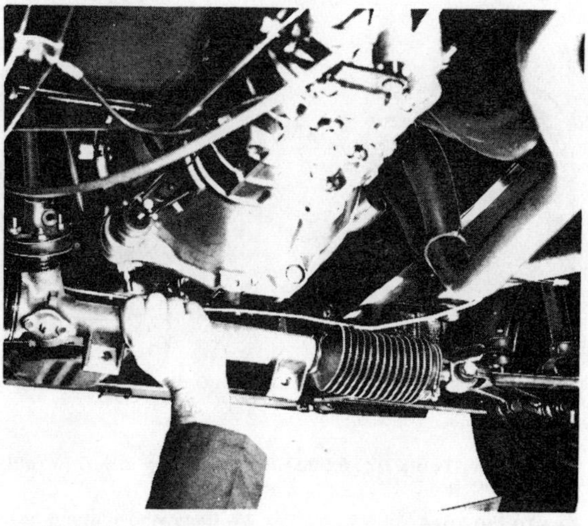

FIG 10:36 Locating the steering gear on the car

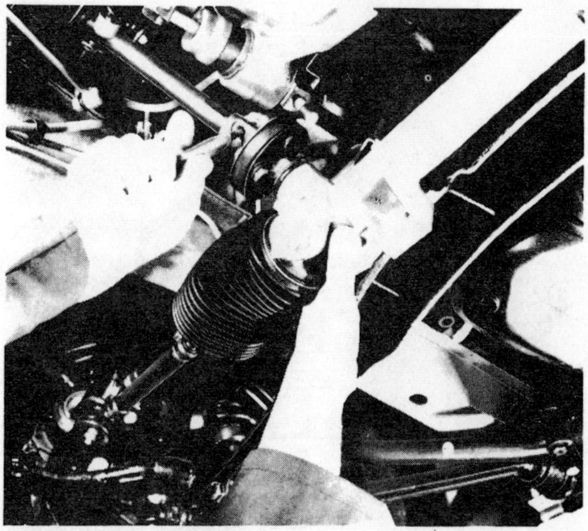

FIG 10:37 Inserting the steering column in the flector collar with the aid of a centre punch as a lever

FIG 10:38 Securing the steering column in the flector

FIG 10:39 Reconnecting the track rod ball joint on the steering wheel side

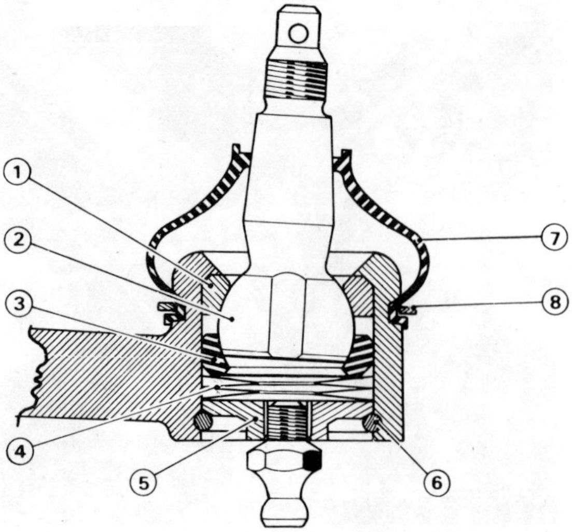

FIG 10:40 A sectional view of a ball joint

Key to Fig 10:40 1 Upper half cup (steel) 2 Ball head 3 Lower half cup (nylon) 4 Belleville washers 5 Ball joint cover 6 Spring clip 7 Rubber boot 8 Clip

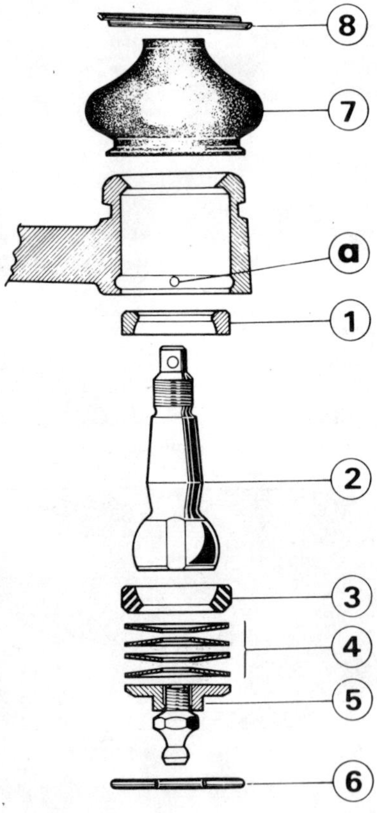

FIG 10:41 An exploded view of a ball joint

Key to Fig 10:41 1 Upper half cup (steel) 2 Ball head 3 Lower half cup (nylon) 4 Belleville washers 5 Ball joint cover 6 Spring clip 7 Rubber boot 8 Clip
a Hole for pin punch

Refit the steering gear to the car as follows:

1 Position the steering wheel spokes vertically. Place the front wheel, on the opposite side to the steering wheel, in the straight-ahead position and turn the other wheel inwards as far as possible (see **FIG 10:35**). Centre the rack in relation to the steering box in the straight-ahead position.
2 Referring to **FIG 10:36,** connect temporarily the track rod ball joint on the opposite side to the steering wheel. Rotate the steering flector a quarter of a turn, to align the flector clamp with the splined end of the steering column.
3 Insert a 6 mm centre punch in the bolt hole on the flector collar. Locate the steering column end in the flector collar by rocking the flector slightly, using the centre punch as a lever as shown in **FIG 10:37.**
4 Secure the steering box to the crossmember. Tighten the screws to a torque of 3.25 kg m (23.5 lb ft), using an 8 mm Allen socket.
5 Secure the steering column in the flector using new nuts, bolts and Blocfor washers. Tighten the nut to a torque of 1 kg m (7.2 lb ft) and lock it by spreading the end of the bolt as shown in **FIG 10:38.**
6 Reconnect the track rod ball joint on the steering wheel side (see **FIG 10:39**), checking the alignment of the two flats on the ball joint housing and the connecting yoke. Position the ball joint pin holes perpendicular to the track rod axis. Fit new Blocfor washers, tighten the nuts to a torque of 4.25 kg m (31 lb ft), and pin carefully both ball joints. Adjust the wheel toe-in as described in **Section 10:8.**

10:5 Track rod ball joints dismantling and reassembly

To overhaul a track rod ball joint, operations are as follows:

1 With the track rod removed as described in **Section 10:3,** clamp the rod in a vice. Referring to **FIG 10:40,** remove the clip 8 and the rubber boot 7.
2 Disengage the spring clip 6, for the ball joint cover, using a pin punch inserted in hole 'a' provided (see **FIG 10:41**).

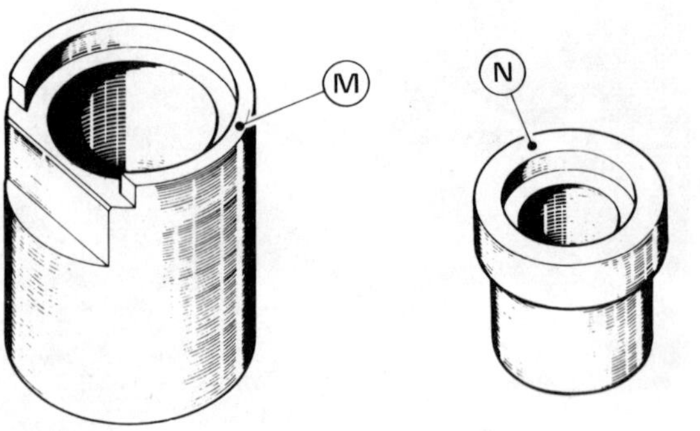

FIG 10:42 Tools No. 8.0907 for renewing steering rack flexible bushes

Key to Fig 10:42 **M** Removing-refitting base **N** Removing-refitting drift

3 Remove the ball joint cover 5, the Belleville washers 4, the lower nylon half cup 3, the ball head 2 and the upper steel half cup 1.

4 To reassemble place the steel half cup 1 in the bottom of the ball joint housing.

5 Locate in position the ball head 2, the nylon half cup 3, new Belleville washers 4, noting the direction of fitment and the ball joint cover 5.

6 Compress the Belleville washers and position a new spring clip 6.

7 Position correctly the ball head with the pin hole perpendicular to the track rod. Fit the rubber boot 7 and the clip **8** and grease the ball joint cover.

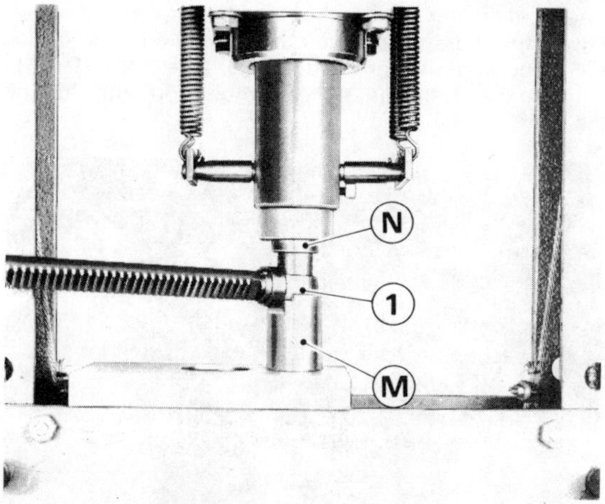

FIG 10:43 Removing a silentbloc from the steering rack eye 1 with the aid of the base M and the drift N

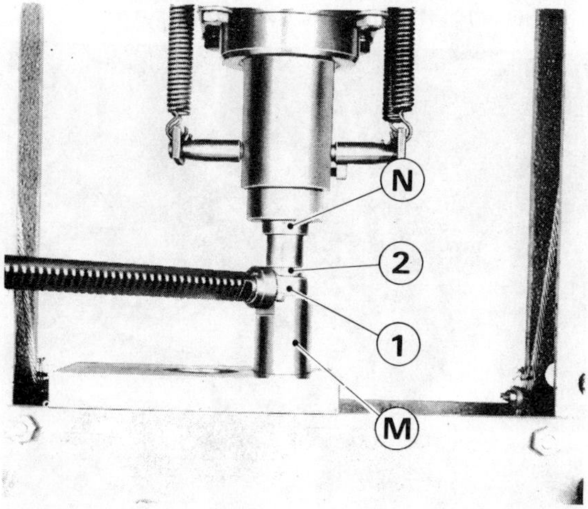

FIG 10:44 Fitting a new silentbloc 2 in the rack eye 1 with the aid of the base M and the drift N

FIG 10:45 Correct adjustment of a silentbloc

FIG 10:46 Removing the gearchange mechanism

Key to Fig 10:46 1 Upper gearchange control rod 2 Selector rod 3 Flector bolt

FIG 10:47 The lower shell removed from the steering column, showing the clip 4 retaining the pin assembling the gearchange control rods

FIG 10:48 Removing the assembly pin with the aid of a 6 mm drift

FIG 10:49 Removing the clamp bolt from the lower collar of the steering column cardan joint

FIG 10:50 The wiring harness disconnected

10:6 Renewal of steering rack flexible bushes

As the removal and refitting of a rack flexible bush normally requires the use of a press it may be desirable to use the facilities of a service agent for this work. Note that as the eye on the pinion end of the rack is not removable, the replacement of the silentbloc can be effected with rack removed from the steering box or with the mechanism assembled.

The tools No. 8.0907 used are shown in **FIG 10:42.** To remove a silentbloc, assemble on the press base plate the base M (see **FIG 10:43**), the steering rack eye 1 and the drift N with the smaller diameter facing the eye. Lower the press piston until the silentbloc falls into the base M.

To fit a new bush, smear with tallow the outside of the silentbloc and the inside of the rack eye. Assemble on the press base plate the base M, the rack eye 1, the new silentbloc 2 (see **FIG 10:44**) and the drift N, with the smaller diameter facing the silentbloc as for removal. Lower the press piston until the chamfered edge of the silentbloc protrudes from the eye (see **FIG 10:45**). Equalize the protrusion of the silentbloc on both sides of the eye if necessary.

FIG 10:51 The wiring harness set free

FIG 10:52 Withdrawing the upper steering column assembly

FIG 10:53 Withdrawing the lower bar of the steering column

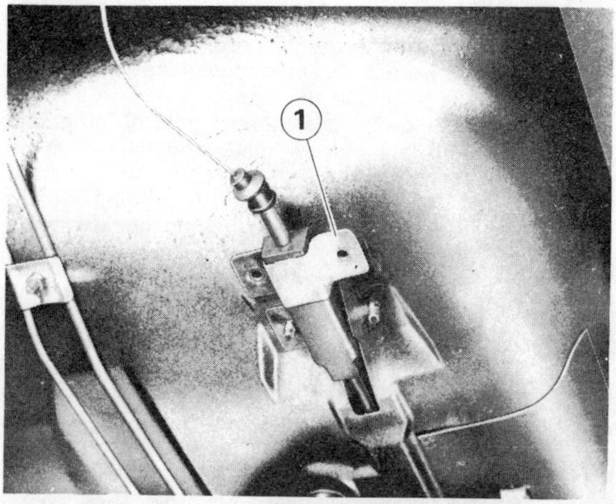

FIG 10:54 The handbrake outer cable stop clamp

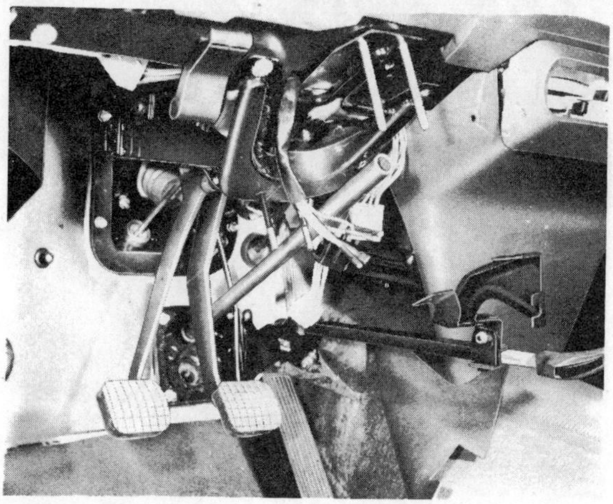

FIG 10:55 Steering column closing plate on scuttle, secured by four nuts

FIG 10:56 Removing the lower gearchange control assembly together with the closing plate

FIG 10:57 Refitting the lower gearchange control assembly together with the handbrake return lever support

FIG 10:58 Reconnecting the gear selector and change control rods to their respective levers

10:7 Steering column removal and refitting

To remove and refit the steering column, operations are undertaken as follows (disregard references to handbrake and gearchange for cars where these controls are floor-mounted):

1 Disconnect the battery. Referring to **FIG 10:46,** release the upper gearchange control rod 1, also the selector rod 2 from its lever. Remove the bolt 3 from the flector.

2 Remove the lower shell from the steering column. Move upwards the clip 4 (see **FIG 10:47**), which retains the pin assembling the gearchange control rods. Remove the pin, using a 6 mm drift, in the manner shown in **FIG 10:48.**

3 Remove the clamp bolt (see **FIG 10:49**) from the lower collar of the steering column cardan joint. Slide the lower part of the steering column downwards until it abuts on the flector.

4 Referring to **FIG 10:50,** disconnect the Neiman anti-theft lock wires and the three connectors on the steering column wiring harness. Remove the two bolts securing the handbrake lever support under the dashboard.

5 Remove the four bearing nuts of the column under the dashboard. Release simultaneously the two parts of the gearchange control rod and the steering column. Lower the handbrake lever support to enable the freeing of the wiring harness of the steering column (see **FIG 10:51**).

6 Withdraw the upper steering column assembly as shown in **FIG 10:52.**

7 Withdraw the lower bar of the steering column as far as possible as shown in **FIG 10:53** and disengage it towards the interior of the car.

8 Remove the handbrake outer cable stop clamp 1 in **FIG 10:54** to enable the withdrawal of the handbrake return lever in relation to the scuttle.

9 Remove the four nuts securing the steering column closing plate to the scuttle. Disengage the handbrake lever support from its securing studs (see **FIG 10:55**) to enable the freeing of the closing plate.

10 Remove the lower gearchange control assembly together with the closing plate and its gasket as shown in **FIG 10:56.**

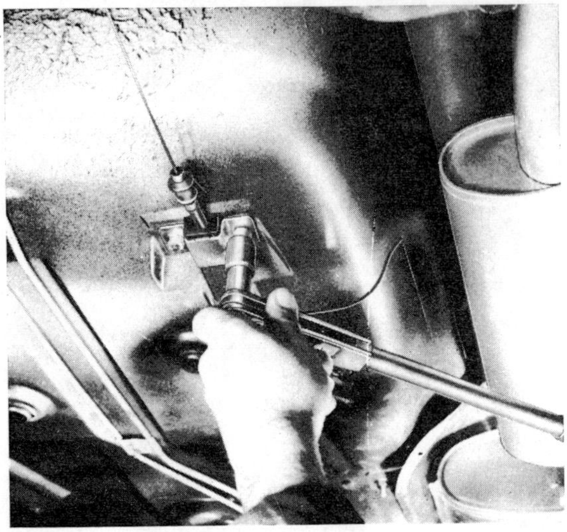

FIG 10:59 Securing the handbrake outer cable clamp to the floor

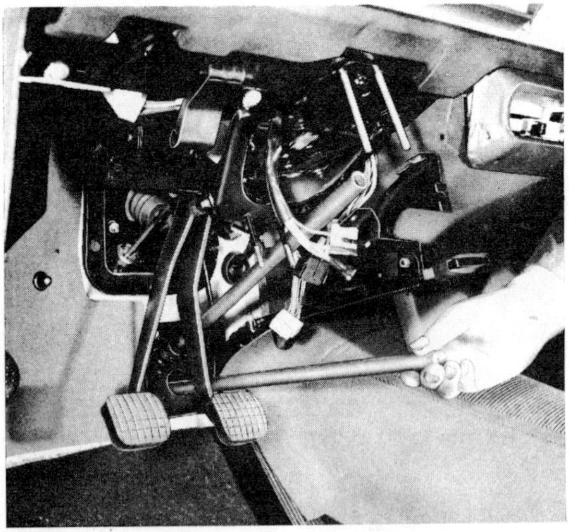

FIG 10:60 Locating the lower steering column rod in its bearing and in the flector collar

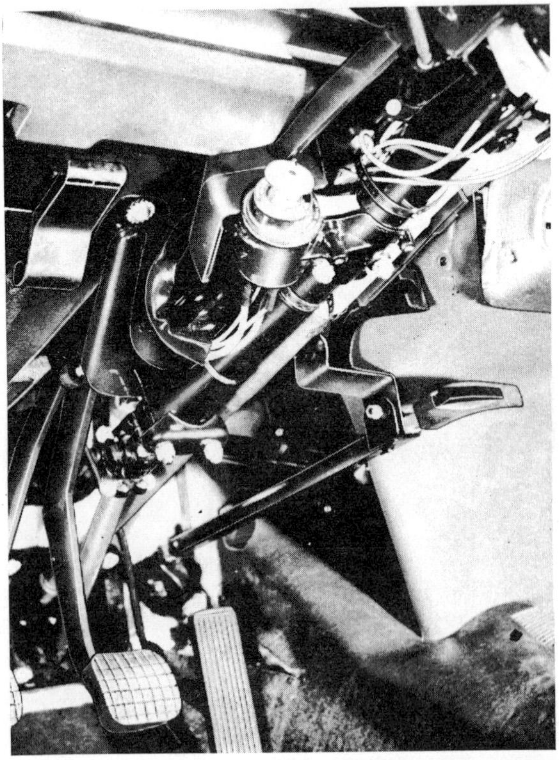

FIG 10:61 Fitting the steering column upper assembly

Refitting operations are as follows:

1 Renew, if necessary, the closing plate gasket. Refit the lower gearchange control assembly together with the handbrake return lever support. Secure the plate and the support using new star washers (see **FIG 10:57**) and tighten the nuts to a torque of 1 kg m (7.2 lb ft).
2 Reconnect the gear selector and change control rods to their respective levers (see **FIG 10:58**) ensuring the correct fitting of the nylon bearing on the ball head of the control rod.
3 Secure the handbrake outer cable clamp to the floor as shown in **FIG 10:59.** Tighten the nuts to a torque of .5 kg m (3.5 lb ft). Ensure the free movement of the handbrake lever, which should have neither free play nor tightness when in the 'at rest' position.
4 Grease thoroughly the lower steering column bush, which is fitted in the sealing plate. Insert the lower steering column rod (see **FIG 10:60**) in its bearing and in the flector collar. Push the rod home into the flector.
5 Referring to **FIG 10:61,** fit the upper assembly of the steering column. Connect simultaneously the two parts of the gearchange control rod and the steering column. Using new star washers, fit and tighten the four nuts, securing the steering column under the dashboard, to a torque of 1 kg m (7.2 lb ft).
6 Fit a new Mecanindus pin, to assemble the gearchange control rods. Position the retaining clip over the pin.
7 Secure the lower part of the cardan joint on the steering column using a new bolt, nut and Blocfor washer. Tighten the nut to a torque of 1 kg m (7.2 lb ft) and lock it by spreading the protruding end of the bolt.
8 Reconnect the Neiman anti-theft lock wires and the three wiring harness connectors on the steering column. Secure the harness under the dashboard.
9 Secure the column in the flector using a new nut, bolt and Blocfor washer. Tighten the nut to a torque of 1 kg m (7.2 lb ft) and lock it by spreading the protruding end of the bolt as shown in **FIG 10:62.**
10 Referring to **FIG 10:63,** secure the handbrake lever support under the dashboard. Reconnect the battery and reset the clock. Check the operation of the lighting, the indicators and the Neiman anti-theft lock.
11 Fit the lower shell of the steering column. Check and adjust, if necessary, the gearchange control rods and the horns.

FIG 10:63 The column shell refitted.

FIG 10:62 Securing the steering column in the flector

FIG 10:64 Adjusting the lefthand track rod 1 whilst holding the ball joint 2

10:8 Adjusting track

To meet the tendency of the front wheels to splay outwards when the car is in motion, the wheels are set slightly inwards to give a toe-in position of 3±1 mm (.12±.04 inch). Toe-in can be precisely determined in service workshops with the car wheels on turntables and using special proprietary equipment, or somewhat less accurately by ordinary measurement. For the latter, both front tyres are inflated to the same pressure with the car on level ground. Measure the distance between the tyres or the rims at wheel centre height at the front. Mark these two points of measurement and then roll the car forward for exactly half a revolution of the wheels, so that the marks finish up at the rear. Measure again between the marked points. The difference between the measurements is the amount of toe-in or toe-out.

Adjustment is made by altering the adjustable track rod length. Referring to **FIG 10:64,** slacken the two clamp nuts on the adjustable track rod 1. Hold the ball joint 2 in position with its two flats horizontal, using a 14 mm open-ended spanner. Then screw or unscrew the track rod to obtain the specified toe-in of 3±1 mm (.12±.04 inch). One turn of the track rod gives approximately 4.5 mm at the wheel rim. Hold the track rod in the position thus found and tighten the clamp nuts to a torque of 1.25 kg m (9 lb ft), at the same time ensuring that the ball socket 2 remains on a horizontal plane.

10:9 Fault diagnosis

(a) Wheel wobble

1 Unbalanced wheels and tyres
2 Slack steering connections
3 Incorrect steering geometry
4 Excessive play in steering gear
5 Steering gear loose on crossmember
6 Worn hub bearings

(b) Wander

1 Check 2, 3, 4 and 5 in (a)
2 Uneven tyre pressures
3 Uneven tyre wear
4 Defective dampers or springs

(c) Heavy steering

1 Check 3 in (a)
2 Very low tyre pressures
3 Neglected lubrication
4 Wheels out of track
5 Steering shaft bent or misaligned
6 Steering shaft bearings tight

(d) Lost motion

1 Loose steering wheel
2 Worn ball joints
3 Play on steering gear
4 Steering gear loose on crossmember

CHAPTER 11

THE BRAKING SYSTEM

11 :1 General description

Disc brakes are fitted on all four wheels, as shown for the front brakes in **FIG 11 :1** and the rear brakes in **FIG 11 : 2.** In rear brakes fitted to convertibles and coupés the disc is mounted inside the hub, but otherwise the main characteristics are the same as for saloon cars. The cast iron disc is attached to the hub by four bolts and fitted with a sheet-metal dished cap. The brake caliper incorporates two pistons on the same side of the disc, the brake pad on the other side being operated by the armature sliding in the caliper body. The brake pads on the rear brakes are of slightly smaller diameter than those at the front.

With the exception of a cable-operated handbrake the brakes are hydraulically operated through a master cylinder by means of a pendant pedal underneath the instrument panel. Assistance is provided by a vacuum servo unit, to reduce considerably the brake pedal effort provided by the driver. The servo unit is attached to the engine compartment rear bulkhead and is directly connected on one side to the brake pedal and to the master cylinder on the other side.

The master cylinder incorporates a brake fluid reservoir which serves both the brake and clutch hydraulic circuits. A float contact in the cap of the master cylinder operates a warning lamp on the instrument panel to give an indication of an excessively low level of fluid in the reservoir. The lamp also serves to signal when the brake pads have reached a stage of wear necessitating their renewal within the next 1000 km (620 mile) or to show that the handbrake has been applied. The reservoir is transparent, with a mark to indicate the maximum level of fluid required.

A brake compensating device which varies fore and aft braking effort according to load is linked to the rear suspension anti-roll bar. It includes a hollow piston of two different sections each fitted with a sealing ring. A hollow plug with a slot on its front face is screwed to the piston to act as a guide for a regulator valve held on its seat by a spring. A lever connects the device to the anti-roll bar by means of a spring, enabling the hydraulic pressure transmitted to the wheel cylinders to be varied according to the load being sustained by the rear axle.

The handbrake operates the brake pads on the rear wheels through a main cable, a compensating lever and two side cables. A self-adjusting mechanism on the rear wheels is provided to take up play and to ensure the effective operation of the handbrake over a long period. Its application is assisted by exerting light pressure on the footbrake at the same time to increase the pressure of the brake pads against the discs.

On estate cars, commercial vehicles and 504L, drum brakes are used instead of discs on the rear wheels. See **Section 11 :14**.

FIG 11 :1 A view of a front disc brake

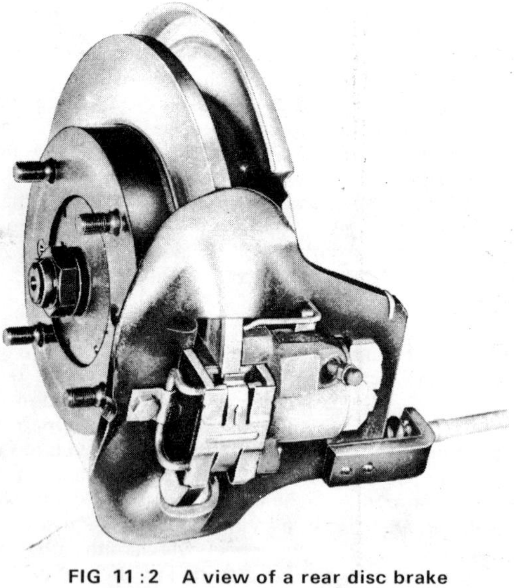

FIG 11 :2 A view of a rear disc brake

11 :2 Routine maintenance, handbrake adjustment

The level of the hydraulic brake fluid in the reservoir which is part of the master cylinder should be inspected at least every 800 km (500 miles) and topped up if necessary to the mark indicated on the outside of the reservoir. Wipe the cap before removing it, as well as the surrounding area, and **use only the Lockheed 55 brake fluid** recommended by the manufacturers. The latter also recommend that the brake system should be completely drained and refilled with the approved fluid every 20,000 km (12,000 miles) or otherwise every year, after which the system will require to be bled as described in **Section 11 :12.**

The disc brakes are self-adjusting. As the lining material of the brake pads becomes worn, fluid in the caliper cylinder and the pipelines to the master cylinder will compensate for the wear, and it follows that no manual adjustment is provided or required.

Adjustment of the handbrake (see **FIG 11 :3**) when necessary is undertaken as follows:

1 Ensure that the lever 3 abuts on the end of its housing and that the rear brake control levers 4 in **FIG 11 :4** abut on their nylon spacers on the pistons.

2 Referring to **FIG 11 :5,** unscrew the locknut and nut on the counter lever control rod. Renew if necessary the cup washers 5 on the traction rod.

3 Refit and tighten the nut to obtain a deflection of the cup washers of 1 to 1.5 mm, then refit and secure the locknut.

11 :3 Brake pads renewal

When brake pad renewal becomes necessary the pads for both brakes on the same axle must be renewed, hence new brake pads are only supplied in sets of four. No alteration should be made to the parts supplied, particularly as regards the separation of the linings from the plates. Whilst renewing brake pads, opportunity should be taken to check the condition of the wheel cylinders, the master cylinder and the brake liners, renewing such items if their continued serviceability appears doubtful. Note that only alcohol or clean brake fluid should be used for cleaning the cylinders or the pistons.

Operations are undertaken as follows:

1 Remove the wheel trims and slacken the wheel nuts.

2 Raise the car and fit firm supports under the cross-members at front and rear.

3 Mark the positions of the wheels on their respective hubs and remove the wheels under attention.

4 Disconnect the brake wear warning lead, then remove the brake pads thrust spring, the retaining fork securing bolt and the retaining fork.

5 Remove the worn pads. If the pads are difficult to withdraw, it is permissible to separate them using a lever placed squarely between the metal lips of the brake pads.

6 Check the surface condition of the brake discs, which must not bear any deep score marks, also the sealing of the wheel cylinders and the condition of the rubber protectors.

7 If suspect, check the disc for any warping which may be present. For this purpose it will be necessary to

remove the caliper (see **Sections 11 : 5** and **11 : 6**) and to use a dial gauge fitted as shown in **FIG 11 : 6** for front brakes and in **FIG 11 : 7** for rear brakes. The dial indicator feeler is set 25 mm from the outer edge of the disc and when the disc is rotated through one turn the maximum amount of warp must not exceed .07 mm. If it does, remove the hub and reposition the disc through a quarter of a turn for front brakes and half a turn for the rear. Secure the disc with new Blocfor washers, refit the hub and recheck the warp. If the limit is still exceeded, check the warp of the hub and renew disc or hub if necessary.

8 Clean the disc and the brake mechanism with alcohol. If the disc is greasy, it should be cleaned carefully with a cloth soaked in trichlorethylene.

9 If the brake calipers have been removed, refit them using new Blocfor washers. Tighten the bolts to a torque of 7 kg m (51 lb ft) for the front brakes and 4.25 kg m (31 lb ft) for the rear brakes.

10 To return the brake pistons in the rear brakes, position, in place of the inner brake pad, the piston positioning key G (see **FIG 11 : 8**) which should be lodged in the groove on the piston as shown in **FIG 11 : 9.**

11 Rotate the piston one eighth of a turn to bring the arm of the key G against the angle of the brake pad guide, in order to release the automatic handbrake play take-up device. Remove the key and make sure that the handbrake lever on the piston is well down on its nylon stop.

12 The front brakes having no mechanical play take-up system, there is no need to rotate the pistons in order to return them. Place the apparatus for returning the front and rear brake pistons E (see **FIG 11 : 8**) as indicated in **FIG 11 : 10.**

13 Fit a tube on the bleed nipple with the other end placed in a small container, then open the nipple one turn to prevent the brake fluid in the reservoir from overflowing.

14 Tighten the knurled screw of the apparatus E by hand until it abuts. Tools such as pliers must not be used. Retighten the bleed nipple and remove the apparatus E.

15 In rear brakes return the piston to its initial position using the key G, then remove the key.

16 Position the new brake pads on each side of the disc. Engage the retaining fork 1 (see **FIG 11 : 11**) and secure it to the armature using a bolt equipped with a new Grower washer. Tighten the bolt to a torque of 1.75 kg m (13 lb ft).

17 Position the thrust spring 2 with the arrow pointing upwards. Reconnect the brake pad wear warning light lead.

18 Proceed in an identical manner for each caliper when replacing the brake pads.

19 Check the brake fluid level and actuate the brake pedal a few times until a strong resistance is felt. This ensures that the brake pads are correctly positioned and bearing on the discs.

20 Refit the wheels and tighten the nuts to a torque of 6 kg m (43.5 lb ft). Carry out a road test.

21 After fitting new brake pads or discs the manufacturers emphasize that it is necessary to bed in the brakes for approximately 3000 km (1800 miles), as immediate intensive use of the brakes could cause future braking instability.

FIG 11 : 3 The handbrake lever 3 and its housing

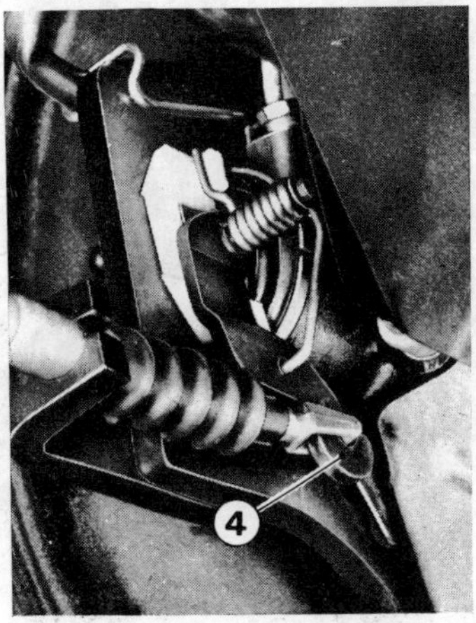

FIG 11 : 4 The handbrake lever 4 and nylon spacer

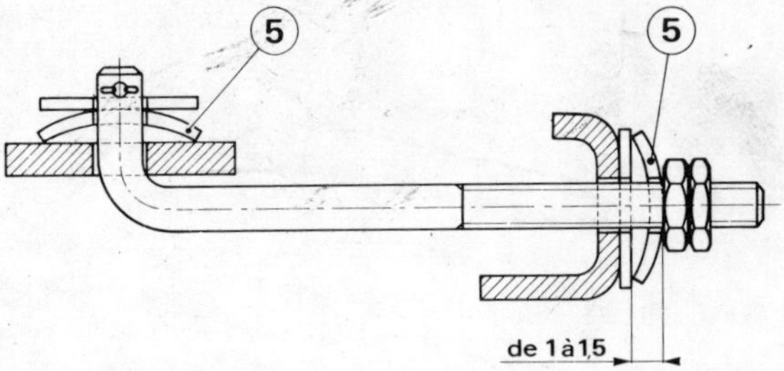

FIG 11 : 5 Handbrake adjusting mechanism showing cup washers 5

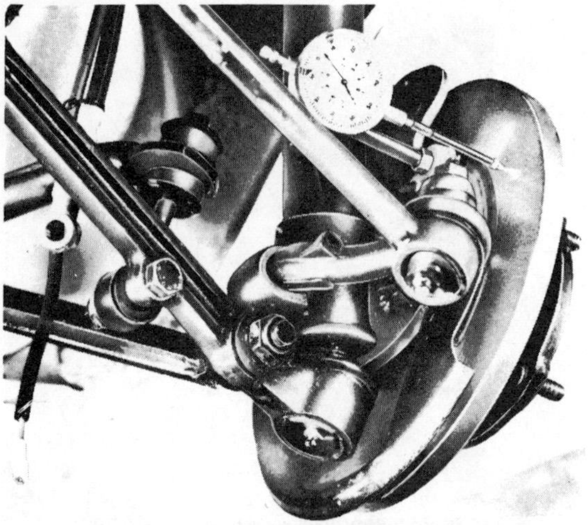

FIG 11 :6 Checking run-out of front disc

FIG 11 :7 Checking run-out of rear disc

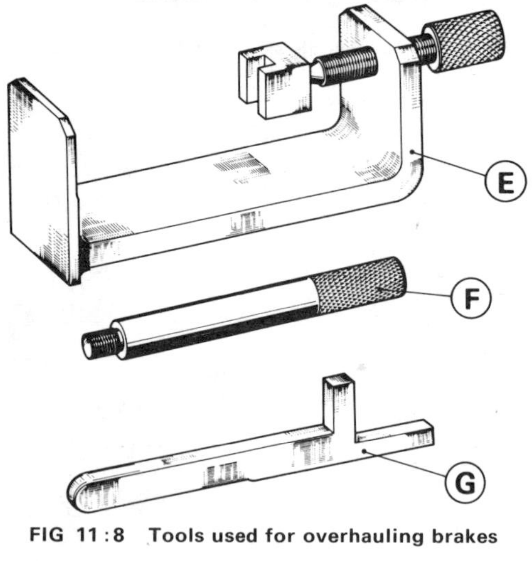

FIG 11 :8 Tools used for overhauling brakes

11 :4 Instructions on servicing hydraulic internals

Absolute cleanliness must be observed in all operations concerned with hydraulic components. When carrying out any work on the hydraulic system ensure that only clean approved brake fluid (see **Section 11 :2**) is used to top up or refill the system. It is inadvisable to re-employ brake fluid which has been extracted from the system during overhaul or bleeding operations. Aeration may persist and it may also be contaminated by traces of solvents in the container used or by particles of dust and grit.

All hydraulic parts must be washed in commercial alcohol, methylated spirits or approved brake fluid. Do not use mineral oils or cleaning fluid extracted from mineral oil such as petrol, paraffin or carbon tetrachloride, as they will cause the rubber seals to swell and become ineffective. Even the slightest trace of mineral oil could soon render the brakes unserviceable.

Pistons and piston seals should be kept away from any possibility of picking up oil or grease. Never replace hydraulic seals which have been used but always fit new seals from a service kit. Always immerse hydraulic components in clean, approved brake fluid when reassembling.

When removing or fitting hydraulic connecting hoses they must not be twisted or permanent damage will result. Always unscrew the union nuts on the metal pipes first. Hold the hexagon on the flexible hose with a second spanner as a precaution against its turning when removing the hose locknut at a bracket.

11 :5 Front brake caliper removal and refitting

To remove and refit a front brake caliper, operations are as follows:

1 Raise the front of the car and fit firm supports under the jacking crossmember. Mark the position of the wheels in relation to the hubs and remove the wheels.
2 Screw the closing plug F (see **FIG 11 :8**) into the master cylinder. Disconnect the brake wear warning lead and the union of the flexible hose from the wheel cylinder body.
3 Remove the caliper after removing the two retaining bolts. If difficulty is encountered, remove the thrust spring and the retaining fork. Separate the brake pads using a lever.

FIG 11 :9 Fitting the piston positioning key G

4 Remove the bleed nipple and drain the brake fluid from the wheel cylinder.
5 To refit the caliper, secure it to the steering swivel using new Blocfor washers (see **FIG 11 :12**). Tighten the bolts to a torque of 7 kg m (51 lb ft).
6 Reconnect the union for the flexible hose using new sealing washers.
7 If removed, refit in the following order:
(a) The brake pads, with the one housing the wear warning lead on the inside.
(b) The retaining fork.
(c) The fork securing bolt equipped with a new Grower washer and tightened to a torque of 1.75 kg m (13 lb ft).
8 Refit the thrust spring with the arrow facing upwards.
9 Reconnect the brake wear warning lead and remove the master cylinder closing plug. Bleed the brake system as described in **Section 11 :12.**
10 Refit the front wheels according to the marks made during removal and tighten the nuts to a torque of 6 kg m (43.5 lb ft). Road test the brakes.

11 :6 Rear brake caliper removal and refitting

To remove and refit a rear brake caliper, proceed as follows:
1 Raise the rear of the car and fit firm supports under the rear crossmember. Remove the wheels and plug the master cylinder as described for front brake calipers.
2 Disconnect the brake wear warning lead, the brake fluid line and the handbrake cable and outer casing.
3 Remove the caliper after removing the two bolts securing the caliper to the knuckle. If difficulty is encountered, remove the thrust spring, the retaining fork and the brake pads.
4 Remove the bleed nipple and drain the cylinder body.
5 To refit the caliper use new Blocfor washers and tighten the securing bolts to a torque of 4.25 kg m (31 lb ft). Reconnect the brake fluid line.
6 Reconnect the handbrake cable and adjust the handbrake as described in **Section 11 :2.** Remove the stopper plug from the master cylinder reservoir.
7 Complete refitting as described in Operations 7 to 10 in **Section 11 :5.**

FIG 11 :10 Bleed nipple slightly opened when using the piston return clamp E

FIG 11 :11 Securing brake pads with the retaining fork 1 and the thrust spring 2

FIG 11 :12 Refitting the caliper

FIG 11 :13 Dismantling a front brake caliper

Key to Fig 11 :13 1 Thrust spring 2 Retaining fork bolt 3 Retaining fork 4 Brake pads

11:7 Front brake caliper overhaul

With the caliper removed as described in **Section 11:5,** its dismantling and reassembly are undertaken as follows:

1 Clamp the caliper in a vice fitted with soft jaws. Referring to **FIG 11:13,** remove the thrust spring 1, the retaining fork securing bolt 2 and the retaining fork 3. Then remove the brake pads 4.

2 Return the pistons as shown in **FIG 11:14,** using the apparatus E (see **FIG 11:8**). Remove the thrust spring 5 from the armature and disengage the armature 6 from the guide grooves in the cylinder body.

3 Remove the spring clips 7 (see **FIG 11:15**) to remove the two protectors 8.

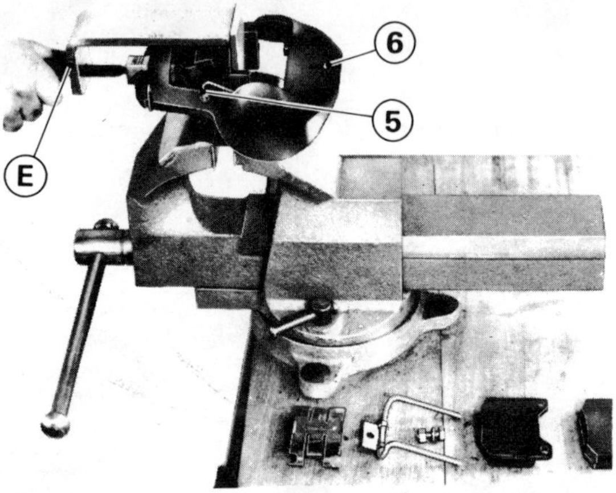

FIG 11:14 Returning the front brake pistons with the apparatus E

Key to Fig 11:14 5 Thrust spring 6 Armature

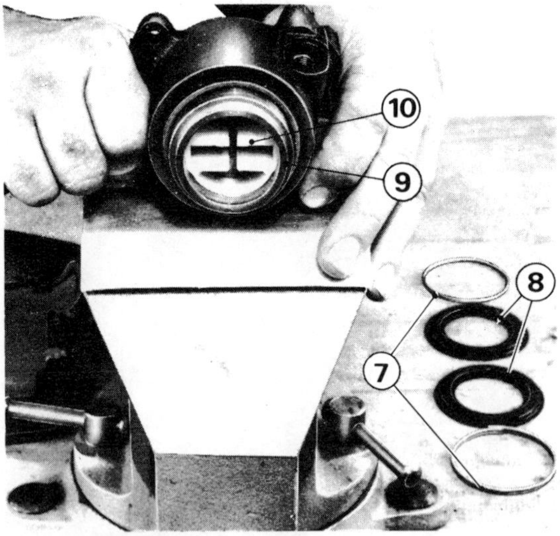

FIG 11:15 Removing front brake caliper pistons

Key to Fig 11:15 7 Spring clips 8 Protectors 9 Pistons 10 Nylon spacer

4 Push the two pistons 9 out of the cylinder and remove the nylon spacer 10 from the piston on the armature side.

5 Remove the sealing rings 1 (see **FIG 11:16**) from the cylinder body and clean the pistons and the cylinder body with alcohol. Renew these items if showing signs of wear, rust or scoring.

6 When reassembling, smear new sealing rings with Lockheed Spagraph grease and position the rings in the grooves inside the cylinder body.

7 Place the nylon spacer in the piston which will be fitted on the armature side.

8 Smear a fine coat of Lockheed Spagraph grease on the pistons and insert them separately in the cylinder body as shown in **FIG 11:17.** Fit the two protector rubbers and their spring clips, the narrow one on the disc side and the thicker one on the armature side.

9 Referring to **FIG 11:18,** refit the thrust plates 1 to the armature if they have been removed.

10 Place against each of the plates a strip 2 of shim plate of .20 mm to facilitate their engagement in the grooves on the cylinder body.

11 Engage the armature in the cylinder body grooves whilst compressing the thrust plates as shown in **FIG 11:18** and then remove the two strips of shim plate.

12 Refit the thrust spring 1 (see **FIG 11:19**) on the upper part of the armature, then firmly position the pistons and the armature using the apparatus E hand tightened. Remove apparatus E and refit the caliper on the car as described in **Section 11:5.**

11:8 Rear brake caliper overhaul

With the caliper removed as described in **Section 11:6,** its dismantling and reassembly are undertaken as follows:

1 Clamp the cylinder body in a vice fitted with soft jaws (see **FIG 11:20**) and remove the thrust spring 1, the retaining fork securing bolt 2 and the retaining fork 3. Then remove the brake pads 4.

FIG 11:16 Removing the sealing rings 1 from the cylinder body

FIG 11 :17 **Inserting the pistons in the cylinder body**

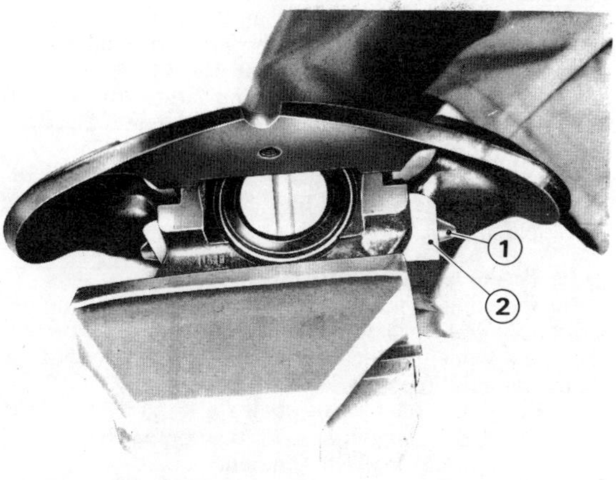

FIG 11 :18 **Fitting the thrust plates 1 with shim strips 2 and engaging the armature in the cylinder body**

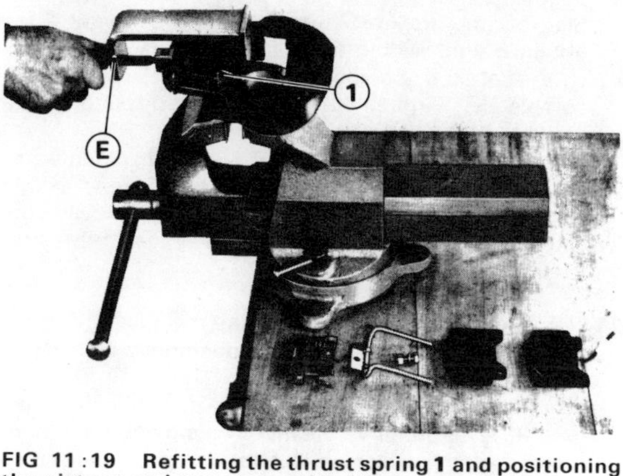

FIG 11 :19 **Refitting the thrust spring 1 and positioning the pistons and armature with the apparatus E**

FIG 11 :20 **Dismantling a rear brake caliper**

Key to Fig 11 :20 1 Thrust spring 2 Retaining fork bolt 3 Retaining fork 4 Brake pads

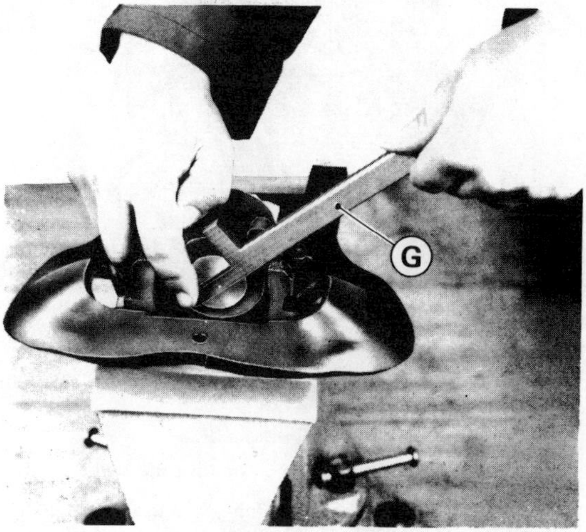

FIG 11 :21 **Rotating the rear brake piston with the key G**

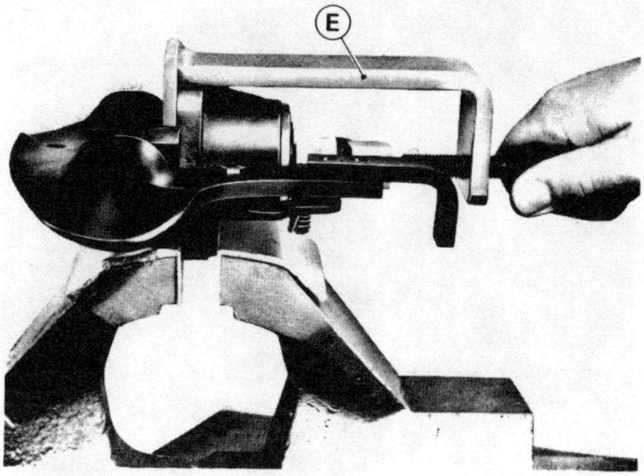

FIG 11 :22 **Returning rear brake pistons with the apparatus E**

FIG 11:23 Sliding the armature from the rear brake cylinder after removing the thrust spring 1

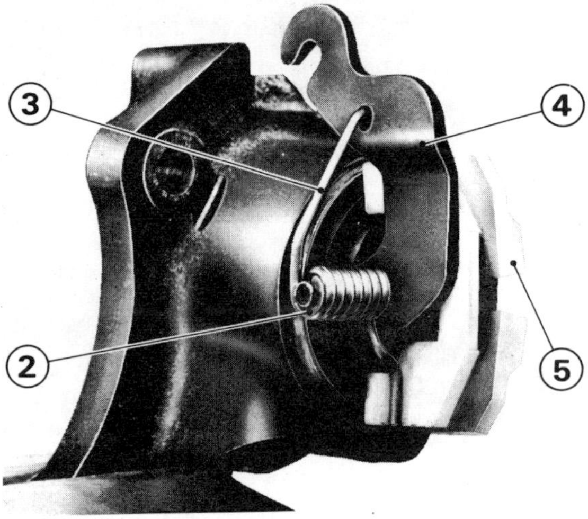

FIG 11:24 Details of handbrake lever

Key to Fig 11:24 2 Truarc ring 3 Lever return spring 4 Lever 5 Nylon spacer

FIG 11:25 Removing the rear brake pistons after removal of the spring clips 6 and the protectors 7

2 Rotate the piston using the positioning key G in the manner shown in **FIG 11:21**. Turn the key until it abuts on the brake pad guide.
3 Return the pistons using the apparatus E (see **FIG 11:22**). Hand tighten the knurled screw until it abuts.
4 Remove the thrust spring 1 (see **FIG 11:23**) from the armature. Slide the armature to disengage it from the grooves in the cylinder body.
5 Remove the Truarc ring 2 (see **FIG 11:24**), and the handbrake lever return spring 3. Raise the handbrake lever 4 and withdraw the nylon spacer 5.
6 Remove the spring clips 6 shown in **FIG 11:25** to withdraw the two piston protectors 7. Then remove the two pistons by pushing on the grooved one.
7 Fit new sealing rings as in Operations 5 and 6 in **Section 11:7.**
8 Smear a fine layer of Lockheed Spargraph grease on the pistons, then fit the piston 1, positioning the handbrake lever as shown in **FIG 11:26.** Continue to fit the piston 2, with its groove inclined at one eighth of a turn from vertical, the two rubber protectors, in their respective positions, the thin spring clip 3 on the disc side and the thick spring clip 4 on the armature side.
9 Raise the handbrake lever (see **FIG 11:27**) in order to position the nylon spacer on the piston.
10 Refit the thrust plates if removed, proceeding as in Operations 9, 10 and 11 in **Section 11:7.**
11 Slide the handbrake return spring 3 (see **FIG 11:28**) onto its pivot and hook up the two ends. Lock the spring on its pivot with a new Truarc ring.
12 Locate the thrust spring 4 on the upper part of the armature as shown in **FIG 11:28.** Refit the bleed nipple, then refit the caliper on the rear knuckle.

11:9 Brake compensator adjustment

For the adjustment of the brake compensator the car should preferably be situated over a pit or on a car lift. The spare wheel should be in place and the petrol tank should be full. Procedure is as follows:

1 Referring to **FIG 11:29,** hook a 5 kg (16 lb) weight on the upper rear extremity of the compensator lever, to the right of the existing notch.
2 Place a 1.4 mm feeler gauge (1.6 mm if the reservoir is empty) as shown in **FIG 11:29** between the extremity of the adjuster screw and the compensator piston.
3 Slacken the locknut, then adjust the screw 1 to obtain a tight sliding fit of the feeler gauge, making sure that the compensator piston is pushed in completely. Tighten the locknut and remove the weight.

Later cars are equipped with a Teves type compensator which is not adjustable. It is operated by a lever attached to the torque tube and controls automatically the hydraulic pressure transmitted to the rear brakes in proportion to the vehicle loading.

11:10 Handbrake cable renewal

To renew the handbrake cable, operations are undertaken as follows:

1 From under the car disconnect the control cable yoke from its lever. Remove the metal clamp and the rubber union fixing the rear end of the primary outer cable to the car floor.

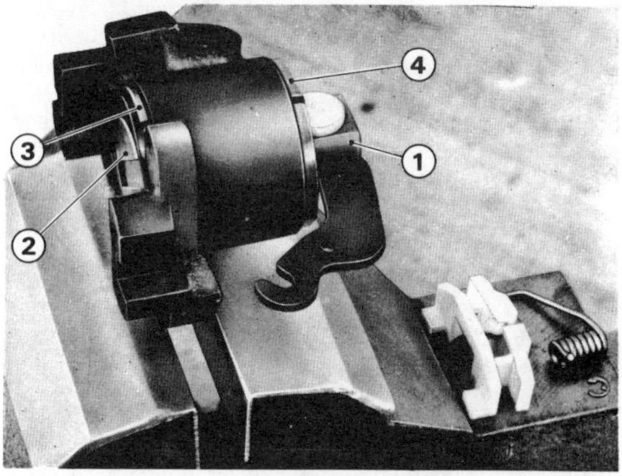

FIG 11:26 Fitting the rear brake pistons

Key to Fig 11:26 1 Piston 2 Piston 3 Spring clip 4 Spring clip

FIG 11:27 Locating the nylon spacer under the handbrake lever

FIG 11:28 Fitting the handbrake return spring **3** and the thrust spring **4**

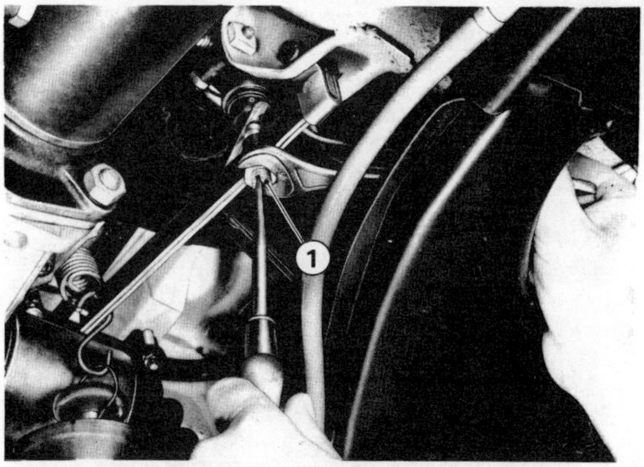

FIG 11:29 Adjusting the brake compensator with a feeler gauge located above the adjusting screw **1**

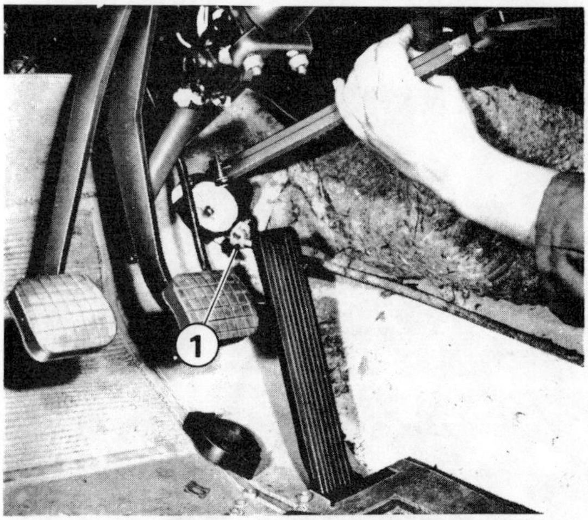

FIG 11:30 Disengaging the handbrake lever housing after removal of the retaining nuts and the cable collar nut **1**

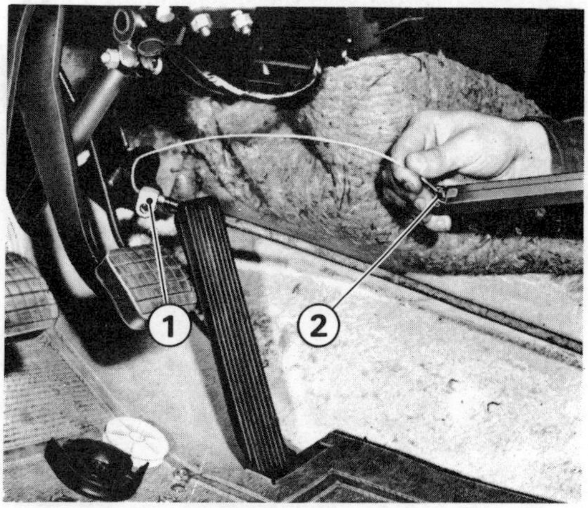

FIG 11:31 Unhooking the cable **2** from the handbrake lever after removing the pulley and the retaining collar **1**

FIG 11:32 Removing the handbrake primary cable through the opening in the floor

FIG 11:33 Inserting a new handbrake primary cable

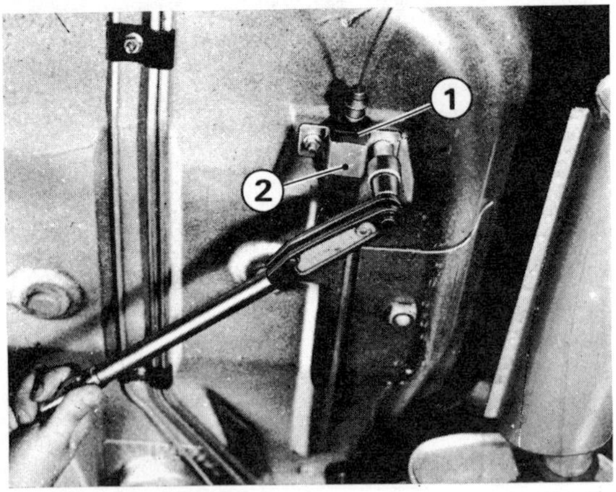

FIG 11:34 Fitting the rubber seal 1 and the metal clamp 2 under the car

2 Inside the car, raise the mat and the soundproofing felt from the gearbox tunnel. Remove the mat and the soundproofing from the rear lefthand floor and unclip the primary cable from under the front seat support.

3 Remove the clip retaining the plastic counter pulley protector. Remove the upper and lower handbrake lever case securing nuts and the primary outer cable retaining collar nut 1 (see **FIG 11:30**). Disengage the handbrake lever/case assembly from the top and then towards the counter pulley.

4 Remove the pulley and the retaining collar 1 (see **FIG 11:31**) from the lower support. Push the handbrake lever fully into its case. Unhook the cable 2 from the lever.

5 Disengage the primary cable towards the rear through the opening in the rear floor of the car as shown in **FIG 11:32.** Recover the securing collar from the primary cable outer casing.

6 Introduce the assembled primary cable through the opening in the floor of the car as shown in **FIG 11:33.** Fit the retaining collar on the front extremity of the outer cable.

7 Reconnect the cable to the handbrake lever in the reverse order to that of dismantling. Reposition the control and counter pulley assembly on the support on the front scuttle.

8 Secure the handbrake lever case in its upper support. Tighten the upper and lower handbrake lever case retaining nuts to a torque of .6 kg m (4.5 lb ft) and the outer cable retaining collar nut on the support to a torque of 1 kg m (7.25 lb ft).

9 Under the car position the rubber seal 1 (see **FIG 11:34**) and the metal clamp 2 and tighten the two securing nuts to a torque of 1 kg m (7.25 lb ft). Secure the yoke to the counter lever using a new splitpin.

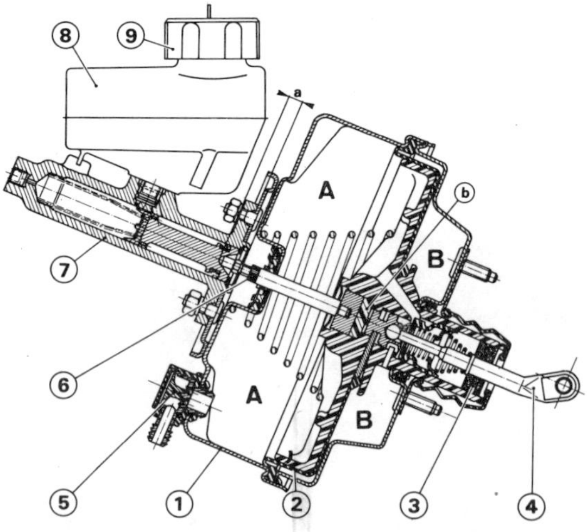

FIG 11:35 A sectional view of the vacuum servo unit

Key to Fig 11:35 **A** Chamber subjected to engine vacuum **B** Chamber linked to atmospheric pressure 1 Shell 2 Diaphragm 3 Air intake filter 4 Thrust rod 5 Vacuum maintaining valve 6 Master cylinder pushrod 7 Master cylinder 8 Brake and clutch fluid reservoir 9 Reservoir cap with brake fluid level indicator **b** Reaction disc

11 :11 Vacuum servo unit

Details of the construction of the vacuum servo unit are shown in **FIG 11 : 35.** At one end the unit is connected to the brake pedal by the thrust rod 4 and at the other end to the master cylinder also shown in the illustration. With the engine running, a partial vacuum depending on inlet depression is supplied to the unit through a non-return valve in the front shell. The diaphragm 2 is thus suspended in vacuum and brake pedal movement admits atmospheric pressure to the rear of the diaphragm, resulting in a pressure difference, which causes the diaphragm and the diaphragm plate to move forward. The brake pedal effort is therefore supplemented by the movement of the diaphragm to operate the master cylinder piston. Providing forward movement of the brake pedal is maintained, the atmospheric port will remain open and assistance in operating the master cylinder provided by the forward movement of the diaphragm. On releasing the brake pedal, the diaphragm spring operates to return the diaphragm, closing the atmospheric port and equalizing the vacuum depression in both chambers. Should for any reason the vacuum assistance fail, the master cylinder will then be operated in the normal manner, although the pedal effort will be greater.

The servo unit rarely develops internal faults and needs no maintenance or servicing. Dismantling the unit calls for special methods and experience and if faulty operation should occur it is advised that a replacement unit should be installed on an exchange basis. Note that the unit is supplied with the master cylinder pushrod 6 preset to a determined protrusion and that under no circumstances must this setting be altered. Also that the rod 6 must never be withdrawn from the reaction disc 'b', as if the disc falls into the unit it would not be possible to refit it in its correct position.

11 :12 Bleeding the system

Bleeding to expel any air which may be present in the hydraulic system may be necessary either after operations on the master cylinder or a front wheel cylinder which have not affected the rear brakes or operations on rear wheel cylinders which have exposed the rear system to the entry of air. Operations in each case require a different procedure.

In the first instance the bleeding can be effected on all four wheels without having to remove the wheels, as follows:

1 Fit a tube, preferably transparent, to one of the bleed nipples and place the other end in a glass jar containing a small quantity of approved brake fluid. During the bleeding operation the end of the pipe must be kept immersed in the fluid and the fluid in the master cylinder reservoir kept topped up.

2 Unscrew the bleed valve and with the help of an assistant depress the brake pedal fully a number of times, pausing after each return stroke, until the fluid entering the jar is clean and free from air bubbles. Then with the pedal held down tighten the bleed valve, top up the reservoir and remove the apparatus.

In the second instance it is necessary to remove the brake pads (see **Section 11 : 3**) and employ the tools shown in **FIG 11 : 8.** Operations are as follows:

1 Engage the end of the key G in the groove on the piston.

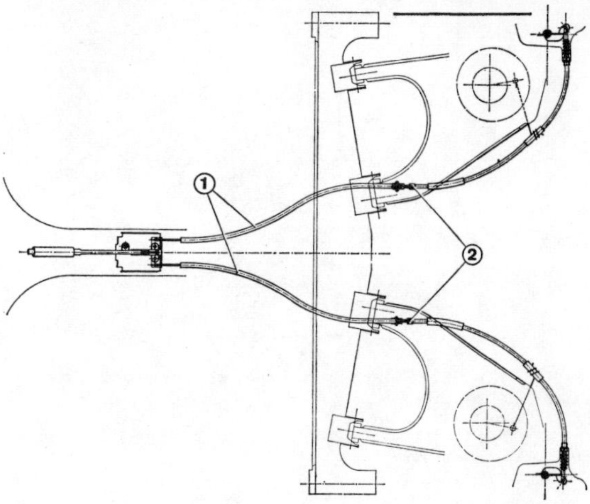

FIG 11 : 36 Layout of the handbrake system with floor mounted lever

2 Pump the brake pedal until the armature of the caliper comes into contact with the outer face of the disc and the key G is pinched between the piston and the other face of the disc. Then proceed with the bleeding as in the previous operations.

3 Pivot the piston one eighth of a turn until the arm of the key G abuts against the angle of the brake pad guide, in order to free the automatic play take up device of the handbrake. Remove the key G.

4 Position the piston return apparatus E as shown in **FIG 11 : 10** and open the bleed nipple one turn to facilitate the return of the pistons.

5 Tighten the knurled screw of the apparatus E by hand until it abuts, then tighten the bleed nipple and remove the apparatus.

6 Return the piston to its initial position using the key G, remove the key and refit the brake pads.

7 Top up the reservoir with approved fluid and refit the wheels.

8 Road test the vehicle, as must always be done after any work on the braking system.

11 :13 Floor mounted handbrake

After chassis No. 1.489.001 the handbrake operating lever is mounted on the floor of the car between the two front seats. The layout of this later system is shown in **FIG 11 : 36**.

Two fixed conduits 1 are welded to the floor and enclose the two operating cables and provide a fixed mounting for the cable outer casings and the adjusting nuts 2.

With this layout the rear crossmember is no longer required to carry the cable conduits nor the compensating bar, which is now at the forward end of the two cables.

Adjustment:

This is simply a matter of adjusting the tension of the cables by means of the two adjusting nuts.

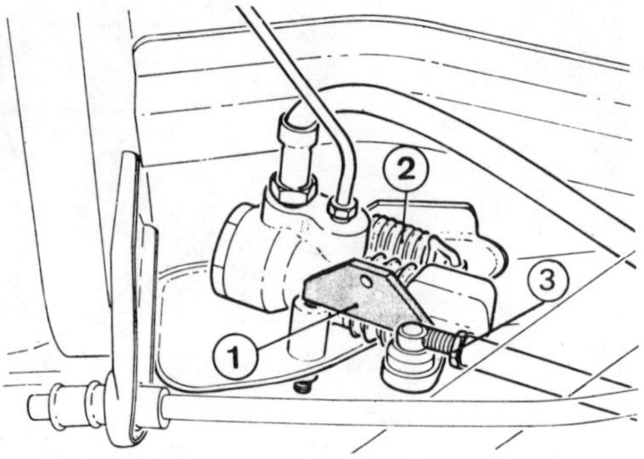

FIG 11:37 Setting the rear brake compensator on rigid rear axle models

Key to Fig 11:37 1 Gauge 80803-1 2 Spring 3 Adjustable connecting rod

11:14 Drum rear brakes

These are fitted to estate cars and commercial vehicles derived from the 504 and also to 504L economy version. They are conventional leading/trailing shoe units hydraulically operated from the foot pedal and include the mechanism for the mechanical application of the parking brake by means of the handlever. No self-adjustment is provided, but each shoe has its own eccentric adjuster on the backplate.

Adjustment:

This is indicated by an increase in the pedal travel required to obtain any given braking effort, it being assumed that the remainder of the system is in order i.e. no air or leaks in the system.

Jack up the rear end of the car and release the handbrake.

Rotate the eccentric adjuster for the primary (front) brake shoe downwards until the wheel cannot be turned by hand.

Apply the foot pedal two or three times to centralize the brake shoe and then turn the adjuster in the opposite direction (upwards) just enough to unlock the brake and allow the wheel to turn without rubbing.

Carry out these operations on the secondary (rear) shoe and then repeat on the other rear wheel, always starting with the primary (front) shoe.

Finally check the adjustment of the handbrake, noting that the normal travel of the handlever should be between seven and eight notches on the ratchet.

Renewing brake shoes:

The friction linings on the brakes should be periodically renewed as necessary. The minimum safe thickness for the linings is 2 to 2.5 mm and any shoe reduced to this dimension should be regarded as worn out and due for replacement. Check also for contamination of the friction material by oil or grease and renew any shoes affected. Do not attempt to clean any such linings as no useful results will be achieved. Note that all four shoes must be renewed together and never just the one that is worn or contaminated otherwise uneven braking will be experienced.

Raise the car on jacks and remove the road wheels.

Slacken off the handbrake and turn each adjuster on the brake backplate to the released position.

Mark the position of the brake drums for later replacement and then remove them by taking out the countersunk headed screws.

Detach the brake shoe return springs and lift off the shoes. Take care not to depress the brake pedal while the shoes are off otherwise the pistons may be ejected from the wheel cylinders with the accompanying oil spillage. This can be prevented by retaining the pistons with rubber bands or a twist of wire.

Clean and inspect the brake mechanism, including the rubbing surfaces of the drums. Slight scoring is permissible, but deeper marks should be removed by machining, provided that only the minimum metal is removed.

The new linings are fitted in the reverse order of removal after lightly greasing any metal working surfaces, being careful not to allow any lubricant to find its way on to the friction linings.

It is recommended that the brakes should be used only lightly for the first 1800 miles (3000 km) to give them time for bedding in.

Compensator adjustment:

The correct setting of the rear brake compensating unit requires the use of a gauge, tool No. 80803-1 as shown in **FIG 11:37** and then procedure is as follows:

First see that the car is unladen but with a full fuel tank and standing on level ground.

Refer to the diagram and note that the gauge 1 must engage in the two holes provided in the compensator. Do **not** touch the retaining nut for the spring 2 on the compensator body.

Unscrew the locking nut on the connecting rod 3 and rotate the rod as necessary to adjust its length to permit the engagement of the gauge in the two holes. Tighten the locknut and remove the gauge.

11:15 Fault diagnosis

(a) 'Spongy' pedal

1 Leak in the system
2 Worn master cylinder
3 Leaking wheel cylinders
4 Air in the system

(b) Brakes grab or pull to one side

1 Distorted disc
2 Wet or oily linings
3 Front suspension loose
4 Worn steering connection
5 Uneven tyre pressures
6 Caliper piston sticking
7 Servo control valve sticking

(c) Brakes dragging

1 Check 1 and 6 in (b)
2 Master cylinder piston sticking

CHAPTER 12

THE ELECTRICAL SYSTEM

12:1 The system, exchange units, test instruments

A 12-volt electrical system is used with a negative earth return. A Ducellier or Paris-Rhone alternator, in conjunction with a voltage regulator, generates an alternating current which is converted to direct current for charging the battery through silicon diodes. These are similar to one-way valves which also prevent the current being returned to the alternator under low voltage conditions. The battery in turn supplies electrical energy to operate the starter motor, the ignition (see **Chapter 3**), the lights and other accessories, of which the general arrangement is shown in the diagram of the wiring system (see **FIG 14:1**) included in the Appendix.

The starter motor, which may be either a Ducellier or Paris-Rhone unit, is of the pre-engaged type with a solenoid which controls both the mechanical and electrical operations of the starter. The headlamps are of trapezoidal form with adjusters for elevation. On fuel injection models special high-performance headlamps are provided, incorporating supplementary halogen lamps. Reversing lights are integrated in rear clusters with stop and direction lights. Other electrical features include two-speed self-parking windscreen wipers controlled by a switch on the dashboard. Electric windscreen washers are operated by a control under the steering wheel and coupled with the windscreen wiper switch. Also provided are a headlamp flasher switch and twin windtone horns.

Major mechanical and electrical defects in the alternator, starter motor and other integral features of the system are best remedied by fitting new units on an exchange basis, but instructions are given on adjustments which can be undertaken with some basic understanding of electrical theory and practice and without elaborate equipment. Electrical adjustments, however, require precise measurement and an accurate voltmeter and ammeter should be available.

12:2 Battery maintenance and testing

Regular attention is essential to keep the battery in good working order and to extend its life. An obvious sign of trouble is the corrosion of the terminals and surrounding parts, causing low output and possibly unsatisfactory starter motor operation. Dust or dirt should brushed away and a weak solution of ammonia and hot water should be used to clean off any signs of corrosion. The top of the battery should always be kept clean and

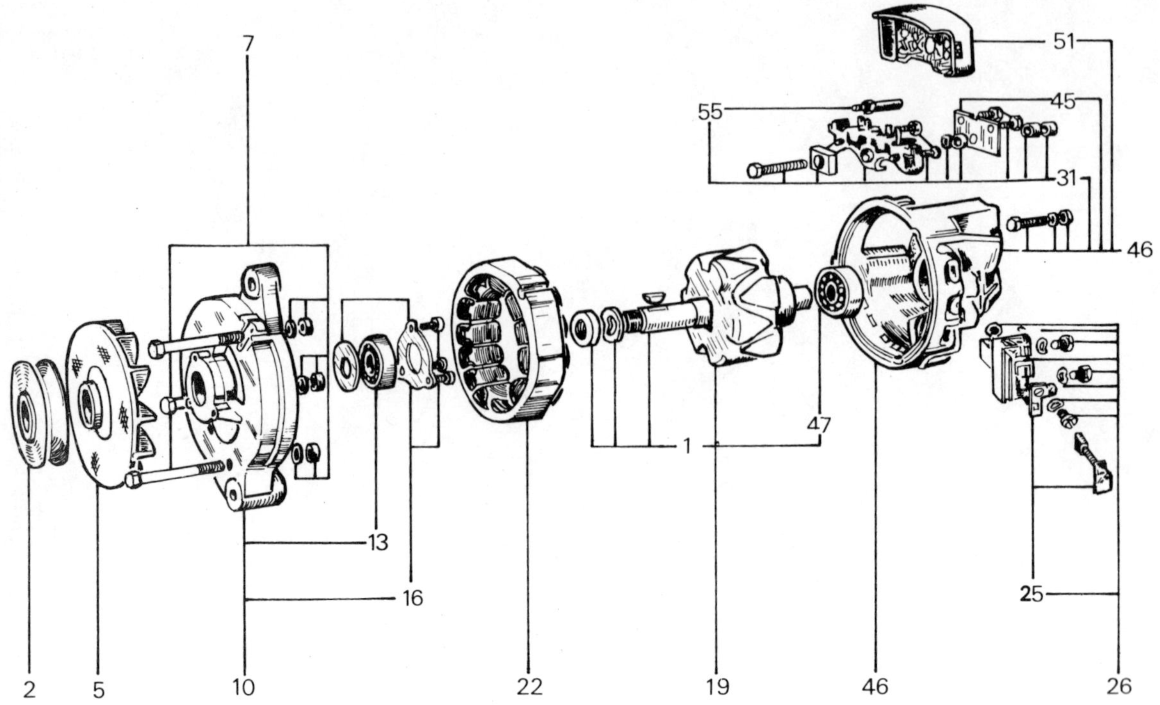

FIG 12:1 An exploded view of the Ducellier alternator

Key to Fig 12:1 1 Pulley mounting 2 Pulley 5 Ventilation fan 7 Assembly rods 10 Drive end bracket 13 Drive end bearing 16 Bearing mounting set 19 Rotor 22 Stator 25 Brushes 26 Brush carrier 31 Push-in terminals 45 Fuse 46, 55 Rear end bracket and diode 47 Rear end bearing 51 Terminal cover

dry. The terminals should be coated with petroleum jelly and anti-sulphuric paint may be used for adjacent parts such as the battery bolts and the clamp frame.

The correct working level of the electrolyte should be maintained at 1 cm above the separators by adding distilled water as necessary. **Never add concentrated acid.** If it is necessary to prepare electrolyte, always add acid to water, **never water to acid.** The condition of the battery can be checked by observing a thermal voltmeter provided on the dashboard, the voltmeter needle moving to the positive side of the centre sector to indicate that charging is proceeding normally. With the engine stopped the needle should reach the beginning of the centre section on the dial when the ignition has been switched on for 40 to 70 seconds. Should the needle descend into the negative red side, the state of the battery and its rate of charge should be investigated. If the needle reaches the positive red side the regulator should be checked.

A master switch is provided on the negative terminal of the battery to isolate the latter when required, disconnection being made by unscrewing the switch about two turns. When reconnecting the supply, reset the electric clock to the correct time and ensure that the control knob returns to its original position and rotates freely. Never leave the clock connected and stopped. A further feature of the battery is that an orifice for a single pin plug is provided on each of the battery terminals to allow for the connection of an inspection lamp or other apparatus, even with the master switch slackened.

It should be noted that with an alternator charging system **certain precautions must be taken,** i.e., (a) never disconnect the alternator/battery lead when the engine is running and (b) when charging the battery disconnect both the positive and negative leads. Under normal operating conditions the alternator output is sufficient to keep the battery charged, but if the car is not used for a long period of time it is good practice to include a monthly charge.

12:3 The alternator and regulator

The advantages of an AC alternator in the electrical system instead of the normal DC generator are that the alternator can operate at higher speeds than the generator and consequently improved performance is obtained at engine idling speeds. Also there is no commutator to require attention and regulation is simplified by providing an instrument only for voltage control.

Dismantling and overhaul operations on the alternator call for special experience and test equipment, especially for electronic details, and it is advised that such work should be undertaken by a qualified service agent. Details of the Ducellier alternator, however, are shown in **FIG 12:1.** The Paris-Rhone alternator is constructed on the same lines but with differences of design of individual components.

The unit consists mainly of a rotor, a stator, a slip ring end shield with two rectifying diodes and a safety fuse in series with each diode, a drive end shield, a pulley and a fan. The current is generated with a stationary armature and a revolving field system. The stator and rotor are housed between the drive and slip ring end shields, the whole assembly being secured by bolts. Two brushes are mounted on the slip ring end shield and bear on the two smooth slip rings. The slip rings replace the commutator on DC generators and because there is no interruption of current to cause sparking the alternator can run at higher speeds. The alternating current generated is rectified, or changed to direct current, by means of the silicon diodes also contained within the slip ring end shield. These diodes do not allow the return of current from the battery to the alternator windings and hence the normal cut-out on DC generators is not required. A fuse element in series with each diode is provided to interrupt the circuit in the event of the diode becoming shortcircuited. The rotor, mounted on ball-bearings, carries the excitation winding which receives the feed through the collector rings and the brushes. The stator consists of a single-phase winding made up of two coils, the ends of which are separately fused and connected together.

The regulator has two terminals, one connected to the positive terminal of the ignition coil and the other connected to the EXC terminal of the alternator. The regulator base plate must be carefully earthed. The main purpose of the regulator is to keep the output voltage of the alternator within defined limits, which is achieved by varying the excitation current of the alternator.

12:4 Testing the alternator and regulator

Whenever work is undertaken on an alternator charging system care must be taken as follows to avoid serious damage to the diodes:

1 All alternator systems have negative earth and the leads of the battery must never be reversed, otherwise the diodes will be burned out and the wiring possibly damaged.
2 Battery leads, or any wires in the charging system, must not be disconnected whilst the engine is running.
3 Disconnect the battery leads if charging the battery from an outside source.
4 The alternator must never be run with the output disconnected.
5 Never check the operation of the unit by short-circuiting either the positive terminal and earth or the excitation terminal and earth.

Faults in the charging system are first to be sought in the condition of the battery, defective wiring connections or the loose adjustment of the driving belt. If the alternator is then suspect, proceed as follows:

1 Connect an ammeter in series on the output circuit, i.e., the thick cable.
2 Disconnect the excitation cable at the alternator to cut off the excitation circuit.
3 Using a separate cable, connect the alternator excitation circuit to the positive terminal of a battery for the full feed (14V) of the excitation circuit.
4 Check the driving belt tension and run the alternator at 3500 rev/min just for the time required to obtain the current reading. If the current reading gives a result not far away from the values indicated on the output diagram in **FIG 12:2,** the alternator is working correctly and the fault lies in the regulator circuit.

To check the regulator, connect as indicated in **FIG 12:3.** Hold for 60 minutes on an output of 15 amp with a 55 amp/hr battery and resistances connected in parallel. After disconnecting the alternator feed and reconnecting it the voltage reading at 5 amp should be 13.4V to 14.4V and at 20 amp 13.2V to 14.2V.

Removal of the alternator is attained by disconnecting the leads from the terminals, slackening the driving belt and unbolting the unit from the engine. A visual check of the stator should be made to ensure that the windings are not burned or damaged. Examine the brushes, which should have a minimum length of 3 mm. Testing of the insulation may be made with the aid of a test lamp in series, after disconnecting the diodes. A similar test may be made between the slip ring and one of the pole clamps, using a 110V source. If the test lamp lights up, the rotor is faulty.

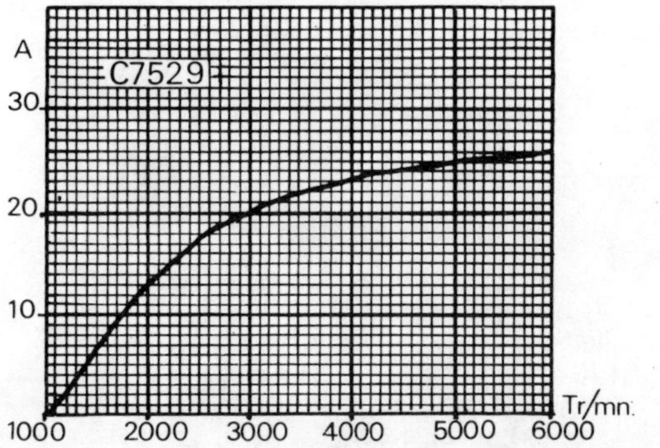

FIG 12:2 Alternator output chart at 14V

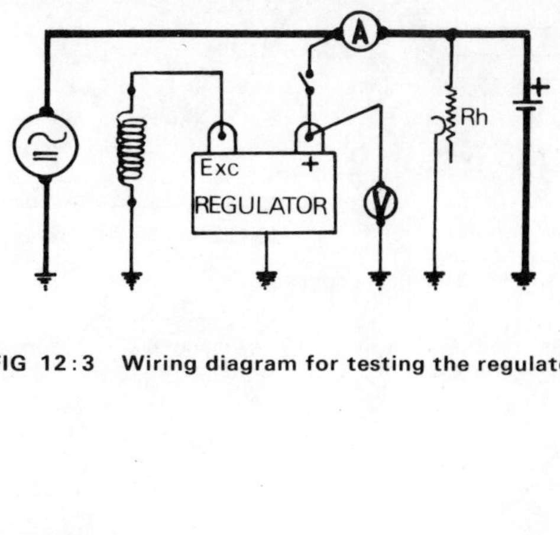

FIG 12:3 Wiring diagram for testing the regulator

12:5 The starter motor

The starter motor may be of either Ducellier or Paris-Rhone manufacture. Both are of the pre-engaged type and similarly constructed, differences being mainly in the manufacturing design of individual parts. An exploded view of a Paris-Rhone motor is shown in **FIG 12:4**.

In operation, when the starter switch is closed the solenoid is energized and the pinion drive moves forwards, causing the pinion to engage with the ring gear on the flywheel. The armature starts turning slowly until at the end of the solenoid stroke the starter receives full current and turns the engine. Release of the starter switch enables the solenoid to withdraw the gear and disconnect the supply to the motor, with the aid of an armature braking device on the commutator end bracket in the Paris-Rhone motor or a freewheel arrangement in the Ducellier type.

Starter motors are generally reliable units which give very little for concern over long periods of operation. When checking starter troubles, first ensure that the battery is in good condition and that all battery and starter connections are in good order. A corroded battery terminal or bad earth connection may have sufficient electrical resistance to make the starter inoperative, though enough current may be available for lamps and accessories. The details given in **FIG 12:4** will guide dismantling and reassembly if required, but if trouble is experienced it is advised that the motor should be renewed on an exchange basis through an accredited service agent.

12:6 Fuse ratings and circuits

The fuse box is fitted under the lefthand side of the dashboard and carries five fuses. The early style is shown in **FIG 12:5** and a list of items protected by the fuses is given below. In 1973 the wiring harnesses were modified and some changes were made to the fused circuits as will be seen from the table below and the wiring diagrams in the **Appendix**.

Early fuse box:

1	5 amp	Side and rear lamps, number plate lamp, instrument panel
2	10 amp	Cigarette lighter, horns, interior lighting, boot, clock
3	10 amp	Reversing and stop lamps, fan
4	10 amp	Flashers, fuel, water temperature, voltmeter, warning lamps for oil pressure, choke and brakes
5	10 amp	Windscreen wiper and washer, heater and accessories

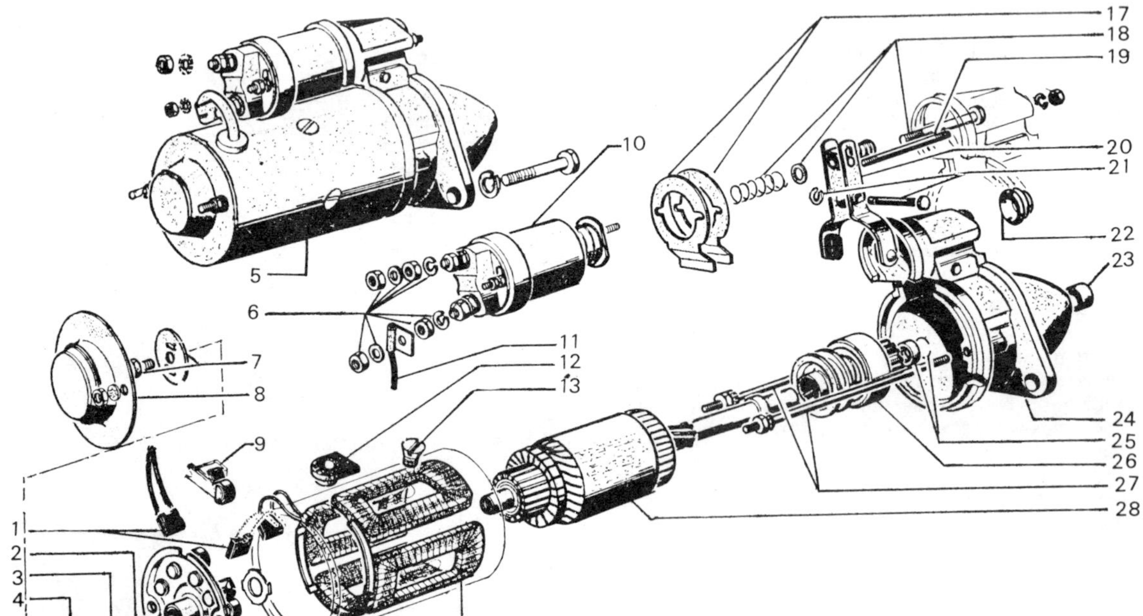

FIG 12:4 An exploded view of the Paris-Rhone starter motor

Key to Fig 12:4 1 Carbon brush 2 Bush 3 Stop spring 4 Stop ring 5 Starter assembly 6 Solenoid terminal set 7 Stop ring plate and screw 8 End cover 9 Brush holder and spring 10 Solenoid 11 Field coil terminal 12 Cable grommet 13 Polepiece screw 14 Windings 15 Friction washer 16 Commutator end bracket 17 Solenoid joint set 18 Adjustment set 19 Solenoid securing stud 20 Operating fork 21 Fork pivot pin assembly 22 Solenoid plug 23 Bush 24 Drive end bracket 25 Pinion stop assembly 26 Pinion and overrunning clutch assembly 27 Through-bolts 28 Armature

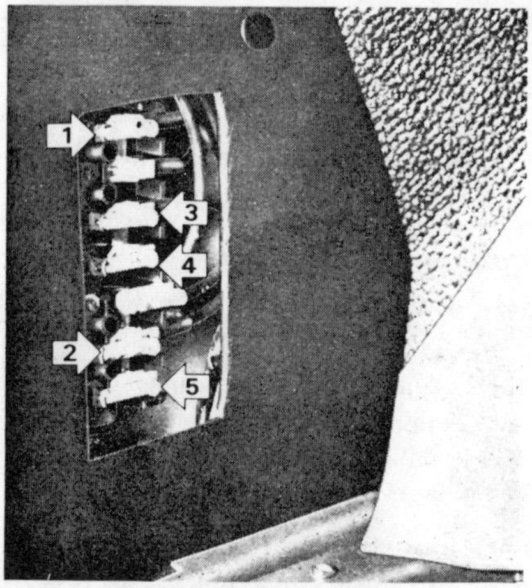

FIG 12:5 The fuse box

Key to Fig 12:5 1 5-amp fuse 2 to 5 10-amp fuses
Circuits covered are described in text

1973 models:

1	5 amp	Side and rear lamps, number plate, instrument panel, heater and side lamp warning lights
2	10 amp	Interior lighting, boot, horns, cigarette lighter, glove box, clock
3	10 amp	(Ignition switch controlled) Stop and reversing lamps, fan
4	15 amp	Heater, windscreen wiper and washer, heated rear window, accessories
5	10 amp	Flashers, voltmeter, fuel and water temperature gauges, oil pressure, choke and brake warning lamps

12:7 Headlamps

The twin-filament headlamp bulbs (see **FIG 12:6**), when dipped, illuminate the side of the road over a greater distance than the centre. To renew a bulb, referring to **FIG 12:7**, free the collar 1 by moving both retaining springs outwards, then remove the connector socket by pulling it axially. Fit the new bulb by positioning the guide boss in the headlight socket. After correctly inserting the bulb, refit both retaining springs on the collar.

If the rear of the car is laden, the dipped light beam may inconvenience oncoming drivers. To avoid this, the light beam of each headlamp may be lowered by turning the control knob 3 a quarter of a turn.

Vertical adjustment is obtained by means of the knurled headscrew 2 and horizontal adjustment by altering the setting of each of the knurled nuts 4. The manufacturers, however, recommend that resetting of the headlamps should only be carried out by an accredited service agent.

On Coupé models a four lamp system is employed. If it is necessary to adjust these without reference to a qualified service station, the adjustment screws are shown in **FIG 12:8**, the two screws 1 being for vertical setting and 2 for lateral alignment. Access to these screws is obtained by first removing the headlamp surround.

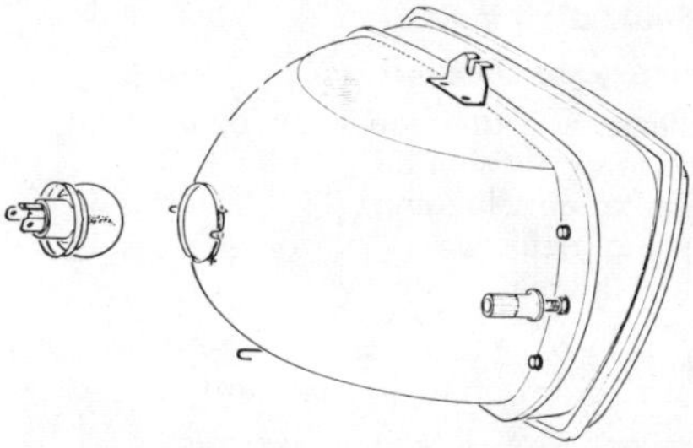

FIG 12:6 A rear view of a headlamp

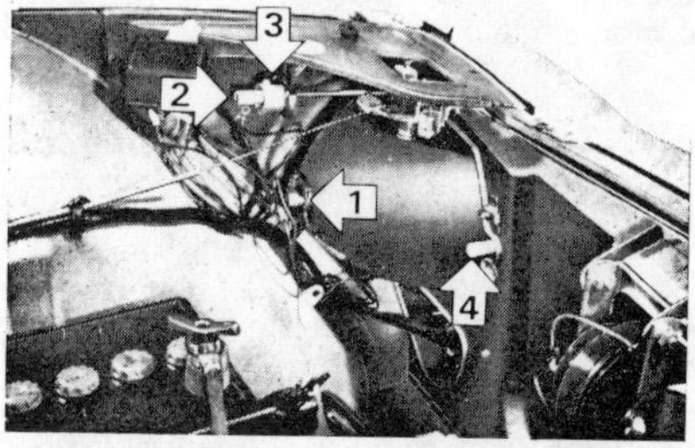

FIG 12:7 Headlamp adjusting screws

Key to Fig 12:7 1 Collar 2 Vertical adjustment 3 Control knob 4 Horizontal adjustment

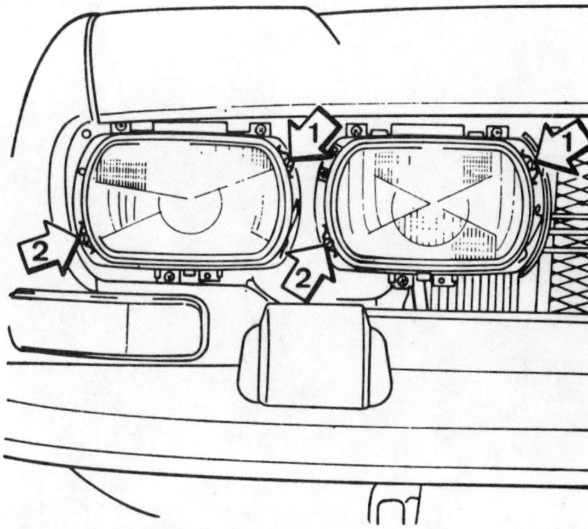

FIG 12:8 Headlamp adjustment on Coupe models with four light units

Key to Fig 12:8 1 Vertical adjustment screws 2 Horizontal adjustment screws

12:8 Fault diagnosis

(a) Battery discharged

1 Terminals or earth connection loose or dirty
2 Lighting circuit shorted
3 Alternator not charging
4 Regulator defective
5 Battery internally defective

(b) Insufficient charging current

1 Loose or corroded battery terminals
2 Alternator driving belt slipping

(c) Battery will not hold charge

1 Low electrolyte level
2 Battery plates sulphated
3 Electrolyte leaking from casing or top sealing compound
4 Separators ineffective

(d) Starter motor lacks power or will not operate

1 Battery discharged
2 Loose connections on battery or starter
3 Faulty earth connection
4 Starter pinion jammed in mesh with flywheel gear
5 Solenoid switch faulty
6 Brushes worn or sticking, leads detached or shorting
7 Commutator worn, burnt or shorted
8 Starter shaft bent
9 Engine abnormally stiff

(e) Starter motor runs but does not turn engine

1 Pinion sticking on screwed sleeve
2 Broken teeth on pinion or flywheel gear

(f) Noisy starter pinion when engine is running

1 Control spring weak or broken

(g) Starter motor inoperative

1 Check 1 and 6 in (d)
2 Armature or field coils faulty

(h) Starter motor rough or noisy

1 Mounting bolts loose
2 Damaged pinion or flywheel ring gear
3 Main pinion spring broken

(j) Lamps inoperative or erratic

1 Battery low, bulbs burned out
2 Faulty earthing of lamps or battery
3 Lighting switch faulty
4 Loose or broken wiring connections

(k) Wiper motor sluggish, taking high current

1 Faulty armature
2 Bearings out of alignment
3 Commutator dirty or shortcircuited

(l) Fuel gauge does not register

1 No battery supply to gauge
2 Gauge casing not earthed
3 Cable between gauge and tank unit earthed

CHAPTER 13

THE BODYWORK

13:1 General description

The steel body is of integral construction with a strong centre section and progressively collapsible extremities. A weatherproof sliding roof is optionally available and the body is guarded against corrosion by a special electrolytic process. The front doors are fitted with anti-burst safety locks and the rear doors with childproof locks. Armrests are integral with the padded door grips. All doors have courtesy light switches. Adjustable headrests and backrests are provided on the front seats, the backrests being fully reclinable as sleeping berths. The spare wheel, housed underneath the floor and accessible from outside, is released from inside the boot.

13:2 Removing door panels

The removal of a door panel requires first the removal of the window regulator handle with the aid of a hook made from piano wire as shown in **FIG 13:1.** Note the position of the handle for refitting, then locate the hook between the handle and its thrust cup to withdraw the spring clip, when the handle can be withdrawn. Remove the inner door opening control lever.

Proceed to unscrew and remove the armrest and unscrew the interior door locking button. Disengage the clips retaining the upper padded panel (see **FIG 13:2**) and raise it to remove it. Remove the upholstery panel to gain access to the interior mechanism of the door.

Refitting of the panel, the armrest, the inner door opening lever and the inner door locking button follows the manner of their removal in each case in reverse. Close the window and fit a new spring clip on the regulator handle. Refit the thrust cup and push the handle on to the shaft in the position occupied before removal.

13:3 Servicing door locks

A view of a front door lock is shown in **FIG 13:3.** To gain access to the lock, remove the upholstery panel as described in the previous Section. Then disconnect the control link 1 (see **FIG 13:4**) at the lock end, remove the three door lock screws and remove the guide plate 2. To remove the lock, insert the key and slide the lock downwards until the locking crank disengages from the catch. Pivot the lock around the slide support, when the lock may then be withdrawn as shown in **FIG 13:5.**

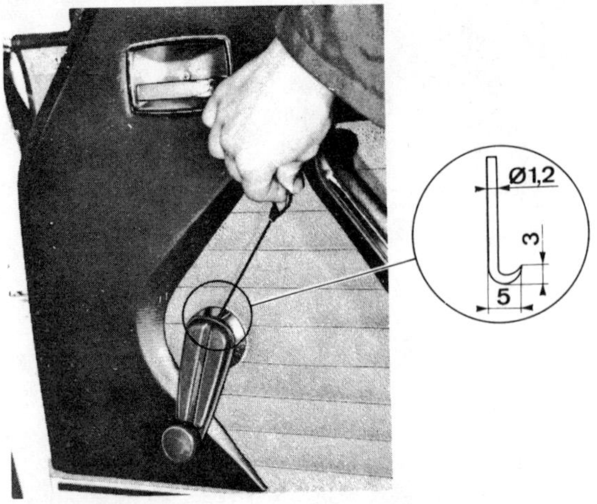

FIG 13:1 Removing the spring clip from a window winder handle. Dimensions in mm

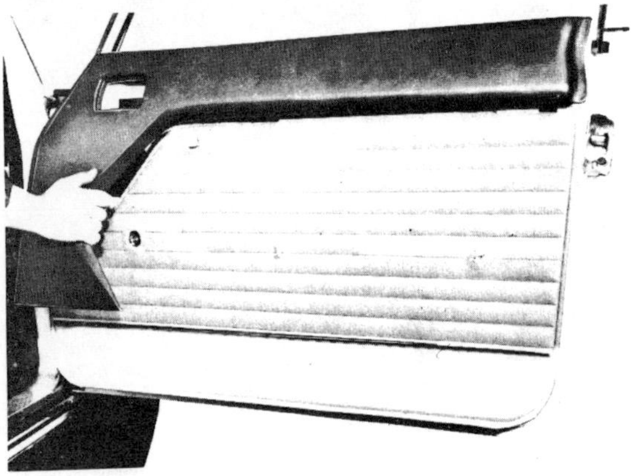

FIG 13:2 Removing a door upper panel

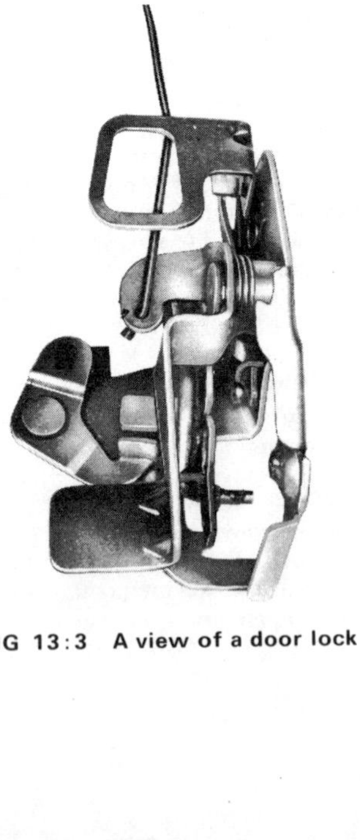

FIG 13:3 A view of a door lock

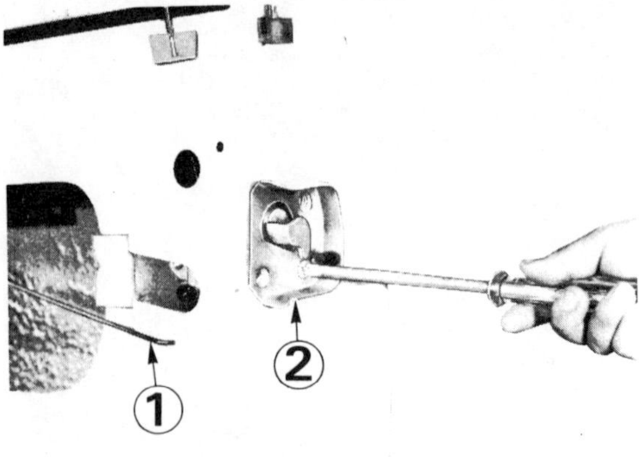

FIG 13:4 Unscrewing a front door lock, showing the control link **1** and the guide plate **2**

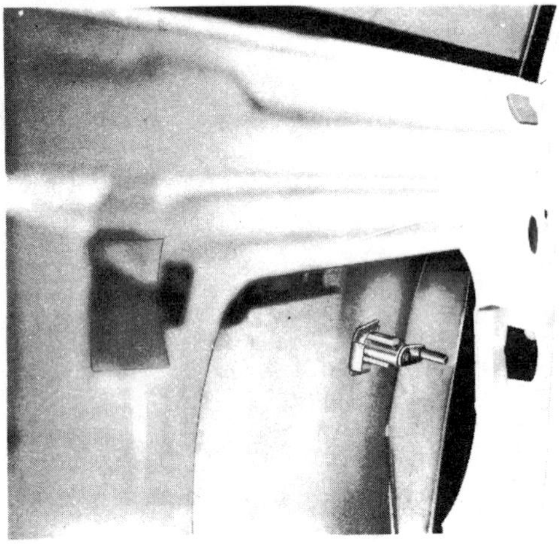

FIG 13:5 The locking crank of a door lock

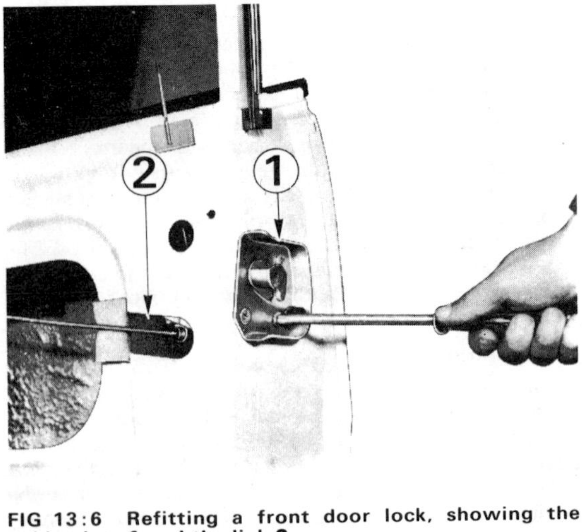

FIG 13:6 Refitting a front door lock, showing the guide plate **1** and the link **2**

Check the operation of the lock mechanism and the condition of all the return springs and grease all the pivots. Place the locking puller in the unlocked position and refit the lock in the reverse order of removal. Make sure that the locking crank engages correctly with the key in the lock.

Couple the guide plate 1 (see **FIG 13:6**) to the lock and tighten the three Philips head screws. Reconnect the link 2 to the lock. Check the operation of the lock in respect of (a) opening from inside and outside, (b) locking from inside and with the key and (c) automatic lock release when the door is closed.

The outer lock is removed by withdrawing the lockstop fork 3 (see **FIG 13:7**) and disengaging it outwards. When refitting, insert the lock taking care to engage the crank in the lock catch 4. Immobilize the lock using the stop fork.

Refit the upholstery panel as previously described and adjust the door catch to obtain a protrusion of 0 to 2 mm in relation to the rear door. Finally check the gap between the upper door frame and the water drip channel, which must be between 4 and 6 mm.

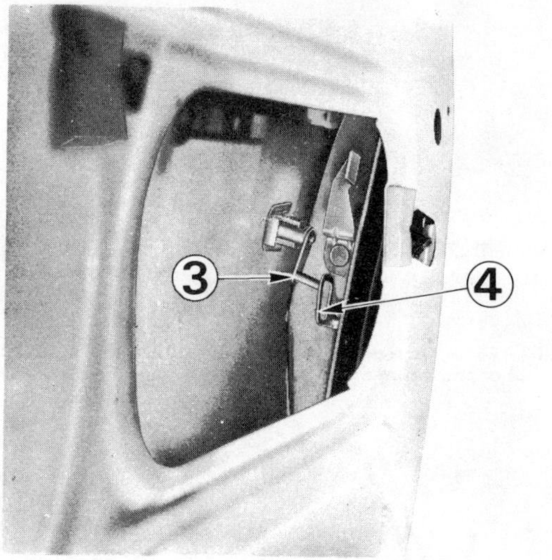

FIG 13:7 **Details of the outer lock, showing the stop fork 3 and the lock catch 4**

13:4 Servicing front window winders, renewing glass

Access to the window winding mechanism is obtained by removing the upholstery panel as previously described. To remove the mechanism, raise the window and detach the retaining nuts. Holding the window in the raised position, push the mechanism in and disengage the rollers from the slide towards the rear. The mechanism may then be withdrawn as shown in **FIG 13:8.**

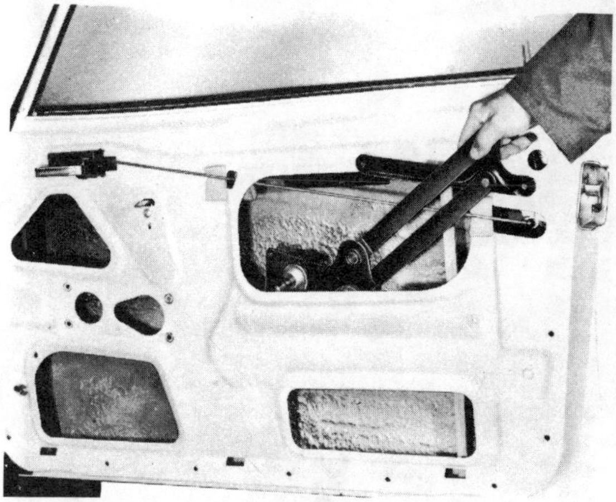
FIG 13:8 **Withdrawing the window winder mechanism from a front door**

With the window in the raised position, lift it towards the front to disengage it from its slides. Continuing to hold it in this position, disengage it upwards as shown in **FIG 13:9.**

FIG 13:9 **Removing a front door window glass**

If the glass is being renewed, clean the window support mounting carefully and coat a new rubber section with talc. Fit the assembly to the glass with the extremity of the mounting 242 mm from the rear of the glass (see **FIG 13:10**).

Examine the outer window seal to ensure that it has no cracks, cuts or permanent distortion. To remove the trim, insert a screwdriver (see **FIG 13:11**) between the plastic clips and the inner edge of the trim. Then disengage it upwards, beginning at the front end. Renew by positioning the plastic clips on the door panel, then place the trim on the clips. Secure the trim by pushing it down by hand.

Remove any broken glass from the bottom of the door and engage the window, tilted towards the front, in the top of the door. Straighten it up to position it in the slides and retain it in the raised position.

Grease the toothed quadrant and its pivots and position the quadrant as shown in **FIG 13:12.** Refit the mechanism in the reverse order of its removal and secure it with the four nuts.

Check the free movement of the glass. Adjust if necessary by positioning the window at its lowest point and slackening the lower slide securing nut 1 (see **FIG 13:13**) on the inner door panel. Bring the slide into contact with the bottom of the window and retighten the nut 1. Refit the panel and other accessories as previously described.

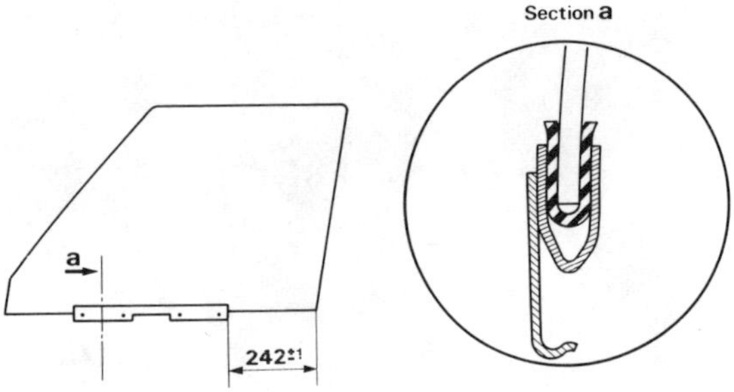

FIG 13:10 A front door window glass and a sectional view of the mounting. Dimensions in mm

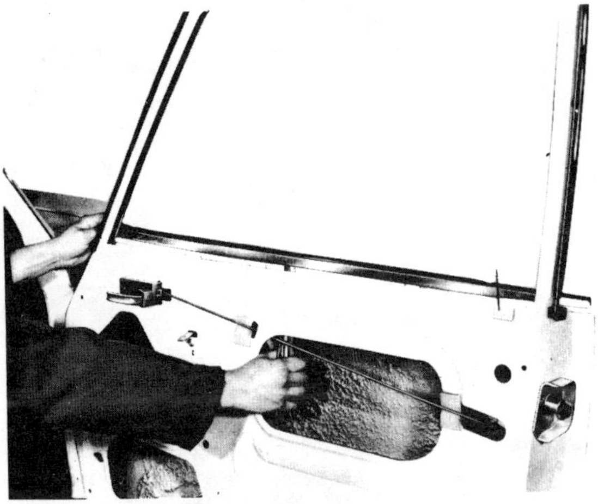

FIG 13:11 Method of removing door trim

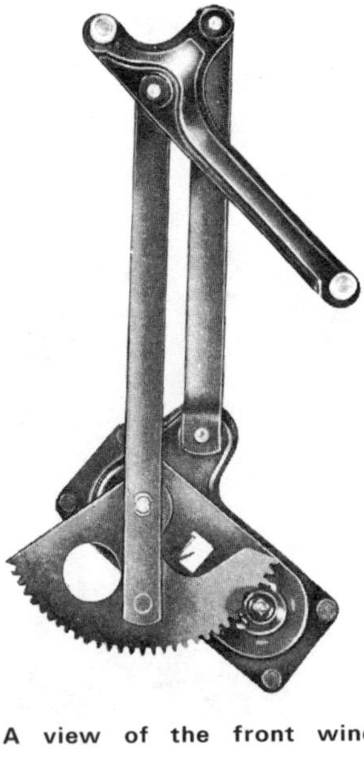

FIG 13:12 A view of the front window winder mechanism

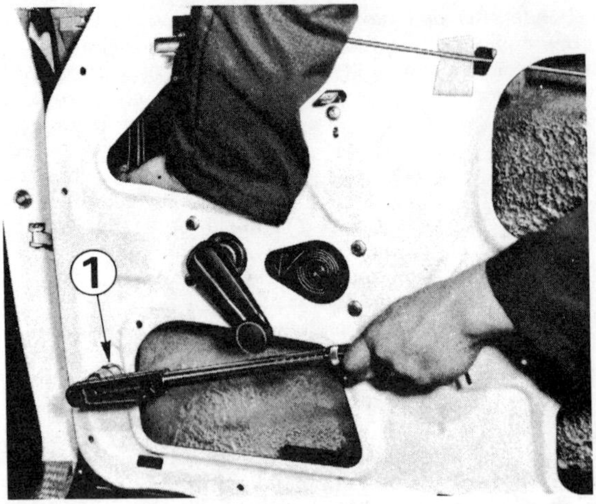

FIG 13:13 Adjusting a front window after insertion

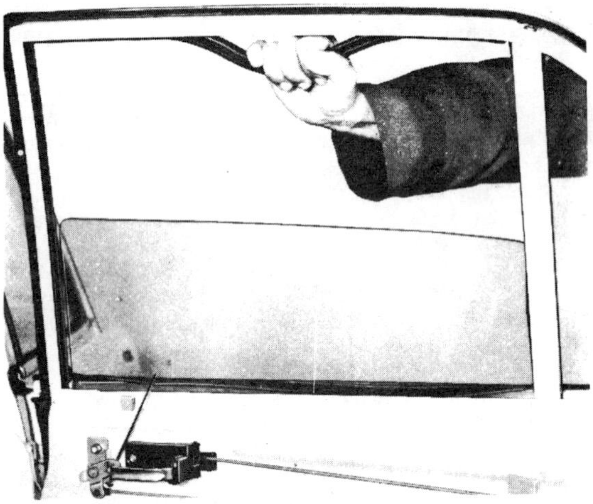

FIG 13:14 Removing the upper glass slide in a rear window

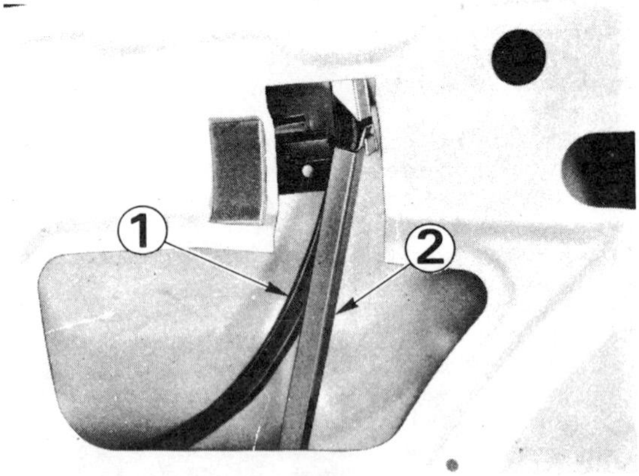

FIG 13:15 Removing a rear window, showing the slide **1** and the rear slide support **2**

13:5 Servicing rear door windows, renewing glass

To detach a movable window and its mechanism, remove the upholstery panel as previously described and then remove the three screws securing the rear slide support. Remove the upper glass slide by firstly unclipping it in the middle (see **FIG 13:14**). Proceed as follows:

1 Raise the window completely with the mechanism and disengage the slide 1 (see **FIG 13:15**) from the lower part of the rear support. Pivot the lower part 2 of the rear slide support forwards, push the top forwards and disengage the support downwards.

2 Hold the window in the raised position, remove the retaining nuts and push the mechanism inwards. Then move it backwards until the shaft appears in the elongated hole in the interior door panel.

3 Using the handle, turn the mechanism (see **FIG 13:16**) to the maximum raised position. Push the mechanism inwards again and move it forwards to disengage the rollers from the slide. Withdraw the mechanism through the upper rear opening in the interior door panel as shown in **FIG 13:17.**

4 Lower the window as much as possible, then push the upper slide support 1 (see **FIG 13:18**) forwards and disengage it upwards. Withdraw the window, in its normal position, through the top of the door.

5 Renew a broken glass as described for a front window in **Section 13:4,** in this case with the extremity of the mounting 18 mm from the rear of the glass.

6 To remove the fixed window, push it hard towards the front and withdraw the glass with its seal (see **FIG 13:19**). Renew the outer window seal if necessary as described in **Section 13:4.**

7 Fit a new seal on the fixed window glass and smear the outer edge with tallow. Fit the glass in its frame, using a rubber hammer if necessary.

8 Remove any broken glass from the bottom of the door and engage the movable window in its normal position, allowing it to rest in the bottom of the door.

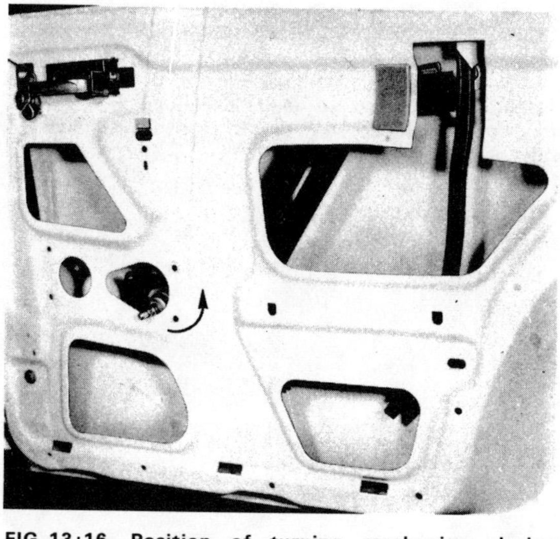

FIG 13:16 Position of turning mechanism during removal of a rear window winder

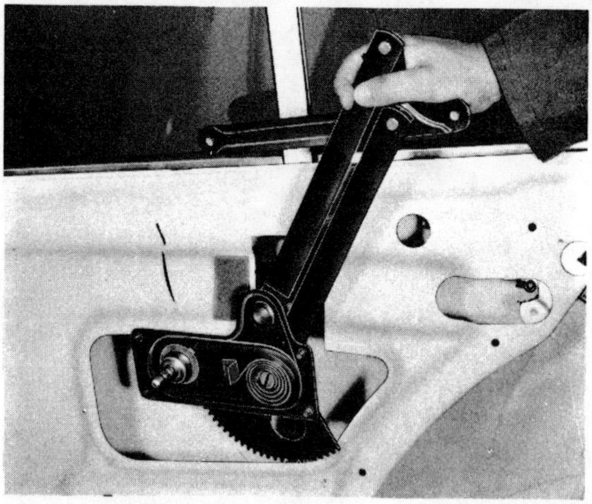

FIG 13:17 Withdrawing the window winder mechanism from a rear door

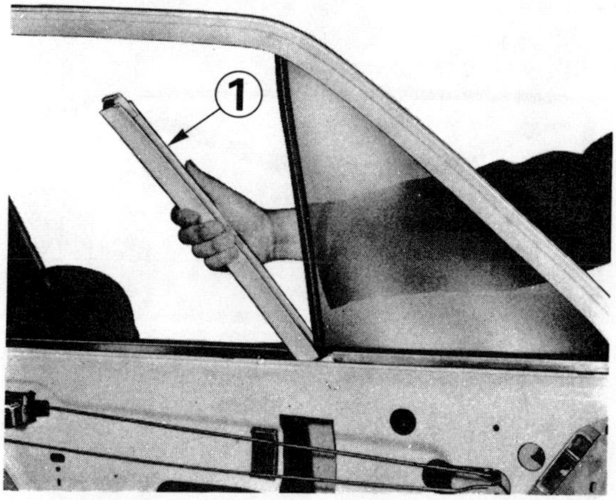

FIG 13:18 Disengaging the upper slide support 1 in a rear window

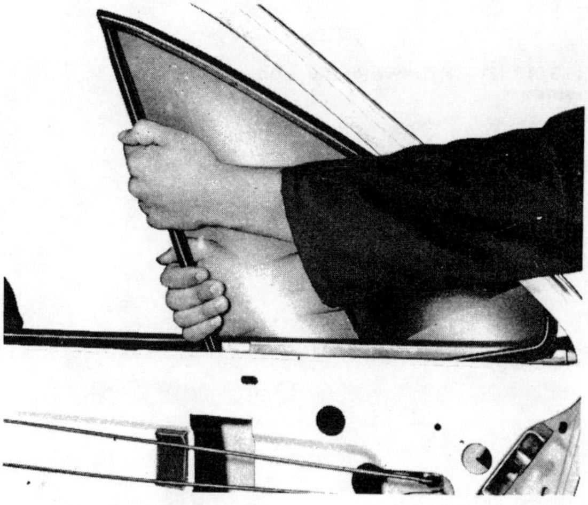

FIG 13:19 Removing a rear fixed window

FIG 13:20 Adjustment of the rear window winder mechanism before refitting in the door

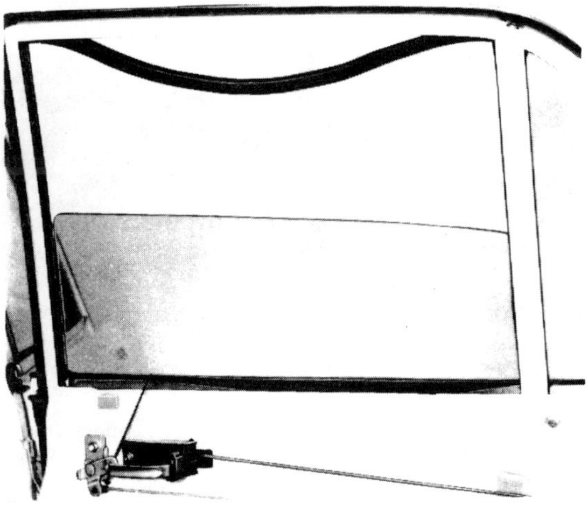

FIG 13:21 Renewing the upper glass slide in a rear window

9 Place the upper rear slide in position, ensuring that it engages correctly on the fixed window seal. Locate the window in its slides and retain it in the fully raised position.

10 Grease the toothed quadrant and position it to obtain a distance of 6 mm between the two arms (see **FIG 13:20**). Refit the mechanism in the reverse order of its removal and secure with the four nuts.

11 Refit the lower slide support as removed, assembling the slide on the lower support. Secure the upper slide support by the two screws, beginning at the top. Lower the window as far as possible with the handle, hold the lower slide support against the glass and tighten the lower mounting screw.

12 Check the free movement of the window and engage the two ends of a new slide in the upper frame (see **FIG 13:21**). Complete the fitting by working from one end to the other. These slides are fitted with glue or clips. Hold the window in the raised position and refit the upholstery panel and accessories.

13:6 Seat belt fixings

Four anchorage points are provided for the installation of the safety belts to be used by the driver and the front passenger. Two of these anchorage points are on the floor behind the seats and the other two are located on the door centre post. A support is provided to which the belt snap buckle is clipped when the belt is not in use.

13:7 Heating and ventilating system

The heating and ventilating system includes a thermostatically-controlled air heater with adjustable output and direction of flow in addition to a fresh air system. A variable speed blower controlled by a rheostat accelerates the air flow when required to obtain efficient defrosting and demisting of the windscreen and side windows. The rear quarter panels incorporate extractor slots designed to direct a flow of air over the rear window to keep it free from mist.

From a fresh air inlet in front of the windscreen the flow is divided into two adjustable outlets above the facia and also below it at each side. Adjustment of the upper outlets proportions the flow passing through the heater element, the thermostatic control of which is designed to maintain a required interior temperature irrespective of the speed of the car. The lower outlets are independent of the blower.

APPENDIX

TECHNICAL DATA

Dimensions are in mm unless otherwise stated

ENGINE DETAILS

Type	4 cylinder in-line ohv, at 45 deg.
Bore and stroke:	
1796 cc	84 x 81
1971 cc	88 x 81
Firing order	1–3–4–2 (No. 1 at flywheel end)
Camshaft:	
Material	Cast iron
Number of bearings	3
Journal diameters (without bearings):	
Rear...	$44^{+.04}_{-0}$
Intermediate	$46^{+.04}_{-0}$
Front	$48^{+.04}_{-0}$
Shaft diameter	26.5
End float	.05 to .14
Connecting rods:	
Material	Forged steel
Type	Matched for weight
Weights (numbered on big-ends):	

No. ...	1	2	3	4	5	6
Weight (g):	611 to 630	631 to 650	651 to 670	671 to 690	691 to 710	711 to 730

Max. difference allowable	20 g
Small-end bore	24.35 to 24.38
Small-end bushes:	
Material	Bronze
Bore when fitted	23.005 to 23.018
Big-end bore	53.655 to 53.674
Big-end shells:	
Material	Steel-backed aluminium with 20% tin
Standard thickness	1.812 to 1.818
Oversize thickness	1.962 to 1.968
Radial clearance	.028 to .075
Crankshaft:	
Material	Steel
Number of bearings	5
Number of counterweights	4
Main bearing journal diameter (without bearings):	
Rear...	$55.00^{+.02}_{-0}$
Intermediate rear	$59.97^{+.02}_{-0}$
Centre	$61.00^{+.02}_{-0}$
Intermediate front	$62.38^{+.02}_{-0}$
Front	$63.22^{+.02}_{-0}$

Main bearing journal diameter:	
Rear ...	51.166 to 51.181
Intermediate rear	56.140 to 56.165
Centre	57.174 to 57.189
Intermediate front	58.548 to 58.573
Front	59.401 to 59.416
Crankpin journal diameter	49.975 to 49.991
Crankpin radial clearance	.01
Main bearing shells:	
Material	Steel-backed aluminium alloy with 20% tin
Bearing thicknesses:	
Standard	1.882 to 1.888
First overhaul	2.032 to 2.035
Second overhaul	2.132 to 2.138
Radial clearances:	
Rear, centre and front	.035 to .081
Intermediate	.035 to .091
Crankshaft end float	.08 to .20
Thrust washers thickness, standard	$2.30^{+.3}_{-0}$
oversize	2.40, 2.45, 2.50 (+.3) (—0)

Cylinder block:	
Material	Cast iron
Type	Renewable cast iron liners
Cylinder bore diameter	86.5
Cylinder liners:	
Type	Graded in four groups according to piston diameters
Identification:	

Liner marking	*Liner bore*	*Piston marking*	*Piston diameter*
I	84.000 to 84.011	A	83.940 to 83.951
II	84.012 to 84.022	B	83.952 to 83.962
III	84.023 to 84.033	C	83.963 to 83.973
IIII	84.034 to 84.044	D	83.974 to 83.984

Cylinder head:	
Material	Aluminium alloy
Combustion chambers	Spherical off-set
Permissible distortion	.05 max.
Gasket type	Metallic sheet with asbestos covering and steel rings around the bores
Sparking plug tube bore diameter	30.695 to 30.698
Sparking plug tube diameter	30.7, oversize 30.9
Valve guide bores:	
Standard	13.970 to 13.995
First oversize	14.200 to 14.225
Second oversize	14.500 to 14.525
Valve guide interference fit	.04
Valve guide inside diameter	8.02 to 8.04 (.2 mm less than nominal diameter)
Valve guide protrusion on head:	
Inlet guides ...	27.5±0.5
Exhaust guides	21.5±0.5

Engine lubrication:

Lubrication system	Pressure feed
Grade of oil	Esso Extra Motor Oil or Esso Uniflo W/30/40 or Multigrade 20/W/40
Oil pump type	Gear
Depth of pinions in body	33.95 to 33.98
Pinion side play	.01 to .08
Oil filter	Fullflow type
Sump capacity...	4 litre
Filter capacity	Approx. .5 litre
Minimum oil level	2.5 litre
Minimum oil pressure	800 g/sq cm

Pistons:

Type	Elliptical solid skirt
Material	Aluminium alloy
Number of rings	2 compression, 1 oil control
Height of ring grooves:	
Upper compression ring	1.50 to 1.55
Lower compression ring	2.00 to 2.02
Oil control ring	4.00 to 4.02
Piston sizes	Graded in four groups A, B, C and D (see Cylinder liners)
Piston permissible weight variation	10 g

Gudgeon pin:

Bore diameter	23.00
Clearance in piston bore	0 to .008
External diameter:	
Standard	$23.005^{+0}_{-.013}$
First oversize	$23.05^{+0}_{-.013}$
Second oversize	$23.10^{+0}_{-.013}$

Piston rings:

	Upper compression ring	*Lower compression ring*	*Oil control ring*
Type ...	Cast iron, chrome plated	Cast iron, bevelled	2 flexible sections with intermediate expander section (not to be shortened)
Height ...	1.490 to 1.475	1.98 to 1.96	3.96±.05
Ring gap	.40 to .55	.40 to .55	20 to 50 each side of expander ring

Valves, springs, pushrods, tappets:

Valve head diameter:	
Inlet...	42.5
Exhaust	35.5
Valve seat angle (cylinder head):	
Inlet...	120 deg.
Exhaust	90 deg.
Valve seat angle (valve):	
Inlet...	120 deg. $^{+15'}_{-0'}$
Exhaust	90 deg. $^{+15'}_{-0'}$
Width of valve bearing face on seat	1.5 maximum

Valve stem diameter:		
Inlet	8.02 —.02	
Exhaust	8.00 —.02	
Valve springs:	*Internal spring*	*External spring*
Free length	41.0	44.5
Fitted length, valve closed	35.8	39.8
Spring load at fitted length	$12.2^{+1.8\ \text{kg}}_{-0.7\ \text{kg}}$	$24.0^{+3.5\ \text{kg}}_{-1.5\ \text{kg}}$
	Inlet	*Exhaust*
Pushrod diameter	$185.4 \pm .5$	$219.3 \pm .5$
length	$6.75^{+.15}_{-.05}$	$6.75^{+.15}_{-.05}$
Tappets:	*Standard*	*Oversize*
External diameter	23.95 to 23.96	24.15 to 24.16
Block bore for tappet	24.00 to 24.03	24.20 to 24.23
Radial clearance	.04 to .08	
Valve timing with a valve clearance of .7 mm, inlet and exhaust, on the cylinder being used:		
Inlet open before TDC	0 deg. 30′	
Inlet closes after BDC	35 deg. 0′	
Exhaust opens before BDC	35 deg. 30′	
Exhaust closes after TDC	10 deg. 0′	

FUEL SYSTEM

Carburetter, 1796 cc engines

Make and type	Solex 34 PBICA 5 with hot water pre-heating system
Choke tube	27
Main jet	145
Correction jet	170
Idling jet	50
Air pilot jet	210
Pump jet	45
Starter jet	160
Emulsion tube	28
Float	5.7 g

Carburetter, 1796 cc engine, USA

	1969	*1970*	
Make and type	Solex 34 PBICA.6	32 PBICA.8	
Choke tube	27	24	24
Main jet	137.5	120	130
Correction jet	200	195	200
Idling jet	52	55	50
Starter jet	160	190	—
Needle valve	1.70	1.50	1.50
Emulsion tube	17	101	17

Carburetter, 1971 cc engine (early)

Make and type	Solex 32-35 SEIEA	
	Primary	*Secondary*
Choke tube	24	27
Main jet:		
Synchromesh	125	137.5
Automatic	122.5	140
Correction jet	140	140
Emulsion tube	ND	SI
Idling jet	55	—
By-pass jet	—	55
Pump jet	40	40
Econostat	—	100
Idle speed	800 rev/min	

Carburetter, 1971 cc engine (later)		
Make and type	Solex 32-35 SEIEA	
	Primary	*Secondary*
Choke tube	24	27
Main jet:		
Synchromesh	125	137.5
Automatic	122.5	140
Correction jet	140	150
Emulsion tube	ND	S1
Idling jet	55/50	—
By-pass jet	—	55
Pump jet	50	35
Econostat	—	100
Carburetter, 1971 cc engine, USA '71		
Make and type	Solex 32-35 SEIEA	
	Primary	*Secondary*
Choke tube	24	27
Main jet:		
Synchromesh	122.5	140
Automatic	120	142.5
Correction jet	140	150
Emulsion tube	ND	S1
Idling jet	50	—
By-pass jet	—	55
Pump jet	40	40
Econostat	—	100
Carburetters, 1971 cc engine, USA '72		
Solex type:	*Primary*	*Secondary*
Synchromesh	32 BICSA 2	34 PBIC 8
Automatic	32 BICSA 2	34 BICSA 2
Choke tube	24	24
Main jet:		
Synchromesh	117.5	112.5
Automatic	112.5	112.5
Correction jet	210	130
Emulsion tube	135	17
Electrovalve	55	50
Idle jet (in choke)	120	210
Pump jet	40	50
Carburetters, 1971 cc engine, USA '73	*Primary*	*Secondary*
Solex type	32 BICSA 2	34 PBIC 8
Choke tube	24	24
Main jet	122.5	122.5
Correction jet	180	210
Emulsion tube	136	137
Electrovalve	55	50
Idle jet (in choke)	120	210
Pump jet	40	50
Econostat	—	90

Fuel pump:	
Type	Guiot type YY, mechanically driven from eccentric on camshaft
Delivery pressure	75 g/sq cm
Fuel tank capacity	56 litre
Air filter	Lautrette, filter element EL.697
Fuel injection system:	
Type	Kugelfischer (optional)

IGNITION SYSTEM

Sparking plugs:	
Size	14 mm, 1.25 pitch
Carburetter engines	AC.44.XL or SEV-Marchal 35.HS
Injection engines	Marchal GT 34 HD or Champion N6Y .AC 41.2 XLS after September 1973
Length	19
Point gap	.60
Distributor:	
Type	Ducellier 4161.B or SEV-Marchal NA.HC
Drive	Skew gear from camshaft
Rotation	Clockwise
Contact breaker points gap	.40 (Marchal 'cassette' points .30)
Coil type	Ducellier 2070.B or SEV-Marchal 3H

COOLING SYSTEM

Radiator:		
Type	Vertical flow, steel tube	
Filler cap release pressure	280 g/sq cm	
Capacity, including heater	7.8 litre	
Fan:		
Type	6-blade plastic, with electro-magnetic clutch	
Thermoswitch engages at	84°C to 90°C	
disengages at	76°C to 82°C	
Solenoid air gap	.35 to .40	
Thermostat:		
Type	Calorstat	
	Standard	*Cold climate*
Opening temperature	74°C to 76°C	87°C to 89°C
Valve lift 7.5 mm at	87°C	97°C
Height with valve closed	53	55

CLUTCH

Type	Single dry plate, diaphragm spring
Actuation	Hydraulic
External diameter	273
Hydraulic fluid	Lockheed 55

SYNCHROMESH GEARBOX

	First	*Second*	*Third*	*Top*	*Reverse*
Ratios:	3.663:1	2.169:1	1.409:1	1.000:1	3.747:1

Lubrication:	
Grade of lubricant	Esso Extra 20.W 30/40
Oil capacity	1.15 litre

AUTOMATIC TRANSMISSION

Type	ZF type 3 HP 12, 3-speed epicyclic with 3-element hydrokinetic torque converter			
Gear ratios:	*First*	*Second*	*Third*	*Reverse*
	2.558:1	1.518:1	1.000:1	2.000:1
Fluid type	Esso A.AQATF.2974.A			
Capacity:				
Transmission only	4.75 to 5.25 litre			
Transmission and oil heat exchanger	5.5 litre			
Weight:				
Unit without oil and converter...	32.5 kg			
Converter	9.5 kg			

FRONT SUSPENSION

Type	Independent. MacPherson struts, coil springs, telescopic dampers, anti-roll bar	
Springs:		
Free length	500	500
Compressed length under load of 318 kg ...	225 to 230	230 to 235
Identification	red/green	white/green
Dampers:		
Fluid type	Esso Oleofluid 40.X	
Capacity	.3 litre	
Anti-roll bar diameter	26	
Wheel alignment (car with tools, oil, water and petrol):		
Castor	2 deg. 40′±30′	
Camber	0 deg. 38′±30′	
Swivel pin inclination	8 deg. 54′±30′	
Toe-in	3 mm±1 mm	

REAR SUSPENSION

Type	Independent coil springs, trailing arms, telescopic dampers, anti-roll bar or rigid axle and coil springs	
Springs:		
Free length	412	412
Compressed length under load of 318 kg ...	324.5 to 329.5	329.5 to 334.5
Identification	yellow/green	blue/white
Dampers	See Front Suspension	
Anti-roll bar diameter	18	

STEERING

Type	Rack and pinion, with two-piece steering shaft
Rack plunger free play	.10±.05 max.
Thickness of shims available for plunger adjustment	.10, .20 and .50
Steering wheel turns, lock to lock	4.5 turns
Maximum steering radius	5.5 m
Lubrication points	Steering knuckle pivots and track arm ball joints each side. Steering rack. Every 5000 km (3000 miles)

BRAKES

Type	Hydraulically operated servo-assisted disc brakes front and rear
Handbrake	Self-adjusting on rear wheels
Pads	Ferodo F.737 yellow or Abex NS.414 black. After 1971, Ferodo EP.2430, one blue, 3 whites, 1 blue
Minimum pad thickness before operation of warning lamp	2.5
Disc run-out	.07 maximum
Servo unit effective ratio	3.3:1
Hydraulic fluid	Lockheed 55

REAR AXLE

Type	Suspended hypoid bevel or rigid hypoid	
	Carburetter	*Fuel injection*
Axle ratios	3.89 : 1	3.78 : 1
Lubricant	Esso gear oil	GX80
Oil capacity	1.2 litre or 1.6 litre	

ELECTRICAL EQUIPMENT

Battery:	
Type	12-volt earth return, negative earth
Capacity	55 amp/hr
Dimensions	250 x 170 x 200 height
Alternator:	
Type	Ducellier 7529A or Paris-Rhone A.13.M.3
Voltage	14 V
Rating	370 W
Rectification	Silicon diodes
Maximum speed	12,000 rev/min
Regulator	Ducellier 8362A, Paris-Rhone AYA.21 or SEV-Marchal VR.14
Starter motor:	
Type	Ducellier 6189A or Paris-Rhone D.8.E.96
Rotation (from driving end)	Clockwise
Average torque at 1000 rev/min	.72 kg m
Current consumption at average torque	280 amp
Windscreen wiper:	
Type	SEV-Marchal or Bosch
No. of speeds	2
Lamp bulbs:	
Headlights	12V 45/40W
Flashers, stop and reversing lights	12V 5W
Panel lights, brake and oil pressure warning lights	12V 4W
Other warning lights	12V 2W
Interior lighting	12V 4W festoon

TIGHTENING TORQUES

	kg m	lb ft
Brakes:		
Front brake caliper to steering swivel	7.0	51
Rear brake caliper to stub axle	4.25	31
Disc to hub	4.75	34
Pad retainers	1.75	13
Clutch:		
Clutch to flywheel bolts	1.5	11
Engine:		
Cylinder head bolts	8.25	60
Connecting rod bolts	4.0	29
Main bearing caps	7.5	54
Crankshaft counterweights	6.75	49
Flywheel	6.75	49
Crankshaft pulley	17.0	123
Camshaft pinion	2.25	16
Crossmember mounting bolts	4.5	33
Sump bolts	1.0	7
Sparking plugs	2.25	16
Gearbox:		
Gearbox to engine	5.5	40
Torque tube to gearbox	6.0	44
Rear housing bolts	1.5	11
Torque converter to support bracket	2.25	16
Support bracket to rear axle	3.25	24
Oil sump to transmission case	1.0	7
Steering gear:		
Steering rack housing to crossmember	3.25	24
Track rod ball joint	4.25	31
Pinion nut	1.5	11
Flexible coupling	1.75	13
Steering wheel	4.5	33
Front suspension:		
Hub to stub axle, pre-tightening	3.0	22
Hub to stub axle, final tightening	1.0	7
Radius arm to suspension arm	4.5	33
Radius arm to crossmember	4.5	33
Stub axle ball joint	4.5	33
Front damper upper bolts	1.0	7
Wheel nuts	6.0	44
Rear suspension:		
Damper lower pivot	4.5	33
Damper upper nylstop nut	1.25	9
Stub axle to suspension arm	4.0	29
Wheel nuts	6.0	44
Rear axle:		
Differential to crossmember	3.75	27
Torque tube to differential	6.0	44
Anti-roll bar link	4.5	33
Hub/knuckle to suspension arm	4.0	29
Damper upper nut	1.25	9
Damper lower nut	4.5	33
Rear arm pivot nut	6.5	47

Key to wiring diagrams

A-Z Connectors **A.C** Cigarette lighter **Al** Distributor **Alt** Alternator **Av** Horn **Bie** Battery **Bo** Coil **C.A.** Horn switch **C.Cli** Flasher unit **C.E.V./L.V.** Windscreen wiper and washer switch **Cli** Flasher **Com** Lighting, washer and wiper switch **C.T** Revolution indicator **Dem** Starter **DIR.AV** Horn and flasher switch **E.C** Boot light **E.Ce** Ashtray light **E.Cl** Heater light **E.I.D** Interior light (right) **E.I.G** Interior light (left) **E.P.B.D** Panel lamp (right) **E.P.B.G** Panel lamp (left) **E.P.P.** Number plate lamp **E.V** Windscreen wiper **E.Va** Electro valve **E.V.P.** Glove box light **F** Fuse **F.P** Door light **I.A.D** Ignition switch **1.Cli** Flasher switch **I.E.C** Boot lamp switch **I.E.V** Windscreen wiper switch **I.E.V.P** Glove box light switch **I.F.M** Handbrake switch **I.L.C** Switch for heated rear window **I.L.V.D** Right window switch **I.L.V.G** Left window switch **I.P.A.V** Door switch (front) **I.P.A.R** Door switch (rear) **I.P.R** Reversing light switch **I.S** Stop lamp switch **I.S.D** Inhibitor switch **JR** Fuel gauge **J.Tr** Fuel tank unit **L** Side and rear lamps **LC** Heated rear window **L.E** Instrument panel lamps **L.V.D** Window motor (right) **L.V.G** Window motor (left) **M** Earth **MO** Clock **M.C.H** Oil pressure transmitter **P.E** Fuel pump **P.F** Brake pad **P.L.V** Windscreen washer **P.R** Reversing light **Pr.C** Dipped headlamp **Pr.R** Main beam **P.T** Water temperature transmitter **R.Bie** Battery switch **Reg** Regulator **R.E.V** Wiper relay **R.L.F** Brake fluid reservoir **R.L** Rheostat **Rh.V.Cl** Fan rheostat **R.Pr** Headlamp relay **T** Wiper intermittent switch **T.Cli** Flasher warning lamp **T.H** Oil pressure warning lamp **T.L.C** Rear window warning lamp **T.P.R** Headlamp warning lamp **T.S** Choke warning lamp **T.S.F** Brake warning lamp **Th.E** Thermometer **Th.V.D.E** Fan thermometer switch (water) **Th.V.D.H** Fan thermo switch (oil) **T.V** Automatic selector panel **V.Cl** Heater fan **V.D** Thermostatic cooling fan **+a.c** Live after contact **+P** Continuously live

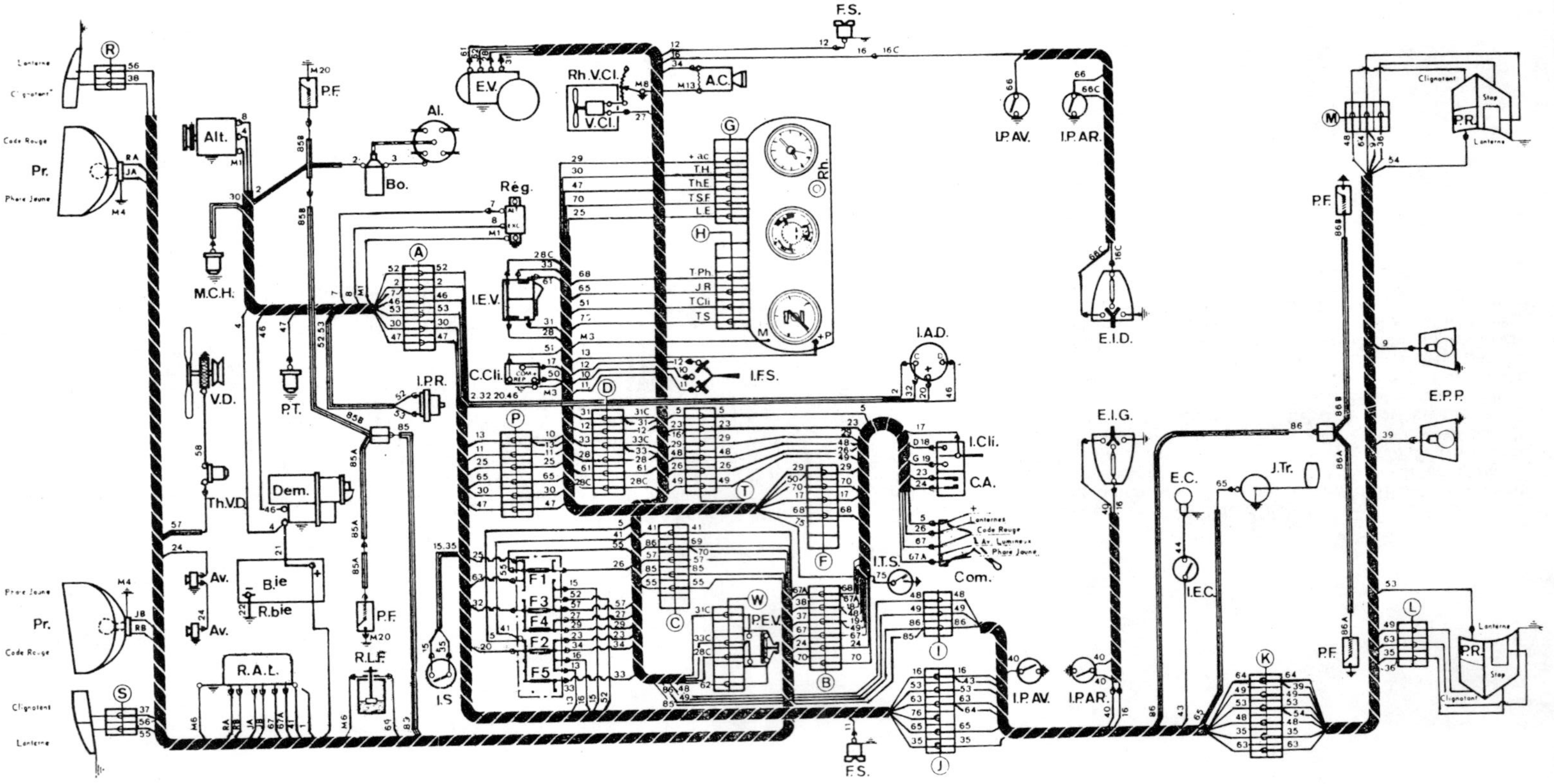

FIG 14:1 Wiring diagram for Peugeot 504 (1969) with carburetter

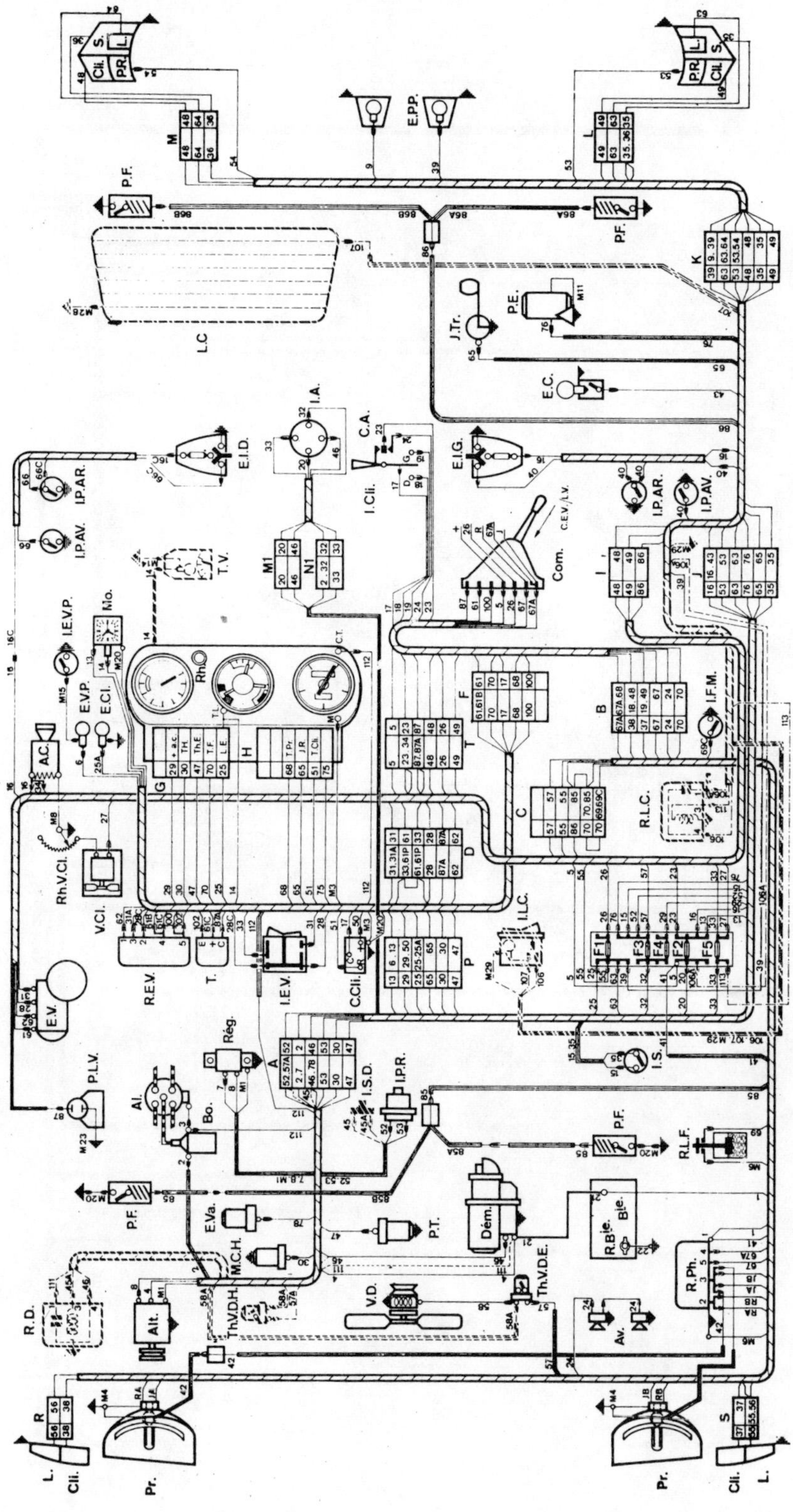

FIG 14:2 Wiring diagram for Peugeot 504 (from 1971) with carburetters

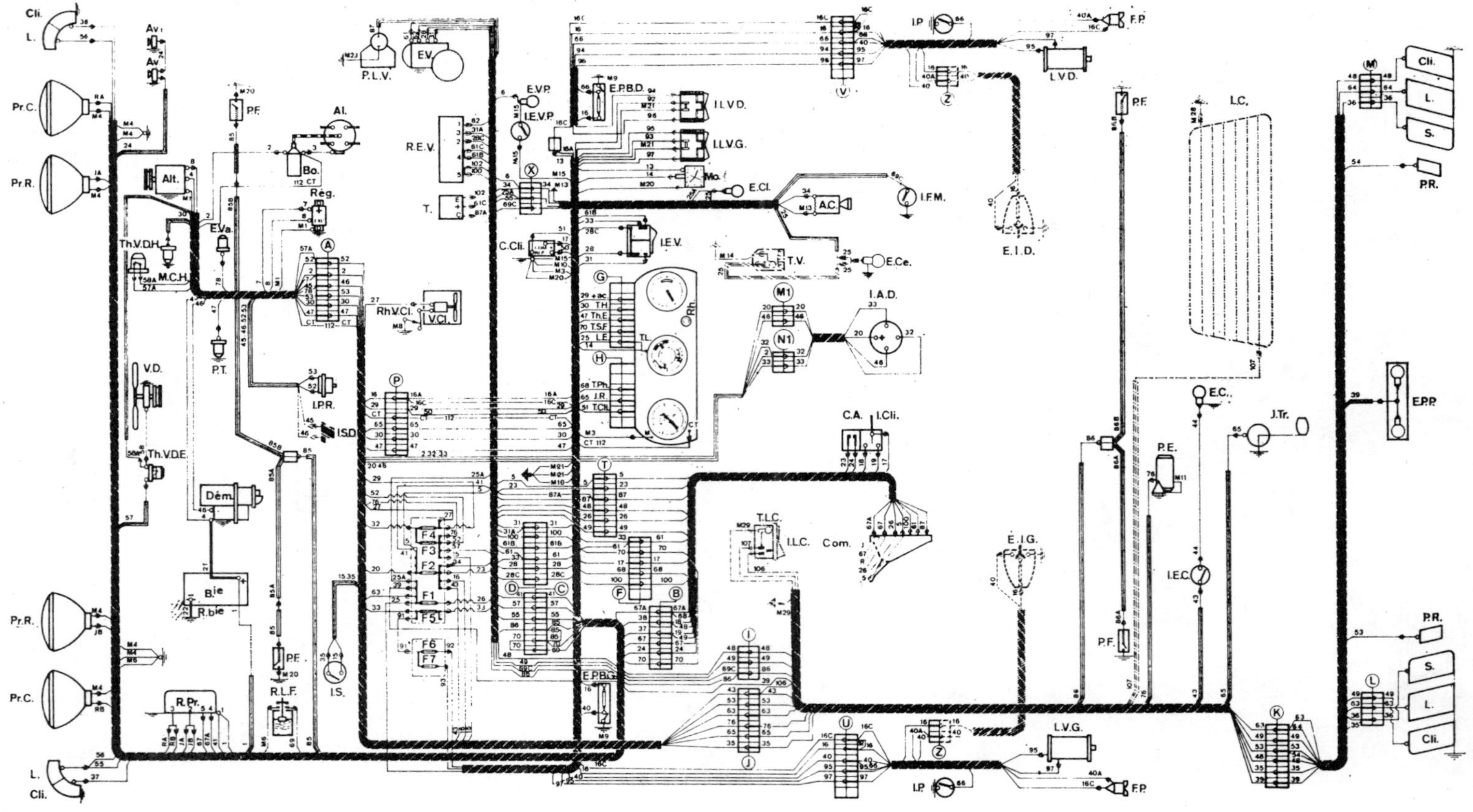

FIG 14:3 Wiring diagram for Peugeot 504 (from 1971) with fuel injection

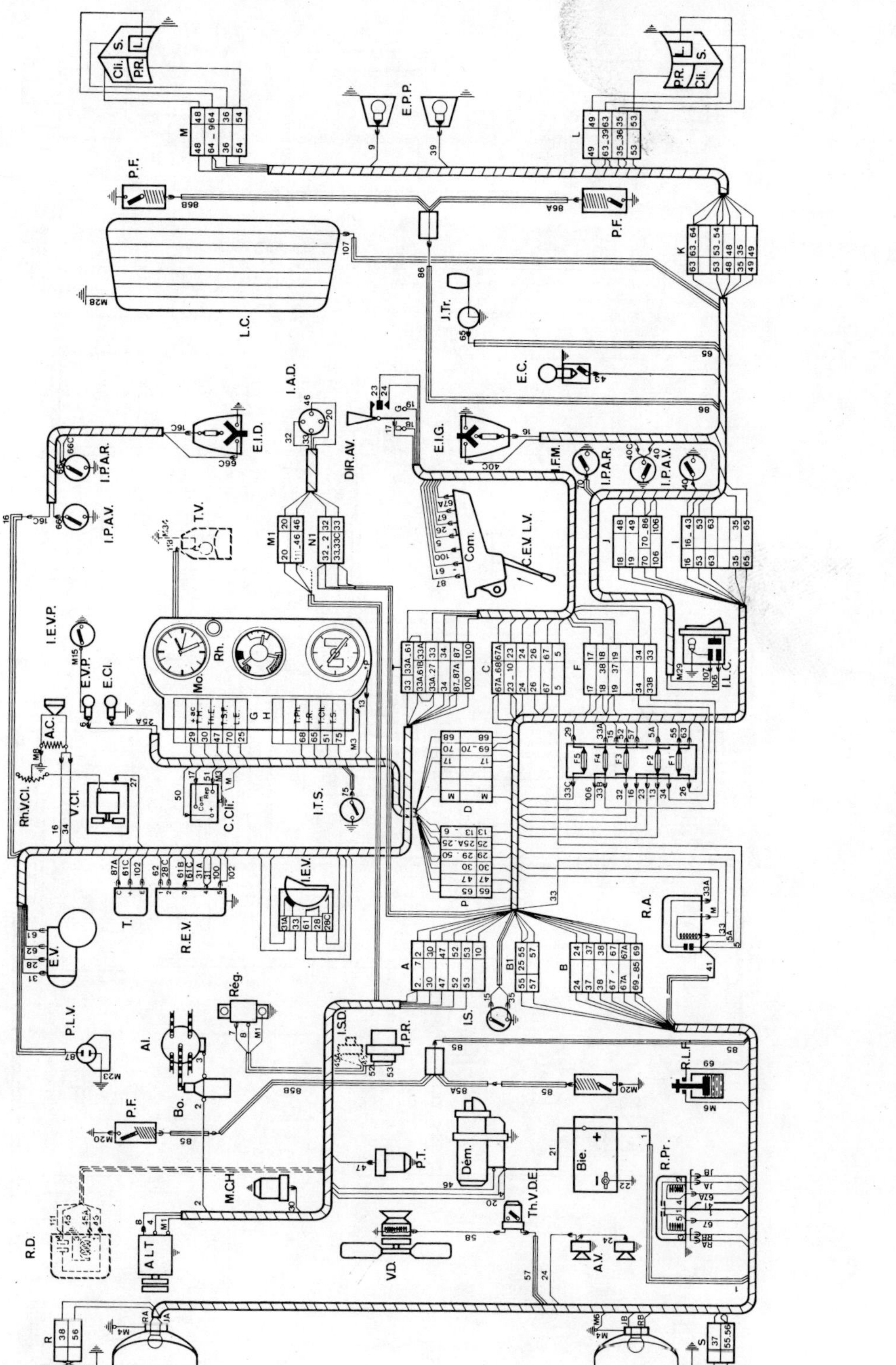

FIG 14:4 Wiring diagram for Peugeot 504 GL (September 1973)

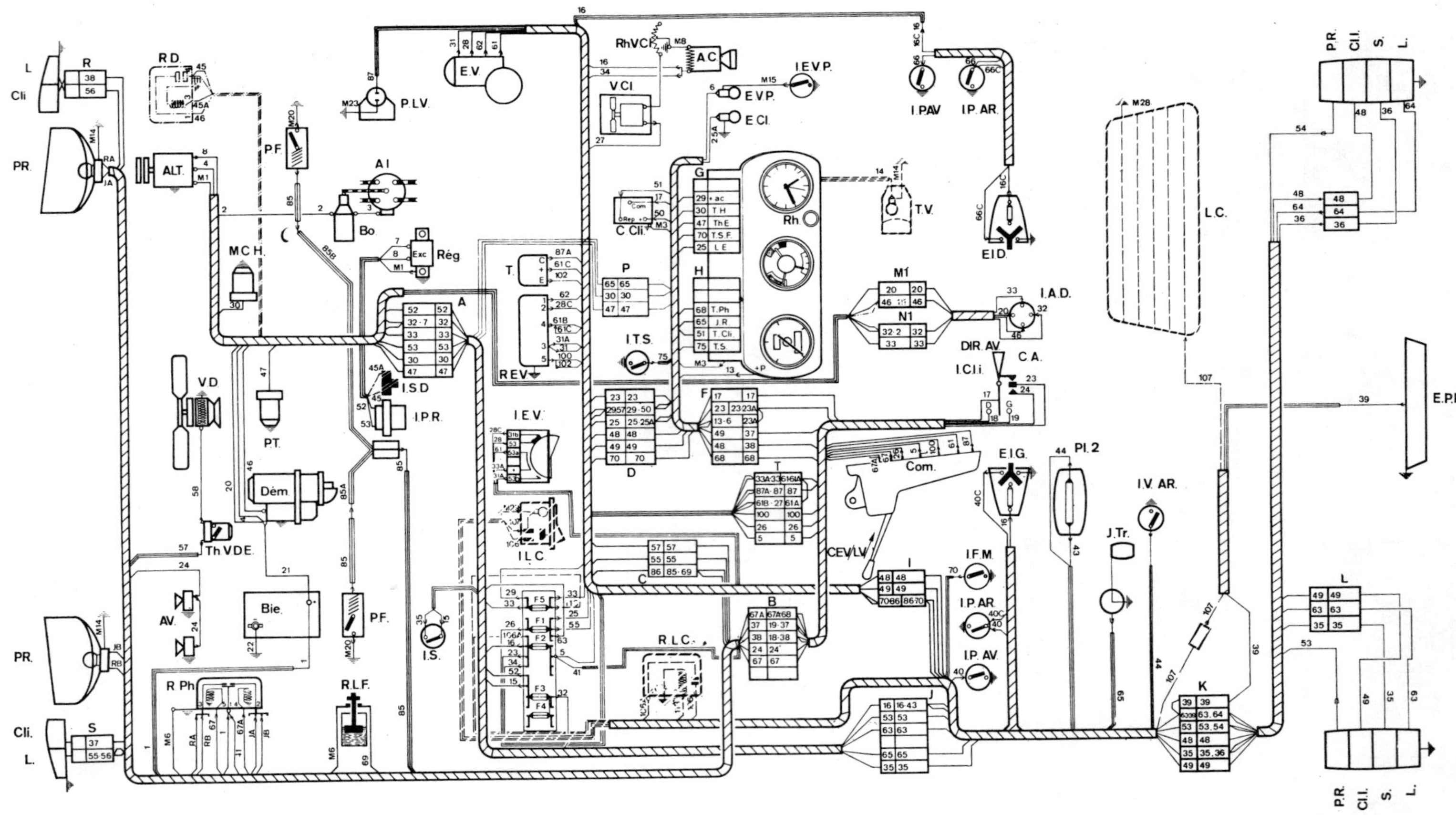

FIG 14:5 Wiring diagram for Peugeot 504 Estate (July 1972)

Inches	Decimals	Millimetres	Inches to Millimetres		Millimetres to Inches	
			Inches	mm	mm	Inches
1/64	.015625	.3969	.001	.0254	.01	.00039
1/32	.03125	.7937	.002	.0508	.02	.00079
3/64	.046875	1.1906	.003	.0762	.03	.00118
1/16	.0625	1.5875	.004	.1016	.04	.00157
5/64	.078125	1.9844	.005	.1270	.05	.00197
3/32	.09375	2.3812	.006	.1524	.06	.00236
7/64	.109375	2.7781	.007	.1778	.07	.00276
1/8	.125	3.1750	.008	.2032	.08	.00315
9/64	.140625	3.5719	.009	.2286	.09	.00354
5/32	.15625	3.9687	.01	.254	.1	.00394
11/64	.171875	4.3656	.02	.508	.2	.00787
3/16	.1875	4.7625	.03	.762	.3	.01181
13/64	.203125	5·1594	.04	1.016	.4	.01575
7/32	.21875	5.5562	.05	1.270	.5	.01969
15/64	.234375	5.9531	.06	1.524	.6	.02362
1/4	.25	6.3500	.07	1.778	.7	.02756
17/64	.265625	6.7469	.08	2.032	.8	.03150
9/32	.28125	7.1437	.09	2.286	.9	.03543
19/64	.296875	7.5406	.1	2.54	1	.03937
5/16	.3125	7.9375	.2	5.08	2	.07874
21/64	.328125	8.3344	.3	7.62	3	.11811
11/32	.34375	8.7312	.4	10.16	4	.15748
23/64	.359375	9.1281	.5	12.70	5	.19685
3/8	.375	9.5250	.6	15.24	6	.23622
25/64	.390625	9.9219	.7	17.78	7	.27559
13/32	.40625	10.3187	.8	20.32	8	.31496
27/64	.421875	10.7156	.9	22.86	9	.35433
7/16	.4375	11.1125	1	25.4	10	.39370
29/64	.453125	11.5094	2	50.8	11	.43307
15/32	.46875	11.9062	3	76.2	12	.47244
31/64	.484375	12.3031	4	101.6	13	.51181
1/2	.5	12.7000	5	127.0	14	.55118
33/64	.515625	13.0969	6	152.4	15	.59055
17/32	.53125	13.4937	7	177.8	16	.62992
35/64	.546875	13.8906	8	203.2	17	.66929
9/16	.5625	14.2875	9	228.6	18	.70866
37/64	.578125	14.6844	10	254.0	19	.74803
19/32	.59375	15.0812	11	279.4	20	.78740
39/64	.609375	15.4781	12	304.8	21	.82677
5/8	.625	15.8750	13	330.2	22	.86614
41/64	.640625	16.2719	14	355.6	23	.90551
21/32	.65625	16.6687	15	381.0	24	.94488
43/64	.671875	17.0656	16	406.4	25	.98425
11/16	.6875	17.4625	17	431.8	26	1.02362
45/64	.703125	17.8594	18	457.2	27	1.06299
23/32	.71875	18.2562	19	482.6	28	1.10236
47/64	.734375	18.6531	20	508.0	29	1.14173
3/4	.75	19.0500	21	533.4	30	1.18110
49/64	.765625	19.4469	22	558.8	31	1.22047
25/32	.78125	19.8437	23	584.2	32	1.25984
51/64	.796875	20.2406	24	609.6	33	1.29921
13/16	.8125	20.6375	25	635.0	34	1.33858
53/64	.828125	21.0344	26	660.4	35	1.37795
27/32	.84375	21.4312	27	685.8	36	1.41732
55/64	.859375	21.8281	28	711.2	37	1.4567
7/8	.875	22.2250	29	736.6	38	1.4961
57/64	.890625	22.6219	30	762.0	39	1.5354
29/32	.90625	23.0187	31	787.4	40	1.5748
59/64	.921875	23.4156	32	812.8	41	1.6142
15/16	.9375	23.8125	33	838.2	42	1.6535
61/64	.953125	24.2094	34	863.6	43	1.6929
31/32	.96875	24.6062	35	889.0	44	1.7323
63/64	.984375	25.0031	36	914.4	45	1.7717

UNITS	Pints to Litres	Gallons to Litres	Litres to Pints	Litres to Gallons	Miles to Kilometres	Kilometres to Miles	Lbs. per sq. In. to Kg. per sq. Cm.	Kg. per sq. Cm. to Lbs. per sq. In.
1	.57	4.55	1.76	.22	1.61	.62	.07	14.22
2	1.14	9.09	3.52	.44	3.22	1.24	.14	28.50
3	1.70	13.64	5.28	.66	4.83	1.86	.21	42.67
4	2.27	18.18	7.04	.88	6.44	2.49	.28	56.89
5	2.84	22.73	8.80	1.10	8.05	3.11	.35	71.12
6	3.41	27.28	10.56	1.32	9.66	3.73	.42	85.34
7	3.98	31.82	12.32	1.54	11.27	4.35	.49	99.56
8	4.55	36.37	14.08	1.76	12.88	4.97	.56	113.79
9		40.91	15.84	1.98	14.48	5.59	.63	128.00
10		45.46	17.60	2.20	16.09	6.21	.70	142.23
20				4.40	32.19	12.43	1.41	284.47
30				6.60	48.28	18.64	2.11	426.70
40				8.80	64.37	24.85		
50					80.47	31.07		
60					96.56	37.28		
70					112.65	43.50		
80					128.75	49.71		
90					144.84	55.92		
100					160.93	62.14		

UNITS	Lb ft to kgm	Kgm to lb ft	UNITS	Lb ft to kgm	Kgm to lb ft
1	.138	7.233	7	.967	50.631
2	.276	14.466	8	1.106	57.864
3	.414	21.699	9	1.244	65.097
4	.553	28.932	10	1.382	72.330
5	.691	36.165	20	2.765	144.660
6	.829	43.398	30	4.147	216.990

NOTES

HINTS ON MAINTENANCE AND OVERHAUL

There are few things more rewarding than the restoration of a vehicle's original peak of efficiency and smooth performance.

The following notes are intended to help the owner to reach that state of perfection. Providing that he possesses the basic manual skills he should have no difficulty in performing most of the operations detailed in this manual. It must be stressed, however, that where recommended in the manual, highly-skilled operations ought to be entrusted to experts, who have the necessary equipment, to carry out the work satisfactorily.

Quality of workmanship:

The hazardous driving conditions on the roads to-day demand that vehicles should be as nearly perfect, mechanically, as possible. It is therefore most important that amateur work be carried out with care, bearing in mind the often inadequate working conditions, and also the inferior tools which may have to be used. It is easy to counsel perfection in all things, and we recognize that it may be setting an impossibly high standard. We do, however, suggest that every care should be taken to ensure that a vehicle is as safe to take on the road as it is humanly possible to make it.

Safe working conditions:

Even though a vehicle may be stationary, it is still potentially dangerous if certain sensible precautions are not taken when working on it while it is supported on jacks or blocks. It is indeed preferable not to use jacks alone, but to supplement them with carefully placed blocks, so that there will be plenty of support if the car rolls off the jacks during a strenuous manoeuvre. Axle stands are an excellent way of providing a rigid base which is not readily disturbed. Piles of bricks are a dangerous substitute. Be careful not to get under heavy loads on lifting tackle, the load could fall. It is preferable not to work alone when lifting an engine, or when working underneath a vehicle which is supported well off the ground. To be trapped, particularly under the vehicle, may have unpleasant results if help is not quickly forthcoming. Make some provision, however humble, to deal with fires. Always disconnect a battery if there is a likelihood of electrical shorts. These may start a fire if there is leaking fuel about. This applies particularly to leads which can carry a heavy current, like those in the starter circuit. While on the subject of electricity, we must also stress the danger of using equipment which is run off the mains and which has no earth or has faulty wiring or connections. So many workshops have damp floors, and electrical shocks are of such a nature that it is sometimes impossible to let go of a live lead or piece of equipment due to the muscular spasms which take place.

Work demanding special care:

This involves the servicing of braking, steering and suspension systems. On the road, failure of the braking system may be disastrous. Make quite sure that there can be no possibility of failure through the bursting of rusty brake pipes or rotten hoses, nor to a sudden loss of pressure due to defective seals or valves.

Problems:

The chief problems which may face an operator are:

1 External dirt.
2 Difficulty in undoing tight fixings.
3 Dismantling unfamiliar mechanisms.
4 Deciding in what respect parts are defective.
5 Confusion about the correct order for reassembly.
6 Adjusting running clearance.
7 Road testing.
8 Final tuning.

Practical suggestions to solve the problems:

1 Preliminary cleaning of large parts—engines, transmissions, steering, suspensions, etc.,—should be carried out before removal from the car. Where road dirt and mud alone are present, wash clean with a high-pressure water jet, brushing to remove stubborn adhesions, and allow to drain and dry. Where oil or grease is also present, wash down with a proprietary compound (Gunk, Teepol etc.,) applying with a stiff brush—an old paint brush is suitable—into all crevices. Cover the distributor and ignition coils with a polythene bag and then apply a strong water jet to clear the loosened deposits. Allow to drain and dry. The assemblies will then be sufficiently clean to remove and transfer to the bench for the next stage.

On the bench, further cleaning can be carried out, first wiping the parts as free as possible from grease with old newspaper. Avoid using rag or cotton waste which can leave clogging fibres behind. Any remaining grease can be removed with a brush dipped in paraffin. If necessary, traces of paraffin can be removed by carbon tetrachloride. Avoid using paraffin or petrol in large quantities for cleaning in enclosed areas, such as garages, on account of the high fire risk.

When all exteriors have been cleaned, and not before, dismantling can be commenced. This ensures that dirt will not enter into interiors and orifices revealed by dismantling. In the next phases, where components have to be cleaned, use carbon tetrachloride in preference to petrol and keep the containers covered except when in use. After the components have been cleaned, plug small holes with tapered hard wood plugs cut to size and blank off larger orifices with grease-proof paper and masking tape. Do not use soft wood plugs or matchsticks as they may break.

2 It is not advisable to hammer on the end of a screw thread, but if it must be done, first screw on a nut to protect the thread, and use a lead hammer. This applies particularly to the removal of tapered cotters. Nuts and bolts seem to 'grow' together, especially in exhaust systems. If penetrating oil does not work, try the judicious application of heat, but be careful of starting a fire. Asbestos sheet or cloth is useful to isolate heat.

Tight bushes or pieces of tail-pipe rusted into a silencer can be removed by splitting them with an open-ended hacksaw. Tight screws can sometimes be started by a tap from a hammer on the end of a suitable screwdriver. Many tight fittings will yield to the judicious use of a hammer, but it must be a soft-faced hammer if damage is to be avoided, use a heavy block on the opposite side to absorb shock. Any parts of the steering system which have been damaged should be renewed, as attempts to repair them may lead to cracking and subsequent failure, and steering ball joints should be disconnected using a recommended tool to prevent damage.

3 It often happens that an owner is baffled when trying to dismantle an unfamiliar piece of equipment. So many modern devices are pressed together or assembled by spinning-over flanges, that they must be sawn apart. The intention is that the whole assembly must be renewed. However, parts which appear to be in one piece to the naked eye, may reveal close-fitting joint lines when inspected with a magnifying glass, and, this may provide the necessary clue to dismantling. Left-handed screw threads are used where rotational forces would tend to unscrew a right-handed screw thread.

Be very careful when dismantling mechanisms which may come apart suddenly. Work in an enclosed space where the parts will be contained, and drape a piece of cloth over the device if springs are likely to fly in all directions. Mark everything which might be reassembled in the wrong position, scratched symbols may be used on unstressed parts, or a sequence of tiny dots from a centre punch can be useful. Stressed parts should never be scratched or centre-popped as this may lead to cracking under working conditions. Store parts which look alike in the correct order for reassembly. Never rely upon memory to assist in the assembly of complicated mechanisms, especially when they will be dismantled for a long time, but make notes, and drawings to supplement the diagrams in the manual, and put labels on detached wires. Rust stains may indicate unlubricated wear. This can sometimes be seen round the outside edge of a bearing cup in a universal joint. Look for bright rubbing marks on parts which normally should not make heavy contact. These might prove that something is bent or running out of truth. For example, there might be bright marks on one side of a piston, at the top near the ring grooves, and others at the bottom of the skirt on the other side. This could well be the clue to a bent connecting rod. Suspected cracks can be proved by heating the component in a light oil to approximately 100°C, removing, drying off, and dusting with french chalk, if a crack is present the oil retained in the crack will stain the french chalk.

4 In determining wear, and the degree, against the permissible limits set in the manual, accurate measurement can only be achieved by the use of a micrometer. In many cases, the wear is given to the fourth place of decimals; that is in ten-thousandths of an inch. This can be read by the vernier scale on the barrel of a good micrometer. Bore diameters are more difficult to determine. If, however, the matching shaft is accurately measured, the degree of play in the bore can be felt as a guide to its suitability. In other cases, the shank of a twist drill of known diameter is a handy check.

Many methods have been devised for determining the clearance between bearing surfaces. To-day the best and simplest is by the use of Plastigage, obtainable from most garages. A thin plastic thread is laid between the two surfaces and the bearing is tightened, flattening the thread. On removal, the width of the thread is compared with a scale supplied with the thread and the clearance is read off directly. Sometimes joint faces leak persistently, even after gasket renewal. The fault will then be traceable to distortion, dirt or burrs. Studs which are screwed into soft metal frequently raise burrs at the point of entry. A quick cure for this is to chamfer the edge of the hole in the part which fits over the stud.

5 **Always check a replacement part with the original one before it is fitted.**

If parts are not marked, and the order for reassembly is not known, a little detective work will help. Look for marks which are due to wear to see if they can be mated. Joint faces may not be identical due to manufacturing errors, and parts which overlap may be stained, giving a clue to the correct position. Most fixings leave identifying marks especially if they were painted over on assembly. It is then easier to decide whether a nut, for instance, has a plain, a spring, or a shakeproof washer under it. All running surfaces become 'bedded' together after long spells of work and tiny imperfections on one part will be found to have left corresponding marks on the other. This is particularly true of shafts and bearings and even a score on a cylinder wall will show on the piston.

6 Checking end float or rocker clearances by feeler gauge may not always give accurate results because of wear. For instance, the rocker tip which bears on a valve stem may be deeply pitted, in which case the feeler will simply be bridging a depression. Thrust washers may also wear depressions in opposing faces to make accurate measurement difficult. End float is then easier to check by using a dial gauge. It is common practice to adjust end play in bearing assemblies, like front hubs with taper rollers, by doing up the axle nut until the hub becomes stiff to turn and then backing it off a little. Do not use this method with ballbearing hubs as the assembly is often preloaded by tightening the axle nut to its fullest extent. If the splitpin hole will not line up, file the base of the nut a little.

Steering assemblies often wear in the straight-ahead position. If any part is adjusted, make sure that it remains free when moved from lock to lock. Do not be surprised if an assembly like a steering gearbox, which is known to be carefully adjusted outside the car, becomes stiff when it is bolted in place. This will be due to distortion of the case by the pull of the mounting bolts, particularly if the mounting points are not all touching together. This problem may be met in other equipment and is cured by careful attention to the alignment of mounting points.

When a spanner is stamped with a size and A/F it means that the dimension is the width between the jaws and has no connection with ANF, which is the designation for the American National Fine thread. Coarse threads like Whitworth are rarely used on cars to-day except for studs which screw into soft aluminium or cast iron. For this reason it might be found that the top end of a cylinder head stud has a fine thread and the lower end a coarse thread to screw into the cylinder block. If the car has mainly UNF threads then it is likely that any coarse threads will be UNC, which are not the same as Whitworth. Small sizes have the same number of threads in Whitworth and UNC, but in the $\frac{1}{2}$ inch size for example, there are twelve threads to the inch in the former and thirteen in the latter.

7 After a major overhaul, particularly if a great deal of work has been done on the braking, steering and suspension systems, it is advisable to approach the problem of testing with care. If the braking system has been overhauled, apply heavy pressure to the brake pedal and get a second operator to check every possible source of leakage. The brakes may work extremely well, but a leak could cause complete failure after a few miles.

Do not fit the hub caps until every wheel nut has been checked for tightness, and make sure the tyre pressures are correct. Check the levels of coolant, lubricants and hydraulic fluids. Being satisfied that all is well, take the car on the road and test the brakes at once. Check the steering and the action of the handbrake. Do all this at moderate speeds on quiet roads, and make sure there is no other vehicle behind you when you try a rapid stop.

Finally, remember that many parts settle down after a time, so check for tightness of all fixings after the car has been on the road for a hundred miles or so.

8 It is useless to tune an engine which has not reached its normal running temperature. In the same way, the tune of an engine which is stiff after a rebore will be different when the engine is again running free. Remember too, that rocker clearances on pushrod operated valve gear will change when the cylinder head nuts are tightened after an initial period of running with a new head gasket.

Trouble may not always be due to what seems the obvious cause. Ignition, carburation and mechanical condition are interdependent and spitting back through the carburetter, which might be attributed to a weak mixture, can be caused by a sticking inlet valve.

For one final hint on tuning, never adjust more than one thing at a time or it will be impossible to tell which adjustment produced the desired result.

NOTES

GLOSSARY OF TERMS

Allen key	Cranked wrench of hexagonal section for use with socket head screws.
Alternator	Electrical generator producing alternating current. Rectified to direct current for battery charging.
Ambient temperature	Surrounding atmospheric temperature.
Annulus	Used in engineering to indicate the outer ring gear of an epicyclic gear train.
Armature	The shaft carrying the windings, which rotates in the magnetic field of a generator or starter motor. That part of a solenoid or relay which is activated by the magnetic field.
Axial	In line with, or pertaining to, an axis.
Backlash	Play in meshing gears.
Balance lever	A bar where force applied at the centre is equally divided between connections at the ends.
Banjo axle	Axle casing with large diameter housing for the crownwheel and differential.
Bendix pinion	A self-engaging and self-disengaging drive on a starter motor shaft.
Bevel pinion	A conical shaped gearwheel, designed to mesh with a similar gear with an axis usually at 90 deg. to its own.
bhp	Brake horse power, measured on a dynamometer.
bmep	Brake mean effective pressure. Average pressure on a piston during the working stroke.
Brake cylinder	Cylinder with hydraulically operated piston(s) acting on brake shoes or pad(s).
Brake regulator	Control valve fitted in hydraulic braking system which limits brake pressure to rear brakes during heavy braking to prevent rear wheel locking.
Camber	Angle at which a wheel is tilted from the vertical.
Capacitor	Modern term for an electrical condenser. Part of distributor assembly, connected across contact breaker points, acts as an interference suppressor.
Castellated	Top face of a nut, slotted across the flats, to take a locking splitpin.
Castor	Angle at which the kingpin or swivel pin is tilted when viewed from the side.
cc	Cubic centimetres. Engine capacity is arrived at by multiplying the area of the bore in sq cm by the stroke in cm by the number of cylinders.
Clevis	U-shaped forked connector used with a clevis pin, usually at handbrake connections.
Collet	A type of collar, usually split and located in a groove in a shaft, and held in place by a retainer. The arrangement used to retain the spring(s) on a valve stem in most cases.
Commutator	Rotating segmented current distributor between armature windings and brushes in generator or motor.
Compression ratio	The ratio, or quantitative relation, of the total volume (piston at bottom of stroke) to the unswept volume (piston at top of stroke) in an engine cylinder.
Condenser	See capacitor.
Core plug	Plug for blanking off a manufacturing hole in a casting.
Crownwheel	Large bevel gear in rear axle, driven by a bevel pinion attached to the propeller shaft. Sometimes called a 'ring gear'.
'C'-spanner	Like a 'C' with a handle. For use on screwed collars without flats, but with slots or holes.
Damper	Modern term for shock-absorber, used in vehicle suspension systems to damp out spring oscillations.
Depression	The lowering of atmospheric pressure as in the inlet manifold and carburetter.
Dowel	Close tolerance pin, peg, tube, or bolt, which accurately locates mating parts.
Drag link	Rod connecting steering box drop arm (pitman arm) to nearest front wheel steering arm in certain types of steering systems.
Dry liner	Thinwall tube pressed into cylinder bore
Dry sump	Lubrication system where all oil is scavenged from the sump, and returned to a separate tank.
Dynamo	See Generator.
Electrode	Terminal, part of an electrical component, such as the points or 'Electrodes' of a sparking plug.
Electrolyte	In lead-acid car batteries a solution of sulphuric acid and distilled water.
End float	The axial movement between associated parts, end play.
EP	Extreme pressure. In lubricants, special grades for heavily loaded bearing surfaces, such as gear teeth in a gearbox, or crownwheel and pinion in a rear axle.

Fade Of brakes. Reduced efficiency due to overheating.

Field coils Windings on the polepieces of motors and generators.

Fillets Narrow finishing strips usually applied to interior bodywork.

First motion shaft Input shaft from clutch to gearbox.

Fullflow filter Filters in which all the oil is pumped to the engine. If the element becomes clogged, a bypass valve operates to pass unfiltered oil to the engine.

FWD Front wheel drive.

Gear pump Two meshing gears in a close fitting casing. Oil is carried from the inlet round the outside of both gears in the spaces between the gear teeth and casing to the outlet, the meshing gear teeth prevent oil passing back to the inlet, and the oil is forced through the outlet port.

Generator Modern term for 'Dynamo'. When rotated produces electrical current.

Grommet A ring of protective or sealing material. Can be used to protect pipes or leads passing through bulkheads.

Grubscrew Fully threaded headless screw with screwdriver slot. Used for locking, or alignment purposes.

Gudgeon pin Shaft which connects a piston to its connecting rod. Sometimes called 'wrist pin', or 'piston pin'.

Halfshaft One of a pair transmitting drive from the differential.

Helical In spiral form. The teeth of helical gears are cut at a spiral angle to the side faces of the gearwheel.

Hot spot Hot area that assists vapourisation of fuel on its way to cylinders. Often provided by close contact between inlet and exhaust manifolds.

HT High Tension. Applied to electrical current produced by the ignition coil for the sparking plugs.

Hydrometer A device for checking specific gravity of liquids. Used to check specific gravity of electrolyte.

Hypoid bevel gears A form of bevel gear used in the rear axle drive gears. The bevel pinion meshes below the centre line of the crownwheel, giving a lower propeller shaft line.

Idler A device for passing on movement. A free running gear between driving and driven gears. A lever transmitting track rod movement to a side rod in steering gear.

Impeller A centrifugal pumping element. Used in water pumps to stimulate flow.

Journals Those parts of a shaft that are in contact with the bearings.

Kingpin The main vertical pin which carries the front wheel spindle, and permits steering movement. May be called 'steering pin' or 'swivel pin'.

Layshaft The shaft which carries the laygear in the gearbox. The laygear is driven by the first motion shaft and drives the third motion shaft according to the gear selected. Sometimes called the 'countershaft' or 'second motion shaft.'

lb ft A measure of twist or torque. A pull of 10 lb at a radius of 1 ft is a torque of 10 lb ft.

lb/sq in Pounds per square inch.

Little-end The small, or piston end of a connecting rod. Sometimes called the 'small-end'.

LT Low Tension. The current output from the battery.

Mandrel Accurately manufactured bar or rod used for test or centring purposes.

Manifold A pipe, duct, or chamber, with several branches.

Needle rollers Bearing rollers with a length many times their diameter.

Oil bath Reservoir which lubricates parts by immersion. In air filters, a separate oil supply for wetting a wire mesh element to hold the dust.

Oil wetted In air filters, a wire mesh element lightly oiled to trap and hold airborne dust.

Overlap Period during which inlet and exhaust valves are open together.

Panhard rod Bar connected between fixed point on chassis and another on axle to control sideways movement.

Pawl Pivoted catch which engages in the teeth of a ratchet to permit movement in one direction only.

Peg spanner Tool with pegs, or pins, to engage in holes or slots in the part to be turned.

Pendant pedals Pedals with levers that are pivoted at the top end.

Phillips screwdriver A cross-point screwdriver for use with the cross-slotted heads of Phillips screws.

Pinion A small gear, usually in relation to another gear.

Piston-type damper Shock absorber in which damping is controlled by a piston working in a closed oil-filled cylinder.

Preloading Preset static pressure on ball or roller bearings not due to working loads.

Radial Radiating from a centre, like the spokes of a wheel.

Radius rod Pivoted arm confining movement of a part to an arc of fixed radius.

Ratchet Toothed wheel or rack which can move in one direction only, movement in the other being prevented by a pawl.

Ring gear A gear tooth ring attached to outer periphery of flywheel. Starter pinion engages with it during starting.

Runout Amount by which rotating part is out of true.

Semi-floating axle Outer end of rear axle halfshaft is carried on bearing inside axle casing. Wheel hub is secured to end of shaft.

Servo A hydraulic or pneumatic system for assisting, or, augmenting a physical effort. See 'Vacuum Servo'.

Setscrew One which is threaded for the full length of the shank.

Shackle A coupling link, used in the form of two parallel pins connected by side plates to secure the end of the master suspension spring and absorb the effects of deflection.

Shell bearing Thinwalled steel shell lined with anti-friction metal. Usually semi-circular and used in pairs for main and big-end bearings.

Shock absorber See 'Damper'.

Silentbloc Rubber bush bonded to inner and outer metal sleeves.

Socket-head screw Screw with hexagonal socket for an Allen key.

Solenoid A coil of wire creating a magnetic field when electric current passes through it. Used with a soft iron core to operate contacts or a mechanical device.

Spur gear A gear with teeth cut axially across the periphery.

Stub axle Short axle fixed at one end only.

Tachometer An instrument for accurate measurement of rotating speed. Usually indicates in revolutions per minute.

TDC Top Dead Centre. The highest point reached by a piston in a cylinder, with the crank and connecting rod in line.

Thermostat Automatic device for regulating temperature. Used in vehicle coolant systems to open a valve which restricts circulation at low temperature.

Third motion shaft Output shaft of gearbox.

Threequarter floating axle Outer end of rear axle halfshaft flanged and bolted to wheel hub, which runs on bearing mounted on outside of axle casing. Vehicle weight is not carried by the axle shaft.

Thrust bearing or washer Used to reduce friction in rotating parts subject to axial loads.

Torque Turning or twisting effort. See 'lb ft'.

Track rod The bar(s) across the vehicle which connect the steering arms and maintain the front wheels in their correct alignment.

UJ Universal joint. A coupling between shafts which permits angular movement.

UNF Unified National Fine screw thread.

Vacuum servo Device used in brake system, using difference between atmospheric pressure and inlet manifold depression to operate a piston which acts to augment brake pressure as required. See 'Servo'.

Venturi A restriction or 'choke' in a tube, as in a carburetter, used to increase velocity to obtain a reduction in pressure.

Vernier A sliding scale for obtaining fractional readings of the graduations of an adjacent scale.

Welch plug A domed thin metal disc which is partially flattened to lock in a recess. Used to plug core holes in castings.

Wet liner Removable cylinder barrel, sealed against coolant leakage, where the coolant is in direct contact with the outer surface.

Wet sump A reservoir attached to the crankcase to hold the lubricating oil.

NOTES

INDEX

NOTES

Alfa Romeo Giulia 1600, 1750, 2000 1962 on
Aston Martin 1921-58
Auto Union Audi 70, 80, Super 90, 1966-72
Audi 100 1969 on
Austin, Morris etc. 1100 Mk. 1 1962-67
Austin, Morris etc. 1100 Mk. 2, 3, 1300 Mk. 1, 2, 3 America 1968 on
Austin A30, A35, A40 Farina 1951-67
Austin A55 Mk. 2, A60 1958-69
Austin A99, A110 1959-68
Austin J4 1960 on
Austin Allegro 1973 on
Austin Maxi 1969 on
Austin, Morris 1800 1964 on
Austin, Morris 2200 1972 on
Austin Kimberley, Tasman 1970 on
Austin, Morris 1300, 1500 Nomad 1969 on
BMC 3 (Austin A50, A55 Mk. 1, Morris Oxford 2, 3 1954-59)
Austin Healey 100/6, 3000 1956-68
Austin Healey, MG Sprite, Midget 1958 on
Bedford CA Mk. 2 1964-69
Bedford CF Vans 1969 on
Bedford Beagle HA Vans 1964 on
BMW 1600 1966 on
BMW 1800 1964-71
BMW 2000, 2002 1966 on
Chevrolet Corvair 1960-69
Chevrolet Corvette V8 1957-65
Chevrolet Corvette V8 1965 on
Chevrolet Vega 2300 1970 on
Chrysler Valiant V8 1965 on
Chrysler Valiant Straight Six 1963 on
Citroen DS 19, ID 19 1955-66
Citroen ID 19, DS 19, 20, 21 1966 on
Citroen Dyane Ami 1964 on
Daf 31, 32, 33, 44, 55 1961 on
Datsun Bluebird 610 series 1972 on
Datsun Cherry 100A, 120A 1971 on
Datsun 1000, 1200 1968 on
Datsun 1300, 1400, 1600 1968 on
Datsun 240C 1971 on
Datsun 240Z Sport 1970 on
Fiat 124 1966 on
Fiat 124 Sport 1966 on
Fiat 125 1967-72
Fiat 127 1971 on
Fiat 128 1969 on
Fiat 500 1957 on
Fiat 600, 600D 1955-69
Fiat 850 1964 on
Fiat 1100 1957-69
Fiat 1300, 1500 1961-67.
Ford Anglia Prefect 100E 1953-62
Ford Anglia 105E, Prefect 107E 1959-67
Ford Capri 1300, 1600 OHV 1968 on
Ford Capri 1300, 1600, 2000 OHC 1972 on
Ford Capri 2000 V4, 3000 V6 1969 on
Ford Classic, Capri 1961-64
Ford Consul, Zephyr, Zodiac, 1, 2 1950-62
Ford Corsair Straight Four 1963-65
Ford Corsair V4 1965-68
Ford Corsair V4 2000 1969-70
Ford Cortina 1962-66
Ford Cortina 1967-68
Ford Cortina 1969-70
Ford Cortina Mk. 3 1970 on
Ford Escort 1967 on
Ford Falcon 6 1964-70
Ford Falcon XK, XL 1960-63
Ford Falcon 6 XR/XA 1966 on
Ford Falcon V8 (U.S.A.) 1965-71
Ford Falcon V8 (Aust.) 1966 on
Ford Pinto 1970 on
Ford Maverick 6 1969 on
Ford Maverick V8 1970 on
Ford Mustang 6 1965 on
Ford Mustang V8 1965 on
Ford Thames 10, 12, 15 cwt 1957-65
Ford Transit V4 1965 on
Ford Zephyr Zodiac Mk. 3 1962-66
Ford Zephyr Zodiac V4, V6, Mk. 4 1966-72
Ford Consul, Granada 1972 on
Hillman Avenger 1970 on
Hillman Hunter 1966 on
Hillman Imp 1963-68
Hillman Imp 1969 on
Hillman Minx 1 to 5 1956-65
Hillman Minx 1965-67
Hillman Minx 1966-70
Hillman Super Minx 1961-65
Jaguar XK120, 140, 150, Mk. 7, 8, 9 1948-61
Jaguar 2.4, 3.4, 3.8 Mk. 1, 2 1955-69
Jaguar 'E' Type 1961-72
Jaguar 'S' Type 420 1963-68
Jaguar XJ6 1968 on
Jowett Javelin Jupiter 1947-53
Landrover 1, 2 1948-61
Landrover 2, 2a, 3 1959 on
Mazda 616 1970 on
Mazda 808, 818 1972 on
Mazda 1200, 1300 1969 on
Mazda 1500, 1800 1967 on
Mazda RX-2 1971 on
Mazda R100, RX-3 1970 on
Mercedes-Benz 190b, 190c, 200 1959-68
Mercedes-Benz 220 1959-65
Mercedes-Benz 220/8 1968 on
Mercedes-Benz 230 1963-68
Mercedes-Benz 250 1965-67
Mercedes-Benz 250 1968 on
Mercedes-Benz 280 1968 on
MG TA to TF 1936-55
MGA MGB 1955-68
MGB 1969 on
Mini 1959 on
Mini Cooper 1961-72
Morgan Four 1936-72
Morris Marina 1971 on
Morris (Aust) Marina 1972 on
Morris Minor 2, 1000 1952-71
Morris Oxford 5, 6 1959-71
NSU 1000 1963-72
NSU Prinz 1 to 4 1957-72
Opel Ascona, Manta 1970 on
Opel GT 1900 1968 on
Opel Kadett, Olympia 993 cc 1078 cc 1962 on
Opel Kadett, Olympia 1492, 1698, 1897 cc 1967 on
Opel Rekord C 1966-72
Peugeot 204 1965 on
Peugeot 304 1970 on
Peugeot 404 1960 on
Peugeot 504 1968 on
Porsche 356A, B, C 1957-65
Porsche 911 1964 on
Porsche 912 1965-69
Porsche 914 S 1969 on
Reliant Regal 1952-73
Renault R4, R4L, 4 1961 on
Renault 5 1972 on
Renault 6 1968 on
Renault 8, 10, 1100 1962-71
Renault 12, 1969 on
Renault 15, 17 1971 on
Renault R16 1965 on
Renault Dauphine Floride 1957-67
Renault Caravelle 1962-68
Rover 60 to 110 1953-64
Rover 2000 1963-73
Rover 3 Litre 1958-67
Rover 3500, 3500S 1968 on
Saab 95, 96, Sport 1960-68
Saab 99 1969 on
Saab V4 1966 on
Simca 1000 1961 on
Simca 1100 1967 on
Simca 1300, 1301, 1500, 1501 1963 on
Skoda One (440, 445, 450) 1955-70
Sunbeam Rapier Alpine 1955-65
Toyota Carina, Celica 1971 on
Toyota Corolla 1100, 1200 1967 on
Toyota Corona 1500 Mk. 1 1965-70
Toyota Corona Mk. 2 1969 on
Triumph TR2, TR3, TR3A 1952-62
Triumph TR4, TR4A 1961-67
Triumph TR5, TR250, TR6 1967 on
Triumph 1300, 1500 1965-73
Triumph 2000 Mk. 1, 2.5 PI Mk. 1 1963-69
Triumph 2000 Mk. 2, 2.5 PI Mk. 2 1969 on
Triumph Dolomite 1972 on
Triumph Herald 1959-68
Triumph Herald 1969-71
Triumph Spitfire, Vitesse 1962-68
Triumph Spitfire Mk. 3, 4 1969 on
Triumph GT6, Vitesse 2 Litre 1969 on
Triumph Stag 1970 on
Triumph Toledo 1970 on
Vauxhall Velox, Cresta 1957-72
Vauxhall Victor 1, 2, FB 1957-64
Vauxhall Victor 101 1964-67
Vauxhall Victor FD 1600, 2000 1967-72

Continued on following page

THE AUTOBOOK SERIES OF WORKSHOP MANUALS

Vauxhall Victor 3300, Ventora 1968-72
Vauxhall Victor FE Ventora 1972 on
Vauxhall Viva HA 1963-66
Vauxhall Viva HB 1966-70
Vauxhall Viva, HC Firenza 1971 on
Volkswagen Beetle 1954-67
Volkswagen Beetle 1968 on
Volkswagen 1500 1961-66
Volkswagen 1600 Fastback 1965-73
Volkswagen Transporter 1954-67
Volkswagen Transporter 1968 on
Volkswagen 411 1968-72
Volvo 120 series 1961-70
Volvo 140 series 1966 on
Volvo 160 series 1968 on
Volvo 1800 1960-73

NOTES

NOTES